The What, Where, When, How & Why
Of Gardening In Florida

Florida
GARDENER'S
GUIDE

TOM MACCUBBIN
GEORGIA B. TASKER

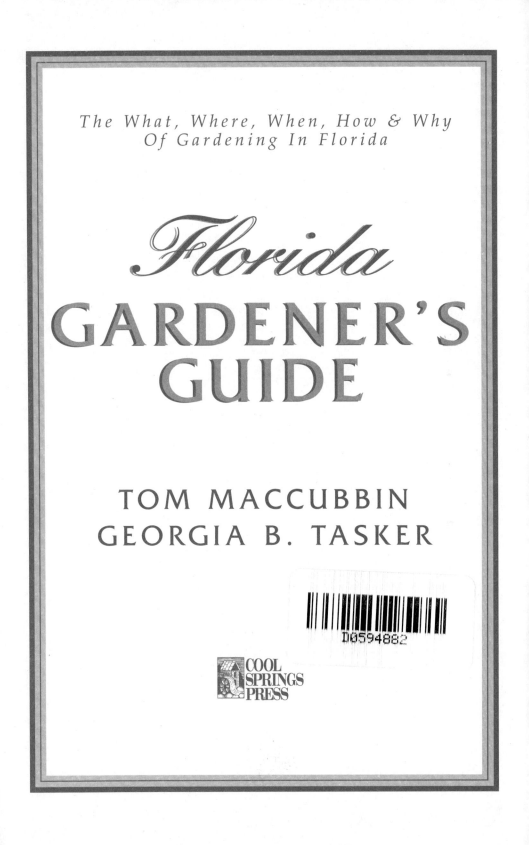

COOL
SPRINGS
PRESS

MacCubbin, Tom and Tasker, Georgia B.
  The Florida Gardener's Guide by MacCubbin, Tom and Tasker, Georgia B.

  p.   cm.
  Includes bibliographical references and index.
  ISBN 1-888608-31-5
  1. Gardening, Florida 2. Florida, Gardening, Guidebooks.
  I. MacCubbin, Tom. II. Tasker, Georiga B.
635.9--dc20
Mac/Tas

Cool Springs Press, Inc.
112 Second Avenue North
Franklin, Tennessee 37064

First printing 1997
Printed in the United States of America
10 9 8 7 6 5

Horticultural Editor: Robert Bowden

On the cover (clockwise from top left): Gloriosa lily, Shell Ginger,Croton, Verbena.

Cover design by Patterson and Graham

Photographs by Horticultural Printers

Map provided by Agricultural Research Service, USDA

Visit the Cool Springs Press website at: www.coolspringspress.com

ACKNOWLEDGMENTS

*T*HIS AUTHOR WOULD LIKE TO ACKNOWLEDGE the information provided on plant growth and care by Tom Wichman and Celeste White, horticulturists at the University of Florida's Orange County Extension Service. Their vast experience in plant culture helped add detailed information to the listings. I would also like to express appreciation to the many University of Florida Extension specialists who have contributed information over the years that increased my knowledge of the plants contained in this book.

—Tom MacCubbin

*G*ARDENERS ARE A GENEROUS GROUP BY NATURE, readily offering cuttings or seeds or plants to those who share their interests. From this wellspring of generosity I have received a great deal of kindly help. I particularly want to thank Don Evans, Don Gann, and Peter Strelkow, who answered harried calls; Debra DeMarco, David Bar-Zvi, Doris Rosebraugh, Dolores Fugina, Bob Fuchs, Jesse Durko, Amy Donovan, Tim Anderson, Monroe Birdsey and Alan Meerow, all of whom fielded questions or tracked down answers as this project proceeded. They, and a long list of others, have been unstinting tutors over the years, though any mistakes or omissions are my own.

—Georgia B. Tasker

The publisher wishes to thank Robert Bowden, Executive Director of the Harry P. Leu Botanical Gardens, Orlando, for serving as horticultural editor of *The Florida Gardener's Guide*.

3

CONTENTS

CONTENTS

INTRODUCTION

Gardening in Florida

W ELCOME TO GARDENING IN FLORIDA, a state of remarkable contrasts. Our state is not all beaches, nor is it all orange groves. It is not all rhododendrons, nor is it all palm trees. It is an exciting and sometimes unexpected mix of all these things. We have regular frosts and occasional hurricanes, beautiful clear days and lots of sweltering ones. We have freshwater marshes, 7000 lakes, sandy ridges, mucky swamps, and more miles of coastal area than just about any other state. To garden here is to experience first-hand the stuff we're made of, from the high pines of the Panhandle to the 25-million-year-old central sandy ridge to the relatively new geology of the southern peninsula.

THE NATURAL TERRAIN IN FLORIDA

The rock beneath our impertinent finger of land is limestone. The peninsula is some 400 miles long and about 100 miles wide (not counting the Panhandle). It is warmed on the southeast by the Gulf Stream and chilled in the northwest by regular arctic fronts.

Gardeners in the northwestern part of the state, north of Tallahassee, know of remnants of Appalachian plants that were pushed south in the last Ice Age meltwater. Imagine coming across mountain laurel and yew trees in ravines and on bluffs around the Apalachicola River—and all this so near white sand and saw palmetto.

Around Gainesville, gardeners are familiar with live oaks hung with Spanish moss, pine trees in the flatwoods, bear grass, deer tongue (wild vanilla), wax myrtle, scrub oak, and sweet bay magnolias that bloom in the summer. The climate is subtropical in this area, where Marjorie Kinnan Rawlings wrote and immortalized Cross Creek and its plants, animals, seasons, and two-footed critters.

When traveling south through the pine landscapes of the Ocala National Forest, you'll come upon one of our rarest landscapes, the scrub, where the sand pine and rosemary, the myrtle oaks and wire grass have staked out their spot on high dunes millions of years

6

Introduction

old. The scrub is arid, desertlike, and populated by many of our most interesting plants and animals, including the endangered scrub jay and the gopher tortoise.

From the chain of lakes that feeds the Kissimmee River which empties into Lake Okeechobee, the land begins to flatten out, to gradually sink toward the sea. Vast pond apple forests once grew south of the lake, before it was diked. At that time water ran from the lake through the sawgrass into the cypress strands and around the tree islands until it reached the Gulf of Mexico on the west coast, or it drained into the Atlantic Ocean on the east through rivers and finger glades.

By the time you reach the southern end of the peninsula, you'll be gardening where temperate and tropical mix in a rich blend, where gumbo limbo, fiddlewood, strongbark, and blolly romance the oak and flirt with the mastic, where a particular kind of slash pine and its companions grow in highly endangered, scattered shards of pine rockland, and where wild coffee snuggles up to the pigeon plum and paradise tree.

On the upper Florida Keys, where West Indian plants make a fragile forest, you'll have to dig into fossilized coral or build a raised bed. The rock here was a reef once, and only a thin layer of leaf litter disguises these stony skeletons. By the time you reach the middle and lower Keys, limestone has resurfaced. Slash pines and silver palms eke out a meager existence, and mangroves surround it all.

This is how we look in our more natural gardens, those we have left and are trying to hang on to.

PLANTED GARDENS IN FLORIDA

Our planted gardens are very different from the natural areas, although there has been a trend toward native gardens in the past decade.

Introduction

Gardening has tended to be more relaxed and leisurely in North Florida than in the southern part of the state. The feverish rush to create instant gardens and overnight jungles that often characterizes garden-making in South Florida is not found here. In northern Florida, gardens are influenced by the Southern states: dogwoods, redbuds, azaleas, camellias, and rhododendrons are prized garden plants, making spring a glorious season. Alfred B. Maclay State Gardens in Tallahassee features azaleas and camellias, and there are displays of these shrubs at Eden State Gardens. Antebellum homes, rolling hills, lakes, and pinelands suffuse many gardens with a sense of history and a connection to the region north of us.

Central Florida has been feeling the ripple effects of Walt Disney World for more than 25 years. The lavish use of color, which is Disney's specialty, is not as intense in home landscapes, but the color impulse is quickened here. In newer neighborhoods, where sunlight is more abundant than in older residential areas, the changing of annual color marks the change of season. In Winter Park, older sections of Orlando, and neighboring small towns, azaleas, laurel oaks, cabbage palms, and sago palms (cycads) are garden mainstays. Bulbs such as day lilies, society garlic, and amaryllis are sources of perennial color, as are roses and crape myrtles. The Harry P. Leu Gardens in downtown Orlando has a huge collection of camellias, roses, palms, cycads, bamboo, and a wonderfully tranquil lakefront walk. Lakes are everywhere—we even have a county named Lake.

Lake Wales, a tiny town south of Orlando, has one of the state's most elegant gardens. This is Bok Tower Gardens, designed by the Frederick Law Olmsted firm which is famous for having designed New York City's Central Park. Bok's carillon, majestically rising atop Iron Mountain (a high point at 295 feet), overlooks reflecting pools and is surrounded by gentle, classic garden walks around huge old azaleas and beneath live oaks. Next door is Pinewood, a home built in 1929 by a Bethlehem Steel executive, Charles Austin Buck. It is on the National Register of Historic Places. William Lyman Phillips designed the garden (Phillips was with the Olmsted firm and designed other gardens in Florida, including Fairchild Tropical Garden in Miami).

Tourist attractions and winter homes of the wealthy have influenced the home gardens on both southern coasts, from McKee Jungle Gardens (now McKee Botanical Gardens), another Phillips design, in Vero Beach . . . to Jungle Larry's Caribbean Gardens near Naples (which was pioneer botanist Henry Nehrling's old garden in the 1920s) . . . to Henry Flagler's White Hall in Palm Beach . . . to Henry Ford's winter home in Fort Myers next door to Thomas Edison's . . . to John Ringling's estate in Sarasota.

On the west coast, the former home of Marie Selby in Sarasota is now a botanical garden specializing in epiphytes, or air plants. The two-story white Selby home is a book and gift shop. The grounds are on a small peninsula that juts into Sarasota Bay, surrounded by mangroves and native plants. Huge ficus are found here—as well as in other areas of the coast, such as the Thomas Edison home in nearby Fort Myers—along with a hibiscus collection, water garden, and bamboo stands.

Thomas Edison, like other early South Florida garden and plant lovers, collected plants from around the world. His home looks onto the Caloosahatchee River; behind it is his large collection of tropical fruit trees. Edison loved palms, and he lined his street of Fort Myers with royal palms, a legacy that still stretches all the way to Fort Myers Beach.

The Deering brothers, among the founders of the giant farm machinery company International Harvester, spent winters in Miami. James built the Italianate palace and formal gardens called Vizcaya; Charles settled farther south and kept his surroundings more natu-

Introduction

ralistic, though he had a mango grove, a lawn sweeping down to Biscayne Bay, and royal palms brought in from the Everglades.

Gardens of contemporary wealthy snowbirds in the town of Palm Beach are kept screened from hoi polloi by enormous hedges of *Ficus benjamina* or weeping fig. Graceful Jamaica coconut palms still exist in this gem-like town, kept alive on antibiotics in order to evade lethal yellowing disease. And there are many famous historic trees documented in a visionary manner at the behest of the Garden Club of Palm Beach. If you manage a glimpse of an estate, expect to see hibiscus, palms, white birds-of-paradise, bougainvillea, broad lawns, sparkling pools, and many relaxed and perfectly groomed gardens. The Society of the Four Arts Garden, a treasure bequeathed to the town of Palm Beach by the garden club back in 1938, is enchanting. It was started to show people how to grow various plants on the island, and today its Japanese garden, water garden, and small formal fountains are all to be cherished.

Fairchild Tropical Garden in Miami (officially in Coral Gables) was begun in the 1930s by palm enthusiast Robert Montgomery and named for David Fairchild, one of this country's most esteemed plant explorers. It has one of the world's best palm collections. The 83-acre garden features long vistas over man-made lakes built by the Civilian Conservation Corps, collections of tropical flowering trees, vines, and shrubs, a conservatory, and a new museum of plant exploration. The garden is considered to be Phillips's masterpiece. In southeastern Florida, palms, cycads, and other plants distributed to Fairchild members have found their way into many home gardens.

Gardeners in Miami Beach, Coral Gables, and Coconut Grove have different garden styles, and they utilize an increasing number of tropical plants to express them. The popularity of crotons, ixoras, and fruit trees is a legacy of early gardeners. Long before Marjory Stoneman Douglas would write *The Everglades: River of Grass*, she

Introduction

and Mabel White Dorn wrote a garden book for South Florida gardeners called *The Book of Twelve*, published in 1928. They presented a dozen trees, shrubs, groundcovers, and vines, and mentioned a dozen more. Dorn was the founder of the South Florida Garden Club.

Today you will find intimate little gardens of exuberant tropical foliage and color in South Beach and more manicured gardens elsewhere. Coral Gables has the wealth to keep gardeners busy clipping and shearing, while Coconut Grove is far more lush, if not overgrown, with many different plants used more playfully.

The look of the Florida Keys, with their vacation mindset, aquamarine waters, and love of bougainvilleas, is tropical-island-pretty, with palms, flowering trees and shrubs, white picket fences, and poinciana trees.

The Latin American influence in South Florida has meant much more use of color and gardens with an abundance of plants. Nurseries have become better sources of plants in the last decade, so the desire to add gingers, heliconias, unusual palms, and flowering plants can be satisfied with an increasing diversity of species.

GARDENING WITH NATIVE PLANTS

Few can resist flowering plants from the tropics or the big, glorious tropical leaves of the aroids and banana families. Yet native plants are on the rise as more gardeners understand the need for habitat restoration and natural gardens for birds, butterflies, and wildlife. In Florida's public areas, native plants are often mandated by law as more and more of the native vegetation disappears to development, particularly in congested South Florida. Many people are planting native trees and shrubs as a hedge against cold, drought, and hurricanes. And there is an increasing awareness of the dangers of too many pesticides, which has made the insect and disease resistance of many natives more appealing.

Introduction

Often the cover of large native trees can be used to create the right microclimate for tropical plants, and gardeners are increasingly sophisticated about using these trees.

CREATE YOUR OWN GARDEN

To create your garden, first think about what you want your garden to do, how you want to use it, how it might fit into your life, and how much of your life you want to fit into it. Consider the appropriateness of the plants you select to reach those goals. Consider the care they might take, the size they might reach, the resources they might require. Anything is possible, but is it practical? Will it require a constant battle against pests and diseases? Constant watering and fertilizing to baby it along? Will your garden be ruined if a freeze hits, or a drought?

A solid framework of native plants appropriate to your area can be an invaluable support for more delicate, sensitive plants, protecting, sheltering, cooling and warming them by turns. If you have a patio, a balcony, or an estate in which to garden, the gardening opportunities are always more powerful than the limitations.

CLIMATE

Soil, climate, and microclimate are the parameters within which you will work. Begin by finding your location on the United States Department of Agriculture's hardiness zone map (page 17). The most recent map divides the state into areas with the same annual minimum temperatures, from Zones 8 through 11. Zones 8, 9, and 10 are subdivided into Zone 8A, Zone 8B, Zone 9A, Zone 9B, Zone 10A, and Zone 10B.

A small wedge of North Florida, in Zone 8A, has minimum winter temperatures of 10 to 15 degrees Fahrenheit, while Zone 11 in the Florida Keys has minimum winter temperatures above 40 degrees. This is quite a difference. Most of the state is considered

Introduction

subtropical, while North Florida is similar to Texas, Louisiana, and Georgia. Extreme southern Florida is tropical, particularly the Zone 10B areas in southern Broward, most of Dade, and the eastern corners of Monroe and Collier counties. Central Florida is often hotter in the summer and cooler in the winter than South Florida, which is favored by southeastern breezes in the summer and far from the impact of most cold fronts in winter.

Florida's winter is December through February; spring is March and April; summer is May through September; autumn is October and November. The widest variation in seasons occurs in the north, the least in the south.

Superimposed on the temperate seasons are the two tropical ones: wet and dry. The rainy season spans May through October, with the beginning and the end of the season having the most rainfall. Thunderstorms and lightning strikes occur more often in Florida than in any other state.

North Florida has more rain in March than Central and South Florida. The dry season of Central and South Florida often ends in drought in April and May before the rains return. The Florida Keys, unlikely as it seems, have considerably less rainfall (about 20 inches less) than South Florida.

A booming population has put a severe strain on the state's freshwater supply, which is rainfed and obtained from underground aquifers. It serves not only Florida's 14 million people, but its agriculture and natural resources. No gardener can afford the luxury of using limitless supplies. While common sense would tell us to group plants by their water needs, we must go a step farther and design gardens that reduce water (and fertilizer) use. Many of the plant entries in this Guide suggest fertilizing plants two or three times a year. Once you become adept at reading plants, you may learn to fertilize only when the plants tell you they require it.

Introduction

Leaves that are generally paler, or yellow between the veins, and plants that produce fewer blooms are three signs of fertilizer need.

Soil

Soils in the northern and western part of the Florida Panhandle tend to be poorly draining clay, while the southern Panhandle and highlands are sloping, sandy-loamy soils, particularly around the Tallahassee hills. The central ridge is sandy with some underlying limestone to the west of the ridge. Most of Central Florida (with the exception of the ridge) is flat, with poorly drained sandy soils; the area is commonly called pine flatwoods.

In South Florida, the central Everglades marshes and swamps are flanked by marl and sand over limestone or outcroppings of limestone. On the West Coast, shells of countless sea creatures have been crushed and washed ashore, making a coarse, calcareous substrate.

The pine flatwoods are characterized by acid sand that doesn't contain many nutrients and doesn't long contain water. Where limestone is near or at the surface, the soil is neutral to alkaline. (Cabbage palms in pine flatwoods, which occur on both coasts, are an indication of lime below acid sands, according to *Ecosystems of Florida*.) Generally, South Florida has alkaline soils, which limit the availability of certain micronutrients to plants.

Most plants prosper in slightly acid to neutral soils, though there is a long list of plants, both native and exotic, that will tolerate high-pH (alkaline) soils. The alkalinity may cause leaf yellowing from magnesium, manganese, or iron deficiency, and foliar sprays of micronutrients are recommended in these areas three or four times a year. Use iron drenches annually to help plants in such soils.

In both sands and rocky soils, certain mineral elements will leach away in heavy rains. (Sandy and rocky soils both require irrigation, but limestone will hold water longer in little niches and crevices.)

14

Introduction

A good many of the newer developments in Coastal and South Florida are built on fill, or land that has been sheared of its organic top layer, and dredged for raising the houses above standing water. The fill material tends to be highly alkaline with extremely poor drainage because of compaction. You may have to build up mounds of good soil to plant in these conditions. Eventually, the roots of trees and shrubs will penetrate the compacted rocky soil and loosen it.

Soil testing is available through the University of Florida's Cooperative Extension Service. Every county has an Extension office, and the listing is under the individual county listings in the telephone directory. Botanical gardens often have pamphlets that tell how to grow certain plants, and they offer classes in gardening. Plant societies are wonderful sources of in-depth information on particular types of plants. Garden clubs can offer newcomers a helping hand with more general horticulture. These are some of the resources you may want to explore when learning to garden in our state.

LIGHT REQUIREMENTS

For best growing results, plants need to be placed where they will receive the proper amount of light. The amount of light suitable for each plant's growing requirements is indicated. The following symbols indicate full sun, partial sun, and shade.

Full Sun   Partial   Shade
            Sun

GARDENING ACROSS THE STATE

Because of the broad range of plants that can be grown in Florida, from temperate in the north to tropical in the south, the Florida Gardener's Guide was written by two authors: Tom MacCubbin,

Introduction

urban horticulturist in Orlando, has written about the more northern and central Florida plants, and Georgia Tasker, Garden Writer
for *The Miami Herald* in Miami, has covered the more southern
ones. Regional information is provided for plants that may be
grown differently in different areas. Some tropical plants may be
grown in Central and North Florida as annuals or container plants,
while some northern flowers may be used as annuals in winter in
South Florida.

Planting times may differ as well. In South Florida, vegetables
and flowers are planted in the winter, while trees and shrubs are
usually planted at the beginning of summer. Summer is the start
of the rainy season, a season which helps in conserving water in
an area that has a burgeoning population, large agricultural industry, and needy natural resources (Everglades National Park, for
example).

Wherever you garden, remember that all our gardens are connected, that our natural areas are affected by what goes on in our
planted yards, and our planted yards benefit from a knowledge of
what grows in our natural areas. So garden carefully, and may you
have all the sun and all the rain you require.

—G.B.T.

USDA HARDINESS ZONE MAP

Florida

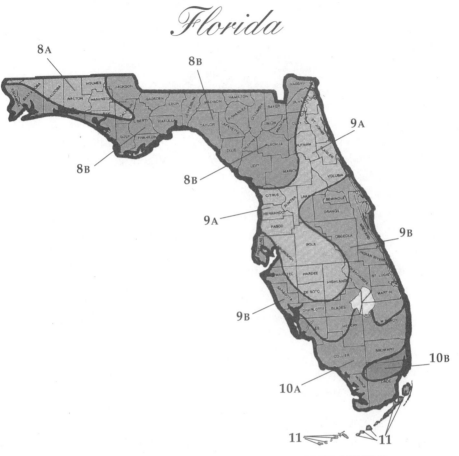

8A

8B

8B

8B

9A

9A

9B

9B

9B

10A

10B

11

11

AVERAGE ANNUAL MINIMUM TEMPERATURE

8A	15° F TO 10° F
8B	20° F TO 15° F
9A	25° F TO 20° F
9B	30° F TO 25° F
10A	35° F TO 30° F
10B	40° F TO 35° F
11	40° F AND ABOVE

17

FLORIDA GARDENERS HAVE LEARNED that a quick way to add color to the landscape is to use annual flowers. Most can be purchased with blooms at local garden centers to bring home and create an instant garden. And the selection of annuals for the landscape is almost endless. As the name annual implies, the plants last only a season or two, but offer plenty of color for six to eight weeks. A few, including geraniums, impatiens, and coleus, continue growing until seasonal changes in temperature cause the plantings to decline.

Plant annual flowers where you need bursts of color. Some gardeners like to add large beds to the landscape; others just want a cluster of a few plants or a pot of flowers. Annuals growing in containers can be added to the balcony, patio, or entrances. Don't forget the tradition of using annuals in windowboxes and hanging baskets.

In Florida you have to learn when to plant certain annuals. There are two main types: the warm-season and the cool-season flowers. Warm-season annuals usually grow well between March and November. Then as the days shorten and temperatures dip into the 40s or lower at night, it's time to add the cool-season types. They are usually planted November through February in most areas of Florida. Some cool-season annuals, including pansies, Johnny jump-ups, calendula, dianthus, and snapdragons, can withstand a light freeze. Obtain a list of annuals for the proper time of the year from your Cooperative Extension Service office to make sure you are staying on schedule.

Chapter One

Most annuals prefer the bright locations with at least six to eight hours of sun. Impatiens are an exception and must have shade to filtered sun during the hotter months. Others, including torenia, coleus, and begonias, can take light shade and still provide good flowers. When picking a location for the flower bed, remember the shifting pattern of the sun throughout the year. During the winter, the sun dips down in the southern horizon to create more shade in many locations.

Give annual flowers some of your best soil. It pays to enrich sandy sites with lots of organic matter. Work in liberal quantities of compost, peat moss, and manure. Till the ground to a depth of 6 to 8 inches before planting. Also test the soil acidity. All annuals prefer a pH around 6.5. Make adjustments as needed following test recommendations.

Some gardeners like to start annuals from seed. It's difficult to pass the seed racks at garden centers and not purchase several packs of flowers to plant. Remember the proper growing season must be followed, and starting flowers from seed takes a little time. Very few seeds can be just tossed in the garden to grow. Most must be sown in pots or cell-packs and take six to eight weeks to be ready for the garden. If you decide to start your own transplants, choose an easy-to-grow annual such as marigolds, salvia, impatiens, or calendula for first attempts. These seeds are large and can be easily seen and handled at planting time. They are also some of the more vigorous varieties.

Use a germinating mix for the sowings, and cover the seed lightly. Keep the seeded containers moist. Most seeds germinate within a week. Then give the seeds the suggested light level noted on the label. Most need full sun immediately. Feed the seedlings with a 20-20-20 or similar fertilizer solution and you should have plants for the garden shortly.

Gardeners wishing to skip seedling culture can find a large selection of transplants at local garden centers. They are usually available at the proper time for planting in Florida. Sometimes garden centers also get unusual Northern flowers including foxglove, delphiniums, and poppies that Florida gardeners can treat like annuals. For years flowers were marketed in cell-packs, but recently, the 4-inch pot has become the standard size for the garden. The plants in these larger pots are usually well rooted and in bloom, ready to create the instant garden.

Check the label of each type of annual selected for the garden to note the spacing needed. Small types like pansies may need only a 6- to 8-inch spacing, but geraniums can be set one foot or more apart. Many of the large growing annuals need some extra room to expand and produce numerous flowering shoots. Check the root-balls of the plants you are purchasing. If the roots have formed a tight web in the ball shape, it may be an old plant and near the end of its life cycle. Plants with tight balls of roots seldom grow out into the surrounding soil. If these are the only plants available, try fluffing the roots apart a little at planting time to encourage growth out into the planting site.

Plant annuals at the same depth that they were growing in the pots or a little higher. If planted too deep, some rot rather quickly. After planting, give the soil a good soaking. Many gardeners also like to add mulch. If you do, keep the mulch back from the stems, and use only a 1- to 2-inch-thick layer. The new plants need every-day watering for the first week or two. Then gradually taper the waterings off to "as needed." When the surface inch of soil starts to feel dry to the touch, it's usually time to water.

Annual flowers also need frequent feedings. Many gardeners like to use a liquid fertilizer solution made from a 20-20-20 or similar product. This should be applied every two to three weeks throughout the growing season. Dry fertilizers of a 6-6-6 or similar analysis can be applied monthly. Gardeners can also use slow-release fertilizers or manure.

Enjoy your annual plantings, and take frequent walks in the gardens to cut bouquets. Check for pests that may be affecting the plantings. The flowers usually have few pests, but some that may affect annuals include caterpillars, mites, and leaf spots. Where needed, hand pick the pests or affected portions from the plants, or use a University of Florida recommended control.

After several months of growth and flowering, most annual flowers decline. It's the culmination of a natural process of flowering and setting seeds. Sometimes you can delay the decline by keeping the old flowers cut off. When most of the plants turn yellow to brown, it's time to replant. Till the soil, work in more organic matter, and select a new selection for the season to put the color back in the flower beds and container gardens.

Ageratum

Ageratum houstonianum

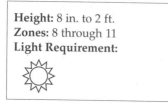

Height: 8 in. to 2 ft.
Zones: 8 through 11
Light Requirement:

The low-growing ageratum is ideal as a compact plant along a walkway or as a carpet of blossoms leading up to shrub plantings. The small flowers are borne in tight clusters that are held well above the plant, creating a blanket of color. Ageratum varieties provide the sometimes all too elusive blue colorations as well as pure whites. The most popular hybrids grow from just 8 in. to more than 2 ft. tall, making many selections also suitable for container plantings and windowboxes.

WHEN TO PLANT

Ageratum is a tender annual that is grown during the warm seasons. Just a little frost or any freezing weather can cause major damage to the plants. Add transplants to the garden whenever you can guarantee temperatures consistently above 32 degrees Fahrenheit, or be ready to protect the plants from cold weather. Plantings can extend into the summer season, but high temperatures and damp, rainy weather often cause the plants to decline.

WHERE TO PLANT

Give ageratum a sunny location for best growth. Locate the plantings where they can be seen and enjoyed. Ageratum can be planted in beds, container gardens, planter boxes, and hanging baskets. In mixed beds they are best used in clusters of 5 or more plants in front of taller plants. They are best planted with a flower of contrasting color or green foliage.

HOW TO PLANT

Ageratum should be planted in a well-prepared garden site. Add plenty of organic matter to sandy soil, and till the ground to a depth of 6 to 8 in. Thoroughly moisten dry soils, then add the transplants. Give ageratum a 12- to 18-in. spacing because most sprawl out over the garden soil. To prevent root rot problems, be sure not to plant too deeply. Immediately after planting, thoroughly moisten the soil.

Many gardeners also like to add a light mulch layer. Just be sure to keep the mulch several inches back from the stems of the plants.

ADVICE FOR CARE

Ageratum need frequent watering for the first few weeks. In sandy soils daily watering may be needed until the roots grow out into the surrounding soil. Gradually reduce watering to times when the surface inch of soil feels dry to the touch, then give the plantings a good soaking. Ageratum growing in containers may need more frequent watering. Check these plants daily, and water when the surface soil feels dry to the touch.

ADDITIONAL INFORMATION

All annuals can have pest problems. Planting the flowers at the proper time of the year and in well-drained soil can prevent most problems. Ageratum may have caterpillars, mites, and garden flea hoppers as pests. Hand pick the pests from the plants. Gardeners can also apply a Bacillus thuringiensis caterpillar control, a soap spray, or product recommended by the University of Florida, following label suggestions.

ADDITIONAL SPECIES, CULTIVARS, OR VARIETIES

New varieties are constantly being developed for the landscape. Some popular varieties include Adriatic, Blue Horizon, Blue Lagoon, Blue Mink, and Hawaii hybrids for plants that grow from just 8 in. to more than 2 ft. tall. Check seed racks and garden catalogs for new introductions.

ADVICE FOR REGIONAL CARE

Gardeners in South Florida can plant ageratum from October through April to take advantage of the long warm season. Central Florida residents may also plant during these months but most likely will lose the plants due to cold during the winter months. North Florida residents should delay plantings until March.

Calendula

Calendula officinalis

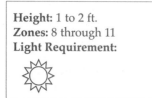

Height: 1 to 2 ft.
Zones: 8 through 11
Light Requirement:

Calendula are bright-flowering plants that, to many gardeners, bear strong resemblance to marigolds. In England, the plant is often "potted up" for flowering during the long, dreary winter months. For this reason, calendula are sometimes referred to as "pot marigolds." Extremely cold weather is not a problem that most Florida gardeners often face. Floridians are therefore able to enjoy the sunshine yellow to bright orange of calendula outside in fall and winter gardens. Calendula provide wonderful masses of color grown in a flower bed but are equally suited in container plantings or in windowboxes. Keep in mind that calendula can grow from 1 to 2 ft. tall. The colorful flowers are usually more than 2 in. in diameter, which makes them quite suitable as cut flowers in floral arrangements.

When to Plant

Grow calendula during the cooler months. The plants are resistant to frost but can be damaged by freezing weather. A period of warm days leading up to the colder weather makes the plants more susceptible to injury.

Where to Plant

Give calendula a sunny location for best growth. Locate the plantings where they can be seen and enjoyed. Calendula can be planted in ground beds, container gardens, planter boxes, and hanging baskets. Since the plants can grow to 2 ft. tall, they may be used as a central feature in beds or planted toward the back of flower gardens.

How to Plant

Calendula should be planted in a well-prepared garden site. Add plenty of organic matter to sandy soil, and till the ground to a depth of 6 to 8 in. Thoroughly moisten dry soils, then add the transplants. Give calendula a 12- to 18-in. spacing. To prevent root rot problems, be sure not to plant too deeply. Immediately after planting, thoroughly moisten the soil. Many gardeners also like to add a light mulch layer. Just be sure to keep the mulch several inches back from the stems of the plants.

ADVICE FOR CARE

Calendula need frequent watering for the first few weeks. In sandy soils daily watering may be needed until the roots grow out into the surrounding soil. Gradually reduce watering to times when the surface inch of soil feels dry to the touch, then give the plantings a good soaking. Calendula growing in containers may need more frequent watering. Check these plants daily, and water when the surface soil feels dry to the touch.

ADDITIONAL INFORMATION

All annuals can have pest problems. Planting the flowers at the proper time of the year and in well-drained soil can prevent most problems. Calendula may have caterpillars as a pest. Hand pick the pests from the plants, or apply a control recommended by the University of Florida, following label suggestions. Some of the beauty of calendula plants is marred by declining blossoms, which very obviously turn brown. Where possible these should be removed to make the plants more attractive and keep the color coming.

ADDITIONAL SPECIES, CULTIVARS, OR VARIETIES

One older variety that seems to grow well in local landscape is Pacific Beauty. It appears to have some resistance to rot problems. Others that should be tried include Bon Bon and Prince. Very few new calendula varieties have been added over the years. Check seed racks and mail-order catalogs for new introductions to try in the garden.

ADVICE FOR REGIONAL CARE

South and Central Florida gardeners can plant calendula throughout most of the winter. North Florida gardeners may want to wait until late winter when the weather is consistently warm to make the first plantings or provide protection from freezing weather. In all areas of the state as the days consistently reach 80 degrees Fahrenheit, calendula rapidly decline.

Celosia

Celosia cristata

Height: 10 to 18 in.
Zones: 8 through 11
Light Requirement:

Few plants offer bright colors in as unique a way as celosia. The plumed celosia sends flower spikes high above the foliage in shades of yellow, orange, red, and pink. Plants with blooms range in height from 10 to 18 in. tall. Feature the unusual plant by itself for warm-season color in a flower bed, or mix it with other plantings to create some bright spots in your landscape. The tall plants make a wonderful central focal point as a backdrop for other lower growing annuals. Celosia also grows well in container gardens. Many gardeners like to cut the flower spikes for use in fresh bouquets. Celosia also dries well, making it suitable for use in dried floral arrangements when the bloom season is over.

WHEN TO PLANT

Celosia is a warm-season annual that's affected by frosts and freezes. It's also affected by rainy, damp weather, which causes the flower clusters to rot. In warmer locations plantings can begin during the fall and continue into spring. Most celosia is removed from flower beds by summer.

WHERE TO PLANT

Give celosia a sunny location for best growth. Locate the plantings where they can be seen and enjoyed. Celosia can be planted in ground beds, container gardens, or planter boxes. Match the colors to other plants, or create contrast with the existing plants.

HOW TO PLANT

Celosia should be planted in a well-prepared garden site. Add plenty of organic matter to sandy soil, and till the ground to a depth of 6 to 8 in. Thoroughly moisten dry soils, then add the transplants. Give celosia a 10- to 12-in. spacing. To prevent root rot problems, be sure not to plant too deeply. Immediately after planting, thoroughly moisten the soil. Many gardeners also like to add a light mulch layer. Just be sure to keep the mulch several inches back from the stems of the plants.

ADVICE FOR CARE

Celosia need frequent watering for the first few weeks. In sandy soils daily watering may be needed until the roots grow out into the surrounding soil. Gradually reduce watering to times when the surface inch of soil feels dry to the touch, then give the plantings a good soaking. Celosia growing in containers may need more frequent watering. Check these plants daily, and water when the surface soil feels dry to the touch. Most of these plants produce sturdy stems, and even though they may have to support some rather large flower clusters, they do not need staking.

ADDITIONAL INFORMATION

All annuals can have pest problems. Planting the flowers at the proper time of the year and in well-drained soil can prevent most problems. Celosia may have caterpillars as pests. Hand pick the pests from the plants, or apply a control recommended by the University of Florida, following label suggestions. Old, faded flowers may mar the beauty of the plants. Where possible, remove the declining blooms to allow new shoots to develop. Celosia gives about 6 to 8 weeks of good color before needing replacement.

ADDITIONAL SPECIES, CULTIVARS, OR VARIETIES

Good varieties for Florida planting include Apricot Brandy, Castle, Century, and Kimono mix. The celosia group also contains cockscomb-type selections of *Celosia cristata*. The blossoms are produced on stocky plants in tight, rounded clusters. Good varieties are found in the Chief mix, Fireglow, Prestige Scarlet, Jewel Box, and Treasure Chest selections. Care is the same as that for plumed celosia.

ADVICE FOR REGIONAL CARE

North Florida gardeners should delay plantings until March or April. Due to the extended spring season in the North, the flowers may last longer, often until summer. Central and South Florida gardeners can plant September through May but must be ready to give winter protection during the colder weather.

Coleus

Coleus × hybridus

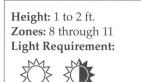

Height: 1 to 2 ft.
Zones: 8 through 11
Light Requirement:

Ranging from lance type to broad, rounded leaves, the foliage of coleus is the focal point of the plant. Coleus offers a veritable feast of colorful foliage with mixes that have every color of the rainbow or varieties with predominantly , pink, green, bronze, or red foliage. The variously shaped leaves are often interestingly edged with a slightly toothed shape to a quite ruffled border. Coleus provides good, reliable eye-catching color whether filling a flower bed or serving as a backdrop for other plantings. The most useful varieties for the landscape are those that grow from 1 to 2 ft. tall. You will find coleus with the most sun tolerance among the newer varieties.

WHEN TO PLANT

Coleus are available at garden centers for year-round planting. Gardeners should remember this is a cold-sensitive plant. With some protection most can grow back after a frost or freeze. Most plantings are made March through October to take advantage of the warm growing season.

WHERE TO PLANT

Give coleus a full-sun to partially shaded location for best growth. Locate the plantings where they can be seen and enjoyed. Coleus can be planted in ground beds, container gardens, and planter boxes. Gardeners used to avoid the hot, sunny spot when planting coleus, but most new varieties have good sun and heat tolerance.

HOW TO PLANT

Coleus should be planted in a well-prepared garden site. Add plenty of organic matter to sandy soil, and till the ground to a depth of 6 to 8 in. Thoroughly moisten dry soils, then add the transplants. Give coleus plants a 12- to 18-in. spacing. To prevent root rot problems, be sure not to plant too deeply. Immediately after planting, thoroughly moisten the soil. Many gardeners also like to add a light mulch layer. Just be sure to keep the mulch several inches back from the stems of the plants. Use small growing varieties in the foreground.

stems of the plants. Use small growing varieties in the foreground. Taller types can be planted in the center of beds or container gardens. Many coleus plantings are also added as a backdrop for other flowers.

ADVICE FOR CARE

Coleus need frequent watering for the first few weeks. In sandy soils daily watering may be needed until the roots grow out into the surrounding soil. Gradually reduce watering to times when the surface inch of soil feels dry to the touch, then give the plantings a good soaking. Coleus growing in containers may need more frequent watering. Check these plants daily, and water when the surface soil feels dry to the touch.

ADDITIONAL INFORMATION

All annuals can have pest problems. Planting the flowers at the proper time of the year and in well-drained soil can prevent most problems. Coleus may have caterpillars and slugs as pests. Hand pick the pests from the plants, use slug bait, or apply another control recommended by the University of Florida, following label suggestions. With the long Florida growing season coleus may grow too tall for the planting site. When this happens, cut the plants back to the desirable height. The plants resume rapid growth to fill in with fresh foliage. Gardeners often use the clippings to root new coleus for the garden.

ADDITIONAL SPECIES, CULTIVARS, OR VARIETIES

Good selections can be found among the Carefree, Fiji, Rainbow, Saber, Wizard, Brilliant, and Fairway varieties. New varieties are constantly being added to the selections available from transplants at garden centers or seed suppliers. Check yearly for the new introductions that you might add to your garden.

ADVICE FOR REGIONAL CARE

North Florida gardeners can expect to replant the coleus after each winter. Unless the plants are given extra winter protection, they are usually lost during the heavy freezes. Central and South Florida gardeners may keep the plants growing for several years.

Dianthus

Dianthus × hybrida

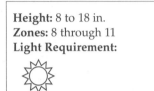

Height: 8 to 18 in.
Zones: 8 through 11
Light Requirement:

Modern dianthus are known to most gardeners as "pinks," partially because so many selections come in a range of pink hues and partially because the fringed edge of each flower petal appears as if it has been trimmed with pinking shears. A perennial plant that is treated as an annual in Florida, most selections of dianthus are either of the species *Dianthus chinensis* or of hybrids of this species with *Dianthus barbatus* (the more northern sweet William). The dianthus grown in Florida are cool-season flowers that can withstand a light frost. Often with just a little protection, the plants can also survive a light freeze. Ranging in size from 8 to 18 in. tall, dianthus are highly useful for a variety of purposes in the landscape. The plants with their pink, white, or red blossoms held well above the foliage can be used as a large mass of color in flower beds or just as a small splash along the walkway. Newer varieties change out the blossom rather quickly so that gardeners don't have to deadhead the declining flowers.

WHEN TO PLANT

Start new plantings during the fall months, and continue through spring. Gardeners in the colder locations are taking a chance that the plants may be lost during winter, but it's worth the risk since the plants have some cold resistance. Most plants are removed by summer, but a few are carried through the hotter months in the cooler locations.

WHERE TO PLANT

Give dianthus a sunny location for best growth. Locate the plantings where they can be seen and enjoyed. Dianthus can be planted in ground beds, container gardens, and planter boxes. Some gardeners get a few plants through the summer by keeping them in planters that can be moved to a cooler location for the hotter months.

How to Plant

Dianthus should be planted in a well-prepared garden site. Add plenty of organic matter to sandy soil, and till the ground to a depth of 6 to 8 in. Thoroughly moisten dry soils, then add the transplants. Give dianthus a 10- to 12-in. spacing. To prevent root rot problems, be sure not to plant too deeply. Immediately after planting, thoroughly moisten the soil. Many gardeners also like to add a light mulch layer. Just be sure to keep the mulch several inches back from the stems of the plants.

Advice for Care

Dianthus need frequent watering for the first few weeks. In sandy soils daily watering may be needed until the roots grow out into the surrounding soil. Gradually reduce watering to times when the surface inch of soil feels dry to the touch, then give the plantings a good soaking. Dianthus growing in containers may need more frequent watering. Check these plants daily, and water when the surface soil feels dry to the touch.

Additional Information

All annuals can have pest problems. Planting the flowers at the proper time of the year and in well-drained soil can prevent most problems. Dianthus may have caterpillars as pests. Hand pick the pests from the plants, or apply a control recommended by the University of Florida, following label suggestions. Some varieties produce a lot of dead flowers all at once while the new blossoms begin to emerge. Some deadheading at this time keeps the flower bed attractive. Dianthus can live for more than one growing season, especially during the cooler months.

Additional Species, Cultivars, or Varieties

Some good performers for the Florida garden include selections from the Baby Doll, Carpet, Charms, Flash, Floral Lace, Ideal, and Telstar varieties. New varieties are constantly being developed by hybridizers. Check garden centers and seed catalogs for the latest introductions to add to your gardens. North Florida gardeners may also be able to grow sweet William, a biennial with similar cultural needs to other dianthus.

Advice for Regional Care

Dianthus are given similar culture throughout the state. Northern plantings may freeze during the winter months. Southern plants are often shorter lived due to the hotter spring and summer seasons.

Dusty Miller

Senecio cineraria

Height: 12 to 18 in.
Zones: 8 through 11
Light Requirement:

The foliage of dusty miller makes a perfect foil for brightly colored annuals in the flower bed. The fuzzy, gray-green leaves give the garden a silvery look. When planted with bright-red salvia or purple petunias, dusty miller provides a tranquil resting spot for the eyes. The shape of the leaves varies between coarsely toothed to lacelike in appearance and adds textural interest to the garden. Plan on the plant growing to between 12 and 18 in. tall. For best performance, plant during the cooler months. Dusty miller proves freezeproof throughout Florida but deteriorates rapidly during summer's rainy days. Few gardeners ever see the flowers, but by late May or June, the plants may open orange blossoms on terminal stems.

WHEN TO PLANT

It's best not to plant dusty miller before the rainy season ends and cool weather begins. For most of Florida the months for planting are October through April. You can expect a fall planting to last until the hot summer season arrives.

WHERE TO PLANT

Give dusty miller a sunny location for best growth. Locate the plantings where they can be seen and enjoyed. Dusty miller can be planted in ground beds, container gardens, and planter boxes. Some gardeners like to make squares, circles, and other patterns out of the dusty miller and then fill in the voids with contrasting annuals. Fancy-leaved types can also be used as border plants for flower beds. In container gardens it's often planted as the central feature around which are planted other annuals.

HOW TO PLANT

Dusty miller should be planted in a well-prepared garden site. Add plenty of organic matter to sandy soil, and till the ground to a depth of 6 to 8 in. Thoroughly moisten dry soils, then add the transplants. Give dusty miller a 10- to 12-in. spacing. To prevent root rot problems, be sure not to plant too deeply. Immediately after planting, thoroughly moisten the soil. Many gardeners also like to add a light mulch layer. Just be sure to keep the mulch several inches back from the stems of the plants.

ADVICE FOR CARE

Dusty miller needs frequent watering for the first few weeks. In sandy soils daily watering may be needed until the roots grow out into the surrounding soil. Gradually reduce watering to times when the surface inch of soil feels dry to the touch, then give the plantings a good soaking. Dusty miller growing in containers may need more frequent watering. Check these plants daily, and water when the surface soil feels dry to the touch.

ADDITIONAL INFORMATION

All annuals can have pest problems. Planting the flowers at the proper time of the year and in well-drained soil can prevent most problems. Dusty miller may have caterpillars as pests. Hand picking the pests from the plants is best. Gardeners can also apply the Bacillus thuringiensis caterpillar control or another control recommended by the University of Florida, following label suggestions. As the hot, damp weather arrives for the summer, most plantings rapidly decline and should be replaced with other annuals.

ADDITIONAL SPECIES, CULTIVARS, OR VARIETIES

Good varieties for the landscape include Cirrus, Silver Dust, and Silver Queen. There have been very few new introductions of dusty miller in recent years. Gardeners should check garden centers, seed racks, and mail order companies for possible new selections that may grow in the home landscape.

ADVICE FOR REGIONAL CARE

South Florida residents may delay dusty miller planting until late fall when the cooler temperatures favor best growth. The plants may also decline soon after the return of hot weather during spring. In North and Central Florida dusty miller often survives into the early summer months.

Geranium

Pelargonium hortorum

Height: 18 to 24 in. tall
Zones: 8 through 11
Light Requirement:

A beloved bedding plant, the geranium produces colorful flowers on plants that are bright green with rounded leaves. The foliage can have zonal marking, which provides added interest. Geranium flowers are produced in clusters at the end of long stems and are held well above the foliage. Many color choices are available, including any shade of pink, red, and lavender plus white and blends. Some members of the genus are perennials, but geraniums in Florida are treated as cool-season annuals. While a few gardeners sneak the plant through the summer with special protection, most geraniums will need to be replaced with warm-season annuals at the start of the summer rainy season.

WHEN TO PLANT

If you are willing to give geraniums winter protection, planting can begin in October. This is an especially good time to form a few container gardens of geraniums that can be protected from the winter weather. Gardeners who have been disappointed by some of North Florida's surprise frosts and freezes usually delay forming large beds until March.

WHERE TO PLANT

Give geraniums a sunny location for best flowering. Actually, the plants tolerate some shade, but don't expect a single blossom until they are moved out into the sun. Locate the plantings where they can be seen and enjoyed. Geraniums can be planted in ground beds, container gardens, and planter boxes. Fill an entire bed, or use these taller growing plants as a backdrop for smaller flowers. In container gardens they make a good central feature.

HOW TO PLANT

Geraniums should be planted in a well-prepared garden site. Add plenty of organic matter to sandy soils, and till the ground to a depth of 6 to 8 in. Thoroughly moisten dry soils, then add the transplants. Give geraniums a 12- to 18-in. spacing. To prevent root rot problems, be sure not to plant too deeply. Immediately after planting, thoroughly moisten the soil. Many gardeners also like to add a light mulch layer. Just be sure to keep the mulch several inches back from the stems of the plants.

ADVICE FOR CARE

Geraniums need frequent watering for the first few weeks. In sandy soils daily watering may be needed until the roots grow out into the surrounding soil. Gradually reduce watering to times when the surface inch of soil feels dry to the touch, then give the plantings a good soaking. Geraniums growing in containers may need more frequent watering. Check these plants daily, and water when the surface soil feels dry to the touch.

ADDITIONAL INFORMATION

All annuals can have pest problems. Planting the flowers at the proper time of the year and in well-drained soil can prevent most problems. Geraniums may have caterpillars as pests. Hand picking the pests from the plants is best. Gardeners may also apply the Bacillus thuringiensis caterpillar control or apply another control recommended by the University of Florida, following label suggestions.

ADDITIONAL SPECIES, CULTIVARS, OR VARIETIES

Good selections for the Florida garden include the Elite, Multibloom, Orbit, Freckles, Maverick Star, and Pinto varieties. Plant breeders are constantly adding new varieties to geranium collections. Check with garden centers and mail-order companies at the beginning of each year for new selections. Geranium gardeners may want to add some of the many scented varieties to the garden. The flowers are often small and inconspicuous, but all have fragrant foliage when crushed. Some of the leaves are very lacy, and others are variegated. Ivy-leaf geraniums are also popular for hanging baskets. These grow well only during the coolest weather.

ADVICE FOR REGIONAL CARE

Geraniums grow well throughout the state. Northern gardeners should plant only in containers until March when beds can be created. These geraniums may last a little longer into the summer season. In South and Central Florida it's worth taking the risk of planting during the fall months and tossing a cover over the beds on colder nights.

35

Impatiens

Impatiens wallerana

Height: 10 to 24 in. tall
Zones: 8 through 11
Light Requirement:

Though the number one bedding plant in the nation for years, impatiens cannot be included among the "cutting edge" plants of the horticultural world. But gardeners should not dismiss the plant as too common for their purposes before considering the usefulness of this shade-loving plant. Impatiens provide color in areas where other flowering plants refuse to bloom. One impatiens plant creates a mound of blossoms normally 1 ft. or more in diameter, thus making it an economical way to fill a large area with color. In warmer locations, impatiens can also grow almost indefinitely. Where the planting is affected by cold, it often grows back either from stems surviving near the ground line or from seeds.

WHEN TO PLANT

Impatiens are added to Florida gardens throughout most of the year. Even in the cooler regions where impatiens may be killed to the ground, they can be planted in tubs or hanging baskets to bring indoors when frost and freezes are expected. The major planting time for North and Central Florida is March through October; for South Florida, use in winter.

WHERE TO PLANT

Give impatiens a shady location for best growth. During the winter months, some varieties can tolerate full-sun locations but decline when the hot, intense sun returns. Locate the plantings where they can be seen and enjoyed. Impatiens can be planted in ground beds, container gardens, planter boxes, and hanging baskets.

HOW TO PLANT

Impatiens should be planted in a well-prepared garden site. Add plenty of organic matter to sandy soil, and till the ground to a depth of 6 to 8 ins. Thoroughly moisten dry soils, then add the transplants. Give impatiens a 12- to 14-in. spacing. To prevent root rot problems, be sure not to plant too deeply. Immediately after planting, thoroughly moisten the soil. Many gardeners like to add a light mulch layer. Just be sure to keep the mulch several inches back from the stems of the plants.

ADVICE FOR CARE

Impatiens need frequent watering for the first few weeks. In sandy soils daily watering may be needed until the roots grow out into the surrounding soil. Gradually reduce watering to times when the surface inch of soil feels dry to the touch, then give the plantings a good soaking. Impatiens growing in containers may need more frequent watering. Check these plants daily, and water when the surface soil feels dry. After months of growth, impatiens usually become tall and lanky. Renew the more desirable growth by pruning the plants back to within 1 ft. of the ground. After a few weeks of warm weather they will be full and in flower again.

ADDITIONAL INFORMATION

All annuals can have pests. Planting the flowers at the proper time of the year and in well-drained soil can prevent most problems. Impatiens may have caterpillars, slugs, and mites as pests. Hand pick the pests from the plants where possible. Gardeners can also apply the Bacillus thuringiensis caterpillar control, a soap spray, slug bait or another appropriate control recommended by the University of Florida, following label suggestions. Nematodes can also be a pest for which there is no easy control. Presently, the best recommendation is to replace the soil in infested beds or grow the plants in containers. Also, you can sink the containers with plants in the soil.

ADDITIONAL SPECIES, CULTIVARS, OR VARIETIES

Some garden favorites include selections from the Dazzler, Accent, Super Elfin, Swirl, Shady Lady, and Tempo hybrids. Plant breeders are constantly developing new varieties, and gardeners should look for new selections to try at garden centers and through mail-order companies. For a special group of impatiens to add to the garden, consider the New Guinea types with colorful leaves and bright flowers. They tolerate full sun from fall through spring but should be given light shade for summer. Some good varieties include the Spectra hybrids and Tango.

ADVICE FOR REGIONAL CARE

North and Central Florida gardeners must be ready to give impatiens protection during the winter months. A cover with light bulbs for heat will minimize the chances of freeze damage on most cold nights. Replace impatiens in summer in South Florida.

Marigold

Tagetes patula

Height: 8 in. to over 1 ft.
Zones: 8, 9, 10, 11
Light Requirement:

There are many gardeners who believe that the marigold should be considered America's National Flower. It is the rose, however, which can lay claim to that distinction after winning out over the marigold for the title in 1986. Still, as runner-up, the marigold is a plant that deserves to be included in many gardens. What is often referred to as the American marigold is actually the African marigold, *Tagetes erecta*. Both the African marigold and the French marigold, *Tagetes patula*, in fact originated in the Americas. Early explorers took the plants to Europe and Africa where they were thereafter considered natives. For Florida gardeners, the best time to grow either type is during the warm seasons. Many gardeners favor the smaller selections that grow 8 to 12 in. tall, but they should not ignore the many good varieties that grow to over 1 ft. tall. Normally seen blooming in yellows or oranges, the adventuresome gardener might seek out a white marigold for a more exotic look. With their compact size, marigolds are suitable for use in flower beds, along walkways, or in container plantings.

WHEN TO PLANT

In the warmer locations, marigold may be planted year-round, but for most areas of the state, this is a warm-season annual that can be added to gardens and planters March through September. Just wait until the cooler weather is over, or be prepared to protect the plants with a cover during periods of frost or freezing weather.

WHERE TO PLANT

Give marigolds a sunny location for best growth. Marigolds can be planted in ground beds, container gardens, and planter boxes. Use taller selections as a backdrop for smaller flowers. Fill containers with marigolds, or use the types as a central feature and then add the other flowers for contrast.

HOW TO PLANT

Marigolds should be planted in a well-prepared garden site. Add

38

plenty of organic matter to sandy soils and till the ground to a depth of 6 to 8 in. Thoroughly moisten dry soils, then add the transplants. Give marigolds a 10- to 18-in. spacing. To prevent root rot problems, be sure not to plant too deeply. Immediately after planting, thoroughly moisten the soil. Many gardeners also like to add a light mulch layer. Just be sure to keep the mulch several inches back from the stems of the plants.

ADVICE FOR CARE

Marigolds need frequent waterings for the first few weeks. In sandy soils, daily waterings may be needed until the roots grow out into the surrounding soil. Gradually reduce watering frequency—when the surface inch of soil feels dry to the touch, give the plantings a good soaking. Marigolds growing in containers may need more frequent waterings. Check these plants daily and water when the surface soil feels dry to the touch.

ADDITIONAL INFORMATION

All annuals can have pest problems. By planting the flowers at the proper time of the year and in a well-drained soil, most problems can be prevented. Marigolds may have caterpillars, garden flea hoppers, mites, and leaf miners as pests. Hand pick the pest from the plants or apply a control recommended by the University of Florida, following label suggestions. Marigolds produce lots of seeds, which gardeners often like to save and plant. Most do germinate, but don't expect to get the same variety, as most marigolds are hybrids and may produce different flower types in the next generation.

ADDITIONAL SPECIES, CULTIVARS, OR VARIETIES

French marigold types for the garden include the Aurora, Bonanza, Hero, Boy, Janie, and Little Devil selections. Good African varieties to try include Antigua, Crush, Excel Jubilee, and Inca. New varieties and colors are constantly being added to the marigold collection. Check at the beginning of the year to find the newest introductions for your garden. Worth growing are the signet marigolds, *Tagetes tenuifolia*. Their flowers are small, but they cover the 12-in.-high and -wide plants.

ADVICE FOR REGIONAL CARE

Northern and Central Florida gardeners must give up marigolds when the weather turns cold. Frost and freezes kill the plants. It's possible to keep the plantings going year-round in southern areas of the state.

Nicotiana

Nicotiana alata

Height: 18 to 24 in.
Zones: 8 through 11
Light Requirement:

Many gardeners are returning to the nostalgic plants that they remember blooming in the gardens of their mothers or grandmothers. Nicotiana, better known as flowering tobacco, is one of those plants that is enjoying renewed attention in modern gardens. Part of the plant's newly enjoyed popularity is certainly due to breeders' efforts to introduce new varieties, which feature better flowering on shorter plants. Nicotiana features colorful spikes of red, pink, or white blossoms. Most varieties grow to a height from 18 to 24 in., making them suitable as a bedding plant alone or as a backdrop for other plants. Nicotiana is striking as an accent feature when a plant or two is placed in the center of a container planting.

WHEN TO PLANT

This is definitely a warm-season annual best planted during the spring season and possibly again for fall. The hot, rainy season destroys the flowers so that most plants are pulled out and replaced during the summer. Nicotiana does not grow well during the cooler winter months.

WHERE TO PLANT

Give nicotiana a sunny location for best growth. Locate the plantings where they can be seen and enjoyed. Nicotiana can be planted in ground beds, container gardens, and planter boxes.

HOW TO PLANT

Nicotiana should be planted in a well-prepared garden site. Add plenty of organic matter to sandy soil, and till the ground to a depth of 6 to 8 in. Thoroughly moisten dry soils, then add the transplants. Give nicotiana a 12- to 18-in. spacing. To prevent root rot problems, be sure not to plant too deeply. Immediately after planting, thoroughly moisten the soil. Many gardeners also like to add a light mulch layer. Just be sure to keep the mulch several inches back from the stems of the plants.

ADVICE FOR CARE

Nicotiana needs frequent watering for the first few weeks. In sandy soils daily watering may be needed until the roots grow out into the surrounding soil. Gradually reduce watering to times when the surface inch of soil feels dry to the touch, then give the plantings a good soaking. Nicotiana growing in containers may need more frequent watering. Check these plants daily, and water when the surface soil feels dry to the touch. The flowering season can be extended by keeping the plants from going to seed. As the flowering stalks finish blooming, cut them back to encourage new shoots to form. Expect 6 to 8 weeks of good color from nicotiana.

ADDITIONAL INFORMATION

All annuals can have pest problems. Planting the flowers at the proper time of the year and in a well-drained soil can prevent most problems. Nicotiana may have caterpillars as pests. Hand picking the pests from the plants is best. Gardeners can also apply the Bacillus thuringiensis caterpillar control or another control recommended by the University of Florida, following label suggestions.

ADDITIONAL SPECIES, CULTIVARS, OR VARIETIES

Good selections for the garden come from the Domino, Nicki, and Starship selections. Plant breeders have shown an interest in nicotiana in recent years, primarily in the addition of better pinks and reds. Check at the beginning of every year for varieties that may grow well in your garden.

ADVICE FOR REGIONAL CARE

North and Central Florida gardeners normally limit the nicotiana plantings to spring gardens. Southern gardeners often plant both spring and early fall.

Pansy

Viola × wittrockiana

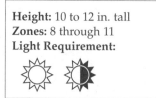

Height: 10 to 12 in. tall
Zones: 8 through 11
Light Requirement:

Gardeners love their pansies. This is the first cool-season annual they look for during the fall months. Most gardeners are a bit impatient, wanting the first pansies as early as September. But in most areas of Florida, that is just too early. Pansies need really cool weather and grow best when night temperatures are in the 50s. They are very hardy and won't mind a frost or freezing weather. After some of Florida's coldest weather, pansies may be the only flowers in the garden still in bloom. Gardeners love the pansies' colorful and cheery flowers. Some appear like little faces looking up from the ground. Others are solid color, which plant breeders say give the best display of color for the garden. Plant a solid bed of pansies, or use them in front of taller plantings. Add the flowering plants to container gardens or hanging baskets. As cut flowers, they are perfect for use in a bouquet.

WHEN TO PLANT

Wait until there is a consistent chill in the air before planting pansies. With too many hot days, the plants quickly decline. Even though garden centers may make pansies available in early fall, it's better to wait until at least late October or November to guarantee good growth. Your pansies should then last well into March. The last time to plant pansies is usually during February.

WHERE TO PLANT

Give pansies a sunny to lightly shaded location for best growth. Plants in full sun will be dense and produce the largest number of flowers. Locate the plantings where they can be seen and enjoyed. Pansies can be planted in ground beds, container gardens, planter boxes, and hanging baskets.

HOW TO PLANT

Pansies should be planted in a well-prepared garden site. Add plenty of organic matter to sandy soil, and till the ground to a depth of 6 to 8 in. Thoroughly moisten dry soils, then add the transplants.

Give pansies a 6- to 8-in. spacing. The plants do not spread out or fill in rapidly. The closest spacing gives the best-looking garden. To prevent root rot problems, be sure not to plant too deeply. Immediately after planting, thoroughly moisten the soil. Many gardeners also like to add a light mulch layer. Just be sure to keep the mulch several inches back from the stems of the plants.

ADVICE FOR CARE

Pansies need frequent watering for the first few weeks. In sandy soils daily watering may be needed until the roots grow out into the surrounding soil. Gradually reduce watering to times when the surface inch of soil feels dry to the touch, then give the plantings a good soaking. Pansies growing in containers may need more frequent watering. Check these plants daily, and water when the surface soil feels dry to the touch.

ADDITIONAL INFORMATION

All annuals can have pest problems. Planting the flowers at the proper time of the year and in well-drained soil can prevent most problems. Pansies may have aphids and slugs as pests. Hand picking the pests from the plants is best. Gardeners may also apply the Bacillus thuringiensis caterpillar control or another control recommended by the University of Florida, following label suggestions. Gardeners should pick bouquets of pansies and remove old blossoms to keep new flowers forming on the plants.

ADDITIONAL SPECIES, CULTIVARS, OR VARIETIES

Some good varieties for the garden include Happy Face, Imperial, Accord, Swiss Giant, Majestic Giants, Crystal Bowl, and Universal selections. Pansies get lots of attention from plant breeders. Check at the beginning of every gardening year for new introductions that might be added to your garden. Besides the traditional pansy, Florida gardeners like to plant the Johnny-jump-up *Viola tricolor*. The blossoms resemble miniature pansies and open several to a shoot. Plantings also sprawl out over the soil to give fuller beds more quickly than the normal pansies.

ADVICE FOR REGIONAL CARE

North Florida gardeners can get a slight jump on most pansy growers by adding pansies to the garden a month or two ahead of schedule. The plants also last longer into the spring season.

Petunia

Petunia × hybrida

Height: 12 to 18 in. tall
Zones: 8 through 11
Light Requirement:

With flowers that range from just over 1 in. to those that are 4 in. in diameter, the petunia offers a wide variety of bedding choices for the cool season. The plant's flowers are available in just about any color of the rainbow. Florida gardeners can choose from the large-flowered grandifloras, mid-sized floribundas, small-flowered multifloras, and new miniature millifloras. In addition, there are varieties with attractive double flowers. Gardeners growing petunias can count on good coverage from any of the varieties they choose. Petunia's spreading habit usually provides dependable coverage from just a few plants. The new milliflora tend to be the most compact, giving an 8- to 10-in.-diameter mound of color. Petunia's ranking as the number one cool-season annual by most Florida gardeners is well deserved. Its ability to take light frosts and its extended bloom period from the fall season right through the spring guarantee color at a time when many gardens need it most.

WHEN TO PLANT

Most gardeners are looking for the first petunias in September, but that may be too early to plant in most areas of the state. When the weather starts to cool during October or November, it's the best time to plant petunias. Most petunia plantings grow throughout the cooler months and last until the hot, damp summer season. When the rainy season returns by late May, most petunias begin to decline and should be replaced with warm-season flowers.

WHERE TO PLANT

Give petunias a sunny location for best growth. Locate the plantings where they can be seen and enjoyed. Petunias can be planted in ground beds, container gardens, planter boxes, and hanging baskets. Select the grandiflora types with large blossoms for close-up observation near walkways and on the patio. Use floribunda, multiflora, and milliflora petunias where you want mounds of flowers. Select the most trailing types for hanging baskets.

How to Plant

Petunias should be planted in a well-prepared garden site. Add
plenty of organic matter to sandy soil, and till the ground to a depth
of 6 to 8 ins. Thoroughly moisten dry soils, then add the transplants.
Give petunias a 10- to 12-in. spacing. To prevent root rot problems,
be sure not to plant too deeply. Immediately after planting, thoroughly moisten the soil. Many gardeners also like to add a light
mulch layer. Just be sure to keep the mulch several inches back from
the stems of the plants.

Advice for Care

Petunias need frequent watering for the first few weeks. In sandy
soils daily watering may be needed until the roots grow out into
the surrounding soil. Gradually reduce watering to times when
the surface inch of soil feels dry to the touch, then give the plantings a good soaking. Petunias growing in containers may need
more frequent watering. Check these plants daily, and water when
the surface soil feels dry to the touch.

Additional Information

All annuals can have pest problems. Planting the flowers at the right
time of the year and in well-drained soil can prevent most problems.
Petunias may have caterpillars and aphids as pests. Hand pick the
caterpillars or apply the Bacillus thuringiensis control. For aphids,
use a soap spray, or another control recommended by the University
of Florida, following label suggestions. Most plantings tend to grow
lanky and full of old blossoms and seed pods in time. Periodically
encourage new growth and extend the life of the plantings with a
rejuvenation pruning to remove the old and declining portions.

Additional Species, Cultivars, or Varieties

Petunia varieties for the garden include Prime Time, Ultra, Frost,
Celebrity, Picotee, Cloud, Madness, Aladdin, Carpet, and Fantasy
selections. Plant breeders are constantly developing new petunia
selections for the garden. Check at the beginning of every gardening
year for new selections that might grow in the home landscape.

Advice for Regional Care

North Florida gardeners can often get a head start on more southern
growers by planting petunias up to a month ahead of schedule.
Plantings in the cooler portions of the state may grow into late
spring and early summer. Plantings in North Florida are likely to
need protection from the sometimes severe freezing weather.

Portulaca

Portulaca grandiflora

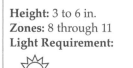

Height: 3 to 6 in.
Zones: 8 through 11
Light Requirement:

The hot, strong Florida sun in summer often proves many a plant's undoing. Not so with portulaca. The moss rose, or Mexican rose as it is sometimes called, loves to provide color in the most sun-drenched areas of the garden. The plump flower buds and spreading growth habit make it a natural for the rock garden or other dry land plantings where a desert look is desired. Many gardeners may remember the older varieties of portulaca that would open during the morning but close down in the heat of the day or when visited by insects. Breeding efforts, however, have now resulted in varieties that provide a full day of color any time the sun shines. The colors of portulaca flowers are vivid and include brilliant reds, pinks, oranges, yellows, creams, and white. The blossoms are available as singles or as doubles. Portulaca grow best during the warm months of spring through summer. The plants open flowers for 6 to 8 weeks before gradually declining.

WHEN TO PLANT

This is definitely a warm-season flower. The plantings seem to feed on Florida's hottest days. Start plantings by April, and continue through the summer months into early fall. Cool weather and short days appear to signal the decline for portulaca plantings.

WHERE TO PLANT

Give portulaca a sun-only location for best growth. Locate the plantings where they can be seen and enjoyed. Portulaca can be planted in ground beds, container gardens, planter boxes, and hanging baskets. The natural trailing habit of portulaca makes it ideal to be viewed from a balcony, porch, or other eye-level or above setting.

HOW TO PLANT

Portulaca should be planted in a well-prepared garden site. Add plenty of organic matter to sandy soil, and till the ground to a depth of 6 to 8 in. Thoroughly moisten dry soils, then add the transplants. Give portulaca an 8- to 10-in. spacing. To prevent root rot problems, be sure not to plant too deeply. Immediately after planting, thoroughly moisten the soil. Many gardeners also like to add a light mulch layer. Just be sure to keep the mulch several inches back from the stems of the plants.

ADVICE FOR CARE

Portulaca needs frequent watering for the first few weeks. In sandy soils daily watering may be needed until the roots grow out into the surrounding soil. Gradually reduce watering to times when the surface inch of soil feels dry to the touch, then give the plantings a good soaking. Portulaca growing in containers may need more frequent watering. Check these plants daily, and water when the surface soil feels dry to the touch. Don't worry if you skip a watering or two; portulaca is quite drought tolerant.

ADDITIONAL INFORMATION

All annuals can have pest problems. Planting the flowers at the proper time of the year and in well-drained soil can prevent most problems. Portulaca may have mites as pests. When present, apply a soap spray or apply a control recommended by the University of Florida, following label suggestions.

ADDITIONAL SPECIES, CULTIVARS, OR VARIETIES

Some good Florida varieties include Afternoon Delight, Sundance, Sundial, and Calypso selections. Check every gardening year for new portulaca selections that may be added to the landscape. A close relative marketed as purslane, *Portulaca oleracea,* is also found at Florida garden centers. The plants have broad, fleshy leaves and lots of small, colorful flowers. It's best used as a groundcover or plant for hanging baskets. Purslane propagates quickly from cuttings.

ADVICE FOR REGIONAL CARE

South Florida gardeners start planting portulaca a few weeks to a month earlier than Central or North Florida gardeners. Portulaca may also last longer into the fall in the South.

Salvia

Salvia splendens

Height: 8 to 18 in.
Zones: 8 through 11
Light Requirement:

A warm-season mainstay of the garden, salvia provides some of the brightest color in the landscape. With lots of rocketlike spikes, salvia can be counted on for almost year-round color in flower beds and containers. For years this plant was known as scarlet sage for its bright-red coloration. Red still continues to be the most popular and reliable color, but breeders have now developed some excellent pinks, whites, and violets for added variety. Depending on the variety chosen, the flowering plant can grow from 8 to 18 in. tall. Salvia gives the best display when planted in clusters for an impressive burst of color.

When to Plant

Salvia can be planted year-round but is susceptible to cold injury. In the warmer areas of the state you can count on several seasons of display life. Some varieties may grow for more than a year. The best time to plant a salvia bed is during the spring months to get a long season of display. Plantings often continue through the summer and early fall months.

Where to Plant

Give salvia a full-sun location for best growth. Locate the plantings where they can be seen and enjoyed. Salvia can be planted in ground beds, container gardens, and planter boxes. Salvias make good feature plants for the flower bed and container gardens. Plant the most colorful selections in an area where they catch the visitor's eye.

How to Plant

Salvias should be planted in a well-prepared garden site. Be careful when purchasing pot-grown plants that they are not overly pot-bound and incapable of growing out into the surrounding soil. Add plenty of organic matter to sandy soil, and till the ground to a depth of 6 to 8 in. Thoroughly moisten dry soil, then add the transplants. Give salvias a 10- to 16-in. spacing. To prevent root rot problems, be sure not to plant too deeply. Thoroughly moisten the soil immediately after planting. Many gardeners also like to add a light mulch layer. Just be sure to keep the mulch several inches back from the stems of the plants.

ADVICE FOR CARE

Salvias need frequent watering for the first few weeks. In sandy soils daily watering may be needed until the roots grow out into the surrounding soil. Gradually reduce watering to times when the surface inch of soil feels dry to the touch, then give the plantings a good soaking. Salvias growing in containers may need more frequent watering. Check these plants daily, and water when the surface soil feels dry to the touch. Salvias can grow tall and lanky after months of flowering. Keep the plants attractive and encourage new shoots by periodically removing the old flower heads and extra-long stems.

ADDITIONAL INFORMATION

All annuals can have pest problems. Planting the flowers at the proper time of the year and in well-drained soil can prevent most problems. Salvia may have caterpillars, mites, and slugs as pests. Hand picking the pests from the plants is best. Gardeners can also apply the Bacillus thuringiensis caterpillar control, use slug bait, or use another control recommended by the University of Florida, following label suggestions.

ADDITIONAL SPECIES, CULTIVARS, OR VARIETIES

Varieties for the Florida garden include Hotline, St. John's Fire, Bonfire, Red Hot Sally, Sizzler, Carabiniere, and Top selections. Plant breeders are constantly adding new salvia varieties. Check at the beginning of every gardening year for new introductions. Several additional species make excellent garden flowers. Species *Salvia farinacea* opens white or purple flowers from March through October. Species *Salvia coccinea* offers year-round red, pink, or white blossoms.

ADVICE FOR REGIONAL CARE

North Florida gardeners can expect salvias to be damaged by winter frosts and freezes. Central Florida gardeners can help most salvia plants survive the winter with just a covering during the cold weather.

Snapdragon

Antirrhinum majus

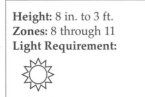

Height: 8 in. to 3 ft.
Zones: 8 through 11
Light Requirement:

The snapdragon is another old-fashioned flower that has been rejuvenated for use in the modern garden. Many gardeners remember the 3-ft. rocket snapdragons that were grown for use in floral arrangements or left to stand tall in flower beds. The larger varieties are still available but are often considered too large for today's landscapes. Now there are lower-growing and more colorful snapdragons from which to choose. Many of these new varieties still have the dragonlike heads of old, but breeders have developed a butterfly series of flower forms. These appear to give a lot more color from the open blooms. New varieties are much more compact, growing from only 8 to 20 in. tall, making them ideal for winter flower beds or containers. One thing that hasn't changed about snapdragons—they are still perfect in a bouquet.

WHEN TO PLANT

Snapdragons are available for fall through early spring plantings. The plants are tolerant of frost and light freezes. They are often one of the first flowers to recover after harsh winter weather. Hot weather causes the plantings to decline. Most beds are removed by early summer and replaced with warm-season color.

WHERE TO PLANT

Give snapdragons a sunny location for best growth. Locate the plantings where they can be seen and enjoyed. Snapdragons can be planted in ground beds, container gardens, and planter boxes. Use the taller varieties for background flowers or the central feature in container gardens. Dwarf types can be used as border plantings or a colorful groundcover.

HOW TO PLANT

Snapdragons should be planted in a well-prepared garden site. Add plenty of organic matter to sandy soil, and till the ground to a depth of 6 to 8 in. Thoroughly moisten dry soils, then add the transplants. Give snapdragons a 10- to 14-in. spacing. To prevent root rot problems, be sure not to plant too deeply. Immediately after planting, thoroughly moisten the soil. Many gardeners also like to add a light mulch layer. Just be sure to keep the mulch several inches back from the stems of the plants. Taller varieties often need staking to support the flower spikes. Use a garden wire or individual stakes to prevent wind damage to the plants.

ADVICE FOR CARE

Snapdragons need frequent watering for the first few weeks. In sandy soils daily watering may be needed until the roots grow out into the surrounding soil. Gradually reduce watering to times when the surface inch of soil feels dry to the touch, then give the plantings a good soaking. Snapdragons growing in containers may need more frequent watering. Check these plants daily, and water when the surface soil feels dry to the touch. This is a plant that is great for cutting bouquets. Removal of the flowers and seed heads encourages new shoots and prevents the rapid decline of plantings.

ADDITIONAL INFORMATION

All annuals can have pest problems. Planting the flowers at the proper time of the year and in well-drained soil can prevent most problems. Snapdragons may have caterpillars as pests. Hand picking the pests from the plants is best. Gardeners can also apply a Bacillus thuringiensis caterpillar control or another control recommended by the University of Florida following label suggestions.

ADDITIONAL SPECIES, CULTIVARS, OR VARIETIES

Some good varieties for the garden include Bells, Chimes, Floral Carpet, Tahiti, Liberty, and Sonnet selections. Gardeners who still want the tall garden types should plant Rocket hybrids. Plant breeders are developing new varieties of snapdragons for the garden. Check at the beginning of the year for new introductions to grow in the garden.

ADVICE FOR REGIONAL CARE

North and Central Florida gardeners should give plantings winter protection to avoid major damage. South Florida gardeners should delay plantings until the cooler weather arrives. In the warmer areas the plantings may not last through spring.

Torenia

Torenia fournieri

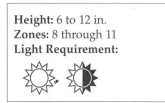

Height: 6 to 12 in.
Zones: 8 through 11
Light Requirement:

A warm-season flowering plant that covers the ground in a blanket of foliage and flowers, torenia is a plant of many names. Often called the summer pansy because the flowers grow best during warm weather when true pansies are long gone, torenia often serves the same landscape needs as its namesake. The wishbonelike shape of the stamens in the blossoms is the source of another name for torenia—the wishbone flower. No matter the name, this plant is a must for the garden due to its tolerance of heat, rain, and light shade. Originally, torenia flowered only in shades of purple, but now the color selections include blue and white plus pink and white blends. All of the flowers are accented with a spot of yellow in the throat of the blossom. Expect the sprawling plants to last for the entire warm season, producing one flush of blooms after another. The plants will start to decline as days shorten and should then be replaced with cool-season color.

WHEN TO PLANT

Start adding torenia to the garden as soon as the cold weather is over. Most gardeners can make the plantings from March through August.

WHERE TO PLANT

Give torenia a full-sun to lightly shaded location for best growth. Locate the plantings where they can be seen and enjoyed. Torenia can be planted in ground beds, container gardens, planter boxes, and hanging baskets. In the landscape fill a bed with only torenia, or use them as a groundcover in front of taller flowers. They can be featured alone in containers or used along the outer edges to hang down over the sides.

HOW TO PLANT

Torenia should be planted in a well-prepared garden site. Add plenty of organic matter to sandy soil, and till the ground to a depth of 6 to 8 in. Thoroughly moisten dry soils, then add the transplants.

Give torenia an 8- to 12-in. spacing. To prevent root rot problems, be sure not to plant too deeply. Immediately after planting, thoroughly moisten the soil. Many gardeners also like to add a light mulch layer. Just be sure to keep the mulch several inches back from the stems of the plants.

ADVICE FOR CARE

Torenia need frequent watering for the first few weeks. In sandy soils daily watering may be needed until the roots grow out into the surrounding soil. Gradually reduce watering to times when the surface inch of soil feels dry to the touch, then give the plantings a good soaking. Torenia growing in containers may need more frequent watering. Check these plants daily, and water when the surface soil feels dry to the touch.

ADDITIONAL INFORMATION

All annuals can have pest problems. Planting the flowers at the proper time of the year and in well-drained soil can prevent most problems. Torenia may have caterpillars and slugs as pests. Hand picking the pests from the plants is best. Gardeners can also apply a Bacillus thuringiensis caterpillar control, use slug bait, or apply another control recommended by the University of Florida, following label suggestions. Larger-growing varieties can become lanky and may need grooming to remain attractive.

ADDITIONAL SPECIES, CULTIVARS, OR VARIETIES

Very few new varieties have been added, but new color combinations have been introduced. Some good varieties include Clown, Happy Faces, and Panda selections. Check yearly for new types to plant in the garden. One eye-catching new species for the garden is *Torenia baillonii* var. Suzie Wong. It makes an excellent basket specimen. Each flower is bright yellow with an almost black center.

ADVICE FOR REGIONAL CARE

Torenia need similar care throughout the state. Northern gardens should delay plantings until consistently warm weather arrives.

Verbena

Verbena × hybrida

Height: 10 to 12 in.
Zones: 8 through 11
Light Requirement:

Verbena provides some of the best garden blues and purples for the landscape while also sporting attractive foliage. With most verbena varieties growing only 10 to 12 in. tall, the wide-spreading plants are ideal for use as a colorful groundcover to fill flower beds. Verbena leaves are deep green and usually have an attractive scalloped edge, which adds to the beauty of the plantings. Although largely popular for its blue and purple flowers, other colors are available, including red, white, and cream selections. Some blossoms also have a cream-colored "eye" as a special accent. Verbena is particularly lovely when filling containers with its vinelike stems of foliage during warm-weather months. The plant is mainly a warm-season annual that tends to trail off in the early winter months.

WHEN TO PLANT

Verbena grows best during the warmer months. Begin plantings during March and continue through October. Most selections give 6 to 8 weeks of good flowering before needing to be replaced.

WHERE TO PLANT

Give verbena a sunny location for best growth. Locate the plantings where they can be seen and enjoyed. Verbena can be planted in ground beds, container gardens, planter boxes, and hanging baskets. Plantings look their best where the vines can hang down over walls and the sides of containers. Use them as a groundcover in front of taller flowers or near the edge of container gardens. Verbena can also be used to complement rock garden plantings.

HOW TO PLANT

Verbena should be planted in a well-prepared garden site. Add plenty of organic matter to sandy soil, and till the ground to a depth of 6 to 8 in. Thoroughly moisten dry soils, then add the transplants. Give verbena a 10- to 14-in. spacing. To prevent root rot problems, be sure not to plant too deeply. Immediately after planting, thoroughly moisten the soil. Many gardeners also like to add a light mulch layer. Just be sure to keep the mulch several inches back from the stems of the plants.

ADVICE FOR CARE

Verbena plantings need frequent watering for the first few weeks. In sandy soils daily watering may be needed until the roots grow out into the surrounding soil. Gradually reduce watering to times when the surface inch of soil feels dry to the touch, then give the plantings a good soaking. Verbena plantings growing in containers may need more frequent watering. Check these plants daily, and water when the surface soil feels dry to the touch.

ADDITIONAL INFORMATION

All annuals can have pest problems. Planting the flowers at the proper time of the year and in well-drained soil can prevent most problems. Verbena may have caterpillars, mites, and garden flea hoppers as pests. Hand pick the pests from the plants, or apply a control recommended by the University of Florida, following label suggestions.

ADDITIONAL SPECIES, CULTIVARS, OR VARIETIES

Plant breeders are constantly developing new varieties for home plantings. Some good varieties include Romance, Peaches and Cream, Amour, Trinidad, and Novalis selections. Check yearly for new selections that might be added to the garden.

ADVICE FOR REGIONAL CARE

Verbena plantings are cold sensitive and may be damaged by frost and freezes in North and Central Florida gardens. Early plantings should be protected from winter injury with covers when cold weather is expected. Southern gardeners may start planting a month or more ahead of schedule due to warmer growing conditions.

Vinca

Catharanthus roseus

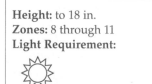

Height: to 18 in.
Zones: 8 through 11
Light Requirement:

Once shunned as too commonplace, vinca is enjoying renewed use in the landscape. A die-hard plant that withstands both heat and drought, vinca provides abundant large blossoms on extremely vigorous plants. Seedlings are often found sprouting in old, neglected gardens and vacant landscapes. Oftentimes called periwinkle, vinca can withstand much on its own but flourishes with conscientious care. For years the flower colors were limited to shades of pink and white, but now there are good reds, deep pinks, and some bicolors from which to choose. Vinca is a good mid-range annual for the rock garden, growing to 18 in. tall and often twice as wide. Vinca thrives during warm months when it is also effective in flower beds, container gardens, and dry land plantings.

When to Plant

Add vincas to flower beds when the cold weather is over. Most plantings can be made from March through September. Vinca is cold sensitive and is usually damaged by frosts and freezing weather. Some plants may survive and grow back during the spring. Most plantings should be replaced during early to mid-fall with cool-season flowers.

Where to Plant

Give vincas a sunny location for best growth. Locate the plantings where they can be seen and enjoyed. Vincas can be planted in ground beds, container gardens, planter boxes, and hanging baskets. Vinca is often treated as an annual groundcover to fill hot, dry beds during the spring and summer season. Give vinca your poor locations, and once it's established, it usually flourishes with minimal care. Plantings require well-drained soil, or they are subject to root and stem rot.

How to Plant

Vinca should be planted in a well-prepared garden site. Add plenty of organic matter to sandy soil, and till the ground to a depth of 6 to

8 in. Thoroughly moisten dry soils, then add the transplants. Give vinca a 12- to 16-in. spacing. To prevent root rot problems, be sure not to plant too deeply. Immediately after planting, thoroughly moisten the soil. Many gardeners also like to add a light mulch layer. Just be sure to keep the mulch several inches back from the stems of the plants.

ADVICE FOR CARE

Vincas need frequent watering for the first few weeks. In sandy soils daily watering may be needed until the roots grow out into the surrounding soil. Gradually reduce watering to times when the surface inch of soil feels dry to the touch, then give the plantings a good soaking. Overwatering of established plants causes rapid decline of vinca. It's better to keep the plants too dry than too wet. Vinca growing in containers may need more frequent watering. Check these plants daily, and water when the surface soil feels dry to the touch.

ADDITIONAL INFORMATION

All annuals can have pest problems. Planting the flowers at the proper time of the year and in well-drained soil can prevent most problems. Mites plus stem and root rot damage may be major problems for vincas. Control mites with a soap spray or another control recommended by the University of Florida, following label suggestions. Stem and root rots are controlled by proper watering.

ADDITIONAL SPECIES, CULTIVARS, OR VARIETIES

Plant breeders are constantly developing new colors and varieties with better pest resistance. Good varieties for the Florida landscape include Cooler, Parasol, Tropicana, Pretty In Rose, Little, and Passion selections. Check at the beginning of every year for new selections that may be planted in home landscapes.

ADVICE FOR REGIONAL CARE

North and Central Florida gardeners usually lose their vinca plantings to winter injury. In South Florida landscapes some varieties may persist for more than a year. These plants often grow lanky and need pruning to maintain a compact and attractive growth habit.

Wax Begonia

Begonia × semperflorens-cultorum

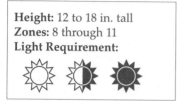

Height: 12 to 18 in. tall
Zones: 8 through 11
Light Requirement:

Begonia is a dependable, minimal-care plant that thrives in a variety of garden situations. Attractive almost the entire year, begonias thrive in the shady spots of the garden along with those receiving full sun. Never before have begonias enjoyed as much popularity in the landscape as today, perhaps because hybridizers have developed some very durable selections. The tidy, mounding plants are available with flowers in a variety of colors including all shades of pinks and reds plus some very pure whites. The plants flower continuously to create spots of color. Most also have the very familiar little spot of yellow stamens in the center of the blossoms. Begonia foliage is very attractive, varying from bright green to bronze in color. All plants are compact and well rounded in shape.

WHEN TO PLANT

Wax begonias have become year-round additions to home landscapes. They are cold sensitive, so gardeners making winter plantings are taking a risk in the colder areas of the state. Begonias establish best if planted before days become consistently hot. Where possible, plant beds March through May to have the plants well rooted in the ground by summer. This helps prevent leaf burn that may result due to inadequate root systems during the hotter months.

WHERE TO PLANT

Give begonia a full-sun to shady location for good growth. Plantings in shady locations may become a little lanky, but they give often needed color in the reduced light areas of the landscape. Locate the plantings where they can be seen and enjoyed. Wax begonias can be planted in ground beds, container gardens, planter boxes, and hanging baskets. Many gardeners fill entire beds with begonias or use them in front of taller flowers. You may wish to create patterns in beds using the different colors of begonia foliage and flowers.

How to Plant

Wax begonias should be planted in a well-prepared garden site. Add plenty of organic matter to sandy soil, and till the ground to a depth of 6 to 8 in. Thoroughly moisten dry soils, then add the transplants. Give wax begonias a 10- to 12-in. spacing. To prevent root rot, be sure not to plant too deeply. Immediately after planting, thoroughly moisten the soil. Many gardeners also like to add a light mulch layer. Just be sure to keep the mulch several inches back from the stems of the plants.

Advice for Care

Wax begonias need frequent watering for the first few weeks. In sandy soils daily watering may be needed until the roots grow out into the surrounding soil. Gradually reduce watering to times when the surface inch of soil feels dry to the touch, then give the plantings a good soaking. Wax begonias growing in containers may need more frequent watering. Check these plants daily, and water when the surface soil feels dry to the touch. Begonias may grow for several seasons to a year or more before declining. Often the plants become lanky and can be pruned back to renew the compact attractive growth habit.

Additional Information

All annuals can have pest problems. Planting the flowers at the proper time of the year and in well-drained soil can prevent most problems. Wax begonias may have caterpillars and slugs as pests. Gardeners can also apply a Bacillus thuringiensis caterpillar control, use a slug bait, a soap spray, or product recommended by the University of Florida, following label suggestions.

Additional Species, Cultivars, or Varieties

Plant breeders are developing new varieties for home planting. Some good varieties for the Florida landscape include the Encore, Varsity, Olympia, Prelude, Victory, Cocktail, Senator, Pizzazz, and Ambassador selections. Check at the beginning of each year for new selections that you might add to the landscape.

Advice for Regional Care

North and Central Florida gardeners usually lose their begonias to frost and freezing weather. Avoid making plantings too late in the year, or be ready to provide cold protection. In South Florida begonias can be planted year-round.

Zinnia

Zinnia elegans

Height: 8 in. to 3 ft.
Zones: 8 through 11
Light Requirement:

The zinnia is a bright, carefree flowering plant with big, long-lasting blossoms. Most zinnias grow a little larger than other garden flowers. Lots of gardeners remember the older varieties such as Giants of California that grew more than 3 ft. tall. They weren't suitable for every garden, but now there are zinnias for every spot. Some grow just 8 in. tall and are ideal for borders, and others in the 12- to 24-in. range find use in background plantings. Of course, you can always fill a bed with zinnias or set them out in a row in a garden. The flowers are big and beautiful, ranging from 2 to 5 in. in diameter. There is an excellent assortment of colors—pinks, reds, oranges, and plums plus white. Zinnias are great to enjoy in the garden or cut to bring indoors. Some gardeners even say the flowers have a slight but pleasing fragrance.

WHEN TO PLANT

Get Florida plantings in the ground during early spring. The weather quickly gets too hot and humid for good zinnia production throughout most of the state. Best plantings are made during March and April to avoid pest problems.

WHERE TO PLANT

Give zinnias a full-sun location for best growth. Locate the plantings where they can be seen and enjoyed. Zinnias can be planted in ground beds, container gardens, and planter boxes. Fill a bed with zinnias, or set taller varieties to the back of the bed as a backdrop for other flowers. In container gardens zinnias are often featured as the central plant.

HOW TO PLANT

Zinnias should be planted in a well-prepared garden site. Add plenty of organic matter to sandy soil, and till the ground to a depth of 6 to 8 in. Thoroughly moisten dry soils, then add the transplants. Give zinnias a 10- to 20-in. spacing, depending on the ultimate size of the variety. To prevent root rot problems, be sure not to plant too deeply. Immediately after planting, thoroughly moisten the soil. Many gardeners also like to add a light mulch layer. Just be sure to keep the mulch several inches back from the stems of the plants. Taller zinnia varieties can be affected by winds that cause limbs to break. Add a stake near the plants to tie up larger stems as they develop.

ADVICE FOR CARE

Zinnias need frequent watering for the first few weeks. In sandy soils daily watering may be needed until the roots grow out into the surrounding soil. Gradually reduce watering to times when the surface inch of soil feels dry to the touch, then give the plantings a good soaking. Zinnias growing in containers may need more frequent watering. Check these plants daily, and water when the surface soil feels dry to the touch. Extend the flowering period by cutting bouquets and removing the declining blossoms.

ADDITIONAL INFORMATION

All annuals can have pest problems. Planting the flowers at the proper time of the year and in well-drained soil can prevent most problems. Zinnias may have caterpillars, leaf spot, and powdery mildew as pests. Caterpillars can be hand picked or treated with a Bacillus thuringiensis control recommended by the University of Florida. Zinnia diseases are best controlled by plantings made during the spring or application of a properly labeled copper fungicide or another University-recommended fungicide.

ADDITIONAL SPECIES, CULTIVARS, OR VARIETIES

Plant breeders are constantly developing new garden varieties. Good varieties for your Florida garden include Dasher, Dreamland, Peter Pan, Pulcino, Small World, Thumbelina, Short Stuff, and Ruffles selections. Check yearly for new selections that might be added to the flower beds. Another zinnia gardeners should add to the landscape is commonly called linearis, *Zinnia angustifolia*. It produces sprawling plants with lots of small orange or white blossoms. Unlike most garden zinnias it's not affected by heat and humidity and can be planted throughout the spring and summer seasons.

ADVICE FOR REGIONAL CARE

North Florida gardeners can enjoy a little longer planting season due to the often cooler spring and early summer weather. Central and South Florida gardeners must plant zinnias early to enjoy the 6 to 8 weeks of good flowering.

CHAPTER TWO

Bulbs

$\mathcal{C}$OULD IT BE THEIR EPHEMERAL QUALITY THAT MAKES US LOVE THEM? Bulbs are plants that have found a niche in time and work quickly to take advantage of it. The temperate bulbs of the northern woods appear in late winter before the snow has melted, rising, flowering, and setting seed before the leaves return to intercept the light. Beginning with the snowdrops, then crocus, the iris, the squill, by turns, accompany the earth to the spring equinox.

Tropical bulbs must work between wet and dry seasons, finding sustenance in the rainy months, storing within the bulbs the means to get through the dry, often resting during drought, sending up flowers as or before the rains return.

Amaryllis have become such popular Christmas plants that we forget they are forced to bloom at that time, and normally bloom in spring. These are the Dutch amaryllis, which are classified botanically as *Hippeastrum*; the true amaryllis is *Amaryllis belladonna*, which has smaller, fragrant pink flowers that appear in the fall.

Caladiums are the summer bulbs in Florida, providing some of the most beautiful leaves anywhere. They are from Central America and northern South America. Early this century, Henry Nehrling, a botanist and plantsman living in Gotha, near Orlando, and then in Naples, created about 1500 caladium hybrids, some of which are still grown today. Freida Hemple may be one of his best-known hybrids.

Rain lilies, both *Zephyranthes* and *Hebranthes*, are delightful little bulbs to have around because their rain-sparked flowers seem to

Chapter Two

appear so suddenly. The foliage is like liriope or lilyturf, and you might try using rain lilies instead of liriope in a nice shaded area. Debra DeMarco, a landscape designer in South Miami, often uses society garlic, another bulb, in place of liriope.

One of the most spectacular of all bulbs is the voodoo lily, *Amorphophallus*. This largest of all flowers from Sumatra, *Amorphophallus titanium*, can stand 5 to 6 feet tall. The first reports of the plant seemed so exaggerated that no one believed it. Smaller species are grown in South Florida from time to time, and they never fail to attract attention when blooming.

Most bulbs are in garden centers (and catalogs) in the fall. If you live in South Florida, you can buy temperate bulbs and store them in the refrigerator's vegetable bin until midwinter. Then plant them for spring flowers, and expect them to last only a season. The *Reader's Digest Illustrated Guide to Gardening* offers this advice for refrigerating bulbs: never put them in the same refrigerator bin as fruit, for the ethylene gas from the fruit will kill the bulbs.

Tropical bulbs may be left in the ground year-round in South Florida. The winter's dry season will give them the rest they need, and you should water sparingly until they begin to put up new leaves, then fertilize and keep the area moist.

Bulbs like a rich soil that drains well, and peat moss, compost, or aged manure can be added to the soil to help it drain and to keep it somewhat moist.

As border plants or bedding plants, as accents, as just the right plant for a special place, bulbs bring a charm of their own to the garden. They can make lovely tabletop flowers when forced. As cuts, they can be spectacular in clear crystal with nothing but themselves for company.

African Iris

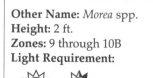

Other Name: *Morea* spp.
Height: 2 ft.
Zones: 9 through 10B
Light Requirement:

Sometimes also called fortnight lily, the African iris is considered a hardy (for a tropical plant) and drought-tolerant bulb. Its 3 outer petals are marked with yellow and are longer than the 3 inner ones. The plants are among the lovely members of the Iris family, most of which originated in tropical America and South Africa. It blooms in the spring and summer in Florida. *Flowers of the World* and other references classify it as *Moraea*. The *Moraea* is from the name of (a) an 18th-century English botanist, Robert More, or (b) the father-in-law of Linnaeus, J. Moraeus. (We do wish these references would get their references straight.) No matter. The iris are planted any time of year, about 6 inches apart, and should be planted in good organic soil. They bloom off and on throughout the season at roughly 2-week intervals, which is why one common name includes the word "fortnight."

WHEN TO PLANT
Plant any time during the year.

WHERE TO PLANT
Plant in full sun. You may want them to have their own bed, or plant them in front of shrubs that tend to get leggy, such as crotons, so they will disguise the bare trunks.

HOW TO PLANT
Enrich the planting hole of the rhizome with organic matter, such as compost, peat moss, and pine-bark mulch. Sand will help increase drainage. Put a little bone meal in the bottom of the planting hole, which should be 2 to 3 in. deep. Cover the hole, and fertilize with 1 to 2 teaspoons of a slow-release fertilizer, and then mulch. Water in well.

ADVICE FOR CARE

If using a granular fertilizer, 2 to 3 pounds per 100 sq. ft. of bulb bed is sufficient. Bulbs already contain enough stored food to go through their first flowering. Rhizomes also store water as well as food, which is one reason these are said to be drought tolerant. But they will profit in their flowering capacity if you water them regularly, 2 to 3 times a week if it does not rain.

ADDITIONAL INFORMATION

Grasshoppers and snails love lilies. The newest product for use to fight grasshoppers is *Nosema locustae*, a protozoa which has various commercially packaged names such as Semaspore or Nolo Bait or Grasshopper Attack. It causes grasshoppers to produce fewer eggs For snails or garden slugs, protect lilies with copper screen barriers or, in dry seasons, with diatomaceous earth.

ADDITIONAL SPECIES, CULTIVARS, OR VARIETIES

Dietes vegeta (or *Moraea iridioides*) has large white flowers with orange/brown and blue markings; 'Lemon Drops' and 'Orange Drops' have yellow or orange markings.

ADVICE FOR REGIONAL CARE

Where cold is a problem, grow tropical bulbs in pots to bring inside in winter.

African Lily

Agapanthus africanus

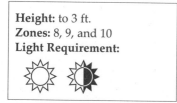

Height: to 3 ft.
Zones: 8, 9, and 10
Light Requirement:

Gardeners who want spring color in a great accent plant will love the durable African lilies. The plants give an eye-catching flower display, shooting up an inflorescence that's topped with a ball-like cluster of blue or white flowers. Each blossom is 1 to 2 in. long. When not in bloom, the plants provide dark-green straplike foliage for year-round greenery. Add African lilies to the perennial flower bed, or spot them among shrub plantings throughout the landscape. Make sure to use them in areas that can be easily seen during the spring flowering season. Some gardeners also like to grow the plants in containers for the patio or entrance area. This makes them mobile so that they can be displayed where desired when they are at their best color.

WHEN TO PLANT

Rhizomes of African lilies are best planted from October through March in the Florida landscape. Container plants in bloom are available from garden centers for planting throughout the year. They can be added to the landscape at any time.

WHERE TO PLANT

Give the African lily a full-sun to partial-shade location. It grows best in areas with 6 to 8 hours of sun and bright light for the remaining portions of the day. The plantings like a moist and improved soil with good drainage. Select areas that do not flood during the rainy season.

HOW TO PLANT

All bulbs should be planted in well-drained soil. African lilies grow well in sandy soils as long as they are given plenty of water and all the nutrients needed for growth. Plants are easier to maintain if the soil is improved with organic matter before planting. Work liberal quantities of compost or peat moss and manure into the planting site. African lilies should be set in the soil with the tops of the rhizomes just below the surface of the ground. Space the rhizomes 12 in. apart. After planting, provide adequate water to thoroughly moisten the soil. A light mulch can be added to maintain soil moisture and supply some nutrients. When planting in containers, use a loose potting mix and large containers.

ADVICE FOR CARE

Keep planting sites moist, watering whenever the surface soil feels dry to the touch. Less water will be needed during the winter months than during the hotter, drier months of the year. The African lily needs a light feeding once in March, May, and September. Gardeners can use a 6-6-6 or similar garden fertilizer, following label instructions for bulbs or perennial plantings. After the plants have flowered, most gardeners cut the old stalks back to near the ground to allow the plant's energy to go into bulb production. Some gardeners allow the plant to continue seed development.

ADDITIONAL INFORMATION

All bulbous plants need division after a few years of growth. African lilies seem to flower best when a bit crowded, however. Limit division to the more vigorous clumps. African lilies are best divided during the fall and winter months. Gently break the rhizome portions apart and reset them in a prepared garden site, or share with friends. Bulbs have a few pests. African lilies may be affected by caterpillars and grasshoppers. Hand pick pests from the plants, or treat them with a pest-control product recommended by the University of Florida, following label instructions.

ADDITIONAL SPECIES, CULTIVARS, OR VARIETIES

Colorful selections of the African lily are often available from garden centers, local growers, and mail-order nurseries. Every year, check for new introductions that are suitable for planting in your landscape.

ADVICE FOR REGIONAL CARE

African lilies grow best in North and Central Florida gardens. In the colder portions of the state, protect them from the more severe freezes. Plantings in South Florida are usually short-lived.

Alstroemeria

Alstroemeria spp.

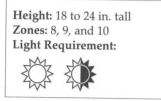

Height: 18 to 24 in. tall
Zones: 8, 9, and 10
Light Requirement:

The lilylike green and red blossoms of alstroemeria, sometimes called the parrot flower, are often used as colorful filler in flower arrangements. Depending on the variety, other selections are available with pink, yellow, and white flower colorations. The 1- to 2-in. blossoms are produced in clusters at the top of a stalk held high above the foliage during late spring and early summer. Even the foliage is very ornamental. The bright-green, oval leaves develop along an upright stem. After the flowers fade, the leaves gradually decline, and the plantings remain dormant until late winter. Alstroemeria makes a great late spring accent when color is often needed. Use it in perennial beds or containers, along walkways, and as an addition to shrub plantings.

WHEN TO PLANT

Alstroemeria is best planted from late winter through spring in Florida gardens. Plants may be available in containers at local garden centers or mail-order nurseries for planting at any time of the year.

WHERE TO PLANT

Give alstroemeria a full-sun to partial-shade location. Consider these plants more for lower light areas. They grow well in areas with 4 to 6 hours of sun and bright light for the remaining portions of the day. A location with filtered sun all day appears to be ideal. The plantings like an enriched soil with good drainage. Select areas that do not flood during the rainy seasons.

HOW TO PLANT

All bulbs should be planted in well-drained soil. Alstroemeria grows well in sandy soil as long as it is given plenty of water and all the nutrients needed for growth. Plants are easier to maintain if the soil is improved with organic matter before planting. Work liberal quantities of compost or peat moss and manure into the planting site. The tuberous roots of alstroemeria should be set 6 to 9 in. deep in the ground. Space the plants about 1 ft. apart. After planting, provide adequate water to thoroughly moisten the soil. A light mulch can be added to maintain soil moisture and supply some nutrients.

ADVICE FOR CARE

Keep planting sites moist, watering whenever the surface soil feels dry to the touch. Less water will be needed during the winter months when the plants are dormant than during the hotter months of the year. Alstroemeria needs a light feeding once in March and May. Gardeners can use a 6-6-6 or similar garden fertilizer, following label instructions for bulbs or perennial plantings. After the plants have flowered, most gardeners cut the old stalks back to near the ground to allow the plant's energy to go into tuberous root production. Some gardeners allow the plant to continue seed development.

ADDITIONAL INFORMATION

All bulbous plants need division after a few years of growth. These plants are best divided during the late winter and spring months. Dig a small clump from a planting, or use individual plants to reset in a prepared garden site or share with friends. Bulbs have a few pests. Alstroemeria may be affected by slugs and cutworms. Hand pick pests from the plants, or treat them with a pest-control product recommended by the University of Florida, following label instructions.

ADDITIONAL SPECIES, CULTIVARS, OR VARIETIES

A number of alstroemeria selections and several species are available from garden centers, growers, and mail-order nurseries. The species *Alstroemeria pulchella*, also marketed as *Alstroemeria psittacina*, appears to grow especially well in Florida gardens. Every year, check for new introductions suitable for planting in your landscape.

ADVICE FOR REGIONAL CARE

Alstroemeria appears to grow best in North and Central Florida. Select varieties from local landscapes or growers to get the hardiest types for South Florida.

Amaryllis

Height: 2 ft.
Zones: 8 through 10B
Light Requirement: during
   hottest part of summer

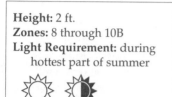

A favorite Christmas present for Florida gardeners, the amaryllis today has become a true knockout, pumped by breeding and able to take all the handling and mishandling that comes from mail-order presents. Apple Blossom and Red Lion are old-time hybrids that are recommended by amaryllis expert Alan Meerow at the University of Florida's Fort Lauderdale Agricultural Research and Education Center. The flowers bloom just a few weeks after planting—or, with mail-order plants, after opening and adding water. Individual flowers don't last terribly long, but they are so beautiful one forgives them for their lack of staying power. Amaryllis not only are being bred larger, they also now come in doubles, thanks to the Dutch. One of the newest of these is a double salmon/light orange flowering amaryllis, *Hippeastrum* 'Smoked Salmon' available from Park Seed. A single bulb will run close to $20.00. A longtime favorite is an orange amaryllis, with flowers that are smaller than some newer hybrids, but that have lots of staying power. I have several pots of these I transplanted from my mother's garden, and they come up year after year. These tropical bulbs are related to daffodils, in the genus *Narcissus* as well as *Clivia*, *Crinum*, *Zephyranthes* (rain lilies), and *Eucharis* (Amazon lily).

WHEN TO PLANT

Plant in September, October, or November, or again in late winter, early spring.

WHERE TO PLANT

Plant in borders, in pots, or in beds before a window.

HOW TO PLANT

Plant in an enriched soil, blending 2 parts peat moss with 1 part sand and 1 part pine-bark mulch or chips, either in the soil or in pots. Meerow recommends digging the whole bed and replacing soil with this mix. Add bone meal to the bottom of the individual planting holes, placing the bulbs just at the soil level or slightly above, spaced a foot or a little more apart. Add a couple of teaspoons of 6-6-6 or slow-release fertilizer for each bulb after backfilling and then mulch to help keep the soil evenly moist.

ADVICE FOR CARE

Fertilize 3 times a year, at the least. When flowers begin to form, spray with a 20-20-20. A foliar micronutrient spray also is helpful, particularly if you see leaves beginning to turn yellow before flowering. After flowering, keep watering the plants until the leaves turn yellow and then allow them to rest. Some may not die back. But when plants seem to go into a slow-down or resting stage, withhold water for a while, or dig and refresh the planting bed. Remove spent flower stalks before the plants form seeds (this occurs quickly). This will direct energy back into bulb formation.

ADDITIONAL INFORMATION

Grasshoppers and snails can demolish amaryllis leaves quickly. The protozoa product containing *Nosema locustae*, mentioned for African iris (Nolo Bait, etc.) can be useful for amaryllis. When the little lubber grasshoppers hatch in crowds of several dozen, step on them immediately. Lubbers go through several moltings on their life's journey from 1/2 in. in size to 2 or 3 in. They're easier to step on when little than when large. Also, check in pots and under mulch for snails. A good snail trap is a board placed on top of mulch in the garden. Search for snails at night, when they eat. Hand pick.

ADDITIONAL SPECIES, CULTIVARS, OR VARIETIES

Butterfly amaryllis, *H. papilio*, is an expensive bulb that can be found in mail-order catalogs and here and there at plant sales. It is a light greenish white overlain with crimson/maroon markings. Another red cousin is the Jacobean lily, *Amaryllis formosissima*, which looks like a cross between an orchid and an amaryllis, with a cinched waist or throat formed by 3 petals.

ADVICE FOR REGIONAL CARE

Plant bulbs in pots to bring indoors when freezing is predicted.

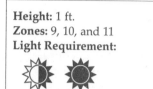

Amazon Lily

Eucharis grandiflora

Height: 1 ft.
Zones: 9, 10, and 11
Light Requirement:

The snow-white blossoms of the Amazon lily held high above the plant resemble those of a large narcissus. Flowering is sporadic but usually occurs during the winter and early spring months. The plant could bloom at almost any time of the year, however. The large, rounded deep-green foliage may reach 6 in. in diameter. This plant works well in the shady gardens of Central and South Florida. Grow it with other perennials, or use it as a groundcover in front of other greenery. Many gardeners prefer to grow the Amazon lily in containers where they can control the water and fertilizer to encourage more reliable flowering. In northern areas of Florida, growing the plants in containers is recommended. Potted Amazon lilies can be grown on the porch or patio or at an entrance.

WHEN TO PLANT

Amazon lilies can be planted at any time of the year. Division of clumps that form rather quickly is best done during the fall through early spring months.

WHERE TO PLANT

Give Amazon lilies a partial-sun to shady location. They grow best in areas with filtered sun but have produced good foliage and flowers in shady areas under trees. Foliage exposed to full sun usually burns. The plantings like an enriched soil with good drainage. Select areas that do not flood during the rainy seasons.

HOW TO PLANT

All bulbs should be planted in well-drained soil. Amazon lilies appear to tolerate sandy soil but are easier to maintain if the soil is improved with organic matter before planting. Work liberal quantities of compost or peat moss and manure into the planting site. Plant the Amazon lily with the tip of the bulb at the surface of the soil. Space bulbs 3 to 4 in. apart. In a container, add 3 to 4 bulbs to an 8-in. pot. After planting, provide adequate water to thoroughly moisten the soil. A light mulch can be added to maintain soil moisture and supply some nutrients with in-ground plantings.

ADVICE FOR CARE
Keep planting sites moist, watering whenever the surface soil feels dry to the touch. Less water will be needed during winter months than during the hotter months of the year. Amazon lilies need a light feeding once in March, May, and September. Gardeners can use a 6-6-6 or similar garden fertilizer, following label instructions for bulbs or perennial plantings. Plants in containers can be fed monthly with a 20-20-20 or similar product at label rates. After the plants have flowered, most gardeners cut the old stalks back to near the ground to allow the plant's energy to go into bulb production.

ADDITIONAL INFORMATION
All bulbous plants need division after a few years of growth. Amazon lilies are best divided during the fall and winter months. Gently break the bulb portions apart and reset them in a prepared garden site, or share with friends. Bulbs have a few pests. Amazon lilies may be affected by caterpillars and slugs. Hand pick pests from the plants, or treat with a pest-control product recommended by the University of Florida, following label instructions. Some plantings are reluctant bloomers. Flowering can usually be encouraged by alternating moist and dry periods for about a month. After the treatment, feed the plants to start growth and flowers.

ADDITIONAL SPECIES, CULTIVARS, OR VARIETIES
Only one type of Amazon lily is usually marketed at garden centers and through mail-order companies as individual bulbs or container plants.

ADVICE FOR REGIONAL CARE
Amazon lilies are quite cold sensitive. North Florida and some colder areas of Central Florida should restrict plantings to container gardens.

Blood Lily

Haemanthus multiflorus

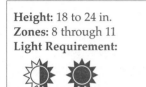

Height: 18 to 24 in.
Zones: 8 through 11
Light Requirement:

Perhaps the name really tells the story about the blood lily flowers. These bright-red attention getters pop up along with the spring foliage to form a 6-in. or larger ball of color. One of Florida's most exotic bulbs, the blood lily can be grown with perennials or added to plantings in front of shrubs. Or it can be grown in containers on a porch or patio or near an entrance. Many gardeners like to add the plants to rest areas where visitors can stop and study the inflorescence made up of many individual blooms. The bright-green foliage sprouts each spring; the long, oval leaves remain attractive until fall when the plants go dormant.

WHEN TO PLANT

Most blood lilies are planted from January through March in the Florida garden. Container plants are often available year-round and can be added to the landscape at any time. Make divisions from fall through early winter when the plants are dormant.

WHERE TO PLANT

Give blood lilies a partial-shade to shady location. They grow best in an area with filtered sun for most of the day but can also be grown under the more intense shade of trees. The plantings like an enriched soil with good drainage. Select areas that do not flood during the rainy seasons.

HOW TO PLANT

All bulbs should be planted in well-drained soil. Blood lilies tolerate sandy soil but are easier to maintain if the soil is improved with organic matter before planting. Work liberal quantities of compost or peat moss and manure into the planting site. Blood lily bulbs should be planted with the tips just below the surface of the soil. Space the bulbs 6 to 8 in. apart. In a 6- or 8-in. pot, several bulbs may be grown. After planting, provide adequate water to thoroughly moisten the soil. A light mulch can be added to maintain soil moisture and supply some nutrients for in-ground plantings.

ADVICE FOR CARE

Keep planting sites moist, watering whenever the surface soil feels dry to the touch. Less water will be needed during the winter months than during the hotter months of the year. Blood lilies need a light feeding once in March, May, and August. Gardeners can use a 6-6-6 or similar garden fertilizer, following label instructions for bulbs or perennial plantings. For container-grown plants, use a 20-20-20 or similar product monthly. After the plants have flowered, most gardeners cut the old stalks back to near the ground to allow the plant's energy to go into bulb production.

ADDITIONAL INFORMATION

All bulbous plants need division after a few years of growth. Blood lilies are best divided during the fall through winter months or immediately after flowering. Gently break the bulb portions apart and reset them in a prepared garden site, or share with friends. Bulbs have a few pests. Blood lilies may be affected by caterpillars and slugs. Hand pick pests from the plants, or treat them with a pest-control product recommended by the University of Florida, following label instructions.

ADDITIONAL SPECIES, CULTIVARS, OR VARIETIES

Only one species of blood lily is commonly marketed in Florida as a bulb or a container-grown plant.

ADVICE FOR REGIONAL CARE

Blood lilies grow well in all areas of Florida. In northern regions, add some extra mulch to the soil for cold protection.

Blue Flag Iris

Iris virginica

Height: to 3 ft.
Zones: 8 to 10B
Light Requirement:

Among the prettiest plants of the wetlands or margins of the wetlands are the blue flags. These ephemeral flowers appear in the spring, and if you're lucky, you'll venture into a park or preserve at just the right time. The flowers are a light lavender-purple with long, yellow-and-white-marked sepals and 3 narrow upright petals. While they are primarily a North Florida species, I have seen them in the Fakahatchee Swamp and at Corkscrew Swamp Sanctuary in Collier County. The flags are rhizomatous plants, not true bulbs, yet they are capable of growing in wet soil, even in pots barely submerged beneath the surface of ponds. Accustomed to growing in muck, these plants are acid lovers. (Muck in Florida is really a decomposed peat of sawgrass and other aquatics. On the edges of freshwater marshes and swamps, it has some rocky and sandy components mixed in with it. When dry, it tends to blow away, particle by particle, and so a lawn or yard built on a 50-50 mix of sand and muck will eventually become just sand, with no nutrient-holding capacity at all.) *Iris virginica* is basically an aquatic plant, along with such others as papyrus (*Cyperus papyrus*), spatterdock (*Nuphar lutea*), and water lilies (*Nymphaea odorata*). Other plants such as pickerelweed (*Pontedaria cordata*) and arrowhead (*Sagittaria lancifolia*) also grow in wet to submerged soils.

WHEN TO PLANT
Plant in the late summer or fall.

WHERE TO PLANT
Plant in low-lying swales, in pots submerged in ponds, or in bog conditions. (Bogs can be created by removing soil to a depth of several inches, lining the area with plastic, then a layer of rocks, then a highly organic mix of peat moss and muck and sand.)

How to Plant

Keep the rhizome within 2 in. of the surface, using a regular garden
potting soil. Cover the surface with rocks before submerging so the
soil won't float off and fish won't dig up the plants. Mix 6-6-6 or
10-10-10 into the soil when planting, and to fertilize later, wrap an
appropriate amount of fertilizer in newspaper and wedge it into the
pot to get it close to the roots. Fertilizer plugs are available for
aquatic use.

Advice for Care

Dig the rhizomes yearly, fall or late winter, separate the rhizomes,
clean, and repot. Use plugs or fertilizer pellets if planting in containers to be submerged, or scatter fertilizer on top of the bog as you
would for any other landscape plant.

Additional Information

At least one pot of blue flag iris in a small pond will give the fish a
hiding place.

Additional Species, Cultivars, or Varieties

Another warm-growing iris is *I. louisiana* which grow to 3 ft. or so
and comes in a range of colors, from blue through yellow, according
to Jacqueline Walker in *The Subtropical Garden*. Bearded iris and
other Japanese or German irises don't grow well in Florida.

Advice for Regional Care

This grows well throughout Florida except in the Keys.

Caladium

Caladium × *hortulanum*

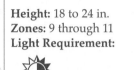

Height: 18 to 24 in.
Zones: 9 through 11
Light Requirement:

Rosy-pink with dark-pink spots; white with wine-colored spots; green veins on white; rosy-red outlined in white, separating into little islands of red against a sea of green . . . these are the caladiums. Aroids by birthright, charmers by God, these plants are far more durable than they look, taking the heat and humidity of summer as if to the station born. And indeed, originating in South America and Trinidad, they have tropical stamina flowing in their veins. The so-called fancy-leaved caladiums are the biggest with the fattest leaves; lance- or strap-leaved caladiums are dwarf with drooping leaves that make them good for hanging baskets. In South and Central Florida, they are magical sources of summer color, mainly planted in beds beneath trees to provide protection from the midday scorching sun. The roots are shallow, coming from the sides of the flattish, round tuber. Little eyes or protuberances develop and can be cut off to start new plants, rather like potatoes. Central Florida is the home to many a caladium farm, where these beautiful leaves make rainbows out of crop fields. An annual caladium festival is held in September in Lake Placid, in South Central Florida off Highway 27 south of Sebring. The festival includes tours of some caladium farms. For tropical flower arrangers, the leaves offer a good source of color and will last quite a long time. Try using them among green foliage to pick up the colors of red or pink gingers.

WHEN TO PLANT
Plant in the late winter or spring.

WHERE TO PLANT
Plant in enriched soil, in the shade, among ferns, alocasias, or around the base of potted plants.

HOW TO PLANT

Set tubers 1 to 2 in. below the soil surface. Use a peat or other type of soil amendment if you wish, and mulch them with pine bark. Water sparingly until the leaves emerge, and then water two or three times a week.

ADVICE FOR CARE

Fertilize them once a month with a balanced fertilizer, such as 6-6-6, or use a slow-release fertilizer. From November to March, reduce fertilizer to bimonthly applications. In South Florida and most of Central Florida, caladiums can stay in the ground year-round. After about 3 years, you may wish to replace the tubers, which tend to get smaller.

ADDITIONAL INFORMATION

In a pot, use a regular sterile potting soil or soilless mix, and add a small amount of slow-release fertilizer, following the directions above.

ADDITIONAL SPECIES, CULTIVARS, OR VARIETIES

There are numerous cultivars of the fancy-leaved caladiums. Some old favorites include 'Candidum', 'Candidum Jr.', 'Freida Hemple', 'Gypsy Rose', 'Pink Beauty', 'Pink Gem', 'Red Frill', 'White Christmas', and 'White Wing'.

ADVICE FOR REGIONAL CARE

In the fall, the leaves die back naturally, and the bulbs can be dug, dried, and saved in a dry place (never the refrigerator because they're tropical) for the following year.

Calla

Zantedeschia spp.

Height: to 2 ft.
Zones: 8, 9, and 10
Light Requirement:

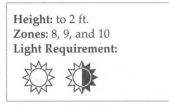

Most Florida gardeners can enjoy the springtime blooms of callas for years without transplanting. Callas call attention to themselves with their large 4- to 6-in. blooms. The white, pink, or yellow blossoms are borne on tall stems that can be left in the garden or cut as bouquets. Add the plantings to a perennial garden, or spot them throughout the landscape in front of other greenery. After flowering, the foliage gradually declines, and the plants go dormant for the fall and winter months.

When to Plant

Callas are best planted from September through January so that they can be ready for spring growth. Some gardeners prefer to dig the rhizomes after the flowers and foliage decline and store them for fall through winter planting.

Where to Plant

Give callas a full-sun to partial-shade location. They will grow best in areas with 6 to 8 hours of sun and bright light for the remaining portions of the day. The plantings like a moist soil with good drainage. Select areas that do not flood during the rainy seasons.

How to Plant

All bulbs should be planted in well-drained soil. Callas grow well in sandy soils as long as they are given plenty of water and all the nutrients needed for growth. Plants are easier to maintain if the soil is improved with organic matter before planting. Work liberal quantities of compost or peat moss and manure into the planting site. Calla rhizomes should be planted 1 to 2 in. deep in the ground. Give each rhizome a 12- to 24-in. spacing. After planting, provide adequate water to thoroughly moisten the soil. A light mulch can be added to maintain the soil moisture and supply some nutrients.

ADVICE FOR CARE

Keep planting sites moist by watering whenever the surface soil feels dry to the touch. Less water is needed during the fall and winter months when the plantings are dormant. Pay special attention to water needs during the hotter, drier months of spring. Callas should be given a light feeding once in March, May, and August. Gardeners can use a 6-6-6 or similar garden fertilizer, following label instructions for bulbs or perennial plantings. After the plants have flowered, cut the old stalks back to near the ground to allow the plant's energy to go into rhizome production.

ADDITIONAL INFORMATION

All bulbous plants need division after a few years of growth. Callas are best divided during the fall through early winter months. Gently break the rhizomes apart and reset them in a prepared garden site, or share with friends. Bulbs have a few pests. Callas may be affected by spider mites and thrips. Treat plants with a pest-control product recommended by the University of Florida, following label instructions. When planting in containers, use large containers and a loose potting mix. Treat as container plantings until the plants flower and the foliage declines. Then keep on the dry side until the spring growing season.

ADDITIONAL SPECIES, CULTIVARS, OR VARIETIES

A number of calla species and varieties may be planted in Florida. The large, white flowering selections appear to grow best. Every year, check for new introductions that might be suitable for planting in your landscape.

ADVICE FOR REGIONAL CARE

Callas grow best in North and Central Florida. Container culture is probably best in South Florida.

Canna

Canna hybrids

Height: 2 to 4 ft.
Zones: 9 through 11;
   C. flaccida to Zone 8
Light Requirement:

The canna is a shining botanical example of multiculturalism. The plants *Canna indica, C. flaccida, C. glauca,* and *C. coccinea* are tropical and subtropical American. In such places as Colombia and Ecuador, the roots are eaten as food, and the leaves are sometimes used for thatching. In 1846, according to *Flowers of the World*, a French consular agent in Chile, one M. Année, collected cannas from South America and took them home to Paris. When they grew well, he began to hybridize them. According to *Gardening in the Tropics* by R. E. Holttum and Ivan Enoch, the plants were then further hybridized in Italy, where the first to become a "modern" canna appeared in 1890. Cannas have since become naturalized in parts of Asia and Africa. *C. flaccida,* the aquatic, yellow-flowering species, is a Florida native (in fact, native to the southeastern United States). Hybridization among species has given us the bold cannas we know today, but it has also made them difficult to maintain. They require a good deal of attention and are subject to such leaf mutilation by the canna leaf roller, a moth larva, that they are not widely grown in South Florida. The exception is at Miami's Parrot Jungle and Gardens, where red cannas have been the signature mass planting around the historic garden's sign for many years. Among the newest releases is Tropicanna, whose multicolored leaves contain burgundy, pink, yellow, and green, changing as the plant ages. The flowers are a thoroughly saturated orange; the color often seduces gardeners. When growing cannas, gardeners will discover whether they're serious or just dabblers.

WHEN TO PLANT
Plant in the late winter to spring.

WHERE TO PLANT
Plant in an area that can be irrigated regularly, in full sun.

How to Plant

Cannas like full sun and a rich soil, so a single planting hole can have organic material (peat moss, compost, aged manure) added to it, or a whole bed can be dug and soil replaced with those ingredients. Plant about 2 ft. apart. Regularly inspect for leaf rollers and fungus.

Advice for Care

Given their marshy origins and even aquatic components, cannas love moist soil and, to be vigorous, require frequent fertilizing. The Parrot Jungle gardeners use a low-nitrogen granular, such as 4-7-5, a small amount monthly, and they supplement that with a weekly spray of 20-20-20. Water 2 or 3 times weekly, early in the morning, so any wet foliage will dry by nightfall to avoid fungal diseases. Spider mites can be a problem in the dry season. Like the frangipani, the canna is subject to rust, a fungus that looks like its name. This can be controlled by sulfur spray or Kocide, a copper fungicide. Dig and divide, then replant every year to keep cannas flowering well.

Additional Information

In South and Central Florida, the plants can be grown in the ground all year. As far south as Palm Beach, they will die down in winter.

Additional Species, Cultivars, or Varieties

In 1992 a dwarf canna, Tropical Rose, was chosen as an All-America Selection that comes true to seed. Until that time, rhizomes were used to propagate dwarf cannas. Tropical Rose was developed in Japan and produces rose-colored flowers. As an added feature, the flowers are self-cleaning—meaning one less chore for the gardener.

Advice for Regional Care

Use as an annual in North Florida and as a perennial in Central Florida, except for *C. flaccida*, the aquatic.

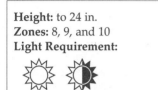

Day Lily

Hemerocallis hybrids

Height: to 24 in.
Zones: 8, 9, and 10
Light Requirement:

Florida boasts of some of the most popular breeders, growers, and varieties of day lilies in the nation. Day lilies sold at plant stores represent just a small portion of selections available from day lily nurseries. Typical color choices are yellow, orange, pink, red, and lavender; however, many flowers are blends, and some have green centers. As the name implies, most day lily blossoms last only a day, but the buds along the stems are numerous and each stalk can continue to open blossoms for weeks. By carefully choosing varieties, you can have day lilies in bloom from March through at least July. Some may bloom sporadically throughout the year. Use day lilies in large beds, rock gardens, perennial borders, and pots. These versatile plants can fit into just about any landscape situation.

WHEN TO PLANT

Day lilies can be added to the landscape at any time of the year as bareroot transplants or container-grown plants. A good time to pick your plants by color is the spring through early summer flowering period. Then you can dig the plants for immediate planting in the landscape.

WHERE TO PLANT

Give day lilies a full-sun to partial-shade location. They grow best in an area with 6 to 8 hours of sun and bright light for the remaining portions of the day. The plantings like an enriched soil with good drainage. Select areas that do not flood during the rainy seasons.

HOW TO PLANT

All bulbs should be planted in well-drained soil. Day lilies grow well in sandy soils as long as they are given plenty of water and all the nutrients needed for growth. Some gardeners give day lilies a drier site where they can exist but don't expect the best growth. Plants are easier to maintain if the soil is improved with organic matter before planting. Work liberal quantities of compost or peat moss and manure into the planting site. Day lilies should be set with the base of the foliage at soil level. It's better to plant a little above the ground than too deep. After planting, provide adequate water to thoroughly moisten the soil. A light mulch can be added to maintain soil moisture and supply some nutrients.

ADVICE FOR CARE

Keep planting sites moist, watering whenever the surface soil feels dry to the touch. Less water will be needed during the winter months than during the hotter, drier months of the spring. Day lilies need a light feeding once in March, May, and September. Gardeners can use a 6-6-6 or similar garden fertilizer, following label instructions for bulbs or perennial plantings. After the plants have flowered, most gardeners cut the old stalks back to near the ground to allow the plant's energy to go into root and stem production. Some gardeners allow the plant to continue seed development.

ADDITIONAL INFORMATION

All bulbous plants need division after a few years of growth. Day lilies can be divided year-round. Gently break the plant portions apart and reset them in a prepared garden site, or share with friends. Day lilies have a few pests. They may be affected by caterpillars, aphids, thrips, and grasshoppers. Hand pick pests from the plants, or treat them with a pest-control product recommended by the University of Florida, following label instructions.

ADDITIONAL SPECIES, CULTIVARS, OR VARIETIES

Numerous selections of day lilies are available from garden centers and growers. Every year, check for new introductions suitable for planting in your landscape. The best day lilies for Florida are the evergreen and semievergreen types. Deciduous varieties that lose their leaves during the winter have been poorer performers in most Florida landscapes.

ADVICE FOR REGIONAL CARE

South Florida growers should check with local garden centers for the best adapted selections. Not all grow well in the hotter sections of the state.

Gladiolus

Gladiolus hybrids

Height: to 2 ft.
Zones: 8 through 11
Light Requirement:

Gardeners love their gladiolus for the tall spikes of color. The flowers come in most colors of the rainbow in addition to some blends. The trumpetlike blooms open from the base of the flower stalk and continue up the stem to the very tip. The flowering process often lasts a week or more. Often the stalks are never allowed to mature in the garden but are cut for bouquets. The lancelike foliage grows straight up. Plant gladiolus in perennial beds and rock gardens, or use them among shrub plantings. Many gardeners plant gladiolus corms in clusters of 6 or more. Others like to place them in rows in a more formal garden. After a few months of growth and flowering, the plants gradually decline for a rest period before starting new growth.

WHEN TO PLANT

Gladiolus can be planted at any time of the year. The bulblike corms are available from January through May for home plantings. Gardeners can dig and store their own bulbs to replant and flower after a few months of rest or when sprouting is noted.

WHERE TO PLANT

Give gladiolus a full-sun location. They grow best in an area with 6 to 8 hours of sun and bright light for the remaining portions of the day. The plantings like an enriched soil with good drainage. Select areas that do not flood during the rainy seasons.

HOW TO PLANT

All bulbs should be planted in well-drained soil. Gladiolus grow well in sandy soils as long as they are given plenty of water and all the nutrients needed for growth. Plants are easier to maintain if the soil is improved with organic matter prior to planting. Work liberal quantities of compost or peat moss and manure into the planting site. Gladiolus corms should be set 2 to 3 in. deep in the ground. Give individual corms a 4- to 6-in. spacing. After planting, provide adequate water to thoroughly moisten the soil. A light mulch can be added to maintain soil moisture and supply some nutrients.

ADVICE FOR CARE

Keep planting sites moist, watering whenever the surface inch of soil feels dry to the touch. Less water will be needed during periods of dormancy. Gladiolus need light feedings monthly during the growing period. Gardeners can use a 6-6-6 or similar garden fertilizer, following label instructions for bulb plantings. After the plants have flowered, most gardeners cut the old stalks back to near the ground to allow the plant's energy to go into corm production. Glads may need staking when the stalks are produced to prevent wind damage. Gladiolus wires for staking are sold at garden centers and through mail-order companies. Gardeners may also tie the flower stalks to horizontal string set along the rows.

ADDITIONAL INFORMATION

All bulbous plants need division after a few years of growth. Many growers dig and divide their corms after every flowering. Gladiolus corms are best divided after the foliage declines, usually 4 to 6 weeks after flowering. At that time the old dry corm portions and small bulbs are separated from the larger corms. All are allowed to air dry before replanting or storing for later planting. Bulbs have a few pests. Gladiolus may be affected by caterpillars, grasshoppers, and thrips. Hand pick pests from the plants, or treat them with a pest-control product recommended by the University of Florida, following label instructions.

ADDITIONAL SPECIES, CULTIVARS, OR VARIETIES

Many varieties—in addition to short and tall forms—of gladiolus are available from garden centers and mail-order nurseries. Every year, check for new introductions that may be suitable for planting in your landscape.

ADVICE FOR REGIONAL CARE

Gladiolus grow well in all areas of Florida but may be affected by cold weather. North and Central Florida plantings are usually restricted to the spring through summer months.

BULBS

Gloriosa Lily

Gloriosa spp.

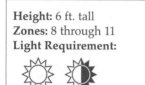

Height: 6 ft. tall
Zones: 8 through 11
Light Requirement:

For a spectacular, colorful flowering plant, add a gloriosa lily near the patio or entrance to the home. The large blooms, which open in an inverted position, are a blend of crimson and yellow colors. The plants start to grow shortly after planting the V-shaped tubers. You can plant gloriosa lilies individually, or you can train several along a wall or fence, since it is one of the few vining bulbous plants. After months of flowering, the plants die back or, in cooler regions, are killed back to the ground by cold weather. The major flowering period is spring through summer in most areas of Florida.

WHEN TO PLANT

Gloriosa lilies are best planted from January through April in Florida landscapes. At this time of year garden centers have pack-aged tubers available for planting. Tubers can be dug and separated from established plantings at any time of the year.

WHERE TO PLANT

Give gloriosa lilies a full-sun to partial-shade location. They grow best in an area with 6 to 8 hours of sun and bright light for the remaining portions of the day. The plantings like an enriched soil with good drainage. Select areas that do not flood during the rainy seasons.

HOW TO PLANT

All bulbs should be planted in well-drained soil. Gloriosa lilies grow well in sandy soils as long as they are given plenty of water and all the nutrients needed for growth. They can withstand periods of drought but die back and then resume growth when damper weather returns. Plants are easier to maintain if the soil is improved with organic matter before planting. Work liberal quantities of com-post or peat moss and manure into the planting site. Gloriosa lilies should be planted 2 to 4 in. deep in the ground. Where more than 1 plant will be added to the same site, space the tubers 12 to 18 in.

apart. After planting, provide adequate water to thoroughly moisten the soil. A light mulch can be added to maintain soil moisture and supply some nutrients.

ADVICE FOR CARE

Keep planting sites moist, watering whenever the surface inch of soil feels dry to the touch. Less water will be needed during the winter months than during the hotter, drier months of the year. Gloriosa lilies grow best with a light feeding once in March, May, and September. Gardeners can use a 6-6-6 or similar garden fertilizer, following label instructions for bulbs or perennial plantings. After flowering, the declining blooms normally drop from the plants, and no trimming is needed. Gloriosa lilies may grow out of bounds and need some trimming of the vining portions to prevent them from growing among other plantings.

ADDITIONAL INFORMATION

All bulbous plants need division after a few years of growth. Gloriosa lilies are best divided during the winter months before new growth begins. Gently break the tuber portions apart and reset them in a prepared garden site, or share with friends. Bulbs have a few pests. Gloriosa lilies may be affected by caterpillars. Hand pick pests from the plants, or treat them with a pest-control product recommended by the University of Florida, following label instructions.

ADDITIONAL SPECIES, CULTIVARS, OR VARIETIES

There are two species of gloriosa lilies usually planted in Florida: *Gloriosa rothschildiana* and *Gloriosa superba*. The species are similar, varying in the amount of crimson and yellow color in the blooms.

ADVICE FOR REGIONAL CARE

Gloriosa lilies grow well in all areas of Florida. Plants go dormant in North and Central Florida when affected by cold. Trim off dead vine portions, and wait for new growth to begin.

Kaffir Lily

Clivia miniata

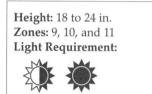

Height: 18 to 24 in.
Zones: 9, 10, and 11
Light Requirement:

Only a few gardeners plant the kaffir lily, also commonly known by its genus name *Clivia*. Perhaps one reason is that the plants are relatively expensive, often costing twenty dollars or more per bulb. But the plants multiply rather rapidly, and you can increase the collection in just a few years. Perhaps another reason for its rare use is that gardeners are not familiar with the bright-orange flowers with a yellowish center. Most are borne atop a 6- to 10-in. stalk, much like an amaryllis. The shade-tolerant kaffir lily can be planted in lower light areas where the selection of flowering plants is quite limited. The bulbs are best clustered together to form a spot of color during the spring months. Use them in perennial beds and among shrub plantings. Kaffir lilies grown in containers display the plants in bloom on porches, patios, and balconies; they can also be brought indoors to enjoy the blooms. Container culture is best in North Florida and portions of Central Florida where the plants may be affected by cold.

When to Plant

Kaffir lilies can be planted any time of the year. Bulbs are most likely to be available during the spring months when the plants are in bloom. They are also available through mail-order companies.

Where to Plant

Give kaffir lilies a partial-shade to shady location. They grow best in an area with filtered sun under tall trees. The plantings like an enriched soil with good drainage. Select areas that do not flood during the rainy seasons.

How to Plant

All bulbs should be planted in well-drained soil. Kaffir lilies grow in sandy soils as long as they are given plenty of water and all the nutrients needed for growth. Plants are easier to maintain if the soil is improved with organic matter before planting. Work liberal quantities of compost or peat moss and manure into the planting site.

Kaffir lily bulbs should be planted with the tips of the bulbs just below the surface of the soil. Space plants 18 to 24 in. apart. For container culture grow 1 bulb in a 6- or 8-in. pot with a loose potting mix. After planting, provide adequate water to thoroughly moisten the soil. A light mulch can be added to maintain soil moisture and supply some nutrients for in-ground plantings.

ADVICE FOR CARE

Keep planting sites moist, watering whenever the surface soil feels dry to the touch. Less water will be needed during the winter months than during the hotter, drier months of the year. Kaffir lilies need a light feeding once in March, May, and September. Gardeners can use a 6-6-6 or similar garden fertilizer, following label instructions for bulbs or perennial plantings. Feed container plantings monthly with a 20-20-20 or similar fertilizer. After the plants have flowered, most gardeners cut the old stalks back to near the ground to allow the plant's energy to go into bulb production. Some gardeners allow the plant to continue seed development. The mature seeds can be sown in a loose potting mix; new plants take 3 years to flower.

ADDITIONAL INFORMATION

All bulbous plants need division after a few years of growth. Kaffir lilies are best divided during the spring months after flowering. Gently break the bulb portions apart and reset them in a prepared garden site or container, or share with friends. Bulbs have a few pests. Kaffir lilies may be affected by caterpillars and grasshoppers. Hand pick pests from the plants, or treat them with a pest-control product recommended by the University of Florida, following label instructions.

ADDITIONAL SPECIES, CULTIVARS, OR VARIETIES

Plant breeders have produced a yellow-flowering kaffir lily. Bulbs are relatively expensive but available from some specialty nurseries.

ADVICE FOR REGIONAL CARE

Kaffir lilies are cold sensitive and best grown in containers in North Florida and the cooler portions of Central Florida. Protect all plantings from freezing temperatures. Keep the plants on the dry side during the winter months.

Louisiana Iris

Iris hybrids

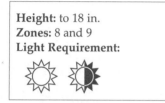

Height: to 18 in.
Zones: 8 and 9
Light Requirement:

Louisiana iris varieties are spring bloomers that come in a variety of colors, including yellows, blues, reds, whites, and purples. The iris plants produce green lancelike leaves typical of the genus. Select a damp area for Louisiana iris plantings. Without a water supply the plants quickly decline. In Florida's sandy soils you may have to create the wet spots using plastic or rubber liners set in the ground to form the oasis. They are ideal for a consistently damp area or a wetland, although plantings can be used in a lightly shaded garden. Gardeners are adding Louisiana iris to container gardens kept moist and planted with other bog plants for use on patios and along walkways.

WHEN TO PLANT

Louisiana iris are best planted from spring through summer in Florida landscapes. They are available as container-grown specimens and as individual rhizomes from aquatic gardens and mail-order nurseries for year-round planting.

WHERE TO PLANT

Give Louisiana iris a sun to partial-shade location. They grow best in an area with 6 to 8 hours of sun and bright light for the remaining portions of the day. The plantings like an enriched damp soil. Plantings can grow in or near standing water, but the rhizomes must be above the water.

HOW TO PLANT

The Louisiana iris is one of the few bulbs that must have a damp to wet soil. To have success with the new plants, bog conditions must be created or already exist. They grow in sandy soils, but most gardeners like to improve the soil with organic matter before planting. Work liberal quantities of compost or peat moss and manure into the planting site. Louisiana iris should be planted with the rhizome at the soil surface and the roots in the ground. Space plants 8 to 12 in. apart. After planting, provide adequate water to keep the soil moist. A light mulch can be added to maintain soil moisture and supply some nutrients.

ADVICE FOR CARE

Keep planting sites moist, watering whenever the surface soil starts to feel dry to the touch. Louisiana iris need a light feeding once in March, May, and September. Gardeners can use a 6-6-6 or similar garden fertilizer, following label instructions for bulbs or perennial plantings. After the plants have flowered, most gardeners cut the old stalks back to near the ground to allow the plant's energy to go into bulb production. Some gardeners allow the plant to continue seed development.

ADDITIONAL INFORMATION

All bulbous plants need division after a few years of growth. Louisiana iris rhizomes are best divided during late spring and summer months after flowering. Gently break the rhizome portions apart, and discard the older, nonproductive sections. Reset the new portions in a prepared garden site, or share with friends. Iris have a few pests. They may be affected by caterpillars and grasshoppers. Hand pick pests from the plants, or treat them with a pest-control product recommended by the University of Florida, following label instructions.

ADDITIONAL SPECIES, CULTIVARS, OR VARIETIES

Many hybrids of the Louisiana iris are available from specialty nurseries and mail-order companies. Every year, check for new introductions suitable for planting in your landscape.

ADVICE FOR REGIONAL CARE

Louisiana iris are best grown in North and Central Florida. South Florida gardens cannot provide the cool weather needed for good growth.

Pride of Burma

Curcuma roscoeana

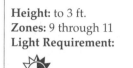

> **Height:** to 3 ft.
> **Zones:** 9 through 11
> **Light Requirement:**

When the *Curcuma* leaves appear, you know tropical spring is in the air. The beautiful understated leaves—not flashy, colored, mottled, or lobed, but simple, with raised veins like ribs—are nice enough to let appear seasonally in the garden by them-selves. The bracts resemble miniature wall sconces back-to-back on a stem, with flowers blooming out of each bract one or two at a time. In the winter, some curcumas go dormant and completely die back. Because of the seasonality, I keep my *Curcuma* hybrids in a container that can be moved out of sight when it becomes a pot of dead leaves. When I remember to, I spritz the dormant pot with water. Once the leaves have appeared, I resume regular watering and fertilizing. The flower bracts are pink to lavender. The *Curcuma* most readily available is Pride of Burma, but other cultivars are finding their way to collec-tors' gardens. The Heliconia Society International is a group that promotes not only heliconias, but relatives such as *Curcuma*, *Alpinia*, *Kaempferia*, and others. The Society started in South Florida and has members around the world, hobby gardeners as well as commercial growers. *Curcuma domestica* is the source of commercial turmeric. The coloring agent, flavoring, and dye are made from the rhizomes. Turmeric has long been used in Oriental and Asian cooking, and was one of the spices that sent Columbus sailing the high seas. Camphor also comes from curcuma rhizomes, specifically from those with pink and blue flowers.

WHEN TO PLANT
Plant in winter to early spring.

WHERE TO PLANT
Plant in a partially shady location with good drainage; morning sun is ideal.

How to Plant

The relatively small rhizomes can be fairly snug in a pot or several inches apart. Enrich the soil with aged manure, compost, or peat, with the addition of perlite or sand for drainage if necessary. The rhizomes should be within 2 or 3 in. of the surface. Loose, leafy mulch is best. Water in after planting and when the leaves emerge.

Advice for Care

Keep soil evenly moist. Fertilize with slow-release fertilizer or a fertilizer formulated for palms with slow-release nitrogen and potassium. Dig and separate the rhizomes in the fall as the plants begin to go dormant. You can keep the rhizomes in sawdust until early spring, planting seasonal color in their spot; or if you don't dig the plants to separate, simply remember where the dormant plants are.

Additional Information

The flower stalks make beautiful cut flowers.

Additional Species, Cultivars, or Varieties

Although not widely available in nurseries, curcumas are gaining in popularity and can be found through mail order or at various plant shows. *Curcuma indora* has an inflorescence topped with pink bracts. The lower bracts remain green. Flowers are yellow.

Advice for Regional Care

Curcumas can be kept in pots in areas where freezing occurs. Some hybrids will do well in cooler climates.

Shell Ginger

Alpinia zerumbet

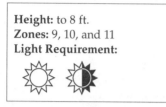

Height: to 8 ft.
Zones: 9, 10, and 11
Light Requirement:

Gardeners in Central and South Florida can enjoy summer color from the shell ginger. As the name implies, individual flowers resemble small seashells about 1 in. long, mainly white with yellow, brown, and red markings. The blossoms are borne in large clusters that remain attractive for weeks. Summer is the major flowering period, but sporadic flowering may occur year-round. The plants are good landscape specimens, producing long, broad, bright-green leaves. Better give this plant plenty of room to grow because the rhizomes increase rapidly. They are best used as a backdrop for other plantings, as space dividers, or as specimen plants.

WHEN TO PLANT

Shell ginger can be added to the landscape at any time of the year. Garden centers make the plants available as rhizomes from late winter through summer. Container specimens are available year-round.

WHERE TO PLANT

Give shell ginger a full-sun to partial-shade location. It's a great plant for the partially shaded garden where few plants with good color are available. Shell ginger grows best in an area with 6 to 8 hours of sun and bright light for the remaining portions of the day. The plantings like an enriched soil with good drainage. Select areas that do not flood during the rainy seasons. Plants can tolerate areas that may be dry for short periods of time.

HOW TO PLANT

All bulbs should be planted in well-drained soil. Shell gingers grow well in sandy soils as long as they are given plenty of water and all the nutrients needed for growth. Plants are easier to maintain if the soil is improved with organic matter before planting. Work liberal quantities of compost or peat moss and manure into the planting site. Shell ginger rhizomes should be planted just below the surface of the soil. Space the plants 12 to 24 in. apart. After planting, provide adequate water to thoroughly moisten the soil. A light mulch can be added to maintain soil moisture and supply some nutrients.

ADVICE FOR CARE
Keep planting sites moist, watering whenever the surface soil feels dry to the touch. Less water will be needed during the winter months than during the hotter, drier months of the year. Shell ginger needs a light feeding once in March, May, and September. Gardeners can use a 6-6-6 or similar garden fertilizer, following label instructions for bulbs or perennial plantings. After the plants have flowered, most gardeners cut the old stalks back to near the ground to allow the plant's energy to go into bulb production.

ADDITIONAL INFORMATION
All bulbous plants need division after a few years of growth. Shell ginger can be divided at any time of the year. Dig clumps to reset or break the rhizome portions apart to plant them individually in a prepared garden site, or share with friends. Bulbs have a few pests. Shell ginger may be affected by caterpillars and grasshoppers. Hand pick pests from the plants, or treat them with a pest-control product recommended by the University of Florida, following label instructions.

ADDITIONAL SPECIES, CULTIVARS, OR VARIETIES
A shell ginger with green-and-yellow foliage of the variety 'Variegata' makes an attractive accent. The plant is a reluctant bloomer in most gardens.

ADVICE FOR REGIONAL CARE
Shell ginger grows best in Central Florida and southward. North Florida gardeners may grow the plants in containers to bring indoors during freezing weather. Even in Central Florida, plants may be affected by cold and need a spring trimming before growth begins.

Swamp Lily

Crinum americanum

Other Names: *Crinum asiaticum*, Tree Lily
Height: 2 ft.
Zones: 8 through 11
Light Requirement:

Crinium americanum and *Crinium asiaticum*, sisters beneath the skin, are spring-blooming tropical lilies with big showy flowers. *Crinum americanum*, the swamp lily, is a bulb native to Florida and Georgia. These lilies stand out against the swampy margins of freshwater marshes like stars in the night. In such vastness, they seem smaller than they are. At home in your garden, you will find they are substantial. They grow to about 2 ft., tall and broad, in a rosette. The flowers are starbursts of white petals with showy stigmas and stamens on long stalks in the center. While *C. americanum* makes a striking garden plant in partial shade or sun, it has a fungus that requires some work: every few weeks it needs a good spray of fungicide. *Crinum asiaticum*, the tree lily, rears itself up on a trunk, with leaves several feet long and stalks of flowers equally large. The stamens have red stems, and flowers are in clusters (technically umbels) on fleshy stalks. This, like the native, likes moist, well-draining soil, although the swamp lily is a perfect candidate for low-lying swales or other areas of the garden where water stands occasionally. These lilies are sturdy characters, but grasshoppers tend to be sturdier. Beginning in March, lubber grasshoppers hatch and emerge from underground nests, and start eating their way through the landscape. Until, that is, they happen on a lily. They can take it to the mat in record time. Use a protozoa with the trade name Nolo Bait, Grasshopper Killer, or Semaspore. Better yet, step on them when they're tiny and all in more or less one area. The bigger they get, the messier the task.

WHEN TO PLANT

Plant any time, but winter is best for flowers in the spring.

WHERE TO PLANT

Plant in sun to partial shade. Plants tend to look just a little nicer in high shade. A low-lying area that has occasionally wet conditions (or a homemade bog) will serve the swamp lily well. A basic rule of thumb for wetland plants: a wetland plant can be grown in dry conditions, but an upland plant cannot be grown in wet conditions.

How to Plant

Enrich the planting hole with 2 parts peat moss, 1 part each sand and pine bark mulch (not large nuggets). Add some bone meal to the bottom, and plant the bulb at the same depth at which it grew in the container, making sure that the neck of the bulb is above the soil line. If planting several, dig a bed at least 6 to 8 in. deep and enrich the entire bed. Space crinum bulbs about 1 to 1 1/2 ft. apart.

Advice for Care

Irrigate regularly to keep the area evenly moist, and fertilize in spring, summer, and fall. Be sure to mulch.

Additional Information

In March, watch for emergence of juvenile lubber grasshoppers (they will be about 1/2 in. long and black with yellow stripes). Step on them, or use a protozoan insecticide.

Additional Species, Cultivars, or Varieties

There are several species and cultivars of *Crinum*, some of them especially attractive with maroon buds and pink stripes, or red stripes. The fragrant flowers of *Crinum* are moth pollinated. *C. amabile* flowers have red buds and red centers; *C. moorei* from South Africa has pink flowers with broad petals. *C. jagus*, an African rain forest bulb, blooms in the spring and fall and smells of vanilla. Alan Meerow, tropical bulb expert at the University of Florida in Fort Lauderdale, recommends the cultivar *C. jagus* 'St. Christopher' with tulip-shaped flowers.

Advice for Regional Care

These lilies can grow into Zone 9 and even into Georgia. Allow them to rest after flowering.

Voodoo Lily

Amorphophallus spp.

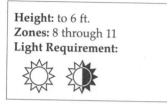

Height: to 6 ft.
Zones: 8 through 11
Light Requirement:

The name "voodoo lily" suggests there might be a little magic in the plant, and there is. It grows from nothing in early spring to a tall plant in just weeks. The leaves are usually deeply cut and up to several feet long and wide. It has an interesting trunk with green streaks and splotches that may be one reason the plant is also called the snake lily. The foliage and thick stems all die back to the ground by fall. Mature plants have spectacular reddish-brown spring flowers that are domed in shape and 1 ft. or more tall. A not-so-pleasant surprise is that flowers may have a very foul odor, but they last just a week or so. Use voodoo lilies along walkways and as an accent feature among shrub plantings. Gardeners often keep them in pots to enhance the patios and entrance areas for the spring through summer months.

WHEN TO PLANT

Voodoo lilies are best planted during the late winter through spring months when the corms are just beginning to grow. Packaged corms can be obtained from garden centers and mail-order companies. Container-grown plants are available from garden centers year-round.

WHERE TO PLANT

Give voodoo lilies a full-sun to partial-shade location. They grow best in areas with 6 to 8 hours of sun and bright light for the remaining portions of the day. The plantings like an enriched soil with good drainage. Select areas that do not flood during the rainy seasons.

HOW TO PLANT

All bulbs should be planted in well-drained soil. Voodoo lilies grow well in sandy soils as long as they are given plenty of water and all the nutrients needed for growth. Plants are easier to maintain and grow to a larger size if the soil is improved with organic matter before planting. Work liberal quantities of compost or peat moss and manure into the planting site. Voodoo lily corms should be planted 3 to 4 in. deep in the ground. Space plants 1 ft. or more apart. After planting, provide adequate water to thoroughly moisten the soil. A light mulch can be added to maintain soil moisture and supply some nutrients.

ADVICE FOR CARE

Keep planting sites moist, watering whenever the surface soil feels dry to the touch. Less water will be needed during the winter months when the plants are dormant than during the hotter, drier months of the spring. Voodoo lilies need a light feeding once in March, May, and August. Gardeners can use a 6-6-6 or similar garden fertilizer, following label instructions for bulbs or perennial plantings. After the plant has flowered, the shriveled blossoms can be removed from the base of the plant.

ADDITIONAL INFORMATION

All bulbous plants need division after a few years of growth. Voodoo lilies are best divided during late winter and early spring months as the corms begin new growth. Remove the corms from the soil and gently break the portions apart, and reset them in a prepared garden site or share with friends. Bulbs have a few pests. Voodoo lilies may be affected by caterpillars and grasshoppers. Hand pick pests from the plants, or treat them with a pest-control product recommended by the University of Florida, following label instructions.

ADDITIONAL SPECIES, CULTIVARS, OR VARIETIES

A number of species and selections of the voodoo lily are available from garden centers and growers. Some grow only a few feet tall, and others grow large enough for a child to stand under. Check for the selections that might be added to your collection.

ADVICE FOR REGIONAL CARE

Voodoo lilies vary as to their hardiness. Most can be grown throughout the state if the soil is mulched after they die back during the fall. All can be grown in containers and brought indoors during freezing weather.

Walking Iris

Neomarica spp.

Height: 3 ft.
Zones: 10B and 11
Light Requirement:

The walking iris is so-named because the flower stalk gradually sinks to the ground and little plants form and root where it falls, allowing the clump to expand or "walk." The yellow-flowering ones do nicely in partial shade, where their gentle color shows up well. Their leaves are flattened and spread, fanlike. These iris are good for a vertical effect in a bed, perhaps over mounds of Mexican bluebells or Mexican heather. They can also be used alone, in an attractive bed where they are tall enough to hold their flowers up for inspection. Like other bulbs, they like a moist and rich bed, although I've seen them thrive in low-lying, untended swales where the weedy muck about in agreeable company.

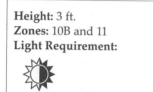

WHEN TO PLANT
Any time of the year.

WHERE TO PLANT
In partial shade, in a foundation planter, a shrub bed or in a Japanese garden-like setting.

HOW TO PLANT
Enrich the planting hole with peat, pine bark mulch and sand so it retains moisture but drains well. Make the planting hole slightly larger than the rootball in the container, and slide off the container, carefully placing the walking iris in the hole. Water in and mulch. From divisions or plantlets, plant just below the surface of the soil.

ADVICE FOR CARE
Walking iris has a low tolerance for droughty conditions, so irrigate twice a week in winter, two to three times in summer if there is not enough rain. Fertilize with slow-release fertilizer in spring, midsummer and fall.

ADDITIONAL INFORMATION
Each flower lasts one day.

ADDITIONAL SPECIES, CULTIVARS, OR VARIETIES
According to *Betrock's Reference Guide to Landscape Plants* by Timothy Broschat and Alan Meerow, *Neomarica caerulea* has blue flowers; *N. gracilis* has white flowers with blue markings; *N. longifolia* is the commonly seen yellow flowering iris.

ADVICE FOR REGIONAL CARE
A tender plant, this will die to the ground in Central Florida in winter but grows back from the rhizome. Walking iris can be replaced with bearded iris, or grown in pots in North Florida.

Zephyr Lily

Zephyranthes spp.

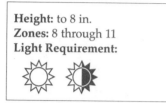

Height: to 8 in.
Zones: 8 through 11
Light Requirement:

Most zephyr lilies are referred to as rain lilies because the flowering season begins at the return of the rainy season. They grow well throughout the state, and the blossoms might remind relocated gardeners of crocus. There are a number of colors available according to the species, and all push their blossoms high above the foliage. Most continue to flower throughout the late spring through early fall months. Zephyr lilies are best planted in clusters as if naturalized in flower beds and perennial gardens. They can also be used along walkways, as a groundcover, and in containers. The bright-green thin foliage is present year-round but may die back during drought if not supplied with adequate water. All zephyr lilies are very drought tolerant but grow best in moist soils.

WHEN TO PLANT

Zephyr lilies can be added to the landscape at any time of the year. Most garden centers and mail-order companies offer packaged bulbs for spring planting. Clumps can be dug and divided to share with friends at any time.

WHERE TO PLANT

Give zephyr lilies a full-sun to partial-shade location. They grow and flower best in an area with 6 to 8 hours of sun and bright light for the remaining portions of the day. The plantings like an enriched soil with good drainage. Select areas that do not flood during the rainy seasons.

HOW TO PLANT

All bulbs should be planted in well-drained soil. Zephyr lilies grow well in sandy soils as long as they are given plenty of water and all the nutrients needed for growth. Plants are easier to maintain and multiply faster if the soil is improved with organic matter before planting. Work liberal quantities of compost or peat moss and manure into the planting site. Zephyr lilies should be planted 1 to 2 in. deep in the ground. Space the bulbs 3 to 4 in. apart. After planting, provide adequate water to thoroughly moisten the soil. A light mulch can be added to maintain soil moisture and supply some nutrients.

ADVICE FOR CARE

Keep planting sites moist, watering whenever the surface soil feels dry to the touch. Less water will be needed during the winter months than during the hotter, drier months of the year. Zephyr lilies need a light feeding once in March, May, and September. Gardeners can use a 6-6-6 or similar garden fertilizer, following label instructions for bulbs or perennial plantings. After the plants have flowered, most gardeners cut the old stalks back to near the ground to allow the plant's energy to go into bulb production. Some gardeners allow the plant to continue seed development. Mature seeds germinate quickly when sown in a loose potting mix.

ADDITIONAL INFORMATION

All bulbous plants need division after a few years of growth. Zephyr lilies are best divided during the fall through spring months. Gently break the bulb portions apart and reset them in a prepared garden site, or share with friends. Bulbs have a few pests. Zephyr lilies may be affected by caterpillars and grasshoppers. Hand pick pests from the plants, or treat them with a pest-control product recommended by the University of Florida, following label instructions.

ADDITIONAL SPECIES, CULTIVARS, OR VARIETIES

Three main species are grown in Florida: *Zephyranthes rosea*, a pink; *Zephyranthes candida*, a white; and *Zephyranthes citrina*, a yellow. The pink is most common, but all can be obtained from specialty nurseries.

ADVICE FOR REGIONAL CARE

Zephyr lilies grow well in all areas of the state with similar care.

CHAPTER THREE

Cycads

Height: 18 in. to 20 ft.
Zones: 10 and 11
Light Requirement:

Even before that matriarchal land mass called Pangaea broke into continents, cycads were here. Perhaps as long as 150 million years ago they spread over most of the earth. Today, in areas such as Florida and southern California, they are prized garden plants, and in their remnant home territories they are highly endangered species.

They look like curious palms; the name cycad comes from a Greek word meaning "palm." Their stems often form trunks and spiky stiff leaves comprise the crowns. There are about 185 species of cycads around the world, primarily found where summers are hot and wet and winters are cool and dry. Australia, South Africa, Central and South America, parts of China and Japan, and some Pacific islands have scattered groups of these plants. Florida has one native cycad, the coontie (*Zamia pumila*).

Some cycads produce one new set of leaves every year, though some slow growers don't get around to leaf production except every 2 or 3 years. We think of these plants as prehistoric, belonging to the Jurassic Age or the Age of Dinosaurs (any dinosaur exhibit worth its salt includes cycads). While they may not be nimble in the evolutionary sense, they are still evolving. In the last 20 years, a new genus has been named, *Chigua* from South America, and a new species of *Bowenia*: *B. serrulata* from Australia.

Like conifers, cycads have seed-bearing cones, and plants are either male or female. The cones produce aromas, from sweet-fruity to wintergreen, and the male cones, which are longer and thinner than the female cones, produce heat, sometimes becoming up to 20 degrees hotter than the surrounding air temperature. (A few female cones do the same thing). In the genus *Zamia*, the temperature change occurs near sundown, before pollen is shed. Male cones of the *Dioon* and *Encephalartos* genera produce heat just after sundown. Scientists believe this quality may be tied to pollen release and the need to attract pollinators.

Chapter Three

The roots of most cycads, called coralloid because they grow up in coral-like shapes, are infested with blue-green algae. These roots fix atmospheric nitrogen at the surface, which is used as a nutrient by the plants.

At Fairchild Tropical Garden in Miami, with one of the world's best cycad collections, you can find an epiphytic cycad growing in the conservatory, *Zamia pseudoparasitica*. *Cycas circinalis*, queen sago, and *C. rumphii*, king sago, are the cycads most often seen in Florida in older landscapes. The queen sago is the larger, both in stature and in leaf size. Many 50- or 60-year-old queen sagos stand 12 to 15 or more ft. tall and develop multiple heads on spreading stems that cluster around the original. King sago is compact, with upright, stiffly held, and sharp leaves.

Dioon species of cycads are native to the New World, or the Americas, and can be found from sea level to 9000 ft. *Dioon edule* has 4- to 5-ft. leaves, pinnately compound, and holds them elegantly up as if in a fountainlike spray. Females of the *Dioon* species have relatively grand cones that are soft and furry, covered with a down, and may last 2 years on the plant. *Dioon edule* may be the slowest growing, and cycad specialists believe it may reach ages approaching 2000 years.

Encephalartos horridus from Africa has wickedly spiny leaflets that are blue-gray once they mature, pinkish when they first flush out. *E. ferox* females add color to the landscape with brilliant-red cones. The seeds are dispersed by mammals, such as monkeys and hornbills.

The name *Encephalartos* is Greek and was assembled this way: *en*, or "in"; *cephale*, meaning "head"; and *artos*, meaning "bread." The inner part of the upper trunk is edible.

The plants in South Africa are fire tolerant and have thick trunks, suckering from the base. Gardeners in South Florida have found it may take 15 to 20 years for one of these to produce a cone, so patience is a must.

Zamia is a West Indies and Latin American group of cycads in the same tribe as *Dioon*. *Zamia* cones are upright, and those of *Z. furfuraceae* break open to release brilliant-red seeds. *Z. furfuraceae* is called the cardboard palm by landscapers because of the texture of its flat, roundish leaves. Its stems are armed with short nodules that make pruning tricky. Florida's only native cycad, *Zamia pumila*, was endangered by overcollecting in the 19th and early 20th centuries, when it was made into starch.

WHEN TO PLANT

Plant in late spring or early summer before the annual flush of new leaves. Leaves form a rosette at the top of the stem. Before new leaves flush, cataphylls, or protective scale-leaves, will appear. When you see these thorny growths, you know it is time to plant or transplant.

WHERE TO PLANT

The most important condition for cycads is excellent drainage. The plants can grow in sun to partial shade, but they will rot in wet soil. A rule of thumb on light is this: blue leaves tolerate sun; blue-green leaves need some shade; green leaves prefer more shade. I once transplanted a *Dioon edule* from shade to sun, and the leaves sunburned. They also stayed on the plant for a couple of years—mistakes are not erased quickly with these plants.

Gardens benefit from cycads because these plants are so architectural. They can be used as specimens, as regal guardians of the entryway, and as accents. Two are small enough to be groundcovers—notably *Zamia pumila* and *Z. fischeri*.

Cycads go with palms like ham with cheese. They can be striking when given a groundcover of rock or mulch or a low-growing flowering cover. They can be stunning when collected in a bed or artfully set on a mound or around a pine. They grow well with aloes.

HOW TO PLANT

Treat a cycad like a palm, and provide a wide hole as deep as the rootball. Backfill without enriching with compost or peat moss. If your soil does not drain especially fast, you may want to build up a mound, incorporating sand into a good potting soil to ensure good drainage.

Chapter Three

CYCADS

ADVICE FOR CARE

A fertilizer formulated for palms can be used on cycads—try a 12-4-12-4 that has slow-release nitrogen and potassium in addition to micronutrients. When new leaves are still soft, apply a foliar micronutrient spray. Yellowing old leaves signal magnesium deficiency; yellowing new leaves are a sign of manganese deficiency and possibly iron deficiency. Scale and mealy bugs can be problems on cycads. Combat pests with insecticidal soap or systemic insecticde sprayed alternately with light horticultural oil. Do not spray with oil in summer; oil can damage leaves in heat above 85 degrees Fahrenheit.

Cycas circinalis and *C. rumphii*, the queen and king sagos, experienced a fungal problem in the early 1990s after the 1989 freeze in South Florida. They have recently been under attack from a deadly scale infestation new to Dade County, particularly in the Coral Gables and Pinecrest areas. The scale is from China and Thailand, and it is extremely difficult to control. It is distinguished by many more male scales, which are long, than female, which are round. Both are white, and the leaves quickly start to look covered with snow. Control scale with consistent use of a light horticultural oil, used alternately with insecticidal soap, systemic insecticide, and Orthene. The scale is much less active in winter than summer. Unfortunately, many old specimens of these plants have been lost to scale.

CHAPTER FOUR

Groundcovers

*C*OULD THERE BE LAWN CHAIRS OR LAWN BOWLING WITHOUT A LAWN? Croquet without grass? Chinch bugs without St. Augustine? No. Could there be happier gardeners without mowing, raking, edging, sweeping, irrigating, and fixing the sprinkler heads? Assuredly.

Give yourself this challenge: enlarge your planting beds 5 to 10 percent each year for the next 5 years and see if you don't love your garden more. This is where groundcovers come in: ferns instead of zoysia, bromeliads instead of chinch bugs, kalanchoe instead of dollar spot. Serendipity instead of a national obsession. Furthermore, and this is not breaking news, groundcovers can reduce the amount of fuel we waste on lawn mowers and fertilizers, the amount of noise we must suffer with leaf blowers, and the hours and hours we spend every Saturday harvesting the crop only to let it decompose, or worse, to throw it away.

We are not completely pro-groundcover, anti-grass. We have dogs that need a place to run. We have parts of the yard we like to visit, and that requires walking across a lawn to get there. We even like the nice contrast grass provides against the groundcovers. But we also like our lives to be our own.

The concept of groundcover may be the most variable in landscaping. A garden with small agaves as accents may have pea rock as a groundcover, while another garden may feature the agaves themselves as the groundcover.

Chapter Four

In the name of creativity, small shrubs can be roped into service. Mexican heather, which is a dwarf shrub, is often used as a groundcover, though it likes attention to look its best. Coontie, the small native cycad, serves well, too. Beargrass, a kind of yucca, is another relatively small plant that might be useful in small areas.

Where is the best place to put groundcovers? Around and beneath trees where grass won't grow; around shrub beds and palms; around the edges of the garden in curving beds to soften the geometry; at the base of shrubs so the plants can serve as a visual link between the flat, floorlike grass and the elevated shrub level; on slopes or grading to keep soil from eroding; on lake fronts; in swales; next to hard surfaces such as patios or decks, again to soften the hard lines of nonliving elements and connect them with living elements.

To successfully prepare an area for groundcovers, first get rid of the grass. There are a couple of ways to do this. One involves covering the area with clear plastic, weighting it down, and allowing the heat to kill the grass. You may not want to wait that long. In that case, you can use Roundup, a herbicide that breaks down quickly. Wait then for the grass to die, remove it, and till the soil, adding compost or peat moss to enrich it. You can add a light application of a slow-release fertilizer at this time, plant the groundcovers and add mulch, then water well.

The goal is to have the edges of the groundcover plants overlap to shade out any weeds. It may take a full growing season or two. In the interim, you'll have to weed and fertilize at appropriate times, keep the soil irrigated, and be patient.

Artillery Plant

Pilea microphylla

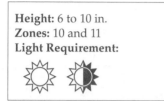

Height: 6 to 10 in.
Zones: 10 and 11
Light Requirement:

Two of the many characteristics that make this West Indies plant useful are its color, which is that of Granny Smith apples, and its texture, which is rather like foam. Together, color and texture make artillery plant a splendid contrast to St. Augustinegrass. It also is durable, taking the rainy season in stride with the dry season, bearing up under heat and not even noticing cold. It looks a little less plump and robust in winter unless you irrigate it, but that's about it (unless a freeze hits, of course). A downside is that some varieties can be weedy. But that comes with the territory of groundcover. Sword ferns, fishtail ferns, wedelia, and certain kalanchoes will do the same thing. After 3 or 4 years, a mat of dead stems forms beneath the new tops, and eventually these have to be cleaned out. It is easier to take out a whole bed of artillery plant and replant. That can be done from cuttings by simply cutting the top 4 or 5 in. off old plants and replanting them in a clump. If growing in moist mulch, the cuttings never even wilt. Artillery plant gets its name from the way the stamens shoot out pollen, in a little cloud, as if the tiniest canon had been fired.

WHEN TO PLANT

Plant at the beginning of the rainy season, which will really help these little plants take off.

WHERE TO PLANT

Artillery plant can be used in many situations, either sunny or somewhat shady.

HOW TO PLANT

Provide good drainage by mixing some sand into the planting bed. Then trowel out a planting hole a little larger than the rootball in the container, and slide the plant from the container into the hole. Fill the planting hole and water. Water well for a few weeks to get this established, if it doesn't rain. For groundcovers, plant about 12 in. apart in staggered rows.

ADVICE FOR CARE

Water in the dry season about once a week. I use artillery plants beneath palms. The whole area gets mulched twice a year, and the palms are fertilized 2 to 3 times a year, so the artillery plants get nutrition by virtue of their location. Periodically, remove old woody stems and replace.

ADDITIONAL INFORMATION

Artillery plant may get a rhizoctonia blight, a fungal disease. When plants are given too much water, they rot out. Snails often hide in the artillery plants, eating them while they're at it. If plants are growing well, they will not show minor damage.

ADDITIONAL SPECIES, CULTIVARS, OR VARIETIES

A related pilea, aluminum plant (*Pilea cadierei*), is dark green with silver markings. From Vietnam, it likes more water and shade, but it spreads quickly. *Pilea* 'Stop Light' has slightly larger round leaves than artillery plant and is a darker color. The little flowers are red, which accounts for the name.

ADVICE FOR REGIONAL CARE

Artillery plant needs protection in winter in Central and North Florida.

Blue Daze

Evolvulus glomeratus

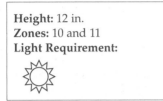

Height: 12 in.
Zones: 10 and 11
Light Requirement:

There was a good deal of excitement a few years ago when blue daze was new to the area, primarily because of the blue color. But blue daze folds up its flowers around midday, so you have to get excited about this first thing in the morning. Nonetheless, it can be utilized in any number of ways: in planters or containers (where its long branches drape over the sides), in borders, in beds, and as groundcover. It grows to about 12 in. tall. Because it is a flowering plant, blue daze gives its best color in full sun. You might consider a swathe of blue daze placed at the feet of pink pentas, which will climb above them. The pentas tend to get leggy, and these plants can disguise that. Yellow shrimp plant, yellow-flowering walking iris, or thryallis might also make good background companions. The plant is in the Convolvulaceae family. The term *convolvo* means to "twine around," and the family is full of vines, such as morning glories (which also close their flowers after midday). *Evolvulus* is from the term *evolvo*, meaning "untwist or unravel." *Evolvulus* is a genus within the family that does not vine or twine.

WHEN TO PLANT
Plant any time in South Florida.

WHERE TO PLANT
Plant in full sun. It is salt tolerant, so it could serve well in seaside gardens or oceanfront condo balconies.

HOW TO PLANT
Space plants about 1 to 1½ ft. apart. If mulching, try to keep the mulch away from plant stalks to reduce the threat of fungus.

Advice for Care

Use a slow-release fertilizer, following package directions. A site that drains well is best to avoid the too-wet conditions that result in disease. Water with a soaker hose. Cut back in spring.

Additional Information

Ed Gilman, in *Betrock's Florida Plant Guide* and Broschart and Meerow in *Betrock's Reference Guide to Florida Landscape Plants* concur that blue daze is moderately drought tolerant and develops fungal disease if kept too wet.

Additional Species, Cultivars, or Varieties

Blue daze has a relative, *Evolvulus purpureo-coeruleus*, that has ultramarine flowers with white centers and purple lines.

Advice for Regional Care

Protect from cold, or use as an annual in areas where frost regularly occurs.

Broad Sword Fern

Nephrolepis biserrata

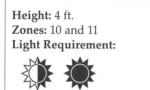

Height: 4 ft.
Zones: 10 and 11
Light Requirement:

Nephrolepis is an often-cultivated genus of epiphytic ferns, made famous by *Nephrolepis exaltata* cv. *Bostoniensis*, or Boston fern. The fronds of these ferns are similar: long and linear with varying sizes of pinnae or leaflets. The broad sword fern is quite a large fern, with fronds sometimes 5 or 6 ft. in length. It will mound up to perhaps 4 ft. This is a fern for really covering a large area. It is versatile enough to take moist to dry conditions, and dense shade to sun. A cultivar of this is the fishtail fern, *Nephrolepis biserrata* cv. *Furcans*. This big, billowy fern has forked ends. It forms beautiful round mounds and holds its own with *Monstera deliciosa*, or Swiss cheese plant, when they meander beneath the oak trees. Allow it to tower over a planting of black velvet begonias, and put mondo grass at the base for an interesting combination. From time to time, you'll have to pull out a clump of this, or it will assert itself as sole owner of the garden. *Nephrolepis exaltata* is the sword fern whose pinnae are fairly widely spaced and form a sharp tip. There are any number of cultivars of this, including 'Fluffy Ruffles' that was a popular hanging basket fern several years ago. *Nephrolepis cordifolia* is sometimes called the tuber sword fern. It is more controlled looking in the landscape, with shorter fronds and smaller, regular pinnae. All of these ferns are wanderers, sending out runners beneath mulch to colonize the garden. You will find yourself pulling up clumps of them once they get started. They're easier to handle, in the long run, than groundcovers that have to be dug and replaced. They take moist (not wet) conditions. These ferns are wonderful beneath trees such as oaks that drop a lot of leaves because they absorb them and turn them to mulch without your turning a hand. They can be used to cover space in your garden while you plant more permanent palms or shrubs. And they are good neighbor plants: you can give them away readily; people are always on the lookout for ferns.

WHEN TO PLANT

Plant at the onset of the rainy season.

WHERE TO PLANT

Plant beneath tree canopies and palms.

HOW TO PLANT

Pull aside mulch, and make some chicken scratches in the soil, setting the clumps near the surface. Bring mulch back around the clumps. Smaller ferns, such as the tuber sword fern, can be planted on 12-in. centers; larger ferns can be set 24 to 36 in. apart.

ADVICE FOR CARE

While these ferns can take drying, they will look better if you irrigate them. With regular watering they will plump up, look lush and full, and spread more quickly. In winter, once or twice weekly watering is best. Three or 4 times a year, spray with a fish emulsion or $1/4$ strength 20-20-20 to keep them super green.

ADDITIONAL INFORMATION

Nephro means "kidney"; *lepis* is "scale." The cases that bear the spores on the undersides of the leaflets are kidney shaped. *Nephrolepis multiflora*, the Asian sword fern, and *Nephrolepis hirsuta* cv. *Superba*, the petticoat fern, are on the invasive exotic plant lists compiled by the Exotic Pest Plant Council. The first is in Category 2, meaning it has the potential to disrupt native communities; the second is in Category 3, indicating it can form dense populations on disturbed sites. All of these ferns will travel and invade. Careful cultivation is required.

ADDITIONAL SPECIES, CULTIVARS, OR VARIETIES

There are many cultivars of these ferns, but the plants mentioned above are easiest to find at nurseries.

ADVICE FOR REGIONAL CARE

Ferns may turn brown over winter if hit by extreme cold or freezing weather, but they will come back. Trim off the brown fronds in the spring.

Bugle Weed

Ajuga reptans

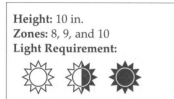

Height: 10 in.
Zones: 8, 9, and 10
Light Requirement:

The name bugle weed sounds like something you had better not turn loose in the landscape, but it's actually a fine groundcover for a variety of light levels. Maybe you like another less-used name—the royal carpet bugle—and could be convinced to use the plant in open areas where you need something that just creeps along. Bugle weed can be used in front of tall plantings. It's ideal near the patio, along walkways, or in perennial beds. The oblong to round leaves range from dark green to purplish in color. Depending on the variety, it produces spring-through-summer blossoms of a white, pink, or purple color. Some gardeners like to grow bugle weed in containers, and others have allowed it to trail from hanging baskets.

WHEN TO PLANT

Bugle weed can be planted at any time of the year. Most plants are available from garden centers in containers year-round. The most stress-free time to plant bugle weed is the late fall through early spring season.

WHERE TO PLANT

Give bugle weed a full-sun to shady location. Air movement around the plants is needed to prevent root rot, especially during the rainy season. The plants like a well-drained soil. Avoid areas that flood during the rainy season or are naturally too wet for good growth.

HOW TO PLANT

Most groundcovers can grow well in the sandy Florida soils. Bugle weed grows more quickly and is easier to maintain if the soil is improved before planting. Where possible, work in several inches of compost or peat moss and manure with the existing soil. Space the plants 10 to 12 in. apart. Dig the hole wider than the rootball but not deeper. Set the plant at the same planting depth as it was growing in the container or a little higher out of the ground. Add soil and water to the hole to have good root-to-soil contact. After planting, water the entire planting site thoroughly. A 2- to 3-in. layer of mulch can be added to keep the soil moist and control weeds. The first feeding may be provided 4 to 6 weeks after planting. Continue watering to keep the soil moist until the plants are established and send roots out into the surrounding soil.

ADVICE FOR CARE

Bugle weed plantings are drought tolerant but grow best with a moist soil. Where extra growth is needed and during periods of severe drought, provide 1/2 to 3/4 in. of water weekly. Feed bugle weed in spring, summer, and early fall. Use a 6-6-6, 12-4-8, or similar garden fertilizer at the rates suggested on the label. Pests are usually few, but bugle weed may be affected by caterpillars and slugs. Hand pick the pests from the plantings, or treat them with a pesticide recommended by the University of Florida Cooperative Extension Service. Rot problems are a major concern during the summer season. Plant in well-drained soils and airy locations to prevent fungal damage.

ADDITIONAL INFORMATION

Bugle weed develops a dense foliage cover without special care. It may slowly invade nearby plantings and may need to be removed to keep it from becoming a problem in the landscape.

ADDITIONAL SPECIES, CULTIVARS, OR VARIETIES

A few selections include 'Alba' with white flowers, 'Atropurpurea' with bronze foliage, and 'Variegata' with cream-and-green foliage. Check your garden center for other selections.

ADVICE FOR REGIONAL CARE

Only partial-sun to shady planting sites are recommended when bugle weed is planted in the southern part of the state. The summer heat may limit its use in the extreme southern portions of the state.

Cast Iron Plant

Aspidistra elatior

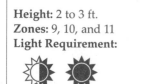

Height: 2 to 3 ft.
Zones: 9, 10, and 11
Light Requirement:

Need a groundcover just for shade? Then you might like the cast iron plant. The name probably says it all. It's durable, takes most soil conditions, and needs limited care. The cast iron plant can beat out most weeds, so once it's established, you won't have to eliminate other unwanted vegetation. Because it cannot take direct sun, it may be the ideal plant for gardeners asking for something for the shade. It produces dark-green foliage that has a tropical and bit exotic look. Each wide leaf grows to 2 ft. long, and there are plenty of them. Use the cast iron plant near the patio, along walkways, or wherever greenery is desired. Plants can be added to containers for porches, balconies, or entrances. Many are used in interiorscapes.

WHEN TO PLANT

Cast iron plants can be added at any time of the year. Most plants are available from garden centers in containers year-round. The most stress-free time to plant is the late fall through early spring season. Plant in spring and early summer in South Florida.

WHERE TO PLANT

Give cast iron plants a partial-shade to shady location. Outdoors it's impossible to find a light level that's too low for these plants. They like a well-drained soil. Avoid areas that flood during the rainy season or are naturally too wet for good growth.

HOW TO PLANT

Most groundcovers can grow well in the sandy Florida soils. Cast iron plants grow more quickly and are easier to maintain if the soil is improved before planting. Where possible, work in several inches of compost or peat moss and manure with the existing soil. Space cast iron plants 12 to 18 in. apart. Dig the hole wider than the root-ball but not deeper. Set the plant at the same planting depth as it was growing in the container or a little higher out of the ground. Add soil and water to the hole to make good root-to-soil contact.

After planting, water the entire planting site thoroughly. A 2- to 3-in. mulch layer can be added to keep the soil moist and control weeds. The first feeding may be provided 4 to 6 weeks after planting. Continue watering to keep the soil moist until the plants are established and send roots out into the surrounding soil.

ADVICE FOR CARE

Cast iron plants are drought tolerant but make the best growth with a moist soil. Where extra growth is needed and during periods of severe drought, provide weekly waterings with $1/2$ to $3/4$ in. of water. Feed cast iron plantings once in spring, summer, and early fall. Use a 6-6-6, 12-4-8, or similar garden fertilizer at the rates suggested on the label. Pests are usually few, but cast iron plants may be affected by caterpillars and slugs. Hand pick the pests from the plantings, or treat them with a pesticide recommended by the University of Florida Cooperative Extension Service.

ADDITIONAL INFORMATION

Plantings grow rather slowly but eventually fill in the bed with a dense stand of foliage. Control is needed to keep the shoots from invading nearby plantings.

ADDITIONAL SPECIES, CULTIVARS, OR VARIETIES

One variety, *Variegata*, often offered at garden centers has green-and-white-striped foliage and appears to grow well in local landscapes.

ADVICE FOR REGIONAL CARE

The cast iron plant is cold sensitive and is frequently damaged in Central Florida by freezing weather. It cannot be grown as a groundcover in the more northern portions of the state but can be established in containers and given winter protection. When the plant is damaged by cold, prune off the brown leaves before spring growth begins.

Creeping Fig

Ficus pumila

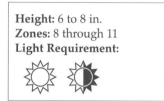

Height: 6 to 8 in.
Zones: 8 through 11
Light Requirement:

Creeping fig is a groundcover that hugs the soil. Its bright-green leaves vary with the stage of plant maturity. When the plants are young and said to be in a juvenile stage of growth, the leaves are small, oval, and 1 in. long. When the plants get older and mature, the leaves are oblong and 2 to 4 in. long. Creeping fig does flower and produce a fig, but the fruit is inedible. Use creeping fig as a groundcover leading up to the turf and walkways or filling in the small spaces from the walkways to the home. As a wall covering, creeping fig climbs buildings and similar structures. Plant creeping fig in hanging baskets, or use it to cover stuffed topiaries.

WHEN TO PLANT

Creeping fig can be planted at any time of the year. Most plants are available from garden centers in containers year-round. The most stress-free time to add creeping fig to the landscape is the late fall through early spring season. Plant during the rainy season in South Florida.

WHERE TO PLANT

Give creeping fig a full-sun to partial-shade location. The plant likes a well-drained soil. Avoid areas that flood during the rainy season or are naturally too wet for good growth.

HOW TO PLANT

Most groundcovers can grow well in the sandy Florida soils. Creeping fig grows more quickly and is easier to maintain if the soil is improved prior to planting. Where possible, work in several inches of compost or peat moss and manure with the existing soil. Space plants 12 to 18 in. apart. Dig the hole wider than the rootball but not deeper. Set the plant at the same planting depth as it was growing in the container or original planting site or a little higher out of the ground. Add soil and water to the hole to make good root-to-soil contact. After planting, water the entire planting site thoroughly. A 2- to 3-in. mulch layer can be added to keep the soil moist and control weeds. The first feeding may be provided 4 to 6 weeks after planting. Continue watering to keep the soil moist until the plants are established and send roots out into the surrounding soil.

ADVICE FOR CARE
Creeping fig plantings are drought tolerant but make the best growth with a moist soil. Where extra growth is needed and during periods of severe drought, provide weekly with 1/2 to 3/4 in. of water. Feed creeping fig once in spring, summer, and early fall. Use a 6-6-6, 12-4-8, or similar garden fertilizer at the rates suggested on the label. Pests are usually few, but creeping fig may be affected by caterpillars. Hand pick the pests from the plantings, or treat them with a pesticide recommended by the University of Florida Cooperative Extension Service.

ADDITIONAL INFORMATION
Creeping fig is an aggressive plant that can climb trees, shrubs, and nearby buildings. Periodic trimming is needed to keep the plantings in bounds.

ADDITIONAL SPECIES, CULTIVARS, OR VARIETIES
Numerous selections of creeping fig have been made for use in the landscape, including varieties *Minima* with all-juvenile foliage, *Quercifolia* with lobed leaves, and *Variegata* with cream-and-green leaves.

ADVICE FOR REGIONAL CARE
Creeping fig grows well in all areas of the state. No special care is needed for the different regions. Plant during the rainy season in South Florida.

Dwarf Carissa

Carissa macrocarpa 'Emerald Beauty'

Other Name: *Carissa macrocarpa* 'Horizontalis'
Height: to 10 ft.
Zones: 10B and 11
Light Requirement:

The Atlantic Ocean and Gulf of Mexico are reasons many of us live in Florida, packed tightly and as close to the shores as we can get. On the East Coast, we boast of summer's southeasterly breezes and remember those Midwest summers of still, hot air and impending tornadoes. But as wonderful as seaside living can be, the people who live next to the shore often are at a loss for salt-tolerant plants in their gardens. Let's see: sea grape, sea oats, coconuts, mangroves, and what? Natal plum, or carissa, from South Africa comes in two sizes: the regular shrub size, which can reach 10 ft. but usually doesn't, and the dwarf form, which can effectively be used as a groundcover in seaside gardens. The plants thrive in sandy soils, even alkaline sandy soils, and their thick, waxy leaves won't be torn by wind. Carissa is in the same family as oleander, frangipani, periwinkle, and allamanda, the Apocynaceae. These have a milky sap (which is sometimes toxic, as is the case with oleander). As groundcovers, the dwarf carissa can be planted on 18- to 24-in. centers. The little shrubs also make good candidates for containers on the million-and-one condo balconies facing the sea, where wind rips and tosses weeping fig trees and other container plants. For condo balconies, salt and wind tolerance are musts. Cactus plants are usually the last resort, but there are other possibilities, including dwarf carissa, jade plant, pony tail, cycads, shore juniper, and Spanish bayonet.

WHEN TO PLANT

Plant in spring, if you can provide irrigation, or at the beginning of the rainy season or throughout the warm months.

WHERE TO PLANT

Plant in full sun.

How to Plant

To use as a groundcover, plant on 2-ft. centers in staggered rows. Enrich the soil with peat, compost, or well-aged manure so that no more than 1/3 of the backfill is organic. Dig a hole as deep as the container and slightly wider; slip the container off the rootball, and position the shrub in the planting hole; water in the backfill. Mulch, keeping the mulch from direct contact with the shrub trunks to prevent disease.

Advice for Care

Water so that the plant's roots stay moderately moist. If in a windy location, this may require watering every other day because wind pulls moisture out of the soil. Three times a year, fertilize with slow-release 14-14-14 or with a granular 6-6-6.

Additional Information

Fruit on regular carissa is often made into jelly.

Additional Species, Cultivars, or Varieties

Ask at your nursery if any other cultivars are available.

Advice for Regional Care

Carissa may be grown in protected areas in Central Florida. Provide cold protection in Central and North Florida.

English Ivy

Hedera helix

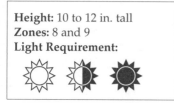
For many gardeners relocated to Florida, the English ivy is the little bit of home they can bring with them. It's a familiar groundcover that can fill the problem spots in the landscapes where some quick-growing greenery is needed. Use it in low-light areas, dry spots, and poor soils. A basic requirement is its need for air circulation to prevent root and stem rot during the rainy season. Many gardeners have replaced turf in shady areas with ivy. It's also good on banks and areas along walkways too small for turf. The bright-green leaves feature about 5 lobes, but many forms and sizes are available. English ivy can be trained to walls and fences, and it can be used in hanging baskets.

WHEN TO PLANT

English ivy can be planted at any time of the year. Most plants are available from garden centers in containers year-round. The most stress-free time to plant is the late fall through early spring season. English ivy may be more difficult to establish in shady areas during the rainy season, which keeps the plantings too moist and encourages rots and leaf spots.

WHERE TO PLANT

Give English ivy a full-sun to shady location. In the more southern portions of the state it appears to grow best in partial-shade to shady locations. The plant likes a well-drained soil. Avoid areas that flood during the rainy season or are naturally too wet for good growth.

HOW TO PLANT

Most groundcovers grow well in the sandy Florida soils. English ivy grows more quickly and is easier to maintain if the soil is improved before planting. Where possible, work in several inches of compost or peat moss and manure with the existing soil. Space plants 18 to 24 in. apart. Dig the hole wider than the rootball but not deeper. Set the plant at the same planting depth as it was growing in the container or original planting site or a little higher out of the ground. Add soil and water to the hole to make good root-to-soil contact. After planting, water the entire planting site thoroughly. A 2- to 3-in. mulch layer can be added to keep the soil moist and control weeds. The first feeding may be provided 4 to 6 weeks after planting. Continue watering to keep the soil moist until the plants are established and send roots out into the surrounding soil.

ADVICE FOR CARE

English ivy plantings are drought tolerant but make the best growth with a moist soil. Where extra growth is needed and during periods of severe drought, provide weekly waterings with $1/2$ to $3/4$ in. of water. Feed English ivy once in spring, summer, and early fall. Use a 6-6-6, 12-4-8, or similar garden fertilizer at the rates suggested on the label. Pests are usually few, but English ivy may be affected by scale insects and mites. Hand pick the pests from the plantings, or treat them with a pesticide recommended by the University of Florida Cooperative Extension Service. Leaf spots and rot problems affect plantings that stay too moist.

ADDITIONAL INFORMATION

English ivy can grow rather rapidly to fill beds. It needs periodic pruning to keep it in bounds and off trees and buildings.

ADDITIONAL SPECIES, CULTIVARS, OR VARIETIES

There are hundreds of varieties of English ivy of varying leaf shapes and leaf colors. Another species worth planting in most areas of Florida is *Hedera canariensis*; its leaves are usually three-lobed, and it grows larger than English ivy. It is used as a groundcover but must be protected from cold in the more northern portions of the state.

ADVICE FOR REGIONAL CARE

English ivy grows well in the northern and central areas of the state. In Central Florida it is best grown in partially shady to shady areas. English ivy does not grow well in South Florida.

Fakahatchee Grass

Tripsicum dactyloides

Height: 2 1/2 to 5 ft.
Zones: All
Light Requirement:

In the last ten years, gardeners all across the country have rediscovered the use of ornamental grasses, and Floridians have been no exception. Natural, informal, and easy to care for, this new approach to some Florida landscapes has created relaxed but sophisticated gardens. Fakahatchee grass, sometimes called Florida gamma grass, is a medium- to olive-green, slender-bladed grass that adds softness to a landscape. It can be grown where there is not enough room for pampas grass. When to use grass? When texture is wanted or when edges need to be softened. Contemporary houses, with strong linear architecture, can be made to fit into the landscape with the addition of grasses that will nicely set off the house while linking it to the earth. Grasses can be used in blocks or arcs to be viewed from a distance. They can be used to make a transition from low to high. They bring a less formal note to a landscape and are effective as meadows or, as in the Everglades, as prairies that move with the wind, that turn color with the season. Grasses on Florida's West Coast can soften the harshness of the bright, white shell substrate and result in a sweeping and unstructured look. Grasses mix well with Geiger trees, which have large leaves and bright-orange flowers; they create gentle mounds around coconut palms, silver palms, and the edges of rectangular pools. Fakahatchee grass is a Florida native, also growing into the Southeast. It grows in pinelands as well as hammocks. The dwarf form is especially useful for home landscapes.

WHEN TO PLANT
Plant any time from spring through fall.

WHERE TO PLANT
Plant in moist areas or in areas where irrigation is possible; select locations in full sun.

How to Plant

If you use this as a groundcover, the clumps can be 3 to 4 ft. apart with full-sized grass, 1 to 2 ft. with dwarf forms. The idea is to have the leaves meet and shade out weeds below.

Advice for Care

Cut the grass back hard in spring (to about 1 ft. for large forms; 6 in. for dwarf), and use the clippings for mulch; choose either a balanced slow-release, such as 14-14-14, or a high-nitrogen fertilizer. Keep the grass well watered throughout the year. If you don't water it in winter, it will turn brown.

Additional Information

Flowers occur in the fall on tall spikes, but they are insignificant, like other grass flowers.

Additional Species, Cultivars, or Varieties

Tripsacum floridana is the dwarf form. It has narrower blades and finer texture than regular Fakahatchee grass.

Advice for Regional Care

Tripsacum grows well throughout the state, but will turn brown in winter in Central and North Florida.

GROUNDCOVERS

Kalanchoe

Kalanchoe blossfeldiana

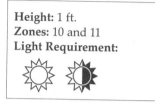

Height: 1 ft.
Zones: 10 and 11
Light Requirement:

When Xeriscaping—landscaping for water conservation—first came into vogue in the late 1980s, its promoters were quick to assure everyone that you didn't have to plant cactus plants to have a water-conserving yard. And that's true. But the use of succulents (remember, all cactuses are succulents but not all succulents are cactuses) is a good strategy for cutting down on water use, whether you are purposely trying to do so or are just fond of the look. Kalanchoes, houseplants for eons, are effective plants to add winter color to those far reaches of your garden where you either don't want to water or water infrequently. The leaves are not as thickly succulent as those of other members of the *Crassula* family (Crassaulaceae), but they store water and are waxy to the touch. The plants are upright when young and somewhat sprawly when full grown. Their size and color make them good candidates for garden edges, where they look pretty against gravel or mulch as well as against greener and more upright plants behind them. A beautiful look is that of yellow-flowering kalanchoe planted in a swathe, accented by *Furcrea foetida*, giant false agave, which is a creamy yellow and green. Both succulents can thrive with infrequent irrigation. The red-flowering kalanchoe may accent a silver Bismarck palm to great effect, while any color might blend well with large cap rocks or limestone boulders in a rock garden area of the landscape.

WHEN TO PLANT
Plant any time.

WHERE TO PLANT
Plant in full sun to partial shade.

HOW TO PLANT
Choose well-draining, sandy soil. The standard nursery topsoil, a 50-50 mix of sand and muck, can be used. Even a 70 percent sand and 30 percent muck mix will do. Space 6 to 10 in. apart.

ADVICE FOR CARE

At the time of planting, use 2 teaspoons of slow-release fertilizer with micronutrients either in the plant hole or on top of the root zones, and water in. Use 6-month slow-release, applying only twice a year. Cut back the flower heads after bloom stops to avoid fungus. Then spray preventively with a fungicide to avoid crown rot.

ADDITIONAL INFORMATION

Kalanchoes are easy to start from cuttings in the spring. Snip off 4 or 5 in., remove the bottom leaves, and root in a peat moss–perlite mix that is kept moist and in the shade. Roots should form in 4 to 6 weeks. Plant outdoors.

ADDITIONAL SPECIES, CULTIVARS, OR VARIETIES

Many cultivars of *Kalanchoe* are sold, and they come in many colors. A species called *K. tomentosa*, the panda plant, with silver-gray, fuzzy leaves makes a nice houseplant, patio plant, or rock garden specimen. *K. pumila* has silver leaves with stalks of pink flowers; use as a houseplant.

Liriope

Liriope muscari

Other Name: Lilyturf
Height: 1 ft.
Zones: All
Light Requirement:
   depending on cultivar

This may be one of the most popular groundcovers of recent years. The dark color and slender leaves that spike up and arch over in a small clump make it a nice contrast to St. Augustine, mulch, shrubs, and trees. The drawback is that you cannot walk on it. But many groundcovers share the same characteristic, so most of us are well trained not to step on it. Lilyturf takes a wide range of conditions, from sun to shade, well watered to dry. It looks great at the base of shrubs that have a tendency to get leggy, such as crotons or ixora. And it contrasts nicely with silver buttonwood. A related species is *Liriope spicata*, or creeping lilyturf. It takes less light, is more cold tolerant, and covers faster than muscari. Liriope is related to other grasslike members of the lily family, *Ophiopogon* or mondo grass. *Ophiopogon japonicus* is finer textured, slower growing, and tiny by comparison, as well as more costly. It makes a wonderful ground-cover, however, and gives a neater-looking landscape than lilyturf. *Chlorophytum*, or spider plant, is also a relative with grasslike leaves. The best-known is the variegated spider plant that produces new plantlets at the end of long stems. A solid green form also is available. Both of these can be used as groundcovers—as container plants or hanging baskets. (The lily family contains many other plants that have narrow leaves and are prized mainly as foliage plants, such as ti plants or *Cordyline terminalis*, a mountain flax from New Zealand, and sanse-vierias.) Lilyturf does get scale; insecticidal soaps and horticultural oils (in winter) can be used to combat them. A variegated lilyturf is being used more often for edgings and groundcovers. It appears too light for effective use in sun. And despite what you may find on local high-ways, blocks of alternating variegated and green lilyturf may not be the best idea unless you intend to create an outdoor checkerboard. It also may be wise to refrain from alternating light and dark lilyturf indi-vidually; the effect can be more jarring than harmonious.

WHEN TO PLANT

Plant in the early summer. The plants are slow growing, and early summer planting will give them a full growing season to take hold.

WHERE TO PLANT

Shade is preferable, although cultivars for sun are available. Be sure to specify where it will be used, and ask for sun-tolerant cultivars if your site is sunny.

HOW TO PLANT

For covering or edging, plant these 8 to 10 in. apart. The dwarf types can be more closely spaced. Sometimes, if containers are quite full in the nursery, you can simply divide them when planting.

ADVICE FOR CARE

Fertilize annually in spring. Keep moist for the first month or so to allow the plant to become established. Water in extremely dry weather.

ADDITIONAL INFORMATION

'Webster Wide Leaf' is susceptible to leaf spot, a fungal disease.

ADDITIONAL SPECIES, CULTIVARS, OR VARIETIES

A number of cultivars of liriope are now sold, including those with silver variegation or gold variegation, and pink, white, blue, or lavender flowers. 'Big Blue' and 'Evergreen Giant' are the tallest, but there also are 'Monroe White', 'Silvery Sunproof', 'Variegata', and 'Variegated Giant'.

ADVICE FOR REGIONAL CARE

In Central and North Florida, protect from freezes.

Mexican Bluebell

Ruellia brittoniana

Height: 2 ft.
Zones: 10 and 11
Light Requirement:

Blue flowers are an acquired taste, and some plants shouldn't be forced to produce them—roses, for instance, or daisies. Just as petunias shouldn't be red-and-white striped, so hibiscus or carnations shouldn't be blue. But ruellia, ah, that's a blue of a different color. The blue flowers of Mexican bluebells are gloriously blue. Like the shadows in the rocks at Grant's Pass near Tucson, just before the sun slips below the desert's horizon, this blue has purple in it. This indeed is the blue of the West, a fierce blue, potent and capable, which, when it darkens on its way into the flower's throat, becomes the purple-blue of mesas, canyons, and the scant shade beneath the ocotillo's long whips. But we can tame it. We in Florida can subdue it with our light, the brilliant and near-white light that washes over all colors with equal power, flattening and curbing them at every turn until they are but a tint of their former selves. So Mexican bluebells really become blue at last, willing to mix with yellows and magenta. Even here, though, a sweep of bluebells is a charming sight. The deli-cate-textured flowers open one at a time on stalks that develop in the axils of the terminal leaves so that each morning flowers are fresh again—providing they have been watered and fed sufficiently. A compact line of Mexican bluebells has been developed, and it is ideal for groundcovers. The dark-green, linear leaves form little mounds. Occasionally the seeds will germinate nearby, helping to spread the plants, or little woody stems can be clipped to propagate them vegetatively.

WHEN TO PLANT
Plant spring through fall.

WHERE TO PLANT
Plant in partial shade (the color will be deeper) to sun. Try them in beds around green and yellow *Schefflera arboricola*.

HOW TO PLANT

Select a sandy mix that drains well but can retain some moisture with a peat component. For groundcovers, plant 12 in. apart in staggered rows. With compact types, plant closer to 6 in. on center.

ADVICE FOR CARE

Water well to establish, and provide with a time-release fertilizer at the time of planting, either in the planting hole or scattered around the root zones. Water a couple of times weekly in winter, every 2 or 3 days in summer if rain is light. Reapply fertilizer in midsummer and in October. The plants will become light green if they are hungry. Cut them back a couple of times a year if you're using the tall variety.

ADDITIONAL INFORMATION

Experienced growers in Central Florida say bluebells are weedy, reseeding everywhere. Use care when planting, and pull unwanted seedlings, lest they escape.

ADDITIONAL SPECIES, CULTIVARS, OR VARIETIES

A mauve-colored cultivar is available; 'Chi-chi' is a good, tall pink.

ADVICE FOR REGIONAL CARE

In North and Central Florida, Mexican bluebells can be taken back to the ground in winter weather, but usually they resprout from basal buds.

Mexican Heather

Cuphea hyssopifolia

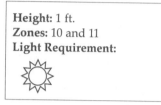

Height: 1 ft.
Zones: 10 and 11
Light Requirement:

Mexican heather is such a little guy that it almost cries to be used as a groundcover or in a raised pot, close to the eye. As a groundcover, its power is lost if you fail to take care of it. The better care it receives, the larger the leaves and the more flowers it will produce. Well cared for, the plants can be nicely grouped in a bed to accent red jatropha, in a complementary scheme, or against yellow-flowering walking iris in an opposite harmony. Mixing colors in the garden is an art, and if you don't have an artist's eye, you can rely on a color wheel from an art supply store. No one will have to know. Bright colors, such as red, orange, and yellow, advance—that is, they seem closer to you than they actually are. Cool colors, in the blue, purple, violet group, appear farther away. The size of this dwarf shrub, combined with the cooler color, should tell you that it must be positioned somewhere within a few feet of the viewer, or it won't be noticed.

WHEN TO PLANT
Plant in the spring. Plant year-round in Central Florida.

WHERE TO PLANT
Plant in full sun to light shade.

HOW TO PLANT
In enriched soil, place plants about 18 in. apart. To the planting soil add compost, peat moss, or aged manure so the ratio is about 1:3 amendment to original soil. Mulch.

ADVICE FOR CARE
Keep Mexican heather well irrigated and fertilized. The plants don't like to dry out completely, or they'll die. Mulching can mediate soil moisture. In addition, the plants are susceptible to nematodes that attack their roots. Nematodes are microscopic worms that can

reduce the vigor of plants and ultimately cause their demise. Nematodes are kept somewhat at bay by keeping plants growing vigorously and by mulching. Fertilize 3 times a year, or use a slow-release fertilizer, such as 13-13-13 or 14-14-14 with micronutrients.

ADDITIONAL INFORMATION
Cuphea, from the highlands of Mexico and Central America, is related to crape myrtle.

ADDITIONAL SPECIES, CULTIVARS, OR VARIETIES
Several cultivars are carried by nurseries, including one called 'Georgia Scarlet', which has flowers shaped like Mickey Mouse. *Cuphea ignea* is carried by one wholesale nursery in Boynton Beach and sold throughout Central Florida. This relative has tubular flowers that are red with a black ring, hence the common name, cigar plant.

ADVICE FOR REGIONAL CARE
Freezing weather will kill branchlets on these little shrubs, but you can prune them back in spring to remove the dead twigs and let them resprout.

Mondo Grass

Ophiopogon japonicus

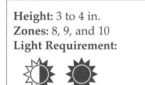

Height: 3 to 4 in.
Zones: 8, 9, and 10
Light Requirement:

Florida gardeners rely upon mondo grass as a groundcover for shady areas. It's not a true grass, but the leaves are linear and give a turflike look to landscapes. As with most groundcovers, it cannot take foot traffic but can be used among stepping-stones for a pathway through the planted areas. The dark-green leaves are about 1/4 in. wide and grow from 6 to 12 in. long. Use mondo grass on hard-to-mow slopes and along walkways. Of course, it can fill in an area near the home, under trees, or in front of shrubs. Mondo grass often appears in Oriental gardens. This durable groundcover grows where other plants cannot take the poorer, drier soils.

WHEN TO PLANT

Mondo grass can be planted at any time of the year. Most plants are available from garden centers in containers year-round. The most stress-free time to add mondo grass to the landscape in Central and North Florida is the late fall through early spring season. At that time of the year it is possible to dig and divide clumps to fill in the voids in the landscape with minimal care.

WHERE TO PLANT

Give mondo grass a filtered-sun to totally shady location. It's hard to find an area in the landscape that has too low a light level for mondo grass. The plants like a well-drained soil. Avoid areas that flood during the rainy season or are naturally too wet for good growth.

HOW TO PLANT

Most groundcovers grow well in the sandy Florida soils. Mondo grass grows more quickly and is easier to maintain if the soil is improved before planting. Where possible, work in several inches of compost or peat moss and manure with the existing soil. Space plants 8 to 10 in. apart. Dig the hole wider than the rootball but not deeper. Set the plant at the same planting depth as it was growing in the container or original planting site or a little higher out of the ground. Add soil and water to the hole for good root-to-soil contact. After planting, water the entire planting site thoroughly. A 2- to 3-in. layer of mulch can be added to keep the soil moist and control weeds. The first feeding may be provided 4 to 6 weeks after planting. Continue watering to keep the soil moist until the plants are established and send roots out into the surrounding soil.

ADVICE FOR CARE

Mondo grass plantings are drought tolerant but make the best growth with a moist soil. Where extra growth is needed and during periods of severe drought, provide weekly waterings with $1/2$ to $3/4$ in. of water. Feed mondo grass once in spring, summer, and early fall. Use a 6-6-6, 12-4-8, or similar garden fertilizer at the rates suggested on the label. Pests are usually few, but mondo grass may be affected by scale insects. Where necessary, apply an insecticide recommended by the University of Florida Cooperative Extension Service.

ADDITIONAL INFORMATION

Mondo grass slowly fills in the bed sites. After several years of growth, it may invade nearby areas. Dig out the plants to fill in bare areas or to share with friends.

ADDITIONAL SPECIES, CULTIVARS, OR VARIETIES

Several selections of mondo grass have been made for Florida landscapes. One commonly available is Nana, a dwarf variety.

ADVICE FOR REGIONAL CARE

Mondo grass grows well throughout all but the most southern portions of Florida. It's quite hardy and needs no special winter care.

Oyster Plant

Rhoeo spathacea

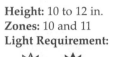

Height: 10 to 12 in.
Zones: 10 and 11
Light Requirement:

Like lilyturf, oyster plant is a widely used groundcover because it is so hardy and forgiving. Maybe it's too forgiving, because you have a hard time getting rid of it. The plant is fairly attractive with green on top of the leaves and rose-purple on the bottom. It is useful in many conditions, able to handle anything you throw at it, including a good boot. In areas with poor soil, not much irrigation, and sun alternating with shade throughout the day, oyster plants are appropriate. In full sun, they can look pretty ratty. They work wonderfully around tree roots that have managed to creep onto the surface because they can grow anywhere and are big enough to hide the anacondalike roots that some trees, such as royal poincianas, can develop. There is a caveat with oyster plants and some related genera: allergy. I am allergic to oyster plants and to its related purple-and-green plants, such as wandering Jew, and probably purple queen, although I haven't tested this yet. Like bright coloration on frogs, the purple should serve as a warning of skin irritants. The sap of the plant can cause enormous patches of hives (and near madness until they stop itching). Remedies include antihistamines and ice, which result in an afternoon nap. When oyster plants are well fertilized and watered, they make striking beds in the proper light. They multiply quickly, and seedlings seem to get big overnight. You have to be conscientious about pulling up seedlings. The plant is on the Category 2 list of the Exotic Pest Plant Council's invasive exotic list. That means it has the potential to disrupt native plant communities.

WHEN TO PLANT

Plant at any time; oyster plants seem oblivious to hardship.

WHERE TO PLANT

Plant under a wide range of conditions, in sun or shade, and even in pots if you are so inclined.

How to Plant

With a trowel, dig a small planting hole that will contain the roots of a containerized plant—or a plant given you by a neighbor. These are across-the-fence plants of the first order, made to just stick in the ground.

Advice for Care

Regular water and fertilizer make these plants shine. Their waxy leaves tend to prevent desiccation in dry spells. High, partial shade is ideal. Thin them to reduce the bed size.

Additional Information

In a bed, space these 1 ft. apart—measuring from the center of one plant to the center of another.

Additional Species, Cultivars, or Varieties

The dwarf oyster plant often looks tidier as a groundcover than its larger brother, and it doesn't seem to pop up unbidden.

Advice for Regional Care

Grow this in a protected area in colder areas of Central Florida. Oyster plants may suffer cold damage but will grow back from basal stems. They are too cold sensitive for North Florida.

Peperomia

Peperomia obtusifolia

Height: 6 to 8 in.
Zones: 10B and 11
Light Requirement:

An ideal groundcover for the north side of your house, this native also does well beneath shade trees. The leaves are ovate to heart-shaped, and there are a number of cultivars and species found in nurseries. While you won't be able to walk on it, the plants can stand some punishment and even survive the family dogs—we speak from experience. What they don't like is to be too wet or too dry. Many species of this plant hail from the West Indies and South America as well as from Florida. They are in the Piperaceae family—that family that gives us commercial pepper, *Piper nigrum*. The flowers of the family occur on upright slender stalks, like the stalks of the aroid family, but smaller—and without the attending modified leaf called the spathe. Known in more temperate climates as houseplants, peperomias are good for indoor cultivation because of their low light requirements. In South Florida, you will come across this humidity-loving plant in sloughs and low hammocks, frequently on old logs. Often on the downside of decomposing, old logs offer an organic medium that drains fast. Try planting a small container in recesses of limestone rocks, where water seems to rush away during rain, but where moisture is held in the interior niches and recesses.

WHEN TO PLANT

Plant in spring, if you will be sure to water regularly—spring is often the driest part of the dry season; or plant at the beginning of the rainy season in late May or June.

WHERE TO PLANT

Plant in shade for a groundcover; in pots for use around the patio; in hanging baskets.

HOW TO PLANT

After a couple of unsucessful attempts, I finally succeeded in growing peperomia beneath palms and on top of mulch. At first, I gave them too much sun; then I gave them too much shade and water. The plants should be treated almost like air plants. They scamper happily across mulch and while they head for the light, they don't really want to grow in it.

ADVICE FOR CARE
The slow-release fertilizer I use on the palms is sufficient for the nearby peperomia.

ADDITIONAL INFORMATION
P. obtusifolia is sometimes called Baby Rubber Plant, because its succulent leaves are like those of rubber trees.

ADDITIONAL SPECIES, HYBRIDS, OR CULTIVARS
At the moment, peperomias are on the wane in popularity, but they do come and go, particularly as houseplants. There is a variegated form of *P. obtusifolia* that has red stems with cream-and-white leaves that are quite attractive. A cultivar called 'Albo-marginata' has white leaf margins; 'Alba' has red leaf markings; 'Watermelon' looks just like a watermelon, as far as color goes. Related houseplants include *P. capaerata* 'Emerald Ripple'. It has smaller leaves and is not as succulent, but has a corrugated leaf texture.

ADVICE FOR REGIONAL CARE
This is a groundcover for South Florida only; but peperomia can be used as an annual or in containers in Central and North Florida.

Purple Queen

Setcreasea pallida

Height: 1 ft.
Zones: 9 through 11
Light Requirement:

Here is a color strong enough for the tropical light of Florida. When beds of this were planted at Fairchild Tropical Garden, the color set the place on its ear, so bold was it, such an upstart in a traditional setting. The beds of purple queen at that botanical garden accent remarkably beautiful blue-gray Bismarck palms, *Bismarckia nobilis*. Between the purple groundcover and the hefty blue palms are rosy-copper bromeliads, *Aechmea blanchetiana*. There is nothing shy about this combination. Try purple queen with silver buttonwood, the genetic sport of the native green buttonwood that is part of the mangrove community. The silver-purple may be given a visual lift with an upright podocarpus. Frances Perry in *Flowers of the World* is clearly scandalized by the plant's colors, describing purple queen as having stems and foliage of "Tyrian purple and the flower cerise—a ghastly combination!" The purple queen today is no longer an embarrassment; the flowers have been toned down to pink and are quite pretty—they seem to lie lightly on the foliage and sparkle. A tough plant, purple queen endures the abuses suffered in median plantings, and even though the individual plants in these public plantings are too far apart to keep the soil (and trash) from showing, they hold up and appear as a solid color from a distance. Snails like the succulence and you may have to put a copper screening around the bed. Snail bait is toxic to pets, so be careful if you elect to use it.

WHEN TO PLANT
Plant any time.

WHERE TO PLANT
Choose a location in full sun with good drainage.

HOW TO PLANT
For an effective groundcover, space the plants 6 in. apart or weeds will creep in. Prepare the whole bed, adding some compost or peat

to it and mixing in well. Set plants in holes dug as deep as the root-ball but 2 or 3 times wider, fill in with soil, and mulch.

ADVICE FOR CARE
Setcresea is tolerant of a wide range of soils, but likes to be watered a couple of times a week to look good. Use a slow-release fertilizer in spring and fall. It may take a couple of years for the purple queen to cover; in the interim, weed and replace mulch every few months.

ADDITIONAL INFORMATION
You can easily propagate this plant from tip cuttings by inserting tender stems a few inches long into moistened peat moss with 50 percent perlite. If the soil is kept moist, you may get these cuttings to root right in the beds rather than go through the intermediate stage of a rooting medium.

ADDITIONAL SPECIES, CULTIVARS, OR VARIETIES
Purple queen is related to wandering Jew (*Zebrina pendula*), to plants in the genus *Tradescantia* (named for John Tradescant, gardener to England's King Charles I), and to *Rhoeo* or oyster plants. All of these plants have sap with the unhappy quality of being a skin irritant. Be careful when working with them.

ADVICE FOR REGIONAL CARE
Cover during freezing weather; prune out damaged parts in spring.

Shore Juniper

Juniperus conferta

Height: 2 ft.
Zones: 8, 9, and 10A
Light Requirement:

Picture a rock garden with a floor of brown and beige river rock, a large accent stone, upright walking iris with yellow flowers, and low-lying blue-green shore juniper. Picture a larger area with a mass of junipers hugging the rocky or sandy ground, pentas with pink flowers in a bold curving wave, and a queen's crape myrtle with its upright racemes of lavender flowers. These are the kinds of serene settings that you can create with shore juniper. They grow not only in gardens in the cooler central parts of the peninsula, but also on the shore because this plant is tolerant even of salt spray. It does not travel well into the hotter parts of the southern tip of the peninsula and the Florida Keys, but it will grow as far south as Zone 10A. The fresh juniper smell and the blue-green of the foliage go a long way toward recommending it; the clincher is its toughness on the ocean front. Where wind is a factor, as it is on the beach, low, ground-hugging plants are among those most likely to succeed in exposed areas. Shore juniper also is drought tolerant. Like all conifers, the shore juniper bears cones in the spring.

WHEN TO PLANT
Shore juniper can be planted at any time of the year in North or Central Florida.

WHERE TO PLANT
Place plants in full sun in sandy or well-draining soils. This plant is tolerant of infertile, sandy soils and will form a carpet in bedding areas.

HOW TO PLANT
To succeed in forming a mat, the junipers should be planted 18 in. apart.

ADVICE FOR CARE

Let this low-growing shrub have its way, and don't prune it. It will require little from you.

ADDITIONAL INFORMATION

Shore juniper is related to Italian cypress in the family Cupressaceae.

ADDITIONAL SPECIES, CULTIVARS, OR VARIETIES

Two cultivars are available in nurseries: 'Blue Pacific', a trailing juniper, and 'Compacta', a compact growing form.

ADVICE FOR REGIONAL CARE

Shore juniper grows well all over the state, although in South Florida, spider mites can be a problem. Mites occur in dry weather; they are sucking insects, and usually cause problems on the lowest branches first. You will notice brown foliage at the base of the plant. Miticides are available, but a hard spray of water should be tried first.

Small Leaf Confederate Jasmine

Trachelospermum asiaticum

Height: 1 ft.
Zones: 8, 9, and 10
Light Requirement:

Many landscape architects choose the small leaf Confederate jasmine as their favorite groundcover due to its versatility. Only a few plants with their vining shoots are needed to fill in relatively large areas of the landscape; the plants are drought tolerant and are not particular about soil type. Most gardeners are familiar with the common Confederate jasmine, so they know what to expect— lots of vines. But this species grows low and is not quite as rampant. Small leaf Confederate jasmine is best used in larger areas where you need a reliable dense mat of greenery, for example, under trees where other ornamentals fail to take root, on slopes, and in median strips. It can be used to hang over walls and to cascade from planters. Although some gardeners coax a few yellow flowers from the home plantings, it is a reluctant bloomer.

WHEN TO PLANT

Small leaf Confederate jasmine can be planted at any time of the year. Most plants are available from garden centers in containers year-round. The most stress-free time to add this jasmine to the landscape is the late fall through early spring season when it can be established with minimal care. Plant in the spring or summer in South Florida.

WHERE TO PLANT

Give small leaf Confederate jasmine a full-sun to partial-shade location. It likes a well-drained soil. Avoid areas that flood during the rainy season or are naturally too wet for good growth.

HOW TO PLANT

Most groundcovers grow well in the sandy Florida soils. Small leaf Confederate jasmine grows more quickly and is easier to maintain if the soil is improved before planting. Where possible, work in several inches of compost or peat moss and manure with the existing soil. Space plants 24 to 36 in. apart. Dig the hole wider than the root-ball but not deeper. Set the plant at the same planting depth as it was growing in the container or original planting site or a little higher out of the ground. Add soil and water to the hole to make good root-to-soil contact. After planting, water the entire planting site thoroughly. A 2- to 3-in. mulch layer can be added to keep the soil moist and control weeds. The first feeding may be provided 4 to 6 weeks after planting. Continue watering to keep the soil moist until the plants are established and send roots out into the surrounding soil.

ADVICE FOR CARE

Small leaf Confederate jasmine plantings are drought tolerant but make the best growth with a moist soil. Where extra growth is needed and during periods of severe drought, water weekly with $1/2$ to $3/4$ in. of water. Feed this jasmine once in spring, summer, and early fall. Use a 6-6-6, 12-4-8, or similar garden fertilizer at the rates suggested on the label. Pests are usually few, but small leaf Confederate jasmine may be affected by scale insects and white flies. Where necessary, apply an insecticide recommended by the University of Florida Cooperative Extension Service.

ADDITIONAL INFORMATION

This plant is easy to grow, but its vining nature calls for periodic trimming to keep it in bounds.

ADDITIONAL SPECIES, CULTIVARS, OR VARIETIES

A number of varieties with colorful foliage and varying leaf patterns have been selected. Gardeners can select from Variegatum with cream-and-green foliage, Bronze Beauty with reddish foliage, and Minima, a dwarf variety.

ADVICE FOR REGIONAL CARE

Small leaf Confederate jasmine grows well in all but the most southern region of Florida. It does not need special winter protection.

Wax Jasmine

Jasminum volubile

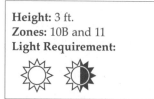

Height: 3 ft.
Zones: 10B and 11
Light Requirement:

Once you know the fragrance of jasmine, you'll always recognize it. And while this form of jasmine is not the one used for perfume (that's *Jasminum officinale*), it is fragrant nonetheless and sweetly pretty with its starry flowers against the green. The wax jasmine is a hardy plant that's able to endure without irrigation or with little supplemental irrigation. It takes full sun without turning yellow. As the state's population continues to climb, house lots get smaller, and water supplies become more unreliable, smaller landscape plants such as this wax jasmine can be doubly useful—as a groundcover, it can reduce the area of your garden devoted to thirsty St. Augustine; as a small shrub, it can serve well in small gardens, such as those of townhouse and zero lot line developments. Other small-scale plants in this category are crown-of-thorns, a poinsettia relative with red or deep-pink round bracts and lots of spines on short stems; dwarf carissa, also with tiny white flowers; holly malpighia or Singapore holly (*Malpighia coccigera*), a dwarf shrub with tiny toothed leaves and occasional outbursts of flowers; dwarf pittosporum (*Pittosporum tobira*); and a prostrate gardenia. Even small trees, such as crape myrtle, caesalpinia, powderpuff, and redberry stopper, can be far more successfully used in little gardens than big plants periodically pruned to within an inch of their lives.

WHEN TO PLANT

Plant in the spring or at the beginning of the rainy season.

WHERE TO PLANT

Choose a location in full sun or partial shade.

HOW TO PLANT

Prepare a large area with the addition of peat or compost. Once the bed components have been mixed to a depth of about 6 or 10 in., you can place the plants (in their containers) 18 to 24 in. apart to determine how they look. Dig the hole, slip the container off the plant, and position the plant, backfilling and watering in as you do so. Mulch all the plants once you have finished planting. Mulch in groundcover beds will even out moisture and reduce weeds.

ADVICE FOR CARE

Water daily for 1 or 2 weeks, reduce watering to every other day for another 2 weeks, then go to 2 times a week. By summer's end, the plants should be growing well. Apply slow-release fertilizer at the time of planting and again in the fall, or a general-purpose 6-6-6 with micronutrients 2 to 3 times a year. Cut back the jasmine quite hard once a year. Again, this is a springtime chore. Fertilize at this time.

ADDITIONAL INFORMATION

Once upon a time, the nursery industry in South Florida called this *Jasminum simplicifolium*, or "Jasmine simp." In recent years, the species has been changed to put it in the right category—often tricky with jasmines. The popularity of this plant, however, has continued to be strong, no matter its current name.

ADDITIONAL SPECIES, CULTIVARS, OR VARIETIES

Jasminum sambac, Arabian jasmine, is recommended for Florida's Gulf Coast by David Bar-Zvi in *Tropical Gardening; J. grandiflorum* produces clusters of large flowers in the summer.

ADVICE FOR REGIONAL CARE

This is not a plant for cold regions.

151

Wedelia

Wedelia trilobata

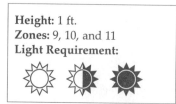

Height: 1 ft.
Zones: 9, 10, and 11
Light Requirement:

In the search to find a colorful groundcover, you should be pleased with wedelia. Its pretty yellow daisy-like flowers open most of the year, and its foliage is bright green. It's suitable for most areas where you need to quickly cover the soil and the planting has to be durable. Use wedelia under trees, on slopes, in hard-to-mow median strips, and in the areas between the street and the sidewalk. Wedelia is very drought tolerant but also survives in moist soils. Plantings in the deeper shade do not flower as well as those in the full sun, but they blossom occasionally. Some gardeners use wedelia in planters and hanging baskets.

WHEN TO PLANT

Wedelia can be planted at any time of the year. Most plants are available from garden centers in containers year-round. The most stress-free time to add wedelia to the landscape is the late fall through early spring season when minimal care is needed. Wedelia can be started by digging clumps or by removing offshoots from established beds in spring through summer.

WHERE TO PLANT

Give wedelia a full-sun to shady location. The plants like a well-drained soil. Avoid areas that flood during the rainy season or are naturally too wet for good growth.

HOW TO PLANT

Most groundcovers grow well in the sandy Florida soils. Wedelia grows more quickly and is easier to maintain if the soil is improved before planting. Where possible, work in several inches of compost or peat moss and manure with the existing soil. Space plants 10 to 12 in. apart. Dig the hole wider than the rootball but not deeper. Set the plant at the same planting depth as it was growing in the container or original planting site or a little higher out of the ground. Add soil and water to the hole to ensure good root-to-soil contact. After planting, water the entire planting site thoroughly. A 2- to 3-in.

mulch layer can be added to keep the soil moist and control weeds. The first feeding may be provided 4 to 6 weeks after planting. Continue watering to keep the soil moist until the plants are established and send roots out into the surrounding soil.

ADVICE FOR CARE

Wedelia is drought tolerant but makes the best growth with a moist soil. Where extra growth is needed and during periods of severe drought, water weekly with 1/2 to 3/4 in. of water. Feed wedelia once in spring, summer, and early fall. Use a 6-6-6, 12-4-8, or similar garden fertilizer at the rates suggested on the label. Pests are usually few, but wedelia may be affected by caterpillars, grasshoppers, and mites. Hand pick the pests from the plantings, or treat them with a pesticide recommended by the University of Florida Cooperative Extension Service.

ADDITIONAL INFORMATION

With proper care wedelia quickly fills a bed. In time it can overgrow the area; it needs periodic trimming to stay in bounds.

ADDITIONAL SPECIES, CULTIVARS, OR VARIETIES

No special selections of this species have been made for Florida landscapes.

ADVICE FOR REGIONAL CARE

Wedelia is limited to the Central and South Florida landscapes. During some winters, it is burned back to the ground by freezing weather. Most landscapers and home gardeners mow or shear the damaged plantings down to near the ground to allow new spring growth.

Orchids

*T*HE SPLENDOR OF ORCHIDS IS ALMOST IMPOSSIBLE TO RESIST if you live in a climate where they can be grown easily. They are among the most romantic of flowers and comprise the largest plant family known, with more than 20,000 species and untold numbers of man-made hybrids.

There are orchids that look like the back ends of female bees, orchids that are moon-faced, orchids that are spiderlike, and orchids that seem to be playing dead. There are some that are leafless and some with minute flowers that develop right on the leaves. Some flowers are hairy, others are covered with warts, some have tails, and others hold up spiraling horns.

Many orchids, such as cattleyas, are air plants, or epiphytes (*epi* means "upon"; *phyte* means "plant"). They grow on other plants, most often tree branches, expanding into clumps by means of a rhizome, or a stem from which roots grow downward and shoots grow up. They are not parasites—they take no nutrients away from the tree on which they grow.

To germinate in nature, orchid seeds have to be infected with a fungus, a fact not known until the turn of the century. It would be years before orchid scientist L. Knudson would discover how to create an artificial medium in agar on which to germinate seed. Once that happened, these once priceless flowers began to soar in popularity. Today, orchids are grown by people in every walk of life.

Some orchids do grow in the ground. These "terrestrials" include *Phaius,* or the nun's orchid; *Haemaris,* the jewel orchids; *Spathoglottis*

orchids, now widely used for mass plantings and as groundcovers in South Florida; the lady slippers; a few Florida natives such as *Bletia*; and ladies tresses, *Spiranthes*.

The epiphytic orchids most easily grown in South Florida are the cattleyas and relatives and hybrids, vandas and several relatives and hybrids, oncidiums, phalaenopsis, dendrobiums, and paphiopedilums. Cattleyas are sympodial, meaning new growth arises at the base of a parent after the parent has flowered, forming a series of stems. Vandas, phalaenopsis, and other orchids are monopodial, meaning they grow on a single stem. Growing in trees, epiphytic orchids have developed special roots that are photosynthetic, yet covered with a silver-gray coating of cells that absorbs water and protects against desiccation. These roots cling tightly to tree bark or clay pots. Pseudobulbs are water-storage organs. Orchids with pseudobulbs, such as cattleyas and oncidiums, require less water than do those without. Orchid flowers, although wildly dissimilar, have several things in common: the pollen is found in two masses that look like round golden drops of resin, and these are attached to a stalk or column. Also in the column is the female stigma, or the reproductive surface. Insects—bees, flies, and moths—move the pollen mass (pollinia) of one orchid to the reproductive surface of another, where the pollen germinates.

Seeds develop in pods and are produced by the millions. They have no endosperm, or the starchy tissue that normally feeds embryos; rather, they depend on fungi for food and germination.

Cattleyas

Cattleya spp.

<table>
<tr><td>

Height: 20 to 40 in.
Zones: 10B and 11 Outdoors
Light Requirements:

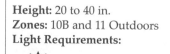

</td></tr>
</table>

This is the queen of orchids, the Mae West of the flowers. And right this minute, two pots of *Cattleya* Mary Felzer are in my living room holding out the most dazzling golden-throated snow-white flowers you can imagine. Their fragrance swills around the room every morning with the dust motes and sunbeams. They are absolutely stunning, these orchids, and to my amazement, I was the one who grew them. Throughout spring and summer, I watched the new shoot develop: the bulge of the "eye" at the base of the last mature stalk; the emergence of the leatherlike leaf; the thickening of the water-storing pseudobulb. Finally, when flower bulbs poked through the protective sheath, swelled, and then unfolded, they seemed newborn butterflies testing the air, pumping fluid into their wings, free at last from the confines of their fetal enclosure. I began growing orchids with cattleyas. They are extraordinarily tough and make good beginner plants. *Cattleya bowringiana, C. intermedia, C. skinneri, C. walkeriana,* and their hybrids are worth trying.

WHEN TO PLANT

"Planting" in the case of cattleyas means potting or repotting, and that should be done in the spring, when the new growth just begins to emerge (late February, early March).

WHERE TO PLANT

Cattleyas like about 50 percent shade and may be kept in a shade house with 50 percent shade cloth covering the plants. They also may be hung in (or attached to) a tree where morning light can reach them or puddles of light pool over them intermittently. To prevent fungus, don't overcrowd your plants. They can take an enormously wide range of temperatures, from upper 90 to upper 30 degrees Fahrenheit. When a freeze is forecast, they should come inside.

HOW TO PLANT

Soak a clean terra-cotta orchid pot (it has extra drainage holes in the bottom rim) in water until air bubbles cease rising to the water's surface. Then fill with an orchid-growing mix to within 1 or 2 in. of the top. Use an orchid mix of chopped tree fern and bark, bark and perlite, or any other medium-textured growing mix for orchids that drains quickly. A cattleya with 4 or 5 "back" bulbs or mature pseudostems (6 or 7 will provide stronger growth) should be positioned on a tall mound of mix. The new growth should be headed toward the center of the pot so the plant may grow for 2 or 3 years before it needs repotting. Hold the oldest back bulb against the pot's edge with one hand, and work to fill medium around it with the other. Press the mix into place with your thumbs so the plant is solidly in place. Use a pot clip to anchor the rhizome into position; remember to remove it after roots develop to secure the orchid. Water and place in a shady spot; keep it drier than undisturbed plants. When growth resumes, put it on a water/fertilizer schedule appropriate to the conditions.

ADVICE FOR CARE

Water cattleyas every 2 or 3 days, allowing the medium to become almost dry. A high-nitrogen (30-10-10) fertilizer is recommended if the medium is primarily bark, since bark will steal nitrogen in its decomposition process. Or use 20-20-20 every 2 weeks throughout the growing season in a medium-coarse orchid mix that contains charcoal, bark, fern, and perlite. In October, when the light begins to change noticeably and plants "harden" their summer's growth, switch to a 10-30-20 or bloom-booster fertilizer, and use it once a month. Resume the 20-20-20 in March, when the eyes begin to swell once more. Humidity is an important consideration for orchids, and cattleyas like a relatively high humidity: 50 to 80 percent.

ADDITIONAL INFORMATION

A plant that doesn't bloom usually isn't getting enough light. The leaves of cattleyas should be yellow green, not deep green.

ADDITIONAL SPECIES, CULTIVARS, OR VARIETIES

Fragrance is a big plus with cattleyas and many of their relatives—the encyclias, brassavolas, and hybrids. The Cattleya alliance of related genera is huge, and they may be bred together, creating what is called "intergeneric hybrids," such as a *Brassavola* × *Cattleya* cross, indicated on the tag by *BC*.

ADVICE FOR REGIONAL CARE

North and Central Florida gardeners can keep orchids outdoors in trees or shade houses during the warmer months. Protection is necessary for Cattleya orchids when temperatures approach freezing.

Dendrobiums

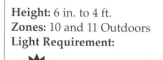

Dendrobium spp.

Height: 6 in. to 4 ft.
Zones: 10 and 11 Outdoors
Light Requirement:

Every 3 years, orchid growers hold a World Orchid Conference at a different location around the globe. In the early 1980s, it was held in Miami. This was an adrenaline rush for orchid fans, who could wander among millions of orchid flowers and glorious exhibits. One sight that I will never forget was that of the stems and flowers of imported dendrobiums in glorious yellows and lavenders, all standing as erect and close together as if they had been startled by the orchid police and told to "Freeze! and put your hands up." One of my favorite dendrobium sights is much less spectacular and occurs in a tree in my yard. It's a white-flowering *Dendrobium phalaenopsis* hybrid. Every fall, it sends out a long and lovely stalk of blossoms that poke their noses out from among tree branches and palm fronds. But what about *Dendrobium phalaenopsis*? Isn't *Phalaenopsis* a genus in and of itself? Well, yes, and that's what makes dendrobiums such a challenge: there are many kinds of confusing dendrobiums. The newest kids on the block are miniature dendrobiums, which can flower (when pushed) when their canes are just a year old. These are being hybridized and produced for the mass market outlets. Nowadays, you can find them at a cost of less than $3.00. Select plants with moist potting medium that has not pulled away from the pot, fresh flowers that have not faded or begun to droop, and canes that are nice and plump. Take them home and after flowers drop, repot into a fast-draining medium.

WHEN TO PLANT
Plant in the spring.

WHERE TO PLANT
Plant on pieces of cork, in pots in quick-draining medium, or on trees in 50 to 70 percent shade in shade houses.

HOW TO PLANT
As with cattleyas, when planting dendrobiums in clay pots, put the oldest back canes against the sides of the pot so new growth heads

toward the center. On cork or trees, use florist's tape (or the colored thin copper wires found inside telephone line) to attach the plant. Allow the tape or wire to remain on the plant until roots securely anchor it to the substrate.

ADVICE FOR CARE

With deciduous plants, withhold most water in winter. There is a fine line between keeping the plant alive and allowing it to dehydrate to the point of death. Every 2 or 3 weeks, splash a small amount of water its way. With evergreen or persistent-leaved plants, reduce the amount of water and fertilizer in winter. When spring arrives, feed and water generously.

ADDITIONAL INFORMATION

When *Dendrobium* is overwatered, it may produce offshoots on the cane. To remove those plants, use a straightedge to cut away a portion of the mother cane with the plantlet, and repot. Use a 20-20-20 weekly or every 2 weeks. I use a few drops of liquid dish detergent to work as a spreader sticker when applying water-soluble fertilizer. This allows the fertilizer to stay on the leaf surface longer.

ADDITIONAL SPECIES, CULTIVARS, OR VARIETIES

Dendrobium nobile is a species from India, China, and Southeast Asia. It is deciduous, losing leaves in winter, flowering in spring, with flowers on short stalks along their bare stems, called canes. A group of this type, which flowers on the canes, is called simply nobile dendrobiums and is successfully grown in Florida. Their flowers are shades of white, yellow, rose, or maroon. These are watered sparingly in winter so that the plants don't die, but don't rot either. *Dendrobium phalaenopsis* and its hybrids bloom from long stems that grow out from between the leaves. The flowers resemble those of the genus *Phalaenopsis*. These are evergreen, churning along robustly in the summer or warm/rainy season, resting somewhat during the winter. Some, such as *D. phalaenopsis*, like it warm all winter; others grow best in warm summers and cool winters. Then there are the intermediate growers that simply rest in winter, while still another group prefers it cool all year.

ADVICE FOR REGIONAL CARE

North and Central Florida orchid growers can keep dendrobiums outside in trees or shade houses during the warm months, but protection is needed when temperatures drop below 50 degrees Fahrenheit.

Epidendrum

Epidendrum spp.

Other Names: *Encyclia,*
  Encyclia
Height: 2 to 3 ft./2 to 6 in.
Zones: 10B and 11 Outdoors
Light Requirement:

In the Fakahatchee Strand of the Big Cypress National Preserve (the Strand is a wooded area on either side of a slough or drainage basin in the Everglades), Florida's orchids still are growing—though in increasingly perilous situations as plant thieves periodically pillage them. In more exposed places alongside trails, they often go unnoticed by tourists, who expect larger plants and flowers. The small, unremarkable *Epidendrum rigidum*, for example, is called the rigid orchid, grows among bromeliads on hammock trees, and it has small, greenish white flowers. Hikers still can see quite a lot of *Epidendrum tampense* (*Encyclia tampensis*), producing sprays of green petals and sepals spotted with magenta, and a white lip also spotted with magenta. Mayakka River State Park, near Sarasota, is full of these beauties—to see them, all you have to do is look up. Once, all epiphytic orchids were called *epidendra*, meaning "on trees." Then in the 18th century, Linneaus classified the 7700 known plants and divided orchids into 8 categories or genera, based on the sexual parts of the flowers. *Epidendrum* was allowed to stay. But in the taxonomic pushing and pulling of species, such old favorites as *Epidendrum cochleatum* and *Epidendrum atropurpurem* have become *Encyclia cochleatum* (and even more recently, *Anachilium cochleatum*) and *Encyclia cordigera*. The chocolate-smelling *Epi. phoenecium* has become *Encyclia phoenicea*. There are epidendrums still around, however, and it turns out that the Florida native called the night-scented orchid, *Epidendrum nocturnum*, is the model, or type, of the rest. The reed-stem epidendrums that wander around in the mulch beneath trees, *Epi. ibaguense*, are hanging in there, but they may soon move into a different genus, or they could fall back into their *Epi. radicans* designation.

WHEN TO PLANT
Plant in the spring when new growth begins.

Where to Plant

Epidendrums are good candidates for growing on oak trees since many grow that way naturally in South Florida.

How to Plant

If using a terra-cotta pot, plant so that slender roots are embedded in a loose, fast-draining mix, such as charcoal and redwood chips.

Advice for Care

Water as you would cattleyas, allowing the plants to almost dry before watering again. Use a soluble 20-20-20 fertilizer every 2 weeks in the growing season. In winter, cut back on water and fertilizer. Use a bloom booster, 10-30-20, monthly in winter.

Additional Information

Epidendrum ibaguense has been hybridized in recent years to have large clusters of brightly colored flowers. They are the easiest to grow. They are called reed-stem because they grow small opposite leaves on upright stems that are thin and sometimes curved. Red and yellow flowers are common, but lavender is quietly beautiful, and the flowers bloom over much of the year. They like an acid soil, so mulch is perfect for them.

Additional Species, Cultivars, or Varieties

Epidendrum nocturnum grows in clumps and has spidery flowers that open one at a time at night. The flowers are large for the genus, about 2 in. long, and they send a lovely fragrance into the darkness. The long throat and fragrance bring night-flying moths to pollinate the plant.

Advice for Regional Care

Central and North Florida orchid growers can keep orchids outside beneath trees or in a shade house during warm months. However, these orchids require some protection when temperatures drop below 50 degrees Fahrenheit.

Oncidium

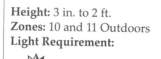

Height: 3 in. to 2 ft.
Zones: 10 and 11 Outdoors
Light Requirement:

"Dancing ladies" is the longtime nickname of *Oncidium* orchids because many of the flowers have wide, skirtlike lips and grow on slender stems that allow them to sway to the rhythm of the breezes. Oncidiums have all the spots, stripes, and clear, bright color you could possibly want to find in plants, but their flowers are produced in small doses. Most of the ladies have yellow skirts, with brown, maroon, or olive sepals and petals tattooed variously in bars and stripes. The plants have round pseudobulbs with long, narrow, thin leaves. I have an often-divided clump of *Oncidium altissimum*, a West Indies orchid, that flowers from its spot in my avocado tree. Part of this clump also grows on the trunk of my triangle palm, and in a fern basket hung sideways at the front of the shade house. This ideal kind of orchid performs consistently with little care. It tolerates all kinds of awful weather, except for freezes. And every spring, a cascade of yellow flowers pours out of the trees. This plant has been in cultivation for more than 200 years. It was taken from the West Indies to England by Captain William Bligh of *Bounty* fame. Mule-ear oncidiums have thick, stiff leaves that look just like what their name suggests. Their pseudobulbs are relatively small. They like to dry thoroughly between waterings. These plants are superior for growing outside in trees or pots. Equitant oncidiums are miniatures, windowsill-sized plants with striking patterns and colors. They bloom when they're only 3 in. tall, and they reach full maturity when they're 4 to 8 in. in height. They produce slender, wiry roots that like to grow up and out of the pots, and they bloom several times a year with branched flower stalks.

***

WHEN TO PLANT

Plant oncidiums after the plants have flowered and new growth begins.

WHERE TO PLANT

Plant in or on tree crotches, limbs, or the trunks of trees and palms. They'll cling. These orchids like more light rather than less.

The full-sized types can be acclimated to tolerate sun, especially morning sun.

HOW TO PLANT

Plant in a fast-draining mix, such as gravel developed for orchids, chunks of tree fern with horticultural charcoal, or a general orchid mix over a layer of polystyrene peanuts.

ADVICE FOR CARE

The secret to growing oncidiums is to let them dry between waterings. Well-fertilized equitants that are faithfully but not too frequently watered put on a grand show for their size, as do the soft-leaved types.

ADDITIONAL INFORMATION

A captivating flower because of its vague insectlike petals that resemble antennae, two blotched sepals, and elaborately ornate yellow-and-brown lip was for many years called *Oncidium papilio*, or butterfly oncidium. In the 1970s it was reclassified in the genus *Psychopsis*, but it still can be found under the *Oncidium* name.

ADDITIONAL SPECIES, CULTIVARS, OR VARIETIES

Oncidium splendidum shows off a quarter-sized butter-yellow lip, with bars of lavender to mahogany on greenish yellow sepals and petals. It's now quite rare in its native Guatemala and Honduras.

ADVICE FOR REGIONAL CARE

North and Central Florida orchid lovers can grow oncidiums out-side during warm months, but bring them in or provide protection when temperature drops below 50 degrees Fahrenheit.

Paphiopedilum

Paphiopedilum spp.

Height: 8 to 30 in.
Zones: All
Light Requirement:

If you love lady slipper orchids, you have to love them warts and all. Warts are part of the package—as are the balloonlike pouches that someone once believed resembled slippers (one or two look more like chicken hearts than something you would put on your feet). Some of these flowers are mystifyingly complex in their structure, and some, with their glistening pouches and bizarre colors, verge on vulgar. Some make spectacular spectacles of themselves, while others can give you the creeps. You cannot help being drawn to them, whether it's to look at the hairs, peer at the warts, admire the spiraling, ribbonlike sepals of *Paphiopedilum pariishii* and *P. philippinese*, or wonder at the splotched and waxy texture of *P. bellatulum*. John Atwood, orchid specialist at Marie Selby Botanical Gardens in Sarasota, once traveled to the 13,000-ft. Mt. Kinabalu in Borneo to find out what pollinated an especially rare paph, *P. rothschildianum*, where it grew among the pitcher plants and mosses on rocky ledges. The answer turned out to be flies, apparently seeking a place to lay eggs. Like *P. rothschildianum*, many of these slippers are cool growers. In temperate North America and Europe, the slipper orchids are called cypripediums. In tropical America, they're phragmepediums. In Asia, they're paphiopedilums. In most cases, the mottled-leaved species are those that will do well in South Florida. But strap-leaved and dwarf paphs also can grow with some care. The whole crowd—phrags, cyps, and paphs—is enjoying a rediscovery of sorts because of two events: one, a rediscovery of paphs in China, including the lovely yellow *Paphiopedilum armeniacum* in one province of China in the early 1980s; the other, the discovery of a red-flowering phragmipedium in Peru by Libby Besse of Sarasota, a plant now named for her, *Phragmipedium besseae*. The notable difference is that these orchids are terrestrials (or in some cases grow on rocks). They like moisture and do not like their roots to dry.

WHEN TO PLANT
Plant before medium gets mushy, after plants have flowered.

Where to Plant

The mottled-leaved slippers and those that produce flowers successively on one stalk are low-light growers, preferring the same place in the shade house as the *Phalaenopsis* orchids, about 70 percent shade. The strap-leaved slippers will flourish in brighter light, such as that given *Cattleya* orchids, about 50 percent shade.

How to Plant

Use a mix that retains moisture, but also drains well. Combine bark, perlite, horticultural charcoal and chopped spaghnum moss. Or mix tree fern, charcoal and perlite in equal parts as you might for orchid seedlings. Repot before the mixture turns to mush—lady slippers are prone to rot if that happens. Repot in the spring—and into a pot the same size; if pot is too large, water will not drain fast enough for these plants and they can get fungus.

Advice for Care

The addition of sphagnum moss to bark, perlite, and charcoal will retain moisture. Paphs grow new shoots after flowering and form clumps in their pots. Each new shoot produces a flower. If you get no flowers, you are giving the plant too much nitrogen or too little light. Switch from a balanced 20-20-20 to a 10-30-20. Or increase the light. Or do both.

Additional Information

Because they are terrestrial, slipper orchids have more delicate roots than epiphytic species. Their roots can be burned by too much salt from too much fertilizer. Many years ago, growers believed that you didn't fertilize the slippers, period. Today, the sentiment is that weak solutions of soluble fertilizer are okay, as is slow-release fertilizer, so the plants don't get a huge dose at one time.

Additional Species, Cultivars, or Varieties

A good beginner's slipper is *P. concolor*, with mottled leaves and a squat little cream-colored flower with red dots. Hybrids of *P. primulinum*, which produces 2 or more flowers on a stalk, each with a sunny-yellow pouch and chartreuse dorsal sepal, also do well.

Advice for Regional Care

Paphiopedilum orchids can be grown outside in North and Central Florida during the warm months, beneath trees, or in shade or lathe houses. When temperatures drop below 50 degrees Fahrenheit, they should have some protection.

Phalaenopsis

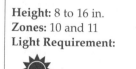

Phalaenopsis spp.

Height: 8 to 16 in.
Zones: 10 and 11
Light Requirement:

Phalaenopsis orchids are called "moth orchids" because of the way they hover in the air on their arching stalks. For pure grace of line, these orchids are the best. With beautifully shaped sepals and petals and intricately lobed and whiskered lips, phals are the essence of sophistication and elegance. And at last they are coming into the world of the everyday plant lover. Their wide, dark-green, and succulent leaves can span 1 ft. or more; their flowers can stay unblemished for weeks when kept inside. Once, white and lavender-pink were the most popular colors, but those days are long since past. Of course the white phalaenopsis will never lose its appeal and grace. Its petals have been perfected, the lips bred to come in yellows, pinks, or spots, and they float magically on the air. But the newest shades include sunset colors of peach, bronze, orange, and yellow with maroon. In addition, the number of flowers is increasing. More than 100 small flowers may hang from many-branched spikes like the daintiest of ornaments. They are not so big and not so ethereal-looking as the large, moon-faced whites, but they are spritely, charming flowers in awesome numbers. The popularity of phals has grown wildly in the last decade, and much of this excitement has come from French breeding, which introduced the spots; from German hybridizing, which added the pinks; and from California crossing, which contributed the stripes. Like vandas, phalaenopsis orchids are monopodial, growing on a single short stem.

WHEN TO PLANT
Plant in the spring after the flowers have died.

WHERE TO PLANT
Keep these plants in the shadowy parts of the shade house. They like more shade than cattleyas or vandas. Shadecloth that screens out 70 percent of the light is recommended, though you can grow them with 50 percent.

How to Plant

Phals like to have their roots moist but not wet. Put another way, they like to be wet and dry slowly. Use a large-grade, loose-draining mix, containing perlite, redwood chips or bark, and tree fern, but add sphagnum to retain moisture.

Advice for Care

When you water *Phalaenopsis* plants, don't let water remain in the crown. Leaves develop from the center of the plant, pushing out and to the side. As new leaves form, a resulting cup in the crown can hold water; avoid leaving water in the cup because it can lead to crown rot. If you grow these under a fiberglass roof, watering is easier to control. As plants enlarge, I find they tend to bend slightly, and this allows water to drain. Use a soluble 20-20-20 every 1 to 2 weeks during the growing season. Fish emulsion occasionally can benefit these orchids. As winter approaches, nighttime temperatures drop into the 60s, and days grow shorter, the plants will begin to set their buds. Therefore, in the waning weeks of October, you may add 1 tablespoon of Epsom salts to a gallon of water and switch to a 10-30-20 bloom-booster fertilizer. The Epsom salts will strengthen the flower spike. This technique is used by commercial growers, who variously recommend one dose of Epsom salts or the use of it with your fertilizer until the spikes are several inches long.

Additional Information

Should crown rot occur, use Kocide 101, 1 tablespoon per gallon, to combat it. Kocide and Captan are general fungicides; Kocide has some bacterial action. Physan 20 also combats fungal and bacterial infections.

Additional Species, Cultivars, or Varieties

Phalaenopsis stuartiana, *P. schilleriana*, and *P. equestris* are parents of many floriferous hybrids. *P. violacaea* is a famous species that imparts small, beefy substance to brightly colored flowers.

Advice for Regional Care

In North and Central Florida, grow phals outside in shade structures during the warm months. The plants should be protected when the temperature drops below 55 degrees Fahrenheit.

Vanda

Vanda spp.

Height: 10 in. to 5 ft.
Zones: 10 and 11
Light Requirement:

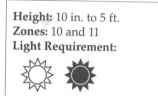

A wonderful thing has happened to the vandas on the way to the orchid show. They have taken on the color of the late summer sky just after sundown, the royal inclinations of amethyst, the sheen of golden Buddhas, and subtleties of milky jade. Some flowers are as big as jar lids; some are as small as quarters; many are as round as the full moon. The plants lurch upward one stiff strappy leaf at a time until they are like ladders; then from the deep recesses of their leaves, they sprout flowers like jewels that are mottled, netted, or spotted, or have darker veins of color. Vandas are grouped by their leaf structure, and the structure determines how much sun they require. 'Miss Joaquim' is a terete type, meaning her leaves are as round as soda straws, a reduction in leaf surface that allows her and other teretes to survive in full sun. Semiterete vandas have hard leaves that grow in a deep V-shape. They take the next brightest conditions and can stand full sun in South Florida's winters. There are flat-leaved or strap-leaved vandas, and they need shade to keep the inner surfaces of their leaves from burning. Vandas are monopodial, meaning they grow on a single stem. They have no water-saving pseudobulbs, and so require daily watering (unless it's cool). They can grow to be enormous plants, and their roots hang straight down from them. Breeding efforts in the last few years, blending vandas with ascocentrums and others, have resulted in smaller plants with more flowers more often throughout the year.

WHEN TO PLANT
Plant in March or April.

WHERE TO PLANT
Plant in wooden slatted baskets. Vandaceous orchids may be grown with or without a medium. Either horticultural charcoal or coarse gravel especially for orchids is the usual medium, which retains some water, as does the wood of the basket. Many people simply grow them in baskets without any medium.

HOW TO PLANT

Soak the plant's roots in water until they become pliable, then carefully wind them around the small basket in which the plant already grows. Put this basket in a larger one. To remove keikis, the small offshoots, snip the base of the plant away from the mother plant when the shoot has several small roots, and wire into a small basket to keep it steady as roots develop. If roots on a large plant are being thrown near the top, a section of the mother plant may be removed and rewired into a slatted basket. Eventually, the bottom will send out keikis.

ADVICE FOR CARE

Orchids in the vandaceous group like to be warm and well watered. Bob Fuchs, an award-winning vanda grower, advises watering them every sunny morning. Water less often in cool weather. Water only in the morning to allow water to dry on the leaves. This is a rule of thumb for everything in your garden. On excessively hot summer afternoons, however, you may mist vandaceous orchids to help cool them. Commercial growers use a very weak fertilizer solution whenever they water. You can get by with soluble 20-20-20 every 2 weeks in the warm months, once a month in winter. Use Kocide when you see fungal spots on the leaves. These are black spots surrounded by a yellow halo. Viral infections cause black spots and streaking on leaves and can affect flowers, causing color breaks or deformities. Little can be done for viruses other than destroying the infected plant and using sterile tools. Never use secateurs (clippers) on more than one orchid without sterilizing them between cuts. Dirty tools spread viruses.

ADDITIONAL SPECIES, CULTIVARS, OR VARIETIES

Plants that have received awards from the American Orchid Society, such as an AM or Award of Merit, often boost the prestige and prices of orchids. If you have patience, you can buy small clones of the awarded plants at reduced prices and wait for them to flower. This is true for all orchids. Species orchids, however, may be more costly because they are becoming so highly endangered in the wild. Be sure, if you purchase a species rather than a hybrid, that the plants have been laboratory produced and not wild collected.

ADVICE FOR REGIONAL CARE

Bring vandaceous orchids inside when temperatures reach 55 to 50 degrees Fahrenheit. In Central and North Florida, they can be grown outside in warm months, hanging in trees or in shade structures.

CHAPTER SIX

Ornamental Grasses

*A*LMOST EVERYONE HAS SOME TURF BUT IT'S NOT THE ONLY GRASS THAT GROWS IN THE LANDSCAPE. You can also use grasses as ornamental plants. Most are native types plus a few species from other countries. Like lawn grasses, the ornamental types are tough—but none makes a good lawn. For one thing, they grow too tall and they form clumps which spread out very slowly. Actually this makes them the ideal landscape plantings as they won't over take the garden with unwanted greenery. Most of the year they have attractive foliage and each offers some unique garden color.

Now the big question is: Where do you use ornamental grasses? Well, they simply double for other ornamental plantings. Taller types, including the fountain grasses, pampas grass and sand cordgrass, can act as view barriers that hide some of the things you would rather not have visitors see such as work areas and ugly fences. They also form good space dividers between areas of the landscape. Others, including muhly grass, purple lovegrass and wiregrass, serve as groundcovers just a foot or two in height. Ornamental grasses can be used as border plantings, along flower beds, or other shrub plantings. Many types also make a great backdrop for annual, perennial and vegetable gardens.

Perhaps where ornamental grasses really shine is as accent features. The foliage alone is different than other ornamentals used in the landscape, being long and thin bladed, easily blown up by the winds to add some interest. Most stems of foliage grow upright with the ends of the leaf blades gracefully turning downward. Some have arching stems with leaves that reach out to touch one another. Most are in bloom when other plantings have stopped providing good seasonal color from midsummer through fall. And the inflorescence is unique, usually creating a feathery plume of color that can range from silver to pink, red, purple and brown. Many of the flowers and seed heads yield feed and nesting materials for wildlife. And who hasn't collected the long plumes from pampas grass? Creative gardeners like to save these flower heads and others to use in dried arrangements.

You can plant clusters of ornamental grasses as barriers or just a few plants as an accent. Perhaps you would like a whole bed of grass to use as a groundcover. The grasses can create a prairie feeling for the landscape and become part of the natural Florida look. As you can guess most are very drought tolerant but do grow best with good care. They are great plants for the dry land setting used to conserve water in the landscape. However, they too tend to go dry during excessively dry periods. Good landscape combinations for grasses include the palmettos, scrub oaks, native wildflowers and dry land hollies.

Ornamental grasses should be planted in well-drained areas of the landscape. Most are accustomed to the drier soils and may decline with wet feet. They also need sunny sites so find an open area with 6 to 8 hours of direct light. Plantings can be made in Florida's infertile sands, but care is often better if the soil is improved with organic matter. Give the grasses plenty of room to grow. It is a good rule to leave a distance equal to the expected height of the plants between neighboring grasses. Remember most are going to reach out and intertwine with each other. Some types with a more upright growth habit should get a little closer spacing. These include the lopsided Indiangrass and sand cordgrass.

Chapter Six

Plant ornamental grasses at the same depth as they were growing in their containers. Those already growing in the landscape can also be divided and set at the same level in the ground. Water the plants well to make good soil-to-root contact. Then keep the soil moist to help the roots grow out into the ground. Apply a two- to three-inch mulch to help prevent weeds. During early growth some weed control is normally needed to keep broadleaf weeds and other grasses from competing with the plantings. Most can be hand pulled from the beds but a non-selective herbicide made for spot weed control among ornamental plantings can also be utilized.

Once the root system is established in the surrounding soil most ornamental grass can exist with minimal care. Native types are especially adapted to surviving with just moisture from rain. They also make needed growth using nutrients found in the rain water plus decaying organic matter deposited on the soil surface. Growth is slow under these conditions and the grasses may not be as attractive as desired in the home landscape but the native look is often sought in natural areas of the landscape. Most gardeners prefer to give the plantings a little better care: watering, especially during periods of drought, or as needed to encourage growth. For the best look most ornamental grasses should receive water from rainfall or irrigation once a week. Applications of lawn fertilizer can be made in February, June or September. It's best to avoid using lawn fertilizers containing a weed killer as the sensitivity of most ornamental grasses to herbicides is unknown.

The grasses make lots of growth spring through summer and by fall most are flowering and producing seeds. The plants also start to decline during fall and into the winter months. Maturing portions of many types turn brown, bronze and reddish—colors often associated with the fall season. During the winter season many of the stems sag and gardeners should make plans to remove the old shoots, foliage and seed heads before spring growth begins.

Sometimes it's best to just trim the plants back close to the ground. Cut the lower growing types to within a few inches of the ground and taller selections to about a foot high. Many grasses have very sharp blades, so be sure to wear protective clothing. Heavy pruning encourages bright, new, green growth as spring begins.

Ornamental grasses are perennials, and after a period of time become crowded. Some types or varieties die out leaving an open center with shoots around the outer edges. Every 3 to 5 years the beds may need rejuvenation. At this time it's best to dig the clumps and divide them into new sections for plantings. Also improve the soil with organic matter and till the ground deeply before adding the grass. Ornamental grasses have few pest problems: caterpillars may feed on the foliage but are normally not numerous enough to need control.

Ornamental grasses add much to the landscape as accent features: their foliage serve as the perfect foils to other landscape plants, and with the wind's cooperation can add movement as another desirable dimension to the garden.

Florida Gamma Grass

Tripsacum floridana

Height: 1 to 2 ft.
Zones: 8, 9, 10, 11
Light Requirement:

If you need a low-growing, clumping grass for sun or light shade, consider Florida gamma grass. Plantings grow between 1 and 2 ft. tall, and are equally as wide. The grass blades are bright green with a narrow white stripe along the midrib. In most areas of the state the grass remains evergreen until frosts and freezes arrive. The 1/2-in.-wide arching leaves add a light, airy feeling to landscapes. Flowering stems are produced above the foliage during the fall and provide some golden-brown color. Use the Florida gamma grass as a groundcover. It's tolerance of most soil types makes it versatile in the landscape. This is a plant for difficult moist conditions when other ornamentals are not suitable. It can be clustered among shrub plantings as a small accent.

WHEN TO PLANT

Florida gamma grass can be planted at any time of the year. Plants are usually available in native-plant nurseries. The grass is usually semidormant during the winter months, but it can be added to the landscape during the cooler months to begin establishing a root system. Perhaps the best planting time for Florida gamma grass is between March and August when the grass is making good growth.

WHERE TO PLANT

All grasses grow best in a full-sun location, but Florida gamma grass also tolerates lightly shaded locations. It can be used under trees in otherwise bright sites, and it can be planted in damp soils that have poor drainage.

HOW TO PLANT

Florida gamma grass can grow in sandy landscape sites, but it makes the best growth when soils are improved with organic matter. Where possible, prepare a bed for planting by working in liberal quantities of compost and peat moss plus manure. Give Florida gamma grass a spacing of 24 to 36 in. If the rootballs are tightly intertwined with roots, they should be lightly loosened to encourage new growth into the surrounding soil. Dig the holes wider but not deeper than the rootball, and set the plants in the ground at the original planting depth. Add soil to the holes with some water to give good root-and-soil contact. After planting moisten the entire planting site and add a 2- to 3-inch mulch layer.

ADVICE FOR CARE

Grasses take minimal care. Once established they can exist with moisture from the rains and nutrients from decaying organic matter. Florida gamma grass makes the best growth if watered during periods of drought. As a general rule, water weekly during the drier times of the year. Florida gamma grass can be fed with a general garden or lawn fertilizer once in February, June, and September. Follow lawn rates or just apply a light scattering of fertilizer.

ADDITIONAL INFORMATION

Florida gamma grass is evergreen in the milder portions of the state. Where frost and freezes are common, it turns brown during the winter months. If needed, schedule a pruning to rejuvenate the planting during late winter. Florida gamma grass can be cut back to within 6 in. of the ground. After the pruning apply the winter feeding to encourage new growth. Caterpillars may feed on the foliage during the growing season but are seldom a serious problem. Where needed, apply a control recommended by the University of Florida for ornamental grasses.

ADDITIONAL SPECIES, CULTIVARS, OR VARIETIES

Fakahatchee grass, *Tripsacum dactyloides*, is another species.

ADVICE FOR REGIONAL CARE

Expect Florida gamma grass to turn brown in the colder areas of the state. In these areas, a late-winter pruning is needed to rejuvenate the plantings.

Fountain Grass

Pennisetum setaceum

Height: to 3 ft.
Zones: 8, 9, 10, 11
Light Requirement:

Fountain grass introduced from Ethiopia is one of the more popular ornamental landscape grasses for home landscapes. Clumps grow to 3 ft. tall and are equally as wide. The foliage is bright green, about 1/4 in. wide. Leaves are arching, often with the outermost rows touching the soil. Fountain grass is added to perennial beds for an accent, and it is often used as a groundcover. Gardeners like the pink to purplish flowers that form from August to October. They are often collected to use in dried flower arrangements. Plantings remain green late into the fall but start to brown with the first hint of winter. Fountain grass is similar to many of its native clump-forming relatives, and it can be used in natural plant settings with a Florida look.

WHEN TO PLANT

Fountain grass can be planted any time of the year. Plants are usually available from garden centers and some mail-order companies. The grass is usually semidormant during the winter months, but it can be added to the landscape to begin establishing a root system. Perhaps the best planting time for fountain grass is between March and August when the grass is making good growth.

WHERE TO PLANT

All grasses grow best in full-sun locations. Plantings of fountain grass should be made in landscape sites that receive 6 to 8 hrs. of full sun and are bright throughout the remaining portions of the day. Fountain grass produces a medium-sized plant and should be planted alone or as backdrop for smaller plantings.

HOW TO PLANT

While fountain grass can grow in the sandy landscape sites, it makes the best growth in soils improved with organic matter. Where possible, prepare a bed for planting by working liberal quantities of compost or peat moss and manure into the soil. Give fountain grass a spacing of 24 to 30 in. If the rootballs are tightly intertwined at planting, loosen the roots a little to encourage new growth into the surrounding soil. Dig the holes wider but not deeper than the root-balls and set the plants in the ground at the original planting depth. Add soil to the holes with some water to give good root-and-soil contact. After planting, moisten the entire planting site and add a 2- to 3-inch mulch layer.

ADVICE FOR CARE

Grasses take minimal care. Once established, they can exist with moisture from rains and nutrients from decaying organic matter. Fountain grass makes the best growth if watered during periods of drought. As a general rule, water weekly during the drier times of the year. Fountain grass can be fed with a general garden or lawn fertilizer once in February, June, and September. Follow lawn rates or just apply a light scattering of fertilizer.

ADDITIONAL INFORMATION

During the fall, fountain grass remains semievergreen for awhile after producing flowers and seedheads. When the first real cold weather arrives, the grass begins to decline and finally turns totally brown. Enjoy the fall color, then schedule a pruning during the winter months to rejuvenate the plants. Fountain grass can be cut back to within 6 to 8 in. of the ground. After the pruning, apply the winter feeding to encourage new growth. Caterpillars may feed on the foliage during the growing season but are seldom a serious problem. Where needed, apply a control recommended by the University of Florida for ornamental grasses.

ADDITIONAL SPECIES, CULTIVARS, OR VARIETIES

A number of varieties of fountain grass are available, including dwarf forms that are ideal for container culture and other types with colorful foliage. The most popular is probably purple-leaf fountain grass, which grows to 5 ft. tall. There are also reddish and copper-leaved forms available.

ADVICE FOR REGIONAL CARE

Throughout the warmer portions of the state, fountain grass may remain semievergreen for most of the winter. In Northern and Central Florida, it turns brown with the first frosts and freezes. It needs rejuvenation pruning by late winter.

Lopsided Indiangrass

Sorghastrum secundum

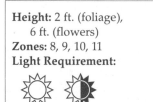

Height: 2 ft. (foliage),
6 ft. (flowers)
Zones: 8, 9, 10, 11
Light Requirement:

Lopsided Indiangrass grows foliage to only 2 ft. tall, but in the fall it can send up flower spikes that grow to 6 ft. in height. This is a native Florida clump-forming grass that ranchers refer to as "wild oats." It has a large seedhead with flowers and seeds borne on one side of the stalk, similar to oats. It's a good fall attraction and should be used as an accent for the landscape, planted in a cluster of 3 or more clumps. You can use the lopsided Indiangrass to create the Florida look in natural settings. The leaves are light- to medium-green. They are about 1/2 in. wide and grow to 24 in. in length. During the fall the plant declines to a golden-brown color that matches the maturing seed stalks. Gardeners like to collect the seed stalks to use in dried flower arrangements.

WHEN TO PLANT

Lopsided Indiangrass can be planted at any time of the year. Plants are usually available from native plant nurseries, and new plants can be started from seeds to grow transplants to be added later. The grass is usually dormant during the winter months, but it can be planted to begin establishing a root system for spring growth. Perhaps the best planting time for lopsided Indiangrass is between March and August when the grass is making good growth.

WHERE TO PLANT

All grasses grow best in a full-sun location, but lopsided Indiangrass is also tolerant of light shade. Plantings are best made in landscapes that receive 6 to 8 hrs. of full sun and are bright throughout the remaining portions of the day. Lopsided Indiangrass is tolerant of varying growing conditions including damp soils.

HOW TO PLANT

While lopsided Indiangrass can grow in sandy landscape sites, it makes the best growth in soils improved with organic matter. Where possible, prepare a bed for planting by adding liberal quantities of compost or peat moss and manure. Give lopsided Indiangrass a spacing of 18 to 24 in. If the rootballs are tightly intertwined at planting, loosen them a little to encourage new growth out into the surrounding soil. Dig the holes wider but not deeper than the rootball, and set the plants in the ground at the original planting depth. Add soil to the holes along with some water to give good root-and-soil contact. After planting moisten the entire planting site and add a 2- to 3-inch mulch layer.

ADVICE FOR CARE

Grasses take minimal care. Once established they can exist with just moisture from rains and nutrients from decaying organic matter. Lopsided Indiangrass makes the best growth if watered during periods of drought. As a general rule water weekly during the drier times of the year. Lopsided Indiangrass can be fed with a general garden or lawn fertilizer once in February, June and September. Follow lawn rates or just apply a light scattering of fertilizer.

ADDITIONAL INFORMATION

During the fall the grass turns golden brown and begins to decline after producing flowers and seedheads. Enjoy the fall colors then during the winter months schedule a pruning to rejuvenate the plants. Lopsided Indiangrass can be cut back to within 4 to 6 in. of the ground. After the pruning apply the winter feeding to encourage new growth. Caterpillars may feed on the foliage during the growing season but are seldom a serious problem. Where needed apply a control recommended by the University of Florida for ornamental grasses.

ADDITIONAL SPECIES, CULTIVARS, OR VARIETIES

Gardeners may also want to plant a similar species know as Indiangrass or gold beard grass, *Sorghastrum nutans*. Plantings turn a yellow to orange during fall and grow to about 5 ft. tall.

ADVICE FOR REGIONAL CARE

Northern and Central Florida plantings may mature earlier than Southern plantings. All need rejuvenation pruning by late winter.

Muhly Grass

Muhlenbergia capillaris

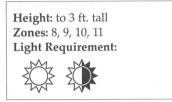

Height: to 3 ft. tall
Zones: 8, 9, 10, 11
Light Requirement:

It's easy to tell when fall arrives by the coloring up of the attractive muhly grass in Florida landscapes. Pink to purple flower clusters form high above the foliage to create an accent planting any gardeners would love. The leaf blades are thin and bright green during the spring and summer months to create mounds of foliage to 3 ft. tall and wide. Use muhly grass in border plantings where some fine delicate foliage is needed. Also add it to perennial gardens and natural settings. It's a great groundcover for the drier areas of the landscape. During late fall after the colorful flowers and seedheads form the plantings turn brown with the onset of colder weather.

WHEN TO PLANT

Muhly grass can be planted at any time of the year. Plants are usually available from native plant nurseries and seed can be used to grow transplants to add to the landscape. The grass is dormant during the winter months but can be transplanted during the cooler times to begin establishing a root system. Perhaps the best planting time for muhly grass is between March and August when the grass is making good growth.

WHERE TO PLANT

All grasses grow best in a full-sun locations but muhly grass does tolerate some light shade. For best flowering plantings of muhly grass should be made in landscape sites that receive 6 to 8 hours of full sun and are bright throughout the remaining portions of the day. Muhly grass is best planted where there is room to add clusters of plants to get the best effect from the fall color.

HOW TO PLANT

Muhly grass grows best in sandy well-drained landscape sites. Where desired gardeners can improve sandy soils with organic matter before planting. Give muhly grass a spacing of 12 to 18 in. If the rootballs are intertwined at planting they can be loosened a little to encourage new growth out into the surrounding soil. Dig the holes wider but not deeper than the rootball and set the plants in the ground at the original planting depth. Add soil to the holes with some water to give good root-and-soil contact. After planting moisten the entire planting site and add a 2- to 3-inch mulch layer.

ADVICE FOR CARE

Grasses take minimal care. Once established they can exist with just moisture from rains and nutrients from decaying organic matter. Muhly grass makes the best growth if watered during periods of drought. As a general rule water weekly during the drier times of the year. Muhly can be fed with a general garden or lawn fertilizer once in February, June and September. Use one half the lawn rates or just apply a light scattering of fertilizer.

ADDITIONAL INFORMATION

During the fall muhly grass begins to decline after producing color-ful flowers and seedheads. Enjoy the fall colors, then during the winter months schedule a pruning to rejuvenate the plants. Muhly grass can be cut back to within a few inches of the ground. After the pruning apply the winter feeding to encourage new growth. Cater-pillars may feed on the foliage during the growing season but are seldom a serious problem. Where needed apply a control recom-mended by the University of Florida for ornamental grasses.

ADDITIONAL SPECIES, CULTIVARS, OR VARIETIES

Numerous muhly grasses grow throughout the United States but have not been thoroughly investigated for cultivation in Florida landscapes.

ADVICE FOR REGIONAL CARE

Northern and Central Florida plantings may brown earlier during the fall due to the arrival of cool weather. Muhly grass growing in all areas of the state does need late winter rejuvenation to produce attractive spring growth.

Pampas Grass

Cortaderia selloana

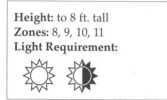

Height: to 8 ft. tall
Zones: 8, 9, 10, 11
Light Requirement:

One of the most sensational ornamentals for the Florida landscape is pampas grass introduced from South America. First, it's a relatively large plant growing to 8 ft. tall and almost as wide. Then, during late summer and fall the plantings fill with plumes of long lasting fluffy white to pink flowers. It's a favorite to cut and add to dried flower arrangements. Use pampas grass alone as an accent or cluster the plants together to form wind breaks and view barriers. It's a good grass to use in coastal areas due to its salt tolerance. The foliage is bright green up to an inch in width and quite sharp. This is one grass to keep away from pedestrian traffic to prevent injuries from just brushing against the foliage. In warmer areas of the state it may remain evergreen throughout the cooler months but it usually turns brown after the first periods of cold weather in most locations.

WHEN TO PLANT

Pampas grass can be planted at any time of the year. Plants are usually available from garden centers or mail-order-nurseries. The grass is semi-dormant during the winter months but can be planted during the cool months to begin to establishing a root system. Perhaps the best planting time for pampas grass is between March and August when the grass is making good growth.

WHERE TO PLANT

All grasses grow best in a full-sun location but pampas grass tolerates some light shade. For best flowers make plantings in landscape sites that receive 6 to 8 hours of full sun and are bright throughout the remaining portions of the day. Pampas grass forms large clumps and needs plenty of room. It's not well suited to small landscapes.

HOW TO PLANT

While pampas grass can grow in sandy landscape sites it makes the best growth in soils improved with organic matter. Where possible prepare a bed for planting by adding compost or peat moss and manure. Give pampas grass a spacing of 36 to 48 in. If the rootballs are intertwined at planting loosen the roots a little to encourage new growth out into the surrounding soil. Dig the holes wider but not deeper than the rootballs and set the plants in the ground at the original planting depth. Add soil to the holes with some water to give good root-and-soil contact. After planting moisten the entire planting site and add a 2- to 3-inch mulch layer.

ADVICE FOR CARE

Grasses take minimal care. Once established they can exist with just moisture from rains and nutrients from decaying organic matter. Pampas grass makes the best growth if watered during periods of drought. As a general rule water weekly during the drier times of the year. Pampas grass can be fed with a general garden or lawn fertilizer once in February, June and September. Follow lawn rates or just apply a light scattering of fertilizer.

ADDITIONAL INFORMATION

During the fall, pampas grass begins to decline after producing flowers and seedheads. Enjoy the fall colors, then during the winter months schedule a pruning to rejuvenate the plants. Pampas grass can be cut back to within a foot of the ground. After the pruning apply the winter feeding to encourage new growth. Caterpillars may feed on the foliage during the growing season but are seldom a serious problem. Where needed apply a control recommended by the University of Florida for ornamental grasses.

ADDITIONAL SPECIES, CULTIVARS, OR VARIETIES

Numerous selections have been made of pampas grass for colorful foliage or flower clusters. Some varietal selections include 'Gold Band', 'Silver Stripe' and 'Sun Stripe' with variegated leaves. Gardeners can also add 'Rubra' with pink flowers to the collection and 'Pumila', a dwarf for perennial beds and containers.

ADVICE FOR REGIONAL CARE

Northern Florida growers can expect winter damage to their plantings. Keep the plants well mulched to prevent plant loss. All pampas grass needs pruning prior to spring growth.

Purple Lovegrass

Eragrostis spectablis

Height: to 2 ft. tall
Zones: 8, 9, 10, 11
Light Requirement:

Catching the wind a foot or more above the foliage, the reddish purple flowers of purple lovegrass create a cloud of color and an excellent accent for the fall landscape. Plant large beds of this native clumping ornamental to enjoy what may be Florida's most attractive grass. It can also be used as a specimen grass for up close study or just enjoyed from a distance. Plantings grow one to two ft. tall and should be used alone or in front of taller growing plants. Leaves of the grass are thin and offer good green growing compact mounds of foliage. During fall the foliage turns a reddish color that adds extra interest to the landscape. Use purple lovegrass as a replacement for one of your not-so-colorful groundcovers or add it to natural landscape areas for a real Florida look. Many gardeners also like to cut and use the colorful inflorescence in dried arrangements.

WHEN TO PLANT

Purple lovegrass can be planted at any time of the year. Plants are usually available from native plant nurseries or transplants can be started from seed to add to the landscape at a later date. The grass is dormant during the winter months but can be planted to establish a root system. Perhaps the best planting time for purple lovegrass is between March and August when the grass is making good growth.

WHERE TO PLANT

All grasses grow best in a full-sun location. Plantings of purple lovegrass should be made in landscape sites that receive at least 6 to 8 hours of full sun and are bright throughout the remaining portions of the day. Purple lovegrass is a lower growing grass and should be planted in front of taller ornamentals so it can be easily seen. It prefers a well-drained soil to prevent roots from rotting.

HOW TO PLANT

Purple lovegrass grows in the sandy landscape sites but makes the best growth in soils improved with organic matter. Where possible prepare a bed for planting with compost or peat moss and manure.

Give purple lovegrass a spacing of 12 to 18 in. If the rootballs are tightly intertwined at planting loosen the roots a little to encourage new growth out into the surrounding soil. Dig the holes wider but not deeper than the rootball and set the plants in the ground at the original planting depth. Add soil to the holes with some water to give good root-and-soil contact. After planting moisten the entire planting site and add a 2- to 3-inch mulch layer.

ADVICE FOR CARE

Grasses take minimal care. Once established, they can exist with just moisture from rains and nutrients from decaying organic matter. Purple lovegrass makes the best growth if watered during periods of drought. As a general rule water weekly during the drier times of the year. Purple lovegrass can be fed with a general garden or lawn fertilizer once in February, June and September. Follow lawn rates or just apply a light scattering of fertilizer.

ADDITIONAL INFORMATION

During the fall, purple lovegrass begins to decline after producing flowers and seedheads. Enjoy the fall colors, then during the winter months schedule a pruning to rejuvenate the plants. Purple lovegrass can be cut back to within 4 to 6 inches of the ground. After the pruning apply the winter feeding to encourage new growth. Caterpillars may feed on the foliage during the growing season but are seldom a serious problem. Where needed apply a control recommended by the University of Florida for ornamental grasses.

ADDITIONAL SPECIES, CULTIVARS, OR VARIETIES

See Elliott lovegrass for another species to add to the landscape.

ADVICE FOR REGIONAL CARE

Northern and Central Florida plantings may decline sooner than Southern Florida plantings due to early frosts and freezes. All do need trimming by late winter to renew the foliage during spring.

ORNAMENTAL GRASSES

Sand Cordgrass

Spartina bakeri

Height: to 5 ft. tall
Zones: 8, 9, 10, 11
Light Requirement:

Sand cordgrass is one of Florida's wetland grasses for use lakeside and in marshlands. Plantings grow upright with a slight curve to the ends of the foliage. Clumps grow to 5 ft. tall and almost as wide. Leaf blades are about a quarter-inch wide, light green on the surface and dark green below. Florida ranchers refer to the clumps in the wetlands as switchgrass, perhaps due to the long flexible stems. Flower heads arise above the foliage May through June and are brown in color. Some gardeners cut the flower heads for use in dried arrangements. Plantings turn brown during the fall to provide some autumn color. Use sand cordgrass in wetland gardens and natural settings where the soil is consistently moist. Lake and canal side gardeners can consider sand cordgrass for use as a space divider, view barrier and accent plantings.

WHEN TO PLANT

Sand cordgrass can be planted at any time of the year. Plants are usually available from native plant nurseries or started from seed for transplants to use at a later date. The grass is usually semi-dormant during the winter months and can be planted to begin establishing a root system. Perhaps the best planting time for sand cordgrass is between March and August when the grass is making good growth.

WHERE TO PLANT

All grasses grow best in a full-sun location. Plantings of sand cordgrass should be made in landscape sites that receive 6 to 8 hours of full sun and are bright throughout the remaining portions of the day. Sand cordgrass is a native bunch grass that has a need for moist soil. It also needs plenty of room to grow and may not be suitable for small landscapes.

HOW TO PLANT

Sand cordgrass needs a moist soil year-round. Select only sites that can be keep moist to make the plantings. Where possible prepare a bed for planting by tilling in compost and peat moss plus manure. Give sand cordgrass a spacing of 48 to 60 inches. If the rootballs are tightly intertwined at planting loosen the roots a little to encourage new growth out into the surrounding soil. Dig the holes wider but not deeper than the rootball and set the plants in the ground at the original planting depth. Add soil to the holes with some water to give good root-and-soil contact. After planting moisten the entire planting site and add a 2- to 3-inch mulch layer.

ADVICE FOR CARE

Grasses take minimal care. Once established, sand cordgrass can exist with just moisture from the wetlands and nutrients from decaying organic matter. In home landscapes water during periods of drought. As a general rule water weekly during the drier times of the year. Sand cordgrass can be fed with a general garden or lawn fertilizer once in February, June, and September. Use one half the lawn rates or just apply a light scattering of fertilizer.

ADDITIONAL INFORMATION

During the fall, sand cordgrass begins to decline, turning a brownish color. Schedule a pruning during the winter months to rejuvenate the plants. Sand cordgrass can be cut back to within a foot of the ground. After the pruning apply a light winter feeding to encourage new growth. Caterpillars may feed on the foliage during the growing season but are seldom a serious problem. Where needed apply a control recommended by the University of Florida for ornamental grasses.

ADDITIONAL SPECIES, CULTIVARS, OR VARIETIES

Other species exist but have not been thoroughly tested in Florida landscapes.

ADVICE FOR REGIONAL CARE

Expect sand cordgrass to turn completely brown in the colder areas of the state. Some green may remain in the base of the plantings in warmer locations.

Wiregrass

Aristida beyrichiana

Height: to 1½ ft. tall
Zones: 8, 9, 10, 11
Light Requirement:

Wiregrass creates the natural Florida look many gardeners are trying to develop in large areas of the landscape. It needs the full sun to produce summer-through-fall fields of golden flower heads. This plant is a natural for wildflower plantings, seeming to give protection to the growing broadleaf plantings. The leaves are wiry, quite thin and upright to arching. With time plants grow to a mounded shape and to 1 and 1½ ft. tall. Perhaps wiregrass's greatest asset is its ability to grow in the poorer soils. It's ideal for use in site restoration plantings.

WHEN TO PLANT

Wiregrass can be planted at any time of the year. Plants are usually available from native plant nurseries and gardeners can also establish good stands from seed. It does not survive well being transplanted from the fields. The grass is dormant during the winter months but can be added to the landscape during the cooler months and begins to establish a root system. Perhaps the best planting time for wiregrass transplants is between March and August when the grass is making good growth.

WHERE TO PLANT

All grasses grow best in a full-sun location. Wiregrass plantings should be made in landscape sites that receive 6 to 8 hours of full sun and are bright throughout the remaining portions of the day. This is a bunch-type grass that is best used in wide open spaces with other wildflowers or used alone as a groundcover.

HOW TO PLANT

Wire grass grows well in the sandy landscape sites where it gets minimal maintenance. This actually helps prevent weeds of unwanted greenery from also becoming established with the grass. Gardeners who do want to prepare a planing site can incorporate organic matter with the sandy soils. Give wiregrass transplants a spacing of 12 to 18 inches. To conserve plant material, a wider spacing can be used and the wiregrass will produce seed that germinates to fill in over the years. When using transplants dig the holes wider but not deeper than the rootball and set the plants in the ground at the original planting depth. Add soil to the holes with some water to give good root-and-soil contact. After planting moisten the entire planting site and add a 2- to 3-inch mulch layer. Wiregrass seed can also be sown in early winter and usually blooms the following fall.

ADVICE FOR CARE
Wiregrass needs minimal care. Once established it can exist with just moisture from rains and nutrients from decaying organic matter. It makes the best growth if watered during periods of drought. As a general rule water weekly during the drier times of the year. Fertilizer is not needed but can be used to speed growth with light feedings of a general garden or lawn fertilizer once in February, June and September. Use one half the lawn rates or just apply a light scattering of fertilizer.

ADDITIONAL INFORMATION
During the fall, wiregrass begins to decline after producing flowers and seedheads. Enjoy the fall colors, then during the winter months schedule a pruning to rejuvenate the plants. In nature, fire burns the fields of grass. Wiregrass can be cut back to within a few inches of the ground. After the pruning a light winter feeding can be made to encourage new growth. Caterpillars may feed on the foliage during the growing season but are seldom a serious problem. Where needed apply a control recommended by the University of Florida for ornamental grasses.

ADDITIONAL SPECIES, CULTIVARS, OR VARIETIES
No other varieties are presently being planted in home landscapes.

ADVICE FOR REGIONAL CARE
Culture of wiregrass is similar throughout the state. It may start the winter decline earlier in Northern and Central Florida due to cool weather. If should be given a rejuvenation pruning each year in all areas of the state.

Palms

*P*ALM TRUNKS, LIKE THOSE OF TREES, ARE INDIVID-
UAL, varying in their degree of lean, sway, and uprightness,
in color and texture, in stoutness and thinness. Fronds or leaves of
palms can be blue-gray or olive-green, yellow-green or deep-green.
The new leaves may emerge red or wine-colored. The fronds are
either pinnate (feather-shaped) or palmate (shaped something like
the palm of your hand). But within these two forms are variations
on a theme: long and graceful pinnae (individual leaflets) or short,
stubby ones; great, round, and stiff palmate fronds or deeply incised
and graceful ones.

The flowers, which are tiny when seen alone, often are pretty
sprays when seen as a whole on the branching flower stalk. Fruit is
scarlet to deep-purple, blue-green or white, yellow or black, and can
range from coconuts to dates to inedible little berries.

Palms are like cats in many ways: you have to get to know them
to see the gradations in character, from sober to puckish, from aloof
to endearing. And one cat by itself will never do; cats must come in
multiples. Unless it is a massive and handsome specimen, a palm by
itself is a lonely character indeed. It cries out for friends, for companionship of kind. Use them in groups. Make them taller and
shorter within the group. Let them mingle like company at a cook-
out. To regiment them militarily is unnatural for them: they grow in
groups and clusters, not in straight rows and long lines. (Royals, by
virtue of their regal bearing, are used singly for property line mark-

Chapter Seven

ers or on either side of an entry. The caveat in doing so is their scale, which may be too large for small properties.)

Some palm trunks are attractively marked, like those of cabada palms, which are green with distinct white rings rather like bamboo. Some palm trunks are clothed in fibers. The lady palms are wrapped in dark-brown to black fibers along their slim trunks. The cabbage or sabal palms have a natural coating of old leaf stems called boots. *Coccothrinax miraguama,* a relative of the Florida silver palm, has matting that seems carefully handwoven on a loom.

In the wild, you find all kinds of things growing in this fiber or in the old leaf stems. I've seen a snake curled in the boot of a cabbage palm, dozing in contentment. Ferns love to germinate there, and bromeliads and orchids can lodge themselves into a boot as naturally as can be. If they don't do this on their own in your garden, you can help them along.

In rain forests, you find all manner of other plants growing on palm fronds, though that seldom occurs in Florida. In your Florida garden, you can train philodendrons up the trunk of a palm for a tropical look.

Many palms are cold tolerant and drought tolerant. In the wild, they can be found on the sides of mountains. Some species can also be flood tolerant.

One of my favorite sights is palm fronds in moonlight. We are accustomed to our plants' shapes and colors in daylight, but at night they take on an ethereal quality. If there is the slightest breeze on a night of the full moon, the fronds (particularly the feathery or pinnate fronds) move magically and most beautifully.

Chapter Seven

My own garden is full of palms, including the quick-growing *Washingtonia* palm used to provide height in the background, and a slow-growing *jefe*, the Bailey palm, *Coprenicia baileyana*. I also have a triangle palm, which, like all other palms, sends up one spear at a time, then somehow moves it into one of three trajectories so that the crown forms a perfect triangle. The bottle palms are flowering now after many years of growing fat bellies, and the upright, handsome foxtails are beginning to produce bright-red seeds. I have four kinds of *Licuala* palms because I love their orbicular, pleated fronds: *Licuala grandis*, with the round, pleated leaf; *L. ramseyii*, with its leaves divided into segments; *L. speciosa*, which sends up offshoots and forms a clump; and *L. lauterbachii*, with widely spaced segments. The hurricane palm, *Dictyospermum album*, two species of *Aiphanes*, several species of *Coccothrinax* and *Thrinax*, cabada, and different species of shade-loving, small palms in the *Chamaedorea* genus also are included in my garden. These palms are in groups, with beds of bromeliads or ferns at their feet. I've attached orchids and bromeliads to the trunks of some; others have been unwitting hosts to ferns.

You have to do some gardening things to grow palms well, especially in alkaline soils or infertile sands. Palms in alkaline conditions often show micronutrient deficiencies, and a palm fertilizer has been formulated especially for them. It is 12-4-12-4, the last 4 being magnesium. The two 12s are nitrogen and potassium needed in equal amounts, and because they both leach from soil, they are in slow-release form in this particular fertilizer. The first 4 is phosphorus, which is especially plentiful in rocky soil of Dade and Broward Counties and the lower Keys. The abundance of phosphorus, which chemically ties up other micronutrients, means little more is needed.

Chapter Seven

Palms have the built-in ability to pull potassium from aging leaves, which is why pruning off old leaves interferes with the nutritional cycle of the plant. Wait until the entire frond has turned brown to prune it if it is not "self-cleaning"—meaning the fronds drop of their own accord.

Most palms require water, fertilizer and, in the event of a freeze, cold protection. But they are lovely creatures to have around, and like cats, once you have them, you'll wonder what you did without them.

Butia Palm

Butia capitata

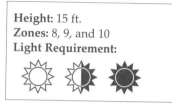

Height: 15 ft.
Zones: 8, 9, and 10
Light Requirement:

Found naturally in South America, butia palms are not native to Florida, although they are certainly one of the state's finest landscape plants. Butias grow ever so slowly, but be warned that they need room to spread out because they grow about as wide as they are tall. Most gardeners know this palm by a few other names, including pindo and jelly palm. The latter comes from the fact that the fruits are edible and the sweeter selections make tasty jelly. Butia palms are best used as specimen and accent plants in large landscapes. The large, featherlike leaves grow to 8 ft. in length. Better selections have a blue-green color, and most twist a little toward the tip. They have an arching habit with the end curling toward the ground. Here is a very hardy and versatile palm that is often planted as a focal point off a patio or to line the streets.

WHEN TO PLANT

Palms make very little growth during the fall through early spring months. In fact, University of Florida studies show that they make almost no root growth. For this reason butia palms dug from fields or landscapes are best moved during the warmer spring through summer months. Well-established container specimens of the butia palm can be added to the landscape at any time of the year, however.

WHERE TO PLANT

Give the butia palm a full-sun location. Although not an especially tall-growing palm, it should be located where it has adequate room to grow in width. It could be planted under most utility wires. The butia palm should be kept at least 10 ft. from sidewalks, driveways, and buildings.

HOW TO PLANT

Butia palms grow well in Florida's sandy soils without any special preparation. Transplant the butia palm by digging a hole 2 to 3 times wider but not deeper than the rootball. Fill in around the rootball with soil while adding adequate water to ensure good root-to-soil contact. Create a berm at the edge of the rootball to help thoroughly wet the rootball at each watering. After planting, add a 2- to 3-in. mulch layer over the root system. Most specimens of the butia palm do not need bracing after planting.

ADVICE FOR CARE

Newly planted butia palms should be kept moist until the roots begin to grow out into the surrounding soil. Make sure the soil does not thoroughly dry for several growing seasons. Once established, the butia palm is very drought tolerant and rarely needs special watering. The butia palm usually obtains needed nutrients from the feedings given lawns and nearby ornamental plantings. To encourage growth and maintain the best color, apply a fertilizer once in March, June, and October. Use a 16-4-8, 12-4-8, or similar palm fertilizer, following label instructions. Periodically, butia fronds decline and need removal. Prune them back as close to the trunk of the palm as possible. The older bases gradually loosen and can be pulled from the plant.

ADDITIONAL INFORMATION

Butia palms vary greatly in growth habits, including palm size, leaf color, and fruiting. They are susceptible to leaf spots and trunk rots that commonly affect palms. These are best controlled by giving the palms proper care, which includes watering only during the drier times of the year.

ADDITIONAL SPECIES, CULTIVARS, OR VARIETIES

Several species of butia palms are found in Florida, but this species is the most popular. Palm nurseries may offer a hybrid with the queen palm, sometimes referred to as the mule palm. It often resembles the queen palm in looks but has the hardiness of the butia palm that gardeners in Central Florida appreciate.

ADVICE FOR REGIONAL CARE

Butia palms grow throughout most of Florida, except for the most southern portion.

Cabbage Palm

Sabal palmetto

Height: to 40 ft.
Zones: 8 through 11
Light Requirement:

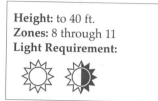

The Florida cabbage palm is the official state tree as declared by the Florida legislature in 1953. (It is also the state tree for South Carolina, adopted in 1939.) The palm is not a true tree but resembles one with its straight, tall growth and big thick trunk. This palm has been more than a towering landscape addition, finding use in making hats, baskets, and roofs for early Native American homes. It has also been a source of food. Many Florida residents are fond of swamp cabbage salad made from the tender portions of the central bud. Even though the cabbage palm is not a true tree, it can be planted to produce shade, especially when several palms are grouped together. Many people like to add a specimen or two near the home or the street to create the look of the tropics often associated with palms. As the older leaves mature and drop or are cut away, the bases often remain on the trunks for added interest.

WHEN TO PLANT

Palms make very little growth during the fall through early spring months. In fact, University of Florida studies show that they make almost no root growth at all. For this reason cabbage palms dug from the wilds, nursery fields, or landscapes are best moved during the warmer spring through midsummer months. Well-established container specimens of the cabbage palm can be added to the land-scape at any time of the year, however.

WHERE TO PLANT

Give the cabbage palm a full-sun to partial-shade location. Don't forget that this tall-growing palm should be located where it has adequate overhead space and is away from electrical wires. It should be kept at least 5 ft. away from sidewalks, driveways, and most buildings. The cabbage palm is very drought tolerant but also tolerates moist soils.

How to Plant

Palms grow well in most Florida soils without special preparation. Except for plants growing in containers, the cabbage palm is dug and moved with very little root system at the base of the palm. University of Florida studies indicate that all roots die back to the base of this palm trunk after digging. Transplant the cabbage palm by digging a hole 2 to 3 times wider but not deeper than the rootball. Fill in around the rootball with soil, and water to ensure good root-to-soil contact. Create a berm at the edge of the rootball to thoroughly wet the rootball at each watering. After planting, add a 2- to 3-in. mulch layer over the root system. Larger specimens of cabbage palms need bracing to prevent wind damage.

Advice for Care

Newly planted cabbage palms should be kept moist until the roots begin growing out into the surrounding soil. Although this is a durable palm, make sure the soil does not dry for several growing seasons. Once established, the cabbage palm needs special watering only during extreme periods of drought. The cabbage palm can be fertilized once in March, June, and October. Use a 16-4-8, 12-4-8, or similar palm fertilizer, following label instructions.

Additional Information

According to university studies, cabbage palms transplant best if all the fronds are removed after planting. Over the years, gardeners have been tempted to set the trunks deeper in the ground, but that practice is now discouraged.

Additional Species, Cultivars, or Varieties

A relative of the cabbage palm, the dwarf palmetto *Sabal minor* is found throughout Florida growing mainly as an understory plant to 6 ft. tall. Where possible, it should be left as a native plant in the landscape. Another relative, the Puerto Rico hat palm *Sabal causiarum* should be considered for larger home sites.

Advice for Regional Care

Cabbage palms grow well throughout the entire state. No special regional care is needed.

Chinese Fan Palm

Livistona chinensis

Height: 20 to 30 ft.
Zones: 9 through 11
Light Requirement:

The faster one bolts through one's allotted hours, the more impatient one might be for others to keep up— even the slow-growing palms. My group of four Chinese fan palms, planted in a tight circle more than 12 years ago to serve as a screen, seems to grow just right. The tallest must be 20 feet, while the shortest is about 10. The shortest has had the disadvantage of being shaded and quickly overtopped by the other three; this has led it to produce elongated leaf stems (which technically is called etoilation). So as a group and seen from a distance, the palms appear to have come right along. Their growth rate, however, is not so important as the fact that I seldom water them, fertilize them only twice a year, and have watched them survive three freezes and a hurricane. The ends of the fronds are divided, and they droop so the ends of each segment seems to be hung with a split ribbon or delicate green icicles. All together, these split ends create a pretty effect. The fruits are a most beautiful blue-green, looking rather like olives. The trunks are still quite full of fibrous leaf trash—old leaf stems and hairs—but one day, this detritus will wear away and trunks will turn a corky brown-gray. And one day, too, the bottom half of the petioles or leaf stems will no longer grow backward-pointing spines that can make pruning seem like a blood drive. Beneath these palms are bromeliads used as groundcovers. They demand little work, but they require thinning and refreshing yearly so the old mother plants can be removed. Ferns, begonias, monsteras, or aroids would be attractive beneath them as well, or a simple mulched bed may be all that is desired.

WHEN TO PLANT
Plant in late spring or early summer.

WHERE TO PLANT
Plant in full sun, with plenty of room around the plant because the crown is large.

How to Plant

Dig a hole as deep as the rootball and 2 or 3 times as wide. Slip the container from the rootball, and position the palm in the ground. Water in backfill, and mulch around the root zone. Water every day for 1 week, every other day for 2 weeks, and every third day for 2 weeks. To keep the rootball moist, keep on that schedule, throughout the first growing season if the rain is insufficient. By planting at the beginning of the rainy season, you reduce irrigation requirements.

Advice for Care

A palm for the armchair gardener, the Chinese fan palm is not fussy and doesn't require babying. If fertilized a couple of times a year, it does quite nicely. You may be motivated to remove brown fronds when the palms are small enough for these to be seen. The longer you can tolerate a brown frond, the better off is the palm, because these plants can pull back potassium from the old leaves as they age. Many palm experts recommend trimming palms only when the leaf stems are as brown as the fronds.

Additional Information

Livistona chinensis has some susceptibility to lethal yellowing disease (see information on the coconut for a full discussion of this). It may also get ganoderma or butt rot, a fungal disease found in older palms. To prevent ganoderma, keep the area around the base of the palm open so that air circulation is unhindered.

Additional Species, Cultivars, or Varieties

Other *Livistona* species, usually described as "robust," include the footstool palm, *L. rotundifolia*, a much taller and faster-growing palm without the green icicle effect on leaf ends; *L. australis*, in the 40- to 60-ft. range; and *L. decipiens*, a fast-growing species from Australia with thin leaf blades that can be torn by wind.

Advice for Regional Care

Grow these palms in containers in areas of Central Florida where freezing temperatures are likely. This is not a palm for North Florida.

Coconut Palm

Cocos nucifera

Height: to 50 ft. or more
Zones: 10B and 11
Light Requirement:

Palm Beach County and Palm Beach, the town, were named for coconuts. So were Coconut Grove and Coconut Creek—but Palm Beach actually has a few of these lithe, Jamaica tall palms left. These are large palms with gray trunks, gracefully held pinnate fronds, and edible fruit or seeds. Here's why this section of South Florida is so palmy with coconuts: A Spanish ship called the *Providentia*, carrying 20,000 coconuts from Havana to Barcelona, ran aground in 1889 at the site of the Palm Beach Bath and Tennis Club. Coconuts spilled everywhere, and the local citizenry couldn't resist planting a few. From the late 19th century into the late 20th century, South Florida's coasts were lined with these palms. We came to love them, even if they originated in Melanesia and not the Caribbean. One of the world's most used and useful plants, the coconut graced our beaches and lined our streets, and they did the same all over the tropical world. They have been made into doormats, raincoats, coffee cups, jewelry, buttons, tobacco boxes, and drums. Coir is the fiber pulled from the husk and made into brooms and brushes; these days, it is chopped and compressed into a potting medium. Copra is the dried meat from which oil is extracted to manufacture margarine, cooking oil, soap, and suntan lotion. Various parts have been used to thatch roofs and walls, stuff mattresses, make clothing, bake cakes, fill candy, and create light and fuel. Yet, as is true of a long list of other good and natural things in South Florida, this bountiful tree has become a victim. It is a victim of an incurable disease, lethal yellowing, which first arrived in Key West in 1955. Spreading up the archipelago, it hit the counties of Dade, Broward, and yes, even Palm Beach, along with the rest of the southern peninsula. Today, Jamaican tall coconuts are all but a memory. In their place are somewhat less graceful, but reliable coconuts, especially the Maypan. The Maypan, a cross between a Malaysian dwarf and a Panama tall, comes close to mimicking the long-lost Jamaican tall, but it doesn't quite hit the mark. It does, however, resist lethal yellowing disease.

200

WHEN TO PLANT
Plant when the certified lethal-yellow-free nuts turn brown and fall
from the tree, or on Malayan dwarf coconuts (which do not fall)
when the outer husk is brown. Shake the nuts to hear internal milk.
If there is none, don't plant. Or, in early summer, plant sprouted
nuts obtained from disease-free nursery stock.

WHERE TO PLANT
Plant in full sun and in an area where the large crown, on its way
to the sky, won't be crowded and where roots have good
drainage.

HOW TO PLANT
Lay the coconut sideways in a thick and damp layer of mulch,
with 2/3 to 1/2 of the husk buried. Keep the mulch moist, and perhaps add a light layer of leaves to soften the husk so the root and
shoot can emerge.

ADVICE FOR CARE
Fertilize every 4 months during the first year with a granular fertilizer formulated for palms. Apply about 3 lb. of fertilizer around the
base of your small palm, and water it in. Apply a nutritional spray
to the leaves every 1 to 3 months during the first year. Fertilize 2 to
3 times a year thereafter.

ADDITIONAL INFORMATION
Coconuts don't like cold weather. Some lower fronds can turn yellow and then brown when weather dips into the 30s; after a freeze,
the palm's lower fronds gradually die. They are quite oblivious to
salt spray on the beach.

ADDITIONAL SPECIES, CULTIVARS, OR VARIETIES
'Red Spicata', 'Dwarf Green', and 'Golden Malayan' also are resistant to lethal yellowing, to varying degrees. To avoid spreading the
disease, never plant a seed from a neighbor's tree. Plant certified
resistant seeds or plants only.

ADVICE FOR REGIONAL CARE
This is not a palm for Central and North Florida.

Florida Silver Palm

Coccothrinax argentata

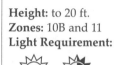

Height: to 20 ft.
Zones: 10B and 11
Light Requirement:

A single-trunked palm with delicate leaves that are very silvery on the undersides, this palm is slow growing and hardy. This graceful Florida and Caribbean native may reach 20 ft. in your children's lifetime. If you travel to Big Pine Key in the Florida Keys and find the Key Deer Refuge, be sure to take the nature trail, even though the trail in summer is boiling hot, oppressed by glaring white light, and untouched by air currents. Limestone rock protruding through the leaf litter passes for soil on this bony little island. But it is precisely these conditions that produce slash pines, silver palms, and deer the size of Lassie. The pines are slender, often crooked or leaning. They rise from a floor of grasses, locustberry, and stones. The palms are slow growing and small, but enduring. (In the Dominican Republic, under different conditions, they grow quite nicely to 60 ft.) This ability to survive on the subsistence diet in these limestone gardens makes the fragile-looking silver palm extraordinarily tough. Rainy-season fires, caused by lightning strikes, are a common feature of Florida pinelands, and blackened trunks of pines and palms are evidence that they can survive these, too. The silver palm's fronds are softly droopy rather than stiff, are deeply incised into 15 or 20 segments, and are gloriously silver on their undersides. Maybe the brilliance of the light has something to do with the intensity of the silver, or maybe not. But in a strong wind, when the fronds are lifted and turned, you will appreciate the color difference.

WHEN TO PLANT
Plant in late spring or early summer.

WHERE TO PLANT
Plant in full sun or light shade in an area with excellent drainage. Because it grows in such fast-draining, dry conditions, overwatering or wet feet can cause disease in this palm.

HOW TO PLANT
Dig a hole large enough to accommodate the rootball. Water daily

for a week; every other day for 2 weeks; every third day for 2 weeks; then just to keep the root zone moist during the first growing season. By planting at the beginning of the rainy season, you reduce irrigation requirements.

ADVICE FOR CARE

Use a palm fertilizer such as 12-4-12-4 with micronutrients 3 times a year—March, June, and October. If you wait long enough, the fronds on the *Coccothrinax* species will fall, leaving the bottom stubs of leaf stems sticking up or out through the trunk fiber.

ADDITIONAL INFORMATION

This palm is good for seaside homes because it is highly salt tolerant. Its drought tolerance makes it an excellent candidate for Xeriscape gardens and native areas without irrigation. Its size makes it suitable for patio and townhouse gardens where space is limited. The silver palm should never be collected from the wild because it is in the protected area of the Key Deer Refuge. Gardeners should buy only nursery-propagated or nursery-grown specimens.

ADDITIONAL SPECIES, CULTIVARS, OR VARIETIES

Coccothrinax is a genus of attractive palms, and one reason for the attractiveness is the interesting trunk fiber. The old man palm, *Coccothrinax crinita* from Cuba, is the hairiest of the bunch, covered with light-brown, thick shaggy fibers that give this palm the look of an elderly gent. Not as slow growing as the silver coccothrinax, the old man is steady and sure-footed. The palmate fronds are stiffer than the fronds of the silver palm. To keep the hair covering intact, the old man is best protected from windy situations. Everglades racers, lovely pewter-colored and slender snakes, have found it convenient to hide in my old man palm over the years. *Coccothrinax miraguama* has very stiff, round fronds and a beautifully matted trunk. If you attach orchids to the old leaf stems, they root quickly into the matting. Miraguama, also from Cuba, has a bluish cast to the leaves and is an erect and beautiful slender palm. A characteristic that distinguishes *Thrinax* from *Coccothrinax* is the color of the fruit: *Thrinax* palms have white fruit, *Coccothrinax* have black fruit.

ADVICE FOR REGIONAL CARE

Grow the silver palm in a container, and protect it from freezing in Central and North Florida.

Lady Palm

Rhapis spp.

Height: 6 to 15 ft.
Zones: 10 and 11
Light Requirement:

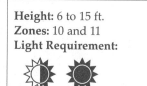

Perhaps it is the slender form or the comeliness of the divided leaves; perhaps it is the pliable and forgiving nature. Perhaps it is the sense of grace she brings to a landscape. Perhaps it is none of these, and we will never know, but this is indeed a lady palm. Chinese or Indochinese, she has been cultivated for more than 300 years in the Orient, and she is favored by the Japanese. She has been made into bonsai or dwarf forms, her feet bound in pots too small. When allowed her head and her feet, she eventually becomes a multitude of stems, crowding together as if for companionship and small talk, all intent on each other's company. *Rhapis* is pronounced "ray-fus." The word means "needle," for the narrow and often pointed segments of the palmately divided fronds. Two species work well in Florida, *R. excelsa* and *R. humilis*, though others are grown here. Excelsa is the large lady palm; she grows to 12 or 14 ft. on slender stems wrapped in black fibers and has rather large segments in her palmate fronds. Given time, she will spread to form hedges. And for sheer elegance, this is one of the most beautiful and durable hedges around, providing you have patience—lady palms are indeed slow growing. *Rhapis humilis* is the slender lady palm, taller than *R. excelsa* but with delicate leaf segments that are more graceful and drooping. Humilis takes more cold than excelsa. It is propagated by division of the rhizomes. There also are some dwarf forms that make exquisite houseplants. They are wonderfully suited to ceramic cachepots, even ceramic bonsai pots, and the named cultivars 'Kodaruma' and 'Gyokuho' will stay quite small. (Lynn McKamey, a member of the International Palm Society and Texas grower of *Rhapis*, says the so-called miniatures 'Koban', 'Daruma', and 'Tenzan' can grow to more than 6 ft. when unrestricted.) I grew a clump for many years in a pot, gave away divisions, and watched those divisions develop into large clumps. Meanwhile, after a year or more of looking sickly, the original lady palm was transplanted into the ground. The yellow and deficient-looking leaves have become deep green again just a few months later, and harmony has been restored.

When to Plant

Plant at the beginning of the rainy season. If transplanting a large clump, root prune 4 to 6 weeks before the moving date; fill in the trench around the rootball, and keep moist until you transplant the palm. Then be diligent about watering so the rootball doesn't dry until the palm puts out new growth. Once established, lady palms may be watered and allowed to become slightly dry before watering again.

Where to Plant

Plant as a hedge or a specimen in a well-draining area where the palms can get partial shade.

How to Plant

Dig a planting hole 3 times as wide, while just as deep, as the rootball. Place the palm in the planting hole so that the root crown is at the same level in the soil as it was in the pot. Backfill, using a hose to water in the soil and eliminate air pockets. Water daily for 1 or 2 weeks, then water every other day for another week or so. After a month, begin watering every 3 to 4 days.

Advice for Care

Use a fertilizer formulated for palms, such as 12-4-12-4, with micronutrients. The extra 4 in the formula ratio indicates 4 percent magnesium. Fertilize a couple of times a year. When hungry, the leaves will begin to turn yellow. When in full sun, the leaves also yellow. Once through the first growing season, the lady palms are able to withstand fairly dry conditions, and watering can be reduced to a minimum except in periods of drought.

Additional Information

Lady palms are excellent indoor palms because they are adapted to low light.

Additional Species, Cultivars, or Varieties

Rhapis subtilis, called the Thailand lady palm, is smaller in height; it grows to about 6 ft. *Rhapis laosensis*, from Laos, has exceptionally thin stems and widely spaced fronds.

Advice for Regional Care

Grow in protected areas of Central Florida, and for colder northern areas of the state, grow in a container.

Pygmy Date Palm

Phoenix roebelenii

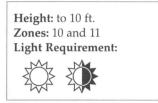

Height: to 10 ft.
Zones: 10 and 11
Light Requirement:

The advantages of being short: one can see through knotholes, slip under gates, get lost in a crowd, wear trousers rolled, rest assured one's feet won't hang over the bed, and never worry about having one's head in the clouds. The advantages of being a short palm: one can escape pruning with long poles, damage in high winds, be free of extenuating circumstances, and spend life never far from the trough. Indeed, the pygmy date palm is far more prized today in South Florida as a result of Hurricane Andrew in 1992 than before the storm, precisely because it was close to the ground. Yet it always has been an untroubling sort, perfectly serviceable and even graceful when it leans rakishly beyond its center of gravity. Its size makes it a useful palm for planters and for those odd little spaces beside a curving walkway and the front entryway that builders sometimes design on purpose, as if daring you to find something proportionately suitable. Its stature also makes it eligible for townhouse yards or patio gardens. Many nurseries plant two or three together nowadays for a decorative effect, and a duo or trio can serve well as a corner planting. The head is quite full when the palms are well tended, and the lower fronds bend down, so the crown is rounded. The caveat with *Phoenix* species is the row of spiny leaflets at the base of each frond. A good field characteristic for identifying a *Phoenix*, the spines are nonetheless brutally sharp—perhaps protecting the seeds that develop among the leaf bases on the female trees. (The pygmy date does not develop edible fruit; only the *Phoenix dactylifera*, or true date, does—and when grown in South Florida, these dates don't develop well.) A wilting disease is found among some types of *Phoenix* palms. Yet the sturdy little pygmy date keeps plugging along.

WHEN TO PLANT

Plant at the beginning of the rainy season, late May or early June, although any time between March and midsummer is fine.

WHERE TO PLANT

Plant in a well-drained area in full sun; use it in a small garden for its scale and fine texture. A groundcover such as purple queen or yellow-flowering lantana would be a good complement to this palm.

HOW TO PLANT

Dig a hole large enough to accommodate the rootball. Water daily for a week; every other day for 2 weeks; every third day for 2 weeks; then just to keep the root zone moist during the first growing season. By planting at the beginning of the rainy season, you reduce irrigation requirements.

ADVICE FOR CARE

Use a fertilizer formulated for palms, such as 12-4-12-4 with micronutrients. This palm and many others are subject to potassium deficiency in Florida soils; to prevent it, use a fertilizer with nitrogen and potassium in slow-release form to keep a steady supply available to the plant. Potassium deficiency in pygmy dates shows up as yellow spots or flecks or banding on the lower, older fronds. It can be confused with magnesium deficiency. In fact, potassium and magnesium should be applied together to correct the deficiency, for potassium alone can cause a magnesium imbalance. Use potassium sulfate with $1/2$ as much magnesium sulfate (about 3 lb. of potassium). Repeat the application 4 times a year. If many fronds are yellow, it can take 1 or more years to eliminate the problem.

ADDITIONAL INFORMATION

The pygmy date palm is from the Mekong River delta in Southeast Asia, and has more need for water than its desert-dwelling relatives. If put on a starvation diet, it will take on a yellow cast and thin its crown in its efforts to alert you to its needs.

ADDITIONAL SPECIES, CULTIVARS, OR VARIETIES

While other members of the *Phoenix* genus are grown in Florida, they are susceptible to lethal yellowing disease, for which there is no cure. Many have withstood the attacks, but many others have succumbed. One of the most beautiful of the group, *Phoenix canariensis*, is susceptible not only to lethal yellowing, but also to ganoderma or butt rot that is found among old species of palms and is spread in the soil as well as by air.

ADVICE FOR REGIONAL CARE

Protect from cold in Central and North Florida, or grow this palm in a container. It grows well in a large container for several years.

Royal Palm

Roystonea elata

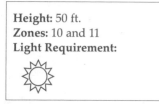

Height: 50 ft.
Zones: 10 and 11
Light Requirement:

There are 2 royal palms that are often confused with each other because they look so similar. One is the native *Roystonea elata*, and the other is *Roystonea regia*. This latter is known as the Cuban royal palm. Experts say the most distinguishable difference is evident in the trunks. The Cuban royal palm has an obvious bulge in the trunk; the Florida royal palm is more uniform. Both are restricted to South Florida. Possibly what catches the attention of many admirers of this palm is the area of long, smooth green trunk at the top, the crownshaft. Gardeners like the leaves that grow to 10 ft. long and more than 3 ft. wide. These majestic palms are best used in large land-scapes. Plant them in clusters as accent features, or line them in rows along a street.

WHEN TO PLANT

Palms make very little growth during the fall through early spring months. In fact, University of Florida studies indicate that they make almost no root growth. For this reason royal palms dug from fields or landscapes are best moved during the warmer spring months through midsummer. Well-established container specimens of royal palms can be added to the landscape at any time of the year.

WHERE TO PLANT

Give royal palm a full-sun location. Don't forget this is a tall-grow-ing palm that should be located where it has adequate overhead space and is away from electrical wires. Keep it at least 5 ft. away from sidewalks, driveways, and the home.

HOW TO PLANT

Royal palms can be planted in Florida's sandy soils but grow best when the soil is enriched with organic matter. Where possible, pre-pare a large planting site by adding compost or peat moss and manure. Transplant the palm by digging a hole 2 to 3 times wider but not deeper than the rootball. Fill in around the rootball with soil while adding water to ensure good root-to-soil contact. Create a berm at the edge of the rootball so that each watering reaches the rootball. After planting, add a 2- to 3-in. mulch layer over the root system. Larger specimens of royal palms need bracing to prevent wind damage.

ADVICE FOR CARE
Newly planted royal palms should be kept moist until the roots begin to grow out into the surrounding soil. Although this is a fast-growing palm, make sure the soil does not thoroughly dry for several growing seasons. Once established, the palms need watering about once a week or whenever the soil begins to dry, especially during periods of drought. Royal palms look and grow the best when fertilized once in March, June, and October. Use a 16-4-8, 12-4-8, or similar palm fertilizer, following label instructions.

ADDITIONAL INFORMATION
Periodically remove older leaves where possible to keep an attractive specimen. Royal palms can exhibit nutrient deficiencies in some South Florida soils. Apply a fertilizer with adequate potassium and minor nutrients needed for growth.

ADDITIONAL SPECIES, CULTIVARS, OR VARIETIES
Hybrids of the 2 royal palm species likely occur, blurring the distinctions between the 2 major types.

ADVICE FOR REGIONAL CARE
Royal palms are limited to South Florida. Winter freezes make it impossible to grow the palms farther north.

Saw Palmetto

Serenoa repens

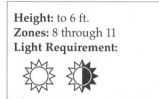

Height: to 6 ft.
Zones: 8 through 11
Light Requirement:

Early settlers probably viewed saw palmettos as a threat to their livelihood. The plants grew in many partially shaded to full-sun locations, had sharp needles on the leaf petioles, and formed almost impermeable thickets. They covered much of the desirable crop and grazing lands. But today gardeners are taking a new look at these plants that can grow in most soils, harbor wildlife, and provide an inexpensive Florida look. In fact, saw palmetto plants are already in place in many landscapes. All you have to do is keep the bulldozer away. Others are adding the saw palmetto to their properties one pot at a time. This clump-forming palm can grow in the sandy to enriched soils throughout the state. It's best used as a low view barrier, a space divider between properties, and an accent plant near patios and along walkways. It's an ideal plant to help create the old Florida look in naturalistic settings. Saw palmettos are almost always planted in clusters of 3 or more.

WHEN TO PLANT

Palms make very little growth during the fall through early spring months. In fact, University of Florida studies show that they make almost no root growth. For this reason the very best planting time for the saw palmetto is the warmer spring months through midsummer, but container-grown specimens can be added to the landscape at any time of the year. Very few saw palmetto specimens are dug from the fields or wilds. Only palm specialists have been successful transplanting the older native clumps of plants.

WHERE TO PLANT

Give the saw palmetto a full-sun to partial-shade location. This palm grows as wide as it is tall, so it needs space to spread out in all directions. Keep it at least 3 to 5 ft. away from sidewalks, driveways, and the home.

HOW TO PLANT

Saw palmettos grow well in Florida's sandy soils without any special site preparation. Transplant the palm by digging a hole 2 to 3 times wider but not deeper than the rootball. Fill in around the rootball with soil while adding water to make good root-to-soil contact. Create a berm at the edge of the rootball to ensure wetting of the rootball at each watering. After planting, add a 2- to 3-in. mulch layer over the root system. This palm usually does not need bracing or staking.

ADVICE FOR CARE

Newly planted saw palmettos should be kept moist until the roots begin to grow out into the surrounding soil. Although this is a very drought-tolerant palm, make sure the soil does not thoroughly dry for several growing seasons. Once established, the saw palmetto does not need special watering but can be given periodic watering along with other landscape plantings. The saw palmetto needs infrequent feedings. Fertilizing other nearby plantings usually is enough to feed the palm plantings, too. Where light feedings are provided in spring and summer, use a 16-4-8, 12-4-8, or similar palm fertilizer, following label instructions.

ADDITIONAL INFORMATION

The saw palmetto gradually increases in size and may overgrow walks and encroach upon other landscape plantings. Prune the plants back as needed. Many gardeners remove the older leaves that brown during the growing season, but doing this is almost impossible with large plantings. Saw palmettos have few pests but may be affected by palmetto weevils and palm leaf skeletonizers. Treat pests with a pesticide recommended by the University of Florida, following label instructions.

ADDITIONAL SPECIES, CULTIVARS, OR VARIETIES

A blue leaf selection of the saw palmetto has been made for landscape plantings. It's being propagated by native plant nurseries.

ADVICE FOR REGIONAL CARE

Saw palmettos grow throughout the state without special care.

Perennials

PERENNIALS ARE LONGER LIVED THAN ANNUALS AND SHORTER LIVED THAN TREES. In some parts of Florida, most things can be made perennial if you work at it, even coleus and impatiens. It is therefore difficult to categorize perennials.

You can expect to get a few years out of these plants, but not a few decades. You can expect many of them to be herbaceous, though some, like pentas, can become woody with age. You can expect them to be accents or groundcovers or vines, too. You may expect that bulbs are sometimes included in perennial listings because they return seasonally but must be replaced from time to time. As with life itself, you can expect the unexpected, and you will not be disappointed.

Perennials are among the elements of your garden that bring it to life, that add richness and dimensionality. They could just as easily not be there; if you never had them, you might never miss them. But if you add perennials, and then remove them, taking them away will make all the difference.

In South Florida, salvia can be grown as a perennial. *Salvia vanhoutteii*, with red flowers emerging from wine- or burgundy-colored tubes or calyces, is a pretty plant to watch grow and enlarge. When it finally reaches shrub size, it can be pruned and shaped as you wish. Its character changes as it ages.

Pentas begin life in the garden looking one way—pert is a description that comes to mind for young pentas. Over the course of 2 or 3 years or more, they become robust, big landscape plants. After a

while in this stage, they must be pruned back quite hard or eliminated altogether and begun again. Or they may be replaced with
another plant that will change the look according to your change
of heart.

This changing aspect of the garden is important, as we all change
our tastes over time. So allow a portion of the garden to be devoted
to perennials that are less labor intensive than annuals, but will not
become permanent, plants that can repeat their performances but be
replaced should they wear out their welcome.

Gaillardias, daylilies, kalanchoes, begonias, walking iris,
Mexican tarragon, milkweed, and phlox are among the plants we
consider perennials, but tropicals may also be included. Consider
the bromeliads that flower every year, send out pups, and then die,
giving up their space to the new generation. Or the costus and
calatheas, the gingers and the rest, which may die back in colder
winter but linger along in mild ones to send out new and exuberant
foliage and flowers in the warm months.

In South Florida, many of the plants called tropicals are perennials: bananas, for instance, which flower and fruit every year to 18
months; gingers and heliconias, which bloom reliably in the warm
months; spathiphyllums, which produce their white flags of peace
during the warm months; and birds-of-paradise.

It is a mistake to assume that they can be left to grow on their
own just because they are perennial. Taking care of them extends
their lives. Refresh a bed; add more mulch; remove spent flowers;
divide the rhizomes or tubers or bulbs; fertilize regularly; water regularly . . . the same good habits of good gardeners are required with
these as with other plants in your care.

Asparagus Fern

Asparagus setaceus

Other Name: *A. densiflorus* 'Sprengeri'
Height: 2 ft.
Zones: All
Light Requirement:

For plants in the lily family that look so delicate, they are tough customers. *Asparagus setaceus* is sometimes called lace-fern because the branchlets are so delicate that they seem to be straight from Belgium. This plant used to be much more commonly seen than it is today. It serves well in pots for the patio and in planters. And its quite beautiful foliage can be cut for flower arrangements. An old name for it is *Asparagus plumosus. Asparagus* 'Sprengeri' suits certain areas perfectly and shouldn't be allowed in others. Where planters have some height, 'Sprengeri' is exactly right for adding a cascade of green. The long, arching stems billow and flow like water, and in early summer they are highlighted by tiny white flowers, followed by red fruit. Both could be used as groundcovers as well as outdoor potted plants, but once they get started, it's hard to get rid of them, so pots or planters are best. They grow on fleshy and fat underground roots, and both have little spines. They love water and might serve well in rocks beside a waterfall or pond. They are South African in origin. They prefer moisture in summer and dry conditions in winter to rest. The little seeds can be transported here and there, and will sprout without difficulty.

When to Plant

Plant in spring when new branchlets are forming. If you divide a clump, this also is best done in spring. Seeds can be planted somewhat earlier, say, later winter or early spring.

Where to Plant

Plant in planters or pots on patios or pool decks or by waterfalls.

How to Plant

If purchasing an asparagus fern in a container intended for a larger terra-cotta pot, use a good, loose potting soil that contains peat, bark, and perlite for drainage. Place terra-cotta shards, polystyrene peanuts, or coarse orchid mix in the bottom 2 or 3 in., and fill with potting soil to a level where the top of the plant's rootball will be within 1 or 2 in. of the top. Fill in around the rootball. Hold the terra-cotta pot with both hands, and firmly tamp it against the ground to help the potting mix settle. Then fill again to bring potting soil to within 1 or 2 in. of the top. Water well.

ADVICE FOR CARE
Asparagus ferns like plenty of water in the growing season. Because terra-cotta is porous, water evaporates quickly from the pots. You may have to water frequently, depending on conditions. Lift the pot to check the weight, or insert a finger into the potting soil to a depth of 1 or 2 in. If the soil feels dry, then water. Water less often in winter. Fertilize with a slow-release 18-18-18 for foliage plants.

ADDITIONAL INFORMATION
A form called *A. densiflorus* 'Myers' has stems that tend to stay upright and foliage that is full at the bottom and narrow at the top. They can look quite unusual, and using them requires a good eye. They are best suited for pots and may be most attractive grouped with other potted plants.

ADDITIONAL SPECIES, CULTIVARS, OR VARIETIES
Dwarf forms are available.

ADVICE FOR REGIONAL CARE
Asparagus ferns can take cold, but bring inside or cover if freeze is expected.

Begonia

Begonia spp.

Height: 2 to 4 ft.
Zones: 10B and 11
Light Requirement:

Flowers change. Just as impatiens have become brighter and geraniums bolder and salvias more diverse in their colors, begonias have undergone a revolution. They're coming back into the landscape. Angel-wing and rhizomatous begonias are being used once again in shady areas of gardens where their leaf shapes, at 2 to 4 ft., hit the spot. Angel-wings, which grow on woody canes, have leaves shaped as if they were plucked from the back of Gabriel preoccupied with blowing that horn. Often spotted with silver, or green on green, or metallic green, the undersides can be plain green, maroon, or pink. And flowers hang on slender stems in shades of pink or white. Rhizomatous begonias have more succulent stems with sometimes-grand leaves close to 1 ft. across. Often the leaf surface is covered with minute hairs and so looks quite velvety. A prime example is 'Black Velvet', a beautiful dark-as-night maroon begonia. Other leaves are quilted, puckered, round, star-shaped, or pointed, with the points slightly off center. In a mixture of shade-loving plants, begonias can shine. Beneath a tree or in a raised bed with excellent drainage, they are quite beautiful. They also can be somewhat tricky. The composition of the bed will spell your success with them. The beds have to drain perfectly, yet retain water. Begonias have delicate roots that stay in the upper 2 or 3 in. of the soil. Tim Anderson, a Miami nurseryman who has grown begonias for many years, says, "They like a lot of water on the dry side." Anderson maintains that wet rocks provide ideal conditions so that roots, which don't like to be completely dry, can have air but stay moist. Use a potting soil with sand or pea rock added. Don't overload it with peat moss or too much organic matter, and avoid muck. Limestone is a porous rock that allows drainage and retains moisture in its crevices, and it can be wonderful for begonias. Cane-type begonias can be pruned to any desired height. The cuttings can be rooted. Rhizomatous begonias can be divided by cutting a piece of rhizome large enough to have several old nodes and two or three leaves, placing this horizontally beneath mulch or on a peat-perlite mix and allowing it to root.

When to Plant
Plant in spring or to midsummer, when plants are actively growing.

Where to Plant
Plant in shade, in raised beds or in areas with excellent drainage.

How to Plant
Build a raised bed, or add rock or even orchid mix to a bed. Pea rock in the bottom of a planting hole will assure good drainage. Mulch.

Advice for Care
Use a slow-release fertilizer to keep a supply of nutrients available to the plants, and keep well watered.

Additional Information
Even wax begonias, used as annuals, are becoming shorter and more floriferous with brighter flowers in pinks and reds.

Additional Species, Cultivars, or Varieties
Begonia popenoei is a large plant excellent for landscape use. It will take bright light to deep shade, and has large, lopsided medium-green leaves. *Begonia nelumbiifolia* has large, round, peltate leaves (the petiole or leaf stem attaches directly into the back of the leaf near the center). Both of these rhizomatous plants produce quite tall stalks (to about 4 ft.) of white flowers in February and March.

Advice for Regional Care
Tuberous begonias do not do well in South Florida. Other types such as angel-wing and rex may best be grown in protected areas, such as southeast corners in North and Central Florida. Cover in cold weather. Otherwise, grow in containers and bring inside.

Bird-of-Paradise

Strelitzia reginae

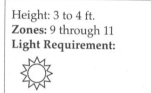

Height: 3 to 4 ft.
Zones: 9 through 11
Light Requirement:

The story of the bird-of-paradise is really the story of man's long search for the Garden of Eden and the hope that botanical gardens might somehow offer some clues to the nature of the Creator. English plant explorers discovered the bird-of-paradise at the Cape of Good Hope in 1773. George III sent them in order to enlarge the Royal Botanic Garden at Kew. George's wife was Queen Charlotte, the duchess of Mecklenburg-Strelitz and a patron of botany. When the bird was taken back to the Kew, Sir Joseph Banks, the king's horticultural advisor and nobody's fool, named it to honor Charlotte: *Strelitzia*, and *reginae*, meaning "queen." The white bird-of-paradise was found on a 1772-75 expedition and named *S. Nicolai*, for Czar Nicholas I of Russia. Related to gingers, bananas, and heliconias, birds-of-paradise are comprised of a bract within which orange sepals and blue, fused petals arise. Inside the petals are the stigma and stamens. The bird head is rather heronlike, recalling the snowy egret's plumes and long, graceful neck with pointed beak. Appropriately, birds pollinate the birds. July and August are the peak flowering months for birds, although some people wonder if the birds will ever bloom. A wives' tale has it that birds-of-paradise must be at least seven before they flower. Good care and proper planting depth will speed up the process. Of course, explorers never found the lost Garden of Eden, the Fountain of Youth, or any other way of achieving immortality. They did find the New World, but that turned out to be less paradisical than initially hoped. Birds-of-paradise, however, remain.

WHEN TO PLANT

Plant in the warm season, May through midsummer, to give the plant ample growing time before winter.

WHERE TO PLANT

Plant in full sun, as an accent or part of a foundation planting or in front of a hedge. Birds-of-paradise have tuberous roots, and they like to clump. Give them space to grow.

218

How to Plant
Enrich the planting hole for the birds with peat moss or well-rotted manure, but don't sink them too deep into the ground. Tubers should be just at the surface. Mulch lightly.

Advice for Care
Birds like to be well fed. Fertilize every month, using a balanced fertilizer, such as 6-6-6. A plant from a 3-gallon container should receive 3 tablespoons of fertilizer; a mature larger plant, 2 cups. Or use a slow-release fertilizer to supple the plant with a constant source of nutrients. Because they have tuberous roots, don't let them sit in water, but provide good drainage. Birds should be well watered and then allowed to dry. Scale insects may be a problem. Cygon 2E is an insecticide useful against a widespread infestation of scale. Malathion is good for small populations.

Additional Information
The bird-of-paradise is the official flower of the city of Los Angeles. Flowers may last several months on plants in the ground.

Additional Species, Cultivars, or Varieties
Strelitzia alba has claret bracts and white flowers; *S. caudata* has pink bracts and white flowers. *S. nicolai,* the giant bird that can grow to 30 ft., has white bracts with blue flowers; *S. parvifolia* has green bracts edged in red, yellow-orange sepals, and electric-blue petals.

Advice for Regional Care
Protect from cold in Central and North Florida. Prune out damage in the spring.

Calathea

Calathea spp.

Height: few in. to 12 ft.
Zones: 10B and 11
Light Requirement:

The beautifully patterned leaves of calathea rise from a short stem. Among the most ornate of plants, the calatheas bear leaves worthy of a graphic designers' hall of fame. Markings usually follow the central vein, branching to side veins. They can be dark green on light green, silver on hunter green, bright pink on dark green, pink and white on dark green . . . the combinations seem quite endless. The undersides of the leaves are frequently red or wine colored. (Marantas, too, are beautifully marked foliage plants. Consider the familiar red-veined prayer plant. There are differences: marantas have only one seed per fruit whereas calatheas have three. Marantas also tend to branch, but calatheas do not. Take comfort in the fact that they're closely related, and if you call a calathea a maranta, it's not as if you called a rose a daisy.) The plants are from tropical America, and while they mix with aroids all right, they seem best suited for their own kind in a bed or, better, displayed individually in pots. Flowers are produced inside bracts; bracts can be spikes or racemes arising among the leaves. One, *Calathea* 'Burle Marx', has unmarked, broad green leaves on long stems and a spike of pale-blue to white cuplike bracts from which white flowers emerge.

WHEN TO PLANT
Plant in spring, especially if you are taking divisions of the tubers.

WHERE TO PLANT
The plants can be grouped in beds beneath trees, such as oaks, since they do well with bright light but not steady direct sun.

HOW TO PLANT
Place the tubers in beds that are a mix of rich organic matter, such as compost or good potting soil, with sand or perlite or another material to enhance drainage.

ADVICE FOR CARE

Use a slow-release fertilizer to keep a good supply of nutrients available to the roots. The patterns will be especially bold if the plants are well fertilized and well watered. Early morning sun is fine, too.

ADDITIONAL INFORMATION

Some of the most beautiful calatheas are *C. insignis*, the rattlesnake plant, which has leaves with undulating edges that are green with a darker midrib; *C. makoyana*, the peacock plant, marked on the upper side with olive- and dark-green spots on the lateral veins and dark-green borders, with a touch of red on the undersides; *C. ornata*, with pink and white lines on lateral veins; and *C. roseopicta*, with red down the central vein, jagged silvery-pink markings near the leaf edges, all on a dark-green background.

ADDITIONAL SPECIES, CULTIVARS, OR VARIETIES

There are many forms of calathea.

ADVICE FOR REGIONAL CARE

Tender tropicals, calatheas like protection in winter. I have a large *C.* 'Burle Marx' in a pot and two in the ground beneath thatch palms, and all did well throughout winter's cold snaps, which sent temperatures into the upper 30s. They fare less well when they dry out.

Leather Fern

Acrostichum danaeifolium

Height: 8 to 10 ft.
Zones: 9, 10, and 11
Light Requirement:

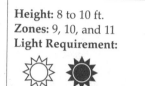

The Arnold Schwarzenegger of ferns, this is the beefiest and largest fern in the United States. Leather fern is a swamp dweller as well as a resident of mangrove zones. The sloughs of the Big Cypress swamp are good places to look for these fellows, as are the estuaries around the southern peninsula. Fronds are pinnately compound, but this fern's leaflets are not the delicate leaflets you normally associate with that description. They are wide, stiff, and dark green. The undersides of fertile leaflets look like suede leather, with rust-colored patches that are the spore capsules. The stems are substantial. Yet when they're curled up as fiddleheads, they are eaten in other parts of the world. Because of its size, the leather fern can be used as a shrub in the right setting. Low hammocks or native plant areas that have moist zones would accommodate the leather fern. It works well in lakefront planting areas where it could mix with the dahoon holly, the sabal palms, and the coastal plain willow. For natural pond areas, sweet bay magnolia, swamp hibiscus, cocoplum, buttonbush, and leather fern are good candidates for your landscape. Plant spider lilies, alligator lilies, rushes, and spartina on the slope that gradually enters your lake or pond, and you have created your own little wetlands system. Leather fern can be grown in a large container. The container can be submerged in a pond, or you can caulk the drainage holes to keep the growing medium wet to moist. Having one of these around lets you imagine that ferns this size were the denizens of prehistory, a tender nibble to a dinosaur.

WHEN TO PLANT
Plant during the warm months of the year.

WHERE TO PLANT
Select moist, low-lying areas.

How to Plant

The type of soil isn't as important as its moisture. Muck—the black, peat-based soil of the Everglades—is fine for this plant, mixed with a little sand. Or a potting soil without much perlite does well. This fern doesn't like to dry out. It will get brown fronds if it does.

Advice for Care

Keep the soil moist. Even though the nutritional requirements for this plant are said to be low, a small amount of slow-release fertilizer or organic fertilizer is beneficial.

Advice for Regional Care

Protect leather ferns from freezing weather.

Pentas

Pentas lanceolata

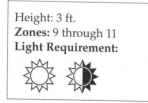

Height: 3 ft.
Zones: 9 through 11
Light Requirement:

With the wild popularity of butterfly gardening, pentas have come into their own. The tiny nectar cups beneath the 5-petaled corollas are a lure for all kinds of hungry butterflies. An old name is Egyptian star-cluster, as the starshaped plants came from Africa and Arabia. Today everyone knows them as pentas. In addition to attracting butterflies, pentas are easy to care for and rapid growers. They tend to get woody and leggy after 3 or 4 years, and you can take cuttings and replace the old plants with new ones. A butterfly garden can take any shape or form. Pentas come in regular and dwarf sizes so you can use them as background shrubs or foreground flowers. The important thing is to include both nectar plants and larval food plants in the design, and to plan for butterflies that are locally plentiful. For example, zebra longwing butterflies in South Florida feed on Spanish needle, lantana, pentas, and flame vine in the early spring. But the zebra longwings also eat pollen, so they will take a mouthful, sit on a nearby leaf, exude a fluid that they mix with pollen, and drink the mixture. To keep them around, you must also supply a passion flower vine because the female lays her eggs on these, and the vine provides food for the caterpillars. Cassius blue butterflies will drink nectar from various sources and lay eggs on necklace pod, plumbago, even lima beans. Cloudless sulfur butterflies lay eggs on cassias and sennas, plants with yellow flowers that match their own color. The nectar and pollen sources should be in the sun, protected from the wind by hedges or small trees. Surround pentas, blue porterweed, salvia, lantana, and milkweeds with shrubs such as firebush, butterfly sage (*Cordia globosa*), and necklace pod and trellises of calico flower, passion vine, a sweetbay magnolia, Bahama cassia, and the twin senna (*Senna polyphylla*). Include a source of water. The butterflies are free.

WHEN TO PLANT
Plant in spring and early summer.

Where to Plant

Plant in full sun to partial shade, where there is good drainage. Mix with other butterfly plants (see above).

How to Plant

Space the plants 12 to 24 in. apart, as they grow quite large and will form a wave of color. Use a trowel to dig a planting hole just larger than the rootball; backfill with soil from the planting hole and water. Water daily for a week or two, gradually tapering off until you water weekly or twice weekly. Use slow-release fertilizer at the time of planting, and again every 3 or 4 months if in South Florida. Six-month slow release will be used up more quickly in South Florida than in cooler areas, unless it is formulated for South Florida conditions.

Advice for Care

Cut back in the early spring to rejuvenate the plants. Pentas require a little care to look their best. Watch for spider mites in winter.

Additional Information

Bright red pentas like some shade.

Additional Species, Cultivars, or Varieties

Additional cultivars are numerous, including 'Cranberry Punch', 'Rose', 'Lilac Mist', and many more. A dwarf pink is available.

Advice on Regional Care

Keep well mulched during winter in Central Florida to help protect basal bud from cold. Also make cuttings of favorite varieties.

Periwinkle

Catharanthus roseus

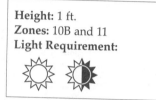

Height: 1 ft.
Zones: 10B and 11
Light Requirement:

Bless their hearts, these naturalized bright little flowers are abandoned-lot hardy. They were among the first flowering plants the pioneers in Florida traded and planted in their gardens. Because the Homesteaders had to construct houses, not tents, as a condition for land, the high, dry pinelands were the first to be settled and logged, almost simultaneously. And there the little flowers flourished. Who knows how they got to Florida, but the women who longed for some tangible beauty around their rough-hewn houses knew to plant periwinkles, which needed nothing more than a smile and a splash of water. That's practically all they need still. The Madagascar periwinkle was one of the stars of the early days of "save the rain forest" campaigns, famous for its alkaloids vincristine and vinblastine, which are used worldwide for treating childhood leukemia and Hodgkin's disease. See, said the conservationists and scientists, we don't know what medicines these plants could render, just look at the periwinkle. But even though interest in screening tropical plants for serviceable goods has grown, deforestation continues. Madagascar, especially, teeters on the edge of biological disaster. Impatiens continue to be the most popular source of garden color in the South, but they are definitely seasonal, while periwinkles bloom year-round. They may not have the cachet of the pampered impatiens—they are little street fighters by comparison—but by using them, you won't be running outside twice a day to water away the limp-wristed wilting to which impatiens succumb. Use periwinkles in sun and partial shade. Plant them in front of the ligustrum hedge or the podocarpus; put them over the septic tank.

WHEN TO PLANT
Plant any time; the beginning of the rainy season is the best time.

WHERE TO PLANT
Plant in beds, in pots, in sandy, dry soil.

How to Plant

Periwinkles can be cut back when they get too straggly. You can root cuttings in March or April, and by May they will be ready to set into beds. Simply use a trowel to lift out soil, inset the pot of periwinkles, and refill the hole. Then water. (Cuttings are easily started. Use a 50:50 mix of peat moss and perlite; wet it thoroughly. Cut periwinkles; remove several pairs of leaves and flowers; insert the cutting into the medium and place it in shade, out of wind, but where you will remember to keep the mix moist. To reduce the need to water, you can put the pots in plastic bags. Insert 1 or 2 bamboo stakes in the pot to keep the plastic from sagging onto the plants, then tie the bag closed. Wait 3 or 4 weeks before checking to see if there are sufficient roots to allow planting.)

Advice for Care

Water to keep the roots moist for a month or so, then gradually taper off, allowing the plant to reduce its water needs. A teaspoon of slow-release fertilizer at planting time is sufficient.

Additional Information

Periwinkles are in the same family as oleander, allamanda, and frangipani. If you look at the flowers, you will notice a resemblance: 5 petals and a tube, with the petals slightly twisting.

Additional Species, Cultivars, or Varieties

Periwinkles have been fancied up by breeding and come in bright new colors. The periwinkle's dark center has been darkened even more by breeding. And while the originals are lanky and rangy, the spiffy new ones are shorter. The originals continue to outperform the hybrids.

Salvia

Salvia spp.

Height: 2 to 3 ft.
Zones: All
Light Requirement:

For splashes of color that keep on performing winter or summer, turn to salvias. You may know them as sage because of the pungent aroma of the leaves. Volatile oils emit the characteristic and particular aroma, including thymes and lavender. Many of the family members are Mediterranean types, more apt to find themselves at home in California than Florida. *Salvia officinalis*, the garden sage used for seasoning, is one of these. But some salvias are from Mexico, Central America, and Brazil. *Salvia coccinea*, the red "tropical sage," is native to Florida, the West Indies, and tropical America. *Salvia splendens* is a Brazilian species known as scarlet sage. Like other ornamental salvias, it has a colorful (in this case, searing scarlet) tubular flower that emerges from an equally colorful calyx—the fused sepals. All told, there are about 750 species of salvias, ranging from annuals to shrubs. Some, of course, reseed themselves and become garden nuisances. Bicolor is one of these, but without too much effort, you can pull the plants while they're tiny. Bicolor is now in its second year in my yard, and when it begins to look bedraggled, I cut it way back. I have mixed the pink bicolor and the vanhoutteii with other red-based colors in a bed, including an azalea, a pink-flowering heliconia. These wander among the *Chamaedorea* palms, lady-of-the-night, and big-leaved begonias. They were joined, by chance, by several bromeliads (*Billbergia pyramidalis* 'Striata') with pink bracts on their flower stalks. For winter color, I mixed red salvia, bush daisies, and white impatiens, and in bowls planted white impatiens with salmon and purple salvia.

WHEN TO PLANT
Plant any time.

WHERE TO PLANT
Plant in flower beds, pots, or mixed plantings. Salvias are lovers of high light, but the higher the light, the more moisture they require,

at least when they are small. Water every couple of days when they are small. The larger they become, the more drought tolerance they develop.

How to Plant
Salvias like a moderately rich soil, so mix peat moss or compost in their planting beds. Use a trowel or spade, depending on the size of the container, and dig a hole slightly larger than the rootball of the salvia. Gently remove the plant from the container, place in the hole, and backfill with enriched soil. Mulch. Alternately, you can scatter seeds removed from flower spikes and sprinkle them into mulch, water, and wait.

Advice for Care
Water once or twice a week, depending on conditions; use a slow-release 14-14-14 fertilizer 3 or 4 times a year, January, March/April, June/July, and October. Cut back when they sprawl out too far.

Additional Information
Salvia is in the same family as coleus, ajuga, and mint (*Mentha spicata* is spearmint).

Additional Species, Cultivars, or Varieties
A well-stocked wholesale nursery in Boynton Beach, Boynton Botanicals, grows 17 different salvias for gardens, and they include *S. coccinea* Bicolor, a charming pink/powder-pink combination; and *S. vanhoutteii*, a big (5 to 6 ft.) plant with deep-maroon calyces and dark-red flowers. *S. madrensis* has yellow flowers, while *S. involucrata*, called rose leaf sage, has fuschia flowers. Blue sage, *S. mexicana*, has blue flowers, and on and on.

Advice for Regional Care
Salvias may be used as annuals in more northern gardens.

Society Garlic

Tulbaghia violacea

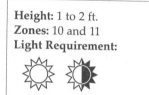

Height: 1 to 2 ft.
Zones: 10 and 11
Light Requirement:

Depending on the reference that you select, you find that society garlic is either in the amaryllis family or in that of the onion, leek, garlic, and chive. The onion/chive set is intriguing because, says Frances Perry in *Flowers of the World*, members of the Alliaceae family occur everywhere around the world with the possible exception of Australia. Why? we wonder. That reference also says that the Alliaceae family is a group of plants intermediate between the amaryllis family and the lily family. There is no question about the charm of society garlic. Round balls of lilac, pink, or white flowers (umbels) top the slender flower stalks that are pleasing to the eye, even if the leaves do have a garlic scent. Mauve, pinks, and blues incline one to think of Gertrude Jekyll's mixed herbaceous borders, yet translating that look to Florida is difficult, given our remarkably bright light and the tendency of pale flowers to wash out. Still, barleria, society garlic, ruellia, pink pentas, plumbago, clock vine, and the seasonally beautiful queen's wreath (*Petrea*), mixed with pink salvia, magenta *Scutellaria*, *Spathoglottis* ground orchids . . . there are great possibilities here. Even alone, lining a pathway or a front walk, society garlic is a pretty flower. In a more tropical vein, a bed of society garlic can surround a silver-blue palm such as a *Latania* for dramatic effect, with the sculptural palm shooting up from a small sea of lilac. Silver buttonwood, silver palms (*Coccothrinax argentata*), and other blue-gray plants should be on your list of mix and match for *Tulbaghia*. If you are more traditionally oriented and want to mix like with like, then try society garlic among your culinary herbs. In South Florida's summer, northern herbs die down, but the flowering garlic will still be a presence among summertime stalwarts, such as Cuban oregano with its beautiful cream-and-light-green leaves.

WHEN TO PLANT
Plant any time.

230

WHERE TO PLANT

Plant in a bed that has good drainage and some organic matter such as compost or peat moss. These plants can take full sun or partial shade.

HOW TO PLANT

As you would plant other rhizomes and bulbs, place society garlic not too far below the surface, with a little bone meal in the bottom of the planting hole; space about 8 to 12 in. apart.

ADVICE FOR CARE

Keep the planting bed moist to get society garlic started, and use a slow-release fertilizer in spring, summer, and fall. Water less in winter.

ADVICE FOR REGIONAL CARE

Plants can be put into containers for winter and brought inside when freezing weather occurs.

Spanish Bayonet

Yucca aloifolia

Height: 8 to 12 ft.
Zones: All
Light Requirement:

A planting of Spanish bayonet, it is reported, once protected the grounds of Marjorie Merriweather Post's Palm Beach estate, Mar-a-Lago, and if it was good enough for her, it ought to be good enough for you in the crime deterrent department. Spanish bayonets are not a pretty sight. A bizarre sight, perhaps even a frightening sight, yes. But if you put your mind to it, you can devise an effectively impenetrable home-protection system without the annoyance of accidental false alarms. Spanish bayonet can be at the center of this. The leaf tips on this plant are memorably sharp. Trunks are usually covered with them. Groups of trunks arise together because they grow on underground stems or rhizomes, which creep along and periodically send up another shoot. In addition to the Spanish bayonet, plants that deter burglars and other strangers include bougainvillea; crown of thorns; limeberry, which hides its spines; and carissa, with twice-pointed thorns. *Aiphanes* palms are savagely armed, even on the undersides of the fronds, as are *Zombia* palms. Throw in some *Aechmea* bromeliads, and you have Fort Knox. A version of Spanish bayonet called 'Marginata' has creamy leaf edges. In a sweeter mood, the spineless yucca, *Y. elephantipes*, keeps its harmless but still pointed leaves at the ends of its multiple trunks, so the effect is more pleasingly architectural than armored. *Y. filamentosa* is a short, trunkless rosette of sharp leaves decorated with curly white hair, and *Y. gloriosa* has red leaf margins and purple stripes on the white flowers.

WHEN TO PLANT
Plant any time.

WHERE TO PLANT
Salt and drought tolerant, yuccas can be grouped with other succulents in areas that are out of reach of the sprinkler system, in seaside gardens, or in beds with plenty of sand.

HOW TO PLANT
Carefully plant them when they are small.

ADVICE FOR CARE
Water until the plants begin to grow; minimal care is needed once the plants are established.

ADDITIONAL INFORMATION
This plant's flowers, which appear in the spring, are moth pollinated by a specific moth, and the two share a unique partnership: a female yucca moth collects pollen from one plant, forms it into a little ball, and carries it inside the flower of another plant. In this second flower, she lays her eggs near the flower's ovaries, then spreads pollen on the stigmas. Caterpillars hatch about the time the seeds ripen and eat most seeds, but not all of them. So the moth and the plant depend on each other for survival.

ADDITIONAL SPECIES, CULTIVARS, OR VARIETIES
Yucca gloriosa and *Y. filamentosa* are Florida natives; *Y. filamentosa* is sometimes called bear grass.

ADVICE FOR REGIONAL CARE
Protect Spanish bayonet from freezing weather in Central and North Florida.

Spineless Century Plant

Agave attenuata

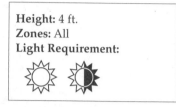

Height: 4 ft.
Zones: All
Light Requirement:

Even in the tropics and subtropics, cactuses and succulents occur because arid conditions are just over the mountain. Parts of Florida, with rocky substrates and lots of sun, can create the need for plants to conserve water even when rain measures in the 30- to 60-in. range, which is why so many plants from the Florida Keys and the Ten Thousand Islands are drought tolerant. Succulents are good at their jobs, filling leaves with water-fat cells. The spineless century plant, from Mexico, is one of the best to have around in small gardens or areas where there are children. Even adults appreciate it when weeding or otherwise working around agaves. Not as big as the *A. americana*, or century plant with spines, this one nonetheless shares other characteristics: its form and its determination to flower in its own sweet time. Century plants, as you well know, flower more frequently than once every 100 years, but they don't flower annually. They are monocarpic: they flower once and then die, so they don't rush into things. When the plant takes a notion to bloom, however, it puts its whole heart into the effort. The flower stalk is branched, and each branch is topped with numerous yellow flowers. Plantlets often form on the branch tips as well. They make wonderful accent plants in areas without irrigation. Grouped with other succulents, such as kalanchoes, or with bromeliads that have a similar form, they can be quite attractive.

WHEN TO PLANT
Plant at any time, except when in flower.

WHERE TO PLANT
Plant in sandy beds, rock gardens, or areas without irrigation. They prefer full sun.

234

How to Plant

Dig a hole as deep as the rootball in the container, but somewhat wider; remove the container from the plant and slip the agave into the planting hole; water in backfill.

Advice for Care

Little care is needed. Water the plants when they are young. Use liquid fertilizer 2 or 3 times a year.

Additional Information

Agave sisalana, the sisal agave, was introduced to the Florida Keys by Dr. Henry Perrine in 1836. Perrine was ambassador to Mexico, and he sent back the plant in hopes of its cultivation for a sisal industry. The plants still grow on Indian Key, which is a state historic site. Perrine was killed by Indians.

Additional Species, Cultivars, or Varieties

Several forms of dwarf century plant are available, including *A. miradorensis,* with fat leaves; *A. angustifolia* 'Woodrowii', with yellow leaf margins; and *A. stricta,* with narrow leaves. A native century plant in Florida, *A. neglecta,* is bluish gray. *A. americana* 'Mediopicta' is a beautiful plant with a cream stripe down the center of each leaf. One can imagine a nice collection of these plants in an atrium.

Advice for Regional Care

Protect these plants from freezes.

Swamp Fern

Blechnum serrulatum

Height:
Zones: All
Light Requirement:

Looking something like a large Boston fern with a perm, the swamp fern has long fronds and long, narrow leaflets with undulating edges. If you visit Corkscrew Swamp Sanctuary, you will find it in abundance, reaching up from the wet muck next to cypress logs and cypress knees, running between the maples and bald cypress, tickling the pop ash and the strangler figs. It loves shade and damp muck. Here at last is a plant that does not require excellent drainage. Swamp fern is not a typical garden component, but a good addition to native gardens, lakeside landscapes, and homemade bogs around homemade ponds. Swamp fern will grow in sun, but not as luxuriantly as it does in that fine and particular scattered shade cast by cypress, maples, and sweetbay magnolias. Like all ferns, this one depends on water for part of its life cycle. Ferns produce minute heart-shaped sexual plants called gametophytes from which sperm and eggs are produced. The sperm must swim to a female organ (either of another gametophyte or its own) to fertilize an egg. When a new plant forms, the gametophyte dies, and what we recognize as a fern grows. Eventually, it will form spores, and when spores are released, they germinate in water and the cycle starts over. (The spore cases, incidentally, are borne on the undersides of leaflets in patterns that often are the distinguishing characteristic of a fern.) If you have a pond and waterfall, you may want to add a few swamp ferns for an authentic Florida feel. Bring in a paurotis palm for a lovely effect. On a lakeshore, it can join leather fern and crinum lilies, buttonbush and wax myrtle, sabal palms and red bay, sweet bay and dahoon holly in a transition zone from hammock to wetland.

WHEN TO PLANT
Plant in spring or during the warm months.

WHERE TO PLANT
Choose shaded locations with wet to moist soil.

236

How to Plant
Keep the rhizome fairly close to the surface of the soil.

Advice for Care
Keep the rhizome damp, and swamp fern will require little else. A high-nitrogen slow-release fertilizer may be added.

Additional Species, Cultivars, or Varieties
B. gibbum is a dwarf tree fern, growing to about 2 ft.

Advice for Regional Care
Protect swamp ferns from freezing weather.

Wild Petunia

Ruellia caroliniensis

Height: 10 to 12 in.
Zones: 10 and 11
Light Requirement:

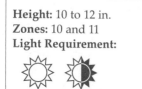

Once, many years before the 1992 hurricane took out the pinelands, wild petunias could be found in Larry and Penny Thompson Park in South Dade County. I know, because old notes from a taxonomy field trip tell me so. The field trip was in August— absolutely the hottest time to be in the pinelands—and I remember the misery. But I also remember the wonder at finding so many plants in what seemed, then, to be a rather uninviting and uninteresting place. Running oak, *Quercus pumila*, was in the understory, along with pineland allamanda, pineland fern (*Anemia adiantifolia*, meaning its fronds resemble maiden hair fern), saw palmetto, and cabbage palms. Wild petunias grew on slender stems with hairy opposite leaves and blue-lavender sessile flowers, which is to say the flowers had no stalk but the ends of the tubes attached directly to the plant. Wild petunias can reseed themselves, given the right opportunity. Twin flower, or *Dyschoriste oblongifolia*, is in every pineland, and puts out 2 flowers for each leaf pair, one opening while the other stays in bud. The pineland morning glory, *Jacquemontia curtissii*, has tiny white starlike flowers, 5 pointed lobes on the corolla (a corolla is made up of fused petals). This little viny thing is native only to the South Florida pinelands and is highly endangered, as is the ecosystem itself. Pale-blue *Jacquemontia tampnifolia* is found in the pinelands of Central and North Florida. White-top sedge, with triangular stems, wanders into pinelands in the wetter areas and meanders along ditches as well. *Dichromena colorata* is its formal name, and it occurs from Florida to Texas and north to Virginia, flowering from early spring to late fall. Yellow-top, *Flaveria linearis*, is a composite—a daisy relative—with disc flowers and ray flowers, the eye and the petals of "she loves me/she loves me not" fame. Also yellow with little buttons of individual flowers is the dwarf pinelands lantana, *Lantana depressa. Piriqueta caroliniana*, known infor-mally as piriqueta, has buttercup-yellow stems and golden feathery stigmas, but you have to be a morning person to catch it because it closes by noon. That's just the beginning. Pick up a Florida wildflower book, and head off into the pinelands and see what you can find. Such a collection of perennials could go a long way toward landscap-ing a native wildflower garden, which, by virtue of its nativeness, would also be a butterfly garden to the sulphurs, skippers, hairstreaks, the Florida buckeye, and other butterflies that naturally go to such places.

WHEN TO PLANT
Plant during the warm season.

WHERE TO PLANT
Choose a sunny, dry location among pines and palmettos.

HOW TO PLANT
Use a trowel to dig a hole slightly larger than the rootball of the containerized ruellia. Gently slip the plant from the container, holding it toward the base of the stem, not by the top. Position the plant in the planting hole, and fill with original soil. Water daily for a week to help the plant become established, then gradually taper off watering. Ruellias are drought tolerant.

ADVICE FOR CARE
Little care is needed after the plant has become established and is growing well.

ADDITIONAL INFORMATION
To get started with a native plant butterfly garden, consult these booklets: *Gardening for Butterflies and Children in South Florida* by Anne Kilmer (contact the *Palm Beach Post*, West Palm Beach, for the booklet); *Butterfly Gardening with Florida's Native Plants* by Craig Huegel, published by the Florida Native Plant Society, P.O. Box 680008, Orlando, Florida 32868; and *Florida Butterflies* by Eugene J. Gerberg and Ross H. Arnett, Jr., Natural Science Publications, Baltimore, Maryland.

ADDITIONAL SPECIES, CULTIVARS, OR VARIETIES
Several nonnative ruellias, which like damp conditions, are found in local nurseries, including *Ruellia amoena*; Mexican bluebell, *R. brittoniana*; several cultivars, 'Compacta', 'Chi Chi,' 'Purple Showers,' and 'Snow Queen'; *R. graecizans*; and *R. squarrosa,* a groundcover.

ADVICE FOR REGIONAL CARE
This native is damaged by cold in Central and North Florida.

240

Ageratum
Ageratum houstonianum

Calendula
Calendula officinalis

Celosia
Celosia cristata

Coleus
Coleus × hybridus

Dianthus
Dianthus × hybrida

Dusty Miller
Senecio cineraria

Geranium
Pelargonium hortorum

Impatiens
Impatiens wallerana

Marigold
Tagetes patula

Nicotiana
Nicotiana alata

Pansy
Viola × wittrockiana

Petunia
Petunia × hybrida

Portulaca
Portulaca grandiflora

Salvia
Salvia splendens

Snapdragon
Antirrhinum majus

Torenia
Torenia fournieri

Verbena
Verbena × hybrida

Vinca
Catharanthus roseus

Wax Begonia
Begonia × semperflorens-cultorum

Zinnia
Zinnia elegans

African Iris
Dietes bicolor

African Lily
Agapanthus africanus

Alstroemeria
Alstroemeria spp.

Amaryllis
Hippeastrum hybrids

Amazon Lily
Eucharis grandiflora

Blood Lily
Haemanthus multiflorus

Blue Flag Iris
Iris virginica

Caladium
Caladium × hortulanum

Calla
Zantedeschia spp.

Canna
Canna hybrids

Day Lily
Hemerocallis hybrids

Gladiolus
Gladiolus hybrids

Gloriosa Lily
Gloriosa spp.

Kaffir Lily
Clivia miniata

Louisiana Iris
Iris hybrids

Pride of Burma
Curcuma roscoeana

Shell Ginger
Alpinia zerumbet

Swamp Lily
Crinum hybrid

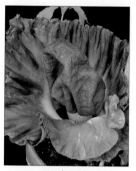

Voodoo Lily
Amorphophallus spp.

Walking Iris
Neomarica spp.

Zephyr Lily
Zephyranthes spp.

Cycads

Artillery Plant
Pilea microphylla

Blue Daze
Evolvulus glomeratus

Broad Sword Fern
Nephrolepis biserrata

Bugle Weed
Ajuga reptans

Cast Iron Plant
Aspidistra elatior

Creeping Fig
Ficus pumila

Dwarf Carissa
Carissa macrocarpa 'Emerald Beauty'

English Ivy
Hedera helix

Fakahatchee Grass
Tripsicum dactyloides

Kalanchoe
Kalanchoe blossfeldiana

Liriope
Liriope muscari

Mexican Bluebell
Ruellia brittoniana

Mexican Heather
Cuphea hyssopifolia

Mondo Grass
Ophiopogon japonicus

Oyster Plant
Rhoeo spathacea

Peperomia
Peperomia obtusifolia

Purple Queen
Setcreasea pallida

Shore Juniper
Juniperus conferta

Small Leaf Confederate Jasmine
Trachelospermum asiaticum

Wax Jasmine
Jasminum volubile

Wedelia
Wedelia trilobata

Cattleyas
Cattleya spp.

Dendrobiums
Dendrobium spp.

Epidendrum
Epidendrum spp.

Oncidium
Oncidium spp.

Paphiopedilum
Paphiopedilum spp.

Phalaenopsis
Phalaenopsis spp.

Vanda
Vanda spp.

Florida Gamma Grass
Tripsacum floridana

Fountain Grass
Pennisetum setaceum

Muhly Grass
Muhlenbergia capillaris

Pampas Grass
Cortaderia selloana

Sand Cordgrass
Spartina bakeri

Butia Palm
Butia capitata

Cabbage Palm
Sabal palmetto

Chinese Fan Palm
Livistona chinensis

Coconut Palm
Cocos nucifera

Florida Silver Palm
Coccothrinax argentata

Lady Palm
Rhapis spp.

Pygmy Date Palm
Phoenix roebelenii

Royal Palm
Roystonea elata

Saw Palmetto
Serenoa repens

Asparagus Fern
Asparagus setaceus

Begonia
Begonia spp.

Bird-of-Paradise
Strelitzia reginae

Calathea
Calathea spp.

Pentas
Pentas lanceolata

Periwinkle
Catharanthus roseus

Salvia
Salvia spp.

Society Garlic
Tulbaghia violacea

Spanish Bayonet
Yucca aloifolia

Spineless Century Plant
Agave attenuata

Swamp Fern
Blechnum serrulatum

Wild Petunia
Ruellia caroliniensis

Climbing Rose
Rosa hybrids

Floribunda
Rosa hybrids

Grandiflora Rose
Rosa hybrids

Hybrid Tea Rose
Rosa hybrids

Miniature Rose
Rosa hybrids

Old Garden Rose
Rosa hybrids

Allamanda
Allamanda cathartica

American Beautybush
Callicarpa americana

Azalea
Rhododendron spp.

Butterfly Bush
Buddleia officinalis

Chenille Plant
Acalypha hispida

Cocculus
Cocculus laurifolius

Cocoplum
Chrysobalanus icaco

Crape Myrtle
Laegerstromia indica

Croton
Codiaeum variegatum

Firebush
Hamelia patens

Gardenia
Gardenia jasminoides

Hibiscus
Hibiscus rosa-sinensis

Hydrangea
Hydrangea macrophylla

Ixora
Ixora coccinea

Lady-of-the-Night
Brunfelsia americana

Ligustrum
Ligustrum japonicum

Nandina
Nandina domestica

Necklace Pod
Sophora tomentosa

Night-Blooming Jessamine
Cestrum nocturnum

Oleander
Nerium oleander

Plumbago
Plumbago auriculata

Sweet Viburnum
Viburnum odoratissimum

Thryallis
Galphimia glauca

Wax Myrtle
Myrica cerifera

Wild Coffee
Psychotria nervosa

Avocado
Persea americana

Bald Cypress
Taxodium distichum

Black Olive
Bucida buceras

Bottlebrush
Callistemon rigidus

Crape Myrtle
Lagerstroemia indica

Geiger Tree
Cordia sebestena

Grapefruit
Citrus × paradisi

Gumbo Limbo
Bursera simaruba

Lignum Vitae
Guaiacum sanctum

Live Oak
Quercus virginiana

Lychee
Litchi chinensis

Mahogany
Swietenia mahagoni

Mango
Mangifera indica

Orange Tree
Citrus sinensis

Pigeon Plum
Coccoloba diversifolia

Red Maple
Acer rubrum

Redberry Stopper
Eugenia spp.

Royal Poinciana
Delonix regia

Satinleaf
Chrysophyllum oliviforme

Sea Grape
Coccoloba uvifera

Slash Pine
Pinus elliottii

Sweetbay
Magnolia virginiana

Sweet Gum
Liquidambar styraciflua

Tabebuia
Tabebuia caraiba

Tabebuia Ipe
Tabebuia impetiginosa

Tangerine
Citrus reticulata

Aglaonema
Aglaonema cultivars

Anthurium
Anthurium spp.

Banana
Musa × paradisica

Bromeliad
Aechmea fasciata

Costus
Costus hybrid

Dracaena
Dracaena fragrans

Elephant Ear
Alocasia spp.

Fern
Adiantum spp.

Ginger
Alpinia spp.

Ginger Lily
Hedychium coronarium

Heliconias
Heliconia spp.

Mussaenda
Mussaenda philippica

Peace Lily
Spathiphyllum spp.

Peperomia
Peperomia spp.

Philodendron
Philodendron spp.

Ti Plant
Cordyline terminalis

Traveler's Tree
Ravenala madagascariensis

Bougainvillea
Bougainvillea spp.

Calico Flower
Aristolochia elegans

Carolina Yellow Jasmine
Gelsemium sempervirens

Confederate Jasmine
Trachelospermum jasminoides

Coral Honeysuckle
Lonicera sempervirens

Coral Vine
Antigonon leptopus

Flame Vine
Pyrostegia venusta

Jade Vine
Stronglyodon macrobotrys

Pandorea
Pandorea jasminoides

Passion Vine
Passiflora spp.

Philodendron
Philodendron spp.

Queen's Wreath
Petrea volubilis

Trumpet Creeper
Campsis radicans

Wisteria
Wisteria sinensis

241

Roses

*W*HAT'S A GARDENER'S FAVORITE FLOWER? Most people would probably put the rose at or near the top of their list. It's also our national flower, and it should be planted proudly.

Many settlers heading into the state tucked away a rose to plant near their new homes. Those homes are often gone now, but amazingly, some Louis Philippe rose plantings—often called the Florida rose—still survive near a chimney or foundation.

One reason roses are so popular is that they have a lot to give. Most modern roses flower continually. Many have a pleasing fragrance, and you can choose almost any color from the rainbow except blue.

Roses grow year-round in Florida. That's why gardeners have to be particular about selecting their plants. It's important to get to know the varieties tested by rosarians living within the state. Most rose societies and your local Extension Service have lists of the good performers.

Some rose selections seem to wear out in the hot, humid summer seasons. It's important to know the rootstock as well as the variety. Until recently, most mail-order companies shipping to Florida did not pick rootstocks for local conditions, and the plants lasted only a year or two. A majority of the Florida gardeners prefer to purchase their roses locally to get the best-adapted plants.

Be sure to ask for a good Florida-performing variety grafted onto a vigorous rootstock. University of Florida evaluations have demonstrated that the *fortuniana* rootstock, also known as the Double

Chapter Nine

White Cherokee rose, produces the most vigorous and longest-lived plants for Florida landscapes. A 'Dr. Huey' rootstock is second best, giving a good flowering plant. Roses grafted on multiflora decline after a year or two of growth, making multiflora the least satisfactory rootstock.

Give roses your best sunny location. Make them the accent plants for the landscape where visitors can stop and enjoy them. This is one time when it really pays to give the soil extra attention. Make sure the site is well drained and enriched before planting.

The list of soil improvements rose growers add to planting sites is extensive. Peat moss, compost, perlite, vermiculite, and manure are among the basics needed to increase the soil's water-holding capacity and provide nutrients for growth. Many growers also add clay particles, alfalfa pellets, bone meal, fish meal, green sand, and similar components. Some even put several sheets of newspaper in the bottom of the hole to hold water in the upper soil layer a little longer.

Roses can be added to the landscape at any time of the year, but Florida plantings are best made at the beginning of the fall or spring months. These are the less stressful times of the year when the plants can root down quickly and produce lots of green growth while still opening flower buds.

Set the new rose in the ground at the same depth it grew in the container or a little higher. Few Florida roses are sold bareroot, but when available, these plants should be set at the original depth as noted along the trunks. Fill in around the roots, watering as you go to ensure good root contact with the soil. Most rose growers like to form a berm at the edge of each rootball to catch water and direct it down to the roots. Finish planting by adding a mulch. Any mulch

will do, including pine needles, bark, or coarse compost. Keep
the new plantings moist, and provide the first feedings in about 2
to 3 weeks.

Gardeners who want to cut lots of bouquets must keep the plantings on a good maintenance schedule. It's best to visit beds daily to
cut flowers for the home or to give to friends. At this time you can
also do minor grooming, removing declining twigs or pinching out
pests. Check the soil for water needs as well. When the surface starts
to feel dry to the touch, it's time to give the plants a $1/2$- to 1-in.
soaking. Well-rooted rose plantings in an improved soil can go 3 to 4
days or more between waterings. New plants need more frequent
irrigation. Microsprinkler or soaker hose irrigation systems keep the
water off the foliage to prevent disease.

Florida roses need a monthly feeding. Many gardeners use a 6-6-6
or similar fertilizer, but others have chosen a higher nitrogen product such as a 12-4-8. Some use liquids, and others use completely
natural products consisting of manure and animal by-products. The
only important guideline seems to be that you maintain a schedule
to keep the plant vigorous and in bloom.

By summer many Florida roses have grown quite tall. Some gardeners use this opportunity to harvest long-stem blooms. Others
allow the plant to grow high overhead with multiple flowering
shoots. In South Florida this is often a time for plants to get a light
trimming. In other areas of the state most gardeners wait until winter to give roses except climbers and miniatures a major pruning.
This involves removing $1/3$ to $1/2$ the height of the plant. Pruners
also trim out the twiggy growths and all diseased portions at this
time. Most hybrid teas and grandiflora and floribunda types are left
with 3 to 7 strong canes to continue growth.

Chapter Nine

Roses do have several pests that growers must contend with to have attractive, long-lived plants. One is the notorious black spot that causes dark, rounded areas, often with a yellow halo, to form on the foliage. It is mainly a disease that appears in the warm, rainy season, but it can appear at other times as well. It's controlled primarily by selecting plants with some resistance and using fungicide treatments. Another major pest is the spider mite that sucks juices from the foliage. Most infestations appear during the drier months between September and May. Controls can be as simple as washing the mites from the underside of the foliage with a strong stream of water. For more persistent mite problems, try applying a soap or oil spray or using one of the synthetic miticides.

Some other pests that may attack roses are thrips, beetles, caterpillars, powdery mildew, and stem cankers. Many can be hand picked or pruned from the plants, but others may need a spray. When applying pesticides, follow label instructions. Weeds can also be a problem in the beds. Most gardeners either pull out the unwanted greenery or spot treat with a nonselective herbicide labeled for use in rose or flower beds. After removing the weeds, renew the mulch layer to control new growths.

Climbing Rose

Rosa Hybrids

Height: 6 to 8 ft. tall
Zones: 8 through 11
Light Requirement:
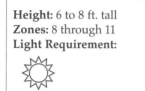

Almost every gardener would like to add a climbing rose to the landscape. It's a quick way to fill a wall, fence, or trellis. Many gardeners like to have a climbing rose to the side of the home or at the entrance to form an accent feature. And climbing roses have lots of limbs, which means there should be bouquets to cut at any time. Gardeners have to be choosy when picking the best climber for the landscape. Some older types are quite colorful but flower only once a year. Perhaps the very best climber for the Florida landscape is Don Juan, a hybrid introduced in 1958 with large, red, fragrant blossoms. Two more that get high ratings among rosarians are America, an orange-pink, and Sombreuil, a double white.

WHEN TO PLANT

Roses can be added to the Florida landscape at any time of the year. But possibly the best time to plant a climber is during the late winter through early spring months. During the cooler months, plantings can establish an extensive root system. They won't be affected by heat to be experienced later in the year. Fall is possibly the next best time for planting the climber.

WHERE TO PLANT

Select only a full-sun location for the climbing rose. Like any vining plant, it's going to reach for the sun. Choose only walls, fences, and trellises that receive 6 to 8 hours of sun per day. Also choose a site where each plant has plenty of room to grow a root system. Climbers can be grown in containers, but the size of the plant is often restricted by the available space. In the ground, roots can grow under sidewalks and other areas that might be bordered by concrete, but you do need some space to water and fertilize the planting.

HOW TO PLANT

It always pays to enrich the planting site before adding the rose bush. Sandy soils especially benefit from lots of organic matter including compost, peat moss, and manure. In Florida it's difficult to work too much into the ground. In damp sites make sure there is good drainage. If the soil is naturally wet, plant the rose bush in a mound of soil or a raised bed. At planting dig the hole wider but no deeper than the rootball. Position the bush so that it is at the same depth it was in the pot or the nursery, and add soil and water together to ensure good root-to-ground contact. Finish the planting by adding a berm to catch water and 2 to 3 in. of mulch.

ADVICE FOR CARE

Encourage the best growth with frequent feedings. Apply fertilizer once a month through the warmer months. Use the rates suggested on the label. During the cooler times of the year, feedings can be reduced to every 6 to 8 weeks. Roses also need lots of water to maintain good growth. Check the soil frequently, and when the surface feels dry to the touch, it's time to water. Most established rose plantings need a good watering every 3 to 4 days. Two pests that can kill a rose bush are black spot, a disease, and mites. When pests are present, use a control available from your local garden center.

ADDITIONAL INFORMATION

Climbing roses get special and limited pruning. There is no heavy trimming during late winter as with the bush-type roses. Allow the long canes to develop with many laterals to bear the roses. After 2 to 3 years of growth, thin out the weak shoots, and prune laterals back to the main stems, leaving just 2 to 3 buds. This encourages new shoots and more flowers from the older plants.

ADDITIONAL SPECIES, CULTIVARS, OR VARIETIES

Several old garden roses are good climbers for the Florida landscape. Most—including the species roses Yellow Lady Banks rose and Cherokee rose—flower only once a year during spring.

ADVICE FOR REGIONAL CARE

Rose care is similar throughout the state of Florida. Residents of North Florida may find more winter injury and need additional pruning after periods of cold. Residents of South Florida may not need to reduce winter feeding but stay on the once-a-month schedule.

Floribunda

Rosa Hybrids

<table>
<tr><td>

Height: to 4 ft.
Zones: 8 through 11
Light Requirement:

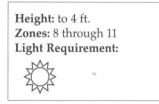

</td><td>

Floribunda roses range in size between the miniatures and the hybrid teas. They are mainly 3 to 4 ft. tall and grow equally wide. They are multipurpose roses, giving lots of small- to medium-sized flowers in a wide assortment of colors. Most

</td></tr>
</table>

flower buds are pointed to slightly rounded and have the hybrid tea look. Some favorites you have probably heard of include Sunflare, French Lace, Europeana, Angle Face, Hannah Gordon, First Edition, and Sunsprite. They are considered very hardy and generally pest resistant. This is a good rose for the smaller garden. Use the plants near the patio or along a walkway, or add them to containers. The flowers can be enjoyed in the garden or cut as bouquets for the home.

WHEN TO PLANT

Add the floribunda rose to the flower bed at any time of the year. Possibly the very best seasons for planting are spring and fall when there are less heat and moisture stress. Some of the best selections also appear at garden centers during the spring and fall months.

WHERE TO PLANT

Select a bright location with at least a half-day of sun. The more sun, the better, and a full-sun location is preferred. Plant the roses where they can be enjoyed in beds near walkways or entrances or off the patio. Container-grown plants can also be added to decks and balconies.

HOW TO PLANT

Prepare a planting site by adding compost, peat moss, and manure to the sandy Florida soils. Containers can be filled with any loose, well-drained potting soil. Some roses are available as bareroot plants, but most are produced in containers for transplanting. Set all roses in the soil at the same depth as they were growing in the field or container. Add water and soil together to fill in around the root-ball. After planting, form a berm of soil around the plant to catch water and direct it down through the roots. Also add a 2- to 3-in.

mulch layer of pine needles, bark, or coarse mulch. Some very
bushy plants may also need staking to prevent frequent wind from
whipping the plants during storms.

ADVICE FOR CARE

All roses need similar care. Keep the soil moist, and apply a fertilizer to in-ground plantings monthly and container gardens weekly.
Use a 12-4-8 or other similar rose fertilizer for in-ground plantings.
A liquid fertilizer can be used with container plantings. Floribunda
roses should receive a pruning during late winter, around January
or February. Cut the plants back 1/3 to 1/2. Also remove twiggy
side shoots, and keep the plants to 3 to 7 main stems.

ADDITIONAL INFORMATION

Common pests of roses include black spot, a disease, and mites that
can affect floribunda plantings. When you see pests, treat the bushes
with an appropriate pesticide. Throughout the growing season,
some grooming may also be needed to remove old flowers, injured
plant portions, and small twiggy growths.

ADDITIONAL SPECIES, CULTIVARS, OR VARIETIES

There are many good floribunda rose varieties. Some others you
may want to try include Playgirl, Ivory Fashion, Nana Mouskouri,
Raspberry Ruffles, and Showbiz. Check with your local rose society
for other good Florida performers. Not all rose varieties perform
well under Florida's growing conditions.

ADVICE FOR REGIONAL CARE

North and Central Florida growers may reduce the feedings to
every 6 to 8 weeks during the late fall and winter months. Also
North Florida plantings might suffer winter damage that needs
pruning before spring growth begins. South Florida growers usually
continue the monthly feeding program but may add an extra pruning during the late summer season.

Grandiflora Rose

Rosa Hybrids

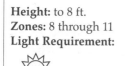

Height: to 8 ft.
Zones: 8 through 11
Light Requirement:

Gardeners who wanted a rose bush a little taller than a hybrid tea and with the full clusters of the floribunda roses got their wish in 1954 with the development of the first grandiflora hybrids. An all-time favorite, Queen Elizabeth was the first of the new group and is today still the standard for this classification. Most blossoms are pointed like the hybrid teas and open as side shoots at the end of the terminal stem. Many stems are long enough to be individually cut for use in bouquets. The plants grow to 8 ft. tall and 4 to 5 ft. wide. They are vigorous and have about the same amount of pest resistance as other modern roses. Since this is a relatively new rose classification, the number of species is rather limited but growing. Some favorites are Gold Medal, Tournament of Roses, Shreveport, Montezuma, and Love.

WHEN TO PLANT

Roses can be planted year-round as container-grown plants. Bareroot specimens sometimes marketed within the state are best planted during the dormant season of January and February. Even container-grown plants seem to get the best start when the temperatures are cooler and there is less need for water. Many gardeners choose to add the plants to the landscape during the fall and early spring months. This is also a time when garden centers have the best selection of plants.

WHERE TO PLANT

Give the rose collection a full-sun location. Enrich sandy soils with organic matter. Most growers add compost, peat moss, and manure to increase the water-holding capacity of the soil and supply some nutrients. Roses should be planted where you need a garden accent. They are best clustered in a bed near walkways at an entrance to the home or off the patio.

How to Plant

Bareroot plants should be set in the ground at the same depth they were growing in the field. Container plants should be set so that the top of the rootball is at or slightly above the soil level. Dig the hole wider but not deeper than the plant, and then add needed water and soil to fill in around the rootball. Complete the planting by constructing a berm under the plants to catch water and direct it down through the rootball. Add a 2- to 3-in. mulch layer. Most gardeners also add a stake or two to keep winds from dislodging the plants during storms.

Advice for Care

Grandiflora roses need good care to produce the expected growth. Feed the plants monthly with a 12-4-8 or similar rose fertilizer. Also keep the soil moist, watering when the surface feels dry to the touch. Since the plants are expected to grow tall and wide, a yearly pruning is definitely needed in January or February. At this time of the year the plants are cut back $1/3$ to $1/2$. Remove small twigs, and reduce the main canes to 3 to 7 in number.

Additional Information

Expect grandiflora roses to be affected by the common rose pests. Two in particular—black spot and mites—can cause major decline. Black spot is mainly a problem during the damp summer months, and mites affect the foliage during the dry times. Apply the appropriate pesticide as needed.

Additional Species, Cultivars, or Varieties

Since this is a relatively new group of roses, only a few varieties have been developed, but more are being added. A few additional varieties worth trying include Pink Parfait, Camelot, White Lightning, Aquarius, Prominent, and Lagerfeld.

Advice for Regional Care

North and Central Florida growers often reduce feedings during the winter months to every 6 to 8 weeks. In these cooler regions of the state some winter damage may occur and need removal from the plants by spring. Southern growers usually continue the monthly feeding program and do some extra pruning toward the end of summer.

Hybrid Tea Rose

Rosa hybrids

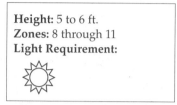

Height: 5 to 6 ft.
Zones: 8 through 11
Light Requirement:

Modern roses began in 1867 with the introduction of the first hybrid tea named La France. All roses prior to this date are considered old varieties, and those produced after this date are the new roses. Hybrid teas have just what the gardener wants: great color, stems of single blossoms, and a bushy plant. Many of the roses you like probably are members of this group, including Pristine, Double Delight, Granada, Uncle Joe, Peace, First Prize, and Cary Grant. The list goes on of mostly vigorous plants that are ideal for the home flower bed. Obtain a list of the best roses for Florida from a local rosarian.

WHEN TO PLANT

Whenever the soil is ready, you can add a hybrid tea rose to the garden or a container. Many are sold in bloom so that you can pick the best colors. Possibly the best time for planting is during spring or fall when the weather is cool. In these seasons most garden centers get a fresh supply of vigorous, easy-to-handle bushes. The only precaution when planting during hotter summer months is that extra care may be needed to make sure they do not lack water.

WHERE TO PLANT

Give hybrid teas a full-sun location in a well-drained garden site. It's best to plant a bed of roses where their needs can be met. Most gardeners also like to locate the plantings where they are the featured attraction. Visitors just naturally like to stop, look, and smell the roses.

HOW TO PLANT

Roses grow best in an enriched soil. Most gardeners add compost, peat moss, and manure to the planting site. Till the soil deeply, and then add the container-grown or bareroot plants. If planting in a container, use a potting soil mix for the growing medium. Position each new rose so that the top of the rootball is even with the soil. If planting bareroot plants, use the color change along the trunk as an indication of how deep to plant. While filling the planting hole, also add plenty of water to provide good root and soil contact. In poorly drained gardens plant the bushes in mounds or raised beds. Complete the plantings by adding a 2- to 3-in. mulch layer over the soil surface.

ADVICE FOR CARE

Roses need frequent feedings and lots of water to flourish. Feed the hybrid teas monthly with a rose fertilizer, following label rates. During cooler winter weather, the time between feedings may be extended to every 6 weeks. Keep the soil moist by watering when the surface of the soil starts to feel dry to the touch. Most established plants need a soaking every 3 or 4 days. Hybrid teas are quite vigorous and may grow 5 to 6 ft. tall. Every year during January or February, roses should be given a pruning to reduce the height by $1/3$ to $1/2$. This is also the time to remove weak stems and limit the bushes to no more than 7 strong stems. Throughout the growing season, gardeners should be constantly giving the plants a light grooming to remove weak stems and direct growth.

ADDITIONAL INFORMATION

Just about all hybrid tea roses are susceptible to black spot, a disease. Black spot attacks mainly during hot, rainy weather but could be present at any time. When severe, spray weekly with a fungicide. Mites are a major problem mainly during dry weather. Light infestations can be washed off the foliage, but if infestations are heavy, apply a miticide. Other pests that may need control include thrips, powdery mildew, aphids, caterpillars, and stem cankers.

ADDITIONAL SPECIES, CULTIVARS, OR VARIETIES

Hybrid teas have been extremely popular garden roses. Many new varieties are produced every year. A few more good performers for Florida include Color Magic, Paradise, Chrysler Imperial, Tropicana, Fragrant Cloud, Swarthmore, and Mister Lincoln.

ADVICE FOR REGIONAL CARE

Rose care is very similar throughout the state. North Florida growers may have to prune out some cold damage, and South Florida growers may add an extra pruning in August. Also, South Florida growers may not need to reduce the feedings during the winter months.

Miniature Rose

Rosa Hybrids

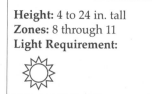

Height: 4 to 24 in. tall
Zones: 8 through 11
Light Requirement:

If you are looking for a rose to grow in a container for the porch, patio, or windowsill, a miniature would make a good selection. Miniatures are also used to fill flower beds as a ground-cover and line walkways. Some miniatures are just inches tall, such as the variety Si with tiny white blossoms. Others, such as Rise 'N' Shine, grow several feet in height. Miniatures all have something in common: blossoms are much smaller than roses in other categories. Miniatures include the rose types of climbers, ramblers, and hybrid tea look-alikes. If you are looking for a good starter collection, you might try Starina, Party Girl, Perrine, Jean Keanneally, Olympic Gold, Debut, Herbie, Red Beauty, and Magic Carrousel.

WHEN TO PLANT

Just about any time you are ready is a good time to add one or more miniature roses to the collection. Very few are sold bareroot. In most instances you are bringing an already well-established plant home to continue growth. Plants given a new container rarely suffer trans-plant shock. Even when added to a flower bed, the plants appear to take root quickly. Also with the year-round interest in miniatures, you are likely to find a good selection at the garden center during all seasons. Many are sold in gift wrap for the holidays.

WHERE TO PLANT

As with all roses the sunny location is best even when plants are grown in the home or on the patio. Find an area with 6 to 8 hours of full sun for the best growth. For a window location, make sure there is good air circulation to reduce the heat buildup and help prevent pests. The very smallest of miniature roses are best left in containers. Leave the taller spreading types for the garden. Give them a site in front of taller plants so that the roses will be in full view. Also plant clusters of miniatures for the best display of blossoms.

How to Plant

Add roses to a container by selecting a pot that's 1 or 2 in. larger than the original container. Giving the plants too large a container can lead to overwatering and root rot. Sometime several plants are added to a large container for a better display of color. In-ground plants should be added to a prepared planting site. As with all rose plantings, sandy soils should be improved with compost, peat moss, and manure. Position the plants at the original growing depth, and add water and soil together to fill in around the root system. With in-ground plantings add a berm to catch water and direct it down through the root system. A 2- to 3-in. mulch of pine needles, bark, or coarse compost can also be added.

Advice for Care

Give miniature roses adequate water to keep the soil moist. Test container gardens daily, and when the surface of the soil starts to dry, it's time to give them a good soaking. In-ground plants can normally go several days between waterings. All plantings need regular feedings. Use a liquid or slow-release fertilizer with container plantings as instructed on the label. In-ground plantings can be fed monthly with a 12-4-8 or similar fertilizer. When the plants become overgrown, most are just given a shearing. Thinning may also be needed to remove old, nonproductive twigs.

Additional Information

Mites seem to be the worst pest of miniature roses. Check in-ground plantings frequently during the drier months. Plants kept in protected locations may have mite problems at any time. Where needed, apply a miticide. Black spot appears to be a less frequent problem but may affect the plants during the rainy season.

Additional Species, Cultivars, or Varieties

Miniature roses are popular among rose growers. New varieties are being released yearly. Most appear to do well throughout the state. Some more to look for include Over the Rainbow, Starglo, Rosmarin, White Angel, Pacesetter, and Kathy.

Advice for Regional Care

Growers in North Florida may reduce feedings during the late fall and winter months. In-ground plantings may suffer some winter damage and need extra pruning.

Old Garden Rose

Rosa Hybrids

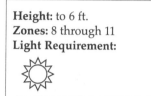

Height: to 6 ft.
Zones: 8 through 11
Light Requirement:

All roses planted prior to 1867 are considered old garden roses. Some are species roses, but many are hybrids within the original Bourbon, China, Noisette, Polyantha, and Tea groups. These were the roses distributed throughout Europe and later taken to the homesteads of settlers in the New World. Fragrance missing in many modern hybrids is often found in the old rose varieties. Some growers feel they also have extra vigor plus pest resistance, having survived for centuries without the benefit of pesticides. Within this very diverse category are bush types growing to 6 ft. tall, climbers, and miniature forms. The colors vary, but many are good pinks including bush types Paul Neyron, Old Blush, Souvenir De La Malmaison, and Rose De Rescht. Some other old roses you might like to add to the Florida garden include the Chestnut rose, Lady Banks rose, Cherokee rose, Louis Philippe, and Green rose.

WHEN TO PLANT

All old garden roses can be added to the landscape year-round. Possibly the very best times to do the planting are during spring and fall. At these times of the year the plant can establish a good root system while the weather is cool and with less need for extra watering.

WHERE TO PLANT

All roses flourish in full-sun locations. Many tolerate a very minimum of a half day of sun with bright light for the rest of the day. Create beds of roses for the best displays near walkways, patios, or the entrance to the home. Since there are many different plant sizes and shapes within this group, pay special attention to spacing and needs for a fence or trellis.

HOW TO PLANT

Give roses your very best soil. Work in lots of organic matter including compost, peat moss, and manure. Roses can be added to the garden as bareroot plants, but most Florida varieties come in pots with well-established root systems. Set the plants in the ground at the same height they were growing in the container. Add soil, and water to fill in around the root system. After the plant is in the ground, construct a berm to hold water and direct it down through the rootball. Also add a 2- to 3-in. mulch layer of pine needles, bark, or coarse compost.

ADVICE FOR CARE

Old garden roses need normal care. Keep the soil moist, and feed monthly with a 12-4-8 or similar rose fertilizer. Bush types should be pruned back during the late winter months of January and February. Most are cut back 1/3 to 1/2. Some plants are quite twiggy and benefit from some thinning at this time. Climbing types are left to grow tall and fill a fence or trellis. Every 2 to 3 years they should be given a renewal pruning.

ADDITIONAL INFORMATION

Many older varieties show resistance to common rose pests. Gardeners should still stay alert to black spot and mites—the two worst pests of roses. Where needed, apply an appropriate pesticide.

ADDITIONAL SPECIES, CULTIVARS, OR VARIETIES

Many varieties of old garden roses are now available for home planting. A few were developed after the 1867 old rose date but are still considered antiques by collectors. Not all, however, flower well in local landscapes. Check with area rose societies to determine the best selections for the garden. The following are a few more old garden roses that perform well in local landscapes: Archduke Charles, Pompon de Paris, Baronne Prevost, Pierre Notting, Champney's Pink Cluster, Cecile Brunner, The Fairy, Duchesse de Brabant, and Sombreuil.

ADVICE FOR REGIONAL CARE

Roses grow well throughout the state. North Florida growers should reduce feedings during late fall through winter to every 6 to 8 weeks. In the North some winter injury may occur that needs additional trimming.

CHAPTER TEN

*F*OR LO, THESE MANY YEARS, I HAVE BEEN TOLD BY HORTICULTURISTS TO THINK OF SHRUBS AS THE WALLS OF THE GARDEN. And so I do, and so they are. They are the space shapers of the garden, the room dividers, the plants that we see at eye level.

Shrubs most often make up the hedges that set off property lines, and they are also used as accents for entryways. These are among the most common reasons for growing them. There are other aesthetic reasons, practical reasons, and of course, the just plain "I want one" reasons.

For small spaces, shrubs are often more convenient than trees. A large shrub (which also may be a small tree) won't have to be brutally pruned should it outgrow its spot; it won't lift the pavers with massive roots; it won't shade out the other plants in the garden.

Shrubs will bring color, and very often alluring fragrance, to an area, be it townhouse garden or suburban yard. Some bring with them fruit, which can be appealing to you or to birds. Some attract butterflies and moths. Carefully selected shrubs will bring fall color (crape myrtles) or winter flowers (*Clerodendron quadriculare*). Others, such as azaleas and rhododendrons, are the very essence of early spring.

An often overlooked function of shrubs is simply to provide greenery. Once you have lived in Florida a few years and travel to the Southwest or Midwest or anywhere in the temperate climate in

Chapter Ten

winter, you understand how vital that green is to our landscape. Snailseed, viburnum, ligustrum, and privet are wonderful plants to use for this purpose.

Using native shrubs can go a long way toward helping not only resident birds, such as the cardinals that nest in shrubs, but also migrants in need of a stopover shelter and food. Provisioning the landscape for wildlife is a vital part of contemporary gardening because so much of the natural area of this country has been covered with cities and farms.

Shrubs also play a key role in butterfly gardening; many of the nectar-bearing flowers that attract butterflies are shrub-borne. One South Florida shrub that comes to mind is *Cordia globosa*. It produces round heads of tiny white flowers and all kinds of skippers, and little butterflies can be found there throughout the day. In Central and North Florida, buddleia is the butterfly bush par excellence.

While we may give special deference to roses, they are in fact shrubs (as well as climbing plants). The returning popularity of old roses is welcome in Florida, where finicky hybrid teas have a hard time with black spot, requiring too many applications of chemicals. Old roses are hardier, less disease prone, and some, such as chinas, teas, and noisettes, flower off and on all year. And many of them can be mixed right in with other shrubs in a border planting.

As our lives have become more hectic and time more precious, there is a greater need to reduce household chores, including those in the garden. One way to do so is to landscape informally, so that shrubs are not clipped and pruned but are allowed to billow and assume their natural shapes. That is not to say pruning is never required, but it will be needed less often if plants can assume hazy or flowing shapes rather than rigid and boxed ones. For such shrubs as gardenia and ixoras, hibiscus and orange jasmine, the flowers are produced on new growth, so regular pruning means fewer flowers.

In recent years, new shrubs have entered our gardening and landscaping vocabulary. *Tibouchina*, for instance, is now widely available. It is popularly called glory bush for its purple flowers. *Mussaenda* is another tropical shrub finding wide use in protected southern areas. Croton is making a comeback; the Thomas Edison / Henry Ford complex in Fort Myers has an abundance of them. In the 1990s new ways to feature croton include mixed borders and grouping several together rather than forming sun-bleached, leggy hedges.

Shrubs are the workhorses of the garden. We can assign them many roles, and they can take them on. But like workhorses, they need a good diet. Fertilize shrubs in spring, summer, and fall (March, June/July, October). Most will need supplemental irrigation in the dry season, at least once a week, possibly less often if mulch has been applied about 3 or 4 in. deep (as with trees, keep mulch away from the trunks of shrubs to avoid disease).

Prune the flowering shrubs after they flower, and the fast-growing big ones in the spring. Watch for aphids, which love new and succulent growth, and use insecticidal soap or 2 tablespoons of detergent in a gallon of water. Shrubs will perform well in return.

Shrubs will bring color, and very often alluring fragrance, to an area . . .

Allamanda

Allamanda cathartica

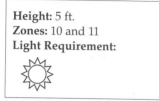

Height: 5 ft.
Zones: 10 and 11
Light Requirement:

Allamanda is one of the plants that cheerily announce the warm season. When its buds begin to form, you know it's spring. This shrub is a faithful and prodigious bloomer through the warm months, bare of flowers only from December to March. While it does not have tendrils with which to cling, it sprawls and reaches with gusto and can be woven over chain link or a wooden trellis or, as I have found, around a mailbox post. Its wholehearted attention to its job, however, means the postman/postwoman sometimes has to look hard to be able to deliver the goods. Originally from Brazil, allamanda is one of the plants that has been carted all over the tropics. With oleander and frangipani, it is a member of the Apocynaceae family, and has this family's characteristic white milky sap. In the allamanda's veins, this sap is toxic, so don't toss any leaves into your salad. The sap has been used in small amounts as a cathartic or purgative—hence the species name. In Florida, this shrub's pollinator is absent, so the plants never set fruit, a bonus for gardeners who do not like dealing with such things. While one of the main uses of vines is to screen or conceal, remember that the flowers on this vine are especially showy, and yellow is a color that draws the eye. Your visitors will see this plant on the toolshed before they notice the more subdued, one-of-a-kind anthurium next to it, however exquisite the other plant may be. Cold weather will knock off some leaves, but the allamanda is a durable plant in almost all conditions. The hottest withering weather may make it wilt.

When to Plant
Plant any time except during the winter.

Where to Plant
Plant in full sun next to a structure that needs screening but can offer support.

How to Plant

Enrich the soil for this vine, mixing compost or peat moss or good potting soil into the planting hole. Water in the backfill and mulch after planting. Keep the root zone moist while the plant becomes established.

Advice for Care

Allamanda grows vigorously in a fairly rich soil, and it loves fertilizer. Its leaves will become chlorotic, or yellow between the veins, when it is hungry. A balanced fertilizer or a 7-3-7 with micronutrients, applied in the spring and fall, can keep the vigor going. Or use a slow-release fertilizer, such as 14-14-14, twice a year. Allamandas are fairly drought tolerant, but they need weekly watering in the dry season. Cut back hard in early spring to remove crossed and woody stems that have become intertwined and tangled. If using this plant as a shrub, you will have to prune it frequently.

Additional Information

If you live in Central Florida, wait to prune until warm weather returns, or unexpected cold may damage or kill the plant.

Additional Species, Cultivars, or Varieties

A purple-flowering plant, *A. violacea*, and a pink species, *A. splendens*, are available. *Allamanda nerifolia* is a shrub.

Advice for Regional Care

In colder parts of the state, grow this plant in a large pot with a trellis so it can be brought inside during cold weather.

American Beautybush

Callicarpa americana

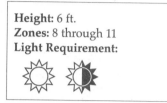

Height: 6 ft.
Zones: 8 through 11
Light Requirement:

American beautybush, also called beautyberry, is a native plant of the southeastern United States. It grows where other shrubs do rather poorly, often in poor soils, and it requires little care. Its pinkish flowers growing along the stems during the spring months can be seen under close inspection. But the real beauty of this shrub is evident during the fall and winter months when the fruits turn a maroon to purplish color in large clusters along the stems. This great accent shrub is possibly best used in naturalistic areas and along walkways. It makes a good space divider and view barrier. Plants can be used in a more formal landscape if kept in bounds and given seasonal pruning. The beautybush can be 6 ft. wide. It remains semievergreen during the winter months. Consider this plant for minimal maintenance landscapes and landscapes getting just natural rainfall. It's frequently planted in clusters of 3 or more to create a major display of fall color.

WHEN TO PLANT

Plants of the American beautybush are best transplanted from one area of the landscape to another between December and February except in South Florida, when it is planted in spring or summer. Most plants sold at garden centers and native plant nurseries are in containers and can be added to the landscape at any time of the year.

WHERE TO PLANT

American beautybush plantings grow well in moist to dry soil locations. A well-drained soil is best. Plantings grow in Florida sand, but where possible, improve the planting site with organic matter before planting to produce the best-looking plants. Enrich a large area with compost or peat moss and manure.

HOW TO PLANT

Dig a hole that's much wider than the rootball but not deeper. Position the American beautybush at the same depth it was growing in the container or original planting site. It may be set a little higher above the soil level, especially in poorly drained locations. Add soil around the rootball with adequate water to make good soil-to-root contact. After planting, form a berm at the edge of the rootball so that water moves down through the root system and then out into the surrounding soil. Also add a 2- to 3-in. mulch layer. No pruning is needed at planting time.

ADVICE FOR CARE

Once established, most shrubs grow well with minimal care. The American beautybush is very drought tolerant and, after the roots of new plants have grown into the surrounding soil, seldom needs special watering. It can also survive with nutrients from mulches and what other trees and shrubs in the area provide. If additional growth is desired, feed once in March, May, and August. Use a 6-6-6, 16-4-8, or similar analysis fertilizer at label rates.

ADDITIONAL INFORMATION

All shrubs need periodic pruning to keep the plantings in bounds and to remove old and diseased portions. The American beautybush grows quite lanky and should be pruned during late winter before new growth begins. Remove older stems, and cut the plantings back to a few feet below the desired height. Some pests that may affect the American beautybush include caterpillars and grasshoppers, but they are seldom a major problem. Many can be hand picked from the plantings, or treat them with a pesticide recommended by the University of Florida, following label instructions.

ADDITIONAL SPECIES, CULTIVARS, OR VARIETIES

Plants of American beautybush that produce white berries are available from some nurseries.

ADVICE FOR REGIONAL CARE

The American beautybush grows well throughout the state with similar care. In South Florida it blooms year-round.

Azalea

Rhododendron spp.

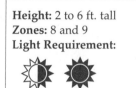

Height: 2 to 6 ft. tall
Zones: 8 and 9
Light Requirement:

Nothing heralds spring's arrival better than azalea plantings. Most gardeners have heard of some old-time favorites such as Duc de Rohan, Formosa, George Lindley Taber, and Southern Charm. Opening bright-pink, red, white, and almost purple blossoms, these are major accent plants for landscapes. Admittedly, sometimes azaleas are used to the point of being overplanted, but who could ask for a more attractive landscape? Azaleas have been a Florida favorite for only about 75 years. Most of the common colorful types are introductions from Japan and Belgium, but recent hybrids have been developed by United States breeders. The more common types for Florida include the Southern Indian, Krume, Satsuki, Rutherford, and Pericat hybrids. The best displays of azaleas are created in large beds where a major flower show greets visitors. Most plantings bloom for 3 to 4 weeks, then fade into the background as a space divider or transition plant. A few selections flicker with blooms throughout the year. Lower-growing azaleas are also used as groundcovers and small hedges along walkways.

WHEN TO PLANT

Azaleas to be transplanted from one area of the landscape to another are best moved between December and February to give the roots time to readjust to the new soil before warmer weather. Most plants sold at garden centers are in containers and can be added to the landscape at any time of the year.

WHERE TO PLANT

Azalea plants prefer a filtered-sun location. They grow good foliage in the shade but usually give poor flower displays. Some selections can adapt to sun, but they lack vibrant green color and suffer during the hotter months. A well-drained soil is best. Where possible, improve the planting site with organic matter before planting. Enrich the bed with compost or peat moss and manure.

HOW TO PLANT

Dig a hole that's much wider than the rootball but not deeper. Position the azalea plant at the same depth as it was growing in the container or original planting site. It may be set a little higher above the soil level, especially in a poorly drained location. Add soil around the rootball with adequate water to make good soil-to-root contact. After planting, form a berm at the edge of the rootball so that water moves down through the root system and then out into the surrounding soil. Add a 2- to 3-in. mulch layer. Pruning is usually not needed at planting time.

ADVICE FOR CARE

Once established, most shrubs grow well with minimal care, but it may be 2 years before azaleas grow a substantial root system. The best plantings have regular feedings and adequate water. Azaleas should be fed once in March, May, and September. Use a 6-6-6, 16-4-8, or similar analysis fertilizer at label rates. Azaleas need frequent watering, especially during periods of drought.

ADDITIONAL INFORMATION

Part of achieving success with azaleas is making sure the plantings have an acid soil. Have the soil tested, and adjust the pH as needed. All shrubs need periodic pruning to keep the plantings in bounds and to remove old and diseased portions. Azaleas need rejuvenation pruning approximately every 3 to 5 years. Pruning to keep the plants in bounds may be needed yearly. Some pests that affect azaleas are caterpillars, lace bugs, and mites. Many can be hand picked from the plantings, or treat them with a pesticide recommended by the University of Florida, following label instructions.

ADDITIONAL SPECIES, CULTIVARS, OR VARIETIES

In addition to the introduced hybrids, Florida is home to 4 native azaleas. The species *Rhododendron austrinum*, *Rhododendron calendulaceum*, and *Rhododendron canescens* are deciduous, and *Rhododendron chapmannii* is an evergreen type. These are medium to large shrubs found mainly in the northern portion of the state.

ADVICE FOR REGIONAL CARE

Native azaleas are limited to the colder areas of the state. They are recommended for North Florida, but some have been planted in the central regions. Most hybrids are limited to North and Central Florida. Azaleas can be grown in partial shade and acid conditions in South Florida; a cultivar called 'Sweet Forgiveness' does well in South Florida.

Butterfly Bush

Buddleia officinalis

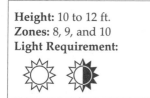

Height: 10 to 12 ft.
Zones: 8, 9, and 10
Light Requirement:

Everyone likes to invite butterflies into the landscape, and one way to put out the welcome mat is to display a colorful plant like the butterfly bush. The species *Buddleia officinalis* grows well in the warmer parts of Florida and opens lilac-colored blossoms during the winter season. Hybrids of *Buddleia davidii* are marketed in the North and Central portions of the state; they have a much broader color range and include reds, pinks, purples, and whites. All butterfly plants can be used individually or clustered in groups of 3 to 5 for a massive effect. Butterfly bushes can be used as hedges and as a backdrop for other flower plantings. Consider forming the outermost edge of the butterfly garden with the shrubs, then add other insect-attracting plants inside.

When to Plant

Plants of butterfly bush are best transplanted from one area of the landscape to another between December and February. Most plants sold at garden centers are in containers and can be added to the landscape at any time of the year.

Where to Plant

Plants of the butterfly bush prefer a full-sun to lightly shaded location. A well-drained soil is best. Where possible, improve the planting site with organic matter before planting. Enrich a large area with compost or peat moss and manure.

How to Plant

Dig a hole that's much wider than the rootball but not deeper. Position the butterfly bush at the same depth it was growing in the container or original planting site. It may be set a little higher above the soil level, especially in a poorly drained location. Add soil around the rootball with adequate water to make good soil-to-root contact. After planting, form a berm at the edge of the rootball so

that water moves down through the root system and then out into the surrounding soil. Add a 2- to 3-in. mulch layer. No pruning is usually needed at planting time.

ADVICE FOR CARE

Once established, most shrubs grow well with minimal care. Feed butterfly bushes once in March, May, and September. Use a 6-6-6, 16-4-8, or similar analysis fertilizer at label rates. Water butterfly bush plantings heavily during August, September and October. Once the plants are allowed to dry out they may collapse and never recover.

ADDITIONAL INFORMATION

All shrubs need periodic pruning to keep the plantings in bounds and to remove old and diseased portions. All butterfly bush plantings can suffer freeze damage and should be pruned hard during late winter or early spring. Many just naturally die back during the winter, much like a perennial. This may be beneficial; when the old growths are removed, the plants send up new flowering shoots for the growing season. Some pests that may affect the butterfly bush include caterpillars and grasshoppers, but they are usually ignored to keep from harming the desirable visiting insects. If infestation is severe, many pests can be hand picked from the plantings.

ADDITIONAL SPECIES, CULTIVARS, OR VARIETIES

Several additional species of butterfly shrubs are cultivated in Florida. One that may be found at garden centers is *Buddleia asiatica* with white fragrant flowers for the winter and spring months. It's suitable for Central Florida. Other good selections include: 'Purple Knight' which grows 6 to 8 ft. tall; and a petite series with plants that grow to 3 ft. tall.

ADVICE FOR REGIONAL CARE

Winter freezes can cause major damage to the more cold-sensitive species. Some may need pruning back to the ground to remove the dead wood, but new growth normally restarts from the base. Spring and early summer are ideal for planting in South Florida.

Chenille Plant

Acalypha hispida

Height: 8 to 10 ft.
Zones: 10B and 11
Light Requirement:

Chenille plant brings an unusual look to the garden—therefore, it is one of those plants that should be used with care. The long strands of flowers, which occur off and on throughout the warm months, have given the plant a secondary name: Red Hot Cat's Tail. The species name, *hispida*, means bristly. Chenille plant, which originally came from the Indonesian area, is related to poinsettia in the spurge family (Euphorbiaceae). This is a huge family with roughly 300 genera and more than 5000 species. White latex sap is one family characteristic, and the family provides us with sources of rubber (*Hevea brasiliensis*), castor oil (*Ricinus communis*), and tapioca (*Manihot esculenta*). With a plant as showy as chenille, positioning it in the landscape may mean allowing it to be a focal point, placing it against an all-green border of shrubs or clustering 3 or 5 together to be "comrades in charm."

WHEN TO PLANT

Plant in spring or just at the beginning of the rainy season (late May to early June) to take advantage of the rains that will keep the root system moist. This plant will become established readily.

WHERE TO PLANT

Plant in full sun to get the best flower production. The chenille plant likes a rich, well-draining soil.

HOW TO PLANT

Add compost, peat moss, or well-aged manure or potting soil to the planting hole, which should be just as deep as the rootball and 2 to 3 times as wide. Slip the container from the rootball, position the shrub in the planting hole, water in the backfill, and cover with mulch to a depth of 3 or 4 in. (To avoid disease, keep the mulch away from the stem of the plant.)

ADVICE FOR CARE

Though not particularly drought tolerant, and not salt tolerant at all, chenille plant nonetheless grows fast and robust with normal care. Fertilize 2 or 3 times a year and don't let the shrub go for weeks on end without water. Water a couple of times a week in summer if rain is not adequate for growth, and once a week in winter. A 6-6-6 fertilizer is fine; use a 7-3-7 in alkaline soils. Prune this shrub after it flowers to keep it in bounds. Attacking insects will be the usual pests that hit shrubs in Florida: aphids on new growth, scale, and mealy bugs. Insecticidal soap can work against aphids and mealy bugs (or you may decide to let ladybugs prey on the aphids, in which case you should expect a buildup of the aphid population before ladybugs are attracted to the plant). Use malathion against scale.

ADDITIONAL INFORMATION

It is the female flowers that are conspicuous on the spike, so the spikes are called pistillate (a pistil is the collective name for the female parts of the flower: the stigma, style, and ovary).

ADDITIONAL SPECIES, CULTIVARS, OR VARIETIES

A. hispida 'Alba' is a variety with white spikes. *Acalypha wilkesiana* is called copper-leaf; it is a species closely related to *A. hispida* and has similar toothed leaves, though they are mottled in red, green, copper, and yellow. *A. wilkesiana* 'Godseffiana' has green leaves bordered in cream or yellow.

ADVICE FOR REGIONAL CARE

A cold-tender plant, chenille will be damaged in Central and North Florida unless protected. Place it in a southeastern location or use a container and cut it back quite hard to keep it small.

Cocculus

Cocculus laurifolius

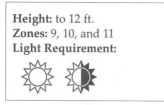

Height: to 12 ft.
Zones: 9, 10, and 11
Light Requirement:

The bright-green color and very shiny appearance of the cocculus leaves appeal to most gardeners. The stems are arching and fairly open in habit, which can be thickened with timely pruning. The plant may be grown just because it's a curiosity. You see, it has another interesting name—the snail seed. The seed resembles a coiled snail shell. It's the most interesting end of the flowering process since the yellow blooms are insignificant. Cocculus make great plants for hedges, shrubby borders, or specimens. Many gardeners use the plants because they are tolerant of most soil conditions and take minimal care. The foliage can be added to arrangements and used to make wreaths, although the leaves are poisonous.

WHEN TO PLANT

Plants of cocculus are best transplanted from one area to another between December and February. Most plants sold at garden centers are in containers and can be added to the landscape at any time of the year; spring or early summer are best in South Florida.

WHERE TO PLANT

Cocculus plants prefer a sunny to partially shaded location. The plants grow in some of Florida's poorer soils. A well-drained soil is best. Where possible, improve the planting site with organic matter before planting. Enrich a large area with compost or peat moss and manure.

HOW TO PLANT

Dig a hole that's much wider than the rootball but not deeper. Position the cocculus plant at the same depth it was growing in the container or original planting site. It may be set a little higher above the soil level, especially in a poorly drained location. Add soil around the rootball with adequate water to make good soil-to-root contact. After planting, form a berm at the edge of the rootball so

that water moves down through the root system and then out into the surrounding soil. Add a 2- to 3-in. mulch layer. No pruning is usually needed at planting time.

ADVICE FOR CARE

Once established, most shrubs grow well with minimal care. Feed cocculus once in March, May, and September. Use a 6-6-6, 16-4-8, or similar analysis fertilizer at label rates. Cocculus plantings are relatively drought tolerant. Most plantings receive adequate moisture from rainfall. When gardeners want to encourage growth and especially during periods of drought, water weekly.

ADDITIONAL INFORMATION

All shrubs need periodic pruning to keep the plantings in bounds and to remove old and diseased portions. Cocculus plants need pruning to keep them compact and full of foliage. One pest that may affect cocculus is scale. Where needed, apply a pesticide recommended by the University of Florida, following label instructions.

ADDITIONAL SPECIES, CULTIVARS, OR VARIETIES

The Carolina snail seed, *Cocculus carolinus,* is native to North Florida. It has a vining growth habit with oval leaves and produces red fruits.

ADVICE FOR REGIONAL CARE

Cocculus suffers cold damage in North Florida in most years and in Central Florida during severe winters. Affected plantings need a late-winter pruning to remove the damaged portions and reshape the plants.

Cocoplum

Chrysobalanus icaco

Height: 3 to 20 ft.
Zones: 9 through 11
Light Requirement:

A medium to large evergreen shrub, cocoplum has an upright or spreading shape and round leaves. Two forms occur: red-tipped and green-tipped. A useful native plant, cocoplum has been popular in South Florida landscaping many years longer than most natives because it is so adaptable and pretty. The round leaves march alternately along the twigs and point skyward. The shrub has a more or less symmetrical shape, and it can become quite full and large inland—indeed, the variety *pellocarpus* forms tree islands in the sloughs of the Everglades and can be found around alligator holes, screening the interior. Along the sand dunes of Hobe Sound, they are much smaller. The coastal form is variety *icaco*. In the nursery business, this sprawling, low cocoplum has the name "variety horizontalis." Along with pigeon plum, gumbo limbo, satinleaf, and mastic, the cocoplum fruit is eaten by birds and wildlife. Throughout the Caribbean, it is eaten by humans, too, and made into jelly. Richard Workman, in *Growing Native*, says the honey from cocoplum flowers is dark and rich. In landscapes, cocoplums make sturdy, dense hedges, both clipped and informal. They take sun or light shade. When creating a native garden or wildlife habitat, cocoplum is a good addition. If you have a low area, a yard that slopes to a lake, or a canal front, you can group cocoplum (var. *pellocarpus*) with dahoon holly, wax myrtle, sweet bay magnolia, and elderberry, and the birds as well as other creatures will forever be grateful.

WHEN TO PLANT

Plant at the beginning of the rainy season, late May / early June, or from March to midsummer if consistent irrigation is practical early on.

WHERE TO PLANT

Use these plants in any number of situations, from background shrubs and screening to clipped hedges.

How to Plant

Dig a hole twice as wide but just as deep as the rootball. If roots in the container are circling, then make several 1/4-in. cuts in the rootball with a sharp knife to promote new, outward root growth. Add compost or peat moss to make up 1/3 of the backfill to enrich the planting hole. Water in backfill to eliminate air pockets. Mulch to a depth of 3 or 4 in., making sure the mulch is several inches away from the trunk of the shrub to prevent fungus.

Advice for Care

Cocoplum benefits from 6-6-6 or 7-3-7 fertilizer twice a year to keep growing vigorously.

Additional Information

The genus name *Chrysobalanus* comes from two words: *chryso*, meaning "gold," and *balanos*, or "acorn." Some species have golden fruit. Those in Florida have pink or white or dark red-purple fruit . . . but as landscape plants, they are worth their weight in gold.

Additional Species, Cultivars, and Varieties

Make use of the *Chrysobalanus icaco* variety and for a low growing form use *Chrysobalanus icaco var. horizontalis*.

Advice for Regional Care

This shrub grows through Central Florida but not into North Florida.

Crape Myrtle

Laegerstromia indica

Height: to more than 20 ft.
Zones: 7 to 10B
Light Requirement:

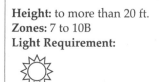

Reliable bloomers that put on a nice show, crape myrtles are from Japan, Korea, and China. Recent breeding efforts in this country have produced many wonderful colors and disease-resistant varieties. The flowers are outstanding in late summer and fall, but come winter, the leaves drop. If bare twigs are not something you can ignore, then plan ahead and mix with other shrubs in the background. Otherwise, you can give it some prominence. A neighbor has a lavender crape myrtle between two small yellow-flowering trees, and when they are in bloom, the combination is stunning. In winter the bare myrtles become nearly invisible against a ficus hedge containing a strategically placed schizopetalum hibiscus with red flowers. Such visual tricks are worth the effort. *Laegerstromia indica* arrived in the United States by way of England in the late 1700s. The shrubs are known as the lilacs of the South. The leaves on the crape myrtle turn yellow and then orange-red before falling in midwinter, and the dried seeds stay on the twig ends, gradually splitting open and falling. After a few years, the bark peels and becomes quite attractive. The plants can sucker at the base and become multistemmed in spite of your best efforts. In deep shade, these are dismal failures. In sun, they are fine performers.

WHEN TO PLANT

Plant at the beginning of the rainy season, late May / early June, or from March to midsummer if consistent irrigation is practical early on.

WHERE TO PLANT

Use in a mixed, informal planting or as specimen plant. Whites tend to get lost in the din; reds, pinks, and lavenders are better noticed. Crape myrtles are drought tolerant and do well in many kinds of soils as long as they don't stand in water.

HOW TO PLANT

Dig a hole just as deep but 1 ft. wider than the rootball (2 to 3 times as wide in rocky ground). If roots in the container are circling, then make several 1/4-in. cuts in the rootball with a sharp knife to promote new, outward root growth. Water in backfill to eliminate air pockets. Build a saucerlike basin of soil around the edge of the planting area to retain water. Mulch to a depth of 3 or 4 in., making sure the mulch is several inches away from the trunk of the shrub to prevent fungus.

ADVICE FOR CARE

Prune in late winter before the new growth begins, as flowering occurs on new branch ends. If too many twigs grow out, thin to shape. Fertilize March, July, and November (make this a low-nitrogen fertilizer, such as 4-6-8). Please do not remove stems larger than pencil-size in diameter. The "dignity " of the plant's shape will remain and the plant will bloom more profusely in a habit more appealing to the eye if these stems are left in place.

ADDITIONAL INFORMATION

The plant was thought to have originated in India, hence its specific name *indica*. George Washington grew crape myrtles in Mount Vernon in the 1790s.

ADDITIONAL SPECIES, CULTIVARS, OR VARIETIES

Three cultivars of *L. indica* and a wild Japanese parent discovered in 1966 (*L. fauriei*) are mildew resistant. Though it has small white flowers, fauriei is highly mildew resistant and more cold tolerant than the straight indica. The cultivars are 'Muskegee', a lavender flowering shrub; 'Natchez' with white flowers; and 'Tuscarora' with coral flowers. The National Arboretum cultivars of *L. indica* developed in the 1970s include 'Catawba', a light lavender that is highly mildew resistant; 'Cherokee', with heavy panicles of red flowers; 'Conestoga', with lavender and pink flowers; 'Powhatan', with clear lavender flowers; 'Potomac', with brilliant pink color.

ADVICE FOR REGIONAL CARE

Crape myrtles grow throughout Florida with similar care.

Croton

Codiaeum variegatum

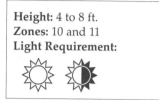

Height: 4 to 8 ft.
Zones: 10 and 11
Light Requirement:

One croton fancier used to collect crotons on trips throughout Florida and ended up with more than 60 different-looking plants—and that was probably just the beginning. Gardeners love the variety of leaf colors, greens, pinks, yellows, and reds, in addition to the assortment of leaf shapes available in the croton genus. Certainly, the plant is a real attention getter that's enjoyed not only in Florida but also throughout the world. It has to be kept consistently warm, however. In cooler portions of the state, protection is needed to survive any dip below 32 degrees Fahrenheit. Use one croton for its colorful foliage, or plant a collection. These relatively narrow plants are ideal for cramped gardens and the small spots between the home and the sidewalk. In the cooler regions of Florida and elsewhere, the plants are often set in containers. Some have been used as foliage plants indoors. You can create croton hedges and use the plants as view barriers.

WHEN TO PLANT

Croton plants are best transplanted from one area to another between December and February. Most plants sold at garden centers are in containers and can be added to the landscape at any time of the year, particularly in spring and early summer in South Florida.

WHERE TO PLANT

Croton plants prefer a full-sun to partial-shade location. Some selections tolerate the lower light levels under a large tree, but the colors are somewhat subdued. A well-drained soil is best. The plants take well to Florida sandy soils. Where possible, improve the planting site with organic matter before planting. Enriching a large area with compost or peat moss and manure ensures the most carefree growth.

HOW TO PLANT

Dig a hole that's much wider than the rootball but not deeper. Position the croton plant at the same depth it was growing in the container or original planting site. It may be set a little higher above the soil level, especially in a poorly drained location. Add soil around the rootball with adequate water to make good soil-to-root contact. After planting, form a berm at the edge of the rootball so that water moves down through the root system and then out into the surrounding soil. Add a 2- to 3-in. mulch layer. No pruning is usually needed at planting time.

ADVICE FOR CARE

Once established, most shrubs grow well with minimal care. Crotons can exist with feedings given nearby plants but make the best growth when fed once in March, May, and September. Use a 6-6-6, 16-4-8, or similar analysis fertilizer at label rates. Crotons are relatively drought tolerant; normal rainfalls are sufficient to maintain them. During periods of extended drought, water the plantings weekly.

ADDITIONAL INFORMATION

All shrubs need periodic pruning to keep the plantings in bounds and to remove old and diseased portions. Crotons also need periodic pruning to produce compact plants with plenty of colorful new shoots. Use the prunings to quickly root new plants. Some pests that may affect crotons include scale, thrips, and mites. Where needed, apply a pesticide recommended by the University of Florida, following label instructions.

ADDITIONAL SPECIES, CULTIVARS, OR VARIETIES

Many croton selections have been made for home planting, but few are sold by name at garden centers. One way to start a collection may be to pick out the attractive colors when available.

ADVICE FOR REGIONAL CARE

Culture in North Florida and parts of Central Florida is restricted to containers due to winter cold. Plant in a loose potting soil, and feed weekly with a 20-20-20 or similar fertilizer during periods of active growth. Give these plants protection from frosts and freezing temperatures.

Firebush

Hamelia patens

Height: 15 ft. or more
Zones: 10 and 11
Light Requirement:

Firebush is a fast-growing shrub with whorls of textured leaves that take on a reddish color in full sun. It has scarlet tubular flowers year-round. Though it may grow to 15 ft. or more, it can be kept much shorter by pruning. A native of the hardwood hammocks of the lower half of Florida, firebush is a valuable plant for its nectar-rich flowers that attract hummingbirds and butterflies. The slender flowers are in clusters toward the ends of the branches, where they are available to those who can hover or alight. Florida is its northernmost territory, and from here it travels down to Brazil. A related species is found in Peru. *Patens* means "spreading," and that it does with vigor, particularly in shade, which makes it lean and lanky. It can be pruned back hard in the spring—and often is pruned back naturally by the caterpillars that are larvae of a sphinx moth, *Xylophanes tersa*. The moth has black hind wings trimmed with yellow triangles. Its larvae, which are green with eyespots on one end and a semicircular tail on the other, feed on members of the coffee family, then pupate in the ground. Hamelia is good at recovering from such plunder, however. And not just from caterpillars, but also from aphids, which find it delectable, and cold wind, which can burn the leaves. Yet it also takes heat and drought like a champ. Mix these plants with wild coffee, necklace pod, spicewood, beautyberry, and other native shrubs in a mixed border. Use them along with some native trees to create a wildlife habitat in a corner of the yard or as a part of the yard you do not irrigate (once the plants are established) in a water-conserving landscape design.

WHEN TO PLANT

Planting just before the rainy season is best; plant in March if you are willing to irrigate often until the rains begin. Transplanting in the high heat of July, August, and September adds an extra burden of stress to the plant.

280

WHERE TO PLANT

Use it as a specimen or in an informal hedge with other native shrubs and trees. Plant in an area that has good drainage.

HOW TO PLANT

Dig a hole twice as wide but just as deep as the rootball. If roots in the container are circling, then make several 1/4-in. cuts in the root-ball with a sharp knife to promote new, outward root growth. Water in the backfill to eliminate air pockets. Mulch to a depth of 3 or 4 in., making sure the mulch is several inches away from the trunk of the shrub to prevent fungus.

ADVICE FOR CARE

Keep the roots moist until the shrub is established. Water daily for the first week; then every other day for 2 weeks; reduce to every 3 or 4 days for 2 weeks. During the first growing season, water weekly if rain is irregular or if the shrub wilts. You may want to prune this back hard to keep it small or to keep it under control.

ADDITIONAL SPECIES, CULTIVARS, AND VARIETIES

Hamelia patens stands without a close next of kin, but it resides within a large family, the Rubiaceae, and is a cousin to many well-known plants such as gardenia, coffee, and ixora.

ADVICE FOR REGIONAL CARE

In Central Florida, the shrub will be damaged by cold. Each spring, prune out the affected area, once new growth has begun to indicate what must be pruned away.

Gardenia

Gardenia jasminoides

Height: approx. 6 ft. high
by 3 or 4 ft. wide
Zones: All
Light Requirement:

The gardenia is a slow-growing evergreen shrub with dark-green leaves and fragrant white flowers in the spring. She sends her intoxicating perfume across the heavy air, and at night even moths that would be drawn to the moon return for the gardenia. For who, once captivated by her powers, can resist this siren? We grant you that some people can't bear to be in the same room with her, but surely, they eat their peas with knives. For our part, we think she is the queen of tropical scents. This regal shrub is named for Dr. Alexander Garden, a Scot by birth who was a South Carolina physician. Because he had the good fortune to correspond with Carl Linnaeus, who named the plants in the 18th century, this Chinese bush in the coffee family remembers him in history. Like other members of the coffee group, she has textured, dark-green leaves and virginal white flowers that are large, most often double, and somewhat roselike in appearance. Gardenias, like their cousins the ixoras, prefer an acid soil, will grow in full sun to light shade, and ought to come with the instructions "to be planted outside the bedroom window." They can be used as specimen shrubs or as part of a mixed border that also might include ixora, azalea, brunfelsia, snowbush, pascuita—shrubs that can have interest from leaves when not in bloom and help accent each other when they are blooming.

WHEN TO PLANT
Plant from March through summer, although late May or early June is the best.

WHERE TO PLANT
Plant in full sun or light shade. Plant it where you can reach it with a hose or in the path of a sprinkler because the soil, ideally, should be kept moist. Fluctuation in soil moisture is one thing that leads to yellowing leaves on this shrub.

HOW TO PLANT

Dig a hole twice as wide but just as deep as the rootball. If roots in the container are circling, then make several 1/4-in. cuts in the rootball with a sharp knife to promote new, outward root growth. Add peat moss or compost to the planting hole so that about 1/3 of the soil is enriched. If you mix too much organic material in the hole in rocky soils, the roots will be disinclined to move out into the rocky substrate. Water in the backfill to eliminate air pockets. Mulch to a depth of 3 or 4 in., making sure the mulch is several inches away from the trunk of the shrub to prevent fungus.

ADVICE FOR CARE

Gardenias are heavy feeders, and in alkaline soils they thrive on high-nitrogen, acid-forming fertilizer. Fertilizer is manufactured especially for azaleas, gardenias, and ixoras. A 12-6-8 or 12-6-10 is appropriate. Small amounts every 2 or 3 months will keep the plant from yellowing. A lack of micronutrients also causes yellow leaves; use a foliar micronutrient spray when this occurs. Often the plants show iron deficiency, and an iron drench once a year is beneficial. Keep the soil evenly moist. Prune lightly after the major flowering period to keep the shrub compact. Should it get leggy, you can rejuvenate it over a period of 3 years by cutting back hard 1/3 of the major branches each year.

ADDITIONAL INFORMATION

Because microscopic worms called nematodes attack gardenia roots, resulting in flower drop or general decline, select cultivars grafted onto *Gardenia thunbergia*. Prune away any suckers from below the graft union. Thrips are attracted to the buds, which are spirally twisted before opening. Thrips are tiny black insects that scrape away plant tissue to cause a wound and then suck juices that leak out. They love *Gardenia* and *Vanda* orchid buds. Malathion is one way to get them. Lacewings and certain predatory mites feed on them. A direct spray of water can knock them off. Small brown marks on the petals are symptoms.

ADDITIONAL SPECIES, CULTIVARS, OR VARIETIES

'Miami Supreme' is the biggest selling cultivar in Florida. It has large flowers, is extremely fragrant, and also grows in partial shade. *Gardenia* 'Radicans' is a dwarf species.

ADVICE FOR REGIONAL CARE

Cold winters can damage gardenias in Central and North Florida. Prune out affected portions after new growth appears in the spring.

283

Hibiscus

Hibiscus rosa-sinensis

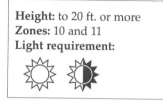

Height: to 20 ft. or more
Zones: 10 and 11
Light requirement:

Hibiscus flowers, like palm trees, say *tropical*. Some of them fairly shout it. Big, flashy, and strong bloomers, hibiscus flowers begin with white and go to mauve, gray, brown, orange, red and yellow, blue, brown with yellow edges, yellow with orange centers . . . combinations that are reminiscent of tie-dyed T-shirts of those long-ago hippie days. Even amateur hibiscus growers seem to have a field day mixing and blending these easily crossed plants, thinking up names as colorful as their paint pots: Tequila Sunrise (yellow with an orange-red center); Silas Wood (brown with yellow edges); Tammy Faye (rosy red with yellow edges). Yet there are people who love the single white, the bright red, the bell-like clarity of the single yellow, the plain pink. Most of the blossoms last only a day, so they don't make great cut flowers, but they perform prolifically in the garden. Hibiscus are robust growers, they flower freely—providing you don't trim off their branch ends—and they provide puddles of brightness throughout those impossibly sticky and steamy summer days.

WHEN TO PLANT
Plant in March through midsummer, with late May and early June as the best times.

WHERE TO PLANT
If planting with others in a hedge, plant them 3 ft. apart from trunk to trunk. A hibiscus planting left unpruned can make a good screen. Find a full-sun location (for most cultivars) and an area where plants won't sit in water because they don't like wet feet. The plants producing blue or gray flowers like partial shade; plants with yellow flowers require shade.

HOW TO PLANT
In South Florida, hibiscus are best grown on Anderson's Crepe rootstock, which withstands nematodes and heat stress. Dig a hole twice as wide but just as deep as the rootball. If roots in the container are

284

circling, then make several 1/4-in. cuts in the rootball with a sharp knife to promote new, outward root growth. Add peat moss or compost to the planting hole so that about 1/3 of the backfill is enriched. If you mix too much organic material in the hole in rocky soils, the roots will be disinclined to move out into the rocky substrate. Water in the backfill to eliminate air pockets. Mulch to a depth of 3 or 4 in., making sure the mulch is several inches away from the trunk of the shrub to prevent fungus.

ADVICE FOR CARE

Once the shrubs are established, most are fairly drought tolerant. You may have to water in the dry season, about once every 3 weeks if there is not any rain. Some cultivars can be less tolerant, however. Watch for wilt. Use a slow-release fertilizer with a 3-1-3 ratio. Bear in mind that slow-release in South Florida may be depleted rather quickly, so that 90-day slow-release may mean 30 days in summer. Hibiscus in alkaline soils can show minor element deficiencies, so a micronutrient foliar spray 3 times a year is advisable. Growers warn not to mix water-soluble 20-20-20 with a micronutrient spray because the phosphorus in the 20-20-20 will tie up micronutrients. Sucking insects, such as whitefly and aphids, can be controlled with an insecticidal soap or 2 tablespoons of liquid Ivory in 1 gallon of water. Soapy solutions may not kill the larvae, and you should repeat the application in 3 to 4 days. Armored scale can attack hibiscus. Prune off the affected area, or if the infestation is widespread, use Cygon. Never use Malathion on hibiscus because it defoliates the shrub.

ADDITIONAL INFORMATION

Pruning hard in early spring will allow the emergence of plentiful new branch tips on which flowers may develop over summer.

ADDITIONAL SPECIES, CULTIVARS, OR VARIETIES

Hibiscus schizopetalus, sometimes called the fringed hibiscus, has upside-down red flowers that hang from long stems. *Hibiscus syriacus* is the rose-of-Sharon that produces blue, single flowers and is deciduous. It does well in alkaline soils.

ADVICE FOR REGIONAL CARE

Hibiscus can be grown in Central Florida in protected areas—such as a sunny southeast side of a house. Any cold damage can be pruned off the plant in the spring. In North Florida, use in containers or as an annual summer planting.

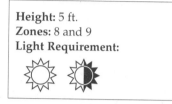

Hydrangea

Hydrangea macrophylla

Height: 5 ft.
Zones: 8 and 9
Light Requirement:

When you think of Easter plants, one shrub that always seems to come to mind is the hydrangea. It's the bright-pink plant that adds the great Easter color, but it also comes in blue. The ball-shaped inflorescences are prominent from mid-spring through early summer. Hydrangeas on display at Easter have been forced and are a little earlier than the landscape plantings. Many named varieties of the hydrangea have been selected, but all are blues or pinks. In fact, you may be able to convince any hydrangea to be either pink or blue by regulating the soil acidity. Many have been selected for the better blue or pink color, however. Hydrangeas are best used in mass displays of 3 or more plants. They can be planted as background shrubs, hedges, or accents. Gardeners like to plant hydrangeas near entrances, off patios, or along walkways.

WHEN TO PLANT

Plants of hydrangeas are best transplanted from one area of the landscape to another from October through February. At that time they are dormant and can begin to establish a root system before spring. Most plants sold at garden centers are in containers and can be added to the landscape at any time of the year.

WHERE TO PLANT

Hydrangeas need protection from the hot, drying sun. They are best planted where they get filtered sun or morning sun and afternoon shade. Select a well-drained soil, but it should be able to hold some moisture. Where possible, improve the planting site with organic matter before planting. Enrich a large area with compost or peat moss and manure.

HOW TO PLANT

Dig a hole that's much wider than the rootball but not deeper. Position the hydrangea plant at the same depth it was growing in the container or original planting site. It may be set a little higher above the soil level, especially in a poorly drained location. Add soil around the rootball with adequate water to make good soil-to-root contact. After planting, form a berm at the edge of the rootball so that water moves down through the root system and then out into the surrounding soil. Add a 2- to 3-in. mulch layer. No pruning is needed at planting time.

ADVICE FOR CARE

Hydrangeas need extra care to grow in most landscapes. Feed plantings once in March, May, and September. Use a 6-6-6, 16-4-8, or similar analysis fertilizer at label rates. Hydrangeas need lots of water; the plants frequently wilt with just a little moisture stress. Check the plantings several times each week, especially during periods of drought. Most plantings need watering every 3 to 4 days during hot weather.

ADDITIONAL INFORMATION

Do you want a blue hydrangea or a pink one? The soil acidity regulates the color. For a blue hydrangea, keep the soil acid, and for a pink one, make sure it's alkaline. All shrubs need periodic pruning to keep the plantings in bounds and to remove old and diseased portions. Hydrangeas need an extra pruning after flowering is complete in early summer. Remove older flower heads, and do any reshaping of the plants. Pruning at other times of the year may remove flower buds. One pest that affects the hydrangea is the caterpillar. Hand pick pests from the plantings, or treat them with a pesticide recommended by the University of Florida, following label instructions.

ADDITIONAL SPECIES, CULTIVARS, OR VARIETIES

Central and North Florida gardeners can also plant the oakleaf hydrangea, *Hydrangea quercifolia*. It grows to about 6 ft. tall and produces a white inflorescence for spring. It, too, prefers filtered sun.

ADVICE FOR REGIONAL CARE

Hydrangeas grow well only in Central and North Florida where they have some cold weather during the winter months. Some years they suffer freeze damage that needs to be pruned out during the early spring season.

Ixora

Ixora coccinea

Other Name: *Ixora* Hybrids
Height: 2¹/₂ ft. to 6 or 10 ft.
Zones: 10B and 11
Light Requirement:

Ixora are evergreen shrubs, ranging in size from dwarf (2¹/₂ ft.) to 6 or even 10 ft. The plants produce many small but bright flowers in large heads throughout the warm season. Once the darling of South Florida builders, ixoras were used in many 1950s subdivisions as foundation plantings. Like crotons, the plants experienced a period of disuse in the 1970s and early 1980s, then came back to the landscapes of the late 1980s and throughout the 1990s. The reasons for this swing had to do with the way the shrubs were originally maintained and the development of new cultivars to make maintenance easier. Ixoras didn't like alkaline soils or nematodes, and they protested these problems by turning their green leaves to yellow. Nor did they like to be next to stucco houses, because rain washing off the highly alkaline concrete only compounded the alkaline conditions. In addition, most people sheared their ixora hedges to pieces, causing leaves to get smaller and smaller, barely able to cover their twigs. It was not a pretty sight. But with the development of cultivars such as *Ixora* 'Nora Grant', which is resistant to nematodes and tolerant of rocky soil, the picture changed. 'Nora Grant' is shapely enough that hard pruning isn't needed. Her flowers are produced in huge, round heads of hot pink, and she is smashing. *Ixora* 'Super King' is another hybrid that fares well. It has large heads of deep-red flowers. 'Super King' is a cultivar of *Ixora duffii*, and although it is susceptible to nematodes, it looks healthier and is a bigger (to about 10 ft.) plant than *I. coccinea*.

WHEN TO PLANT
Plant at the beginning of the rainy season, late May to early June.

WHERE TO PLANT
Plant this in full sun for best flower production. Good drainage is important. These shrubs make good hedges or flowering specimens. Combine them with palms for a pleasant tropical look. Use as a

walkway hedge. Plant artillery fern or variegated liriope at their feet for a pleasant contrast and good transition from grass to hedge.

How to Plant

Dig a hole twice as wide but just as deep as the rootball. If roots in the container are circling, then make several 1/4-in. cuts in the root-ball with a sharp knife to promote new, outward root growth. Add peat moss or compost to enrich the planting hole so that about 1/3 of the backfill is organic. Water in the backfill to eliminate air pockets. Mulch to a depth of 3 or 4 in., making sure the mulch is several inches away from the trunk of the shrub to prevent fungus.

Advice for Care

Ixoras like fertilizer to keep producing those big balls of flowers called umbels. Like gardenias and azaleas, they prefer acid soil, so they benefit from mulch and high-nitrogen fertilizer. Lightly prune to shape; ixoras perform best when not sheared.

Additional Information

Micronutrient deficiencies are often seen in alkaline soils, particu-larly magnesium deficiency, making older leaves yellow, manganese deficiency, causing yellowing in new leaves, and iron deficiency, causing general yellowing but leaving green veins. One or two handfuls of Epsom salts around the root zone when you fertilize will help with the magnesium problem. An iron drench once a year is beneficial. Manganese sulfate combats yellowing of new leaves, and the sulfate helps make soil acid as well. Use a micronutrient foliar spray.

Additional Species, Cultivars, or Varieties

Ixora javanica produces orange flowers. There also are yellow and white cultivars, but they are not widely available.

Advice for Regional Care

Very cold weather, in the upper 30s, will cause leaves to develop brown spots. If freezing occurs, wait until spring before pruning so you can allow the emergence of new leaves to indicate how far back twigs and branches were damaged.

Lady-of-the-Night

Brunfelsia americana

Height: to 10 ft.
Zones: 10B and 11
Light Requirement:

On the softest summer nights, when the moon is hazy through the humidity and the screech owls call in little whinnies from the poincianas, the sweet scent of cloves may drift or linger. Unlike jasmine, with its sometimes cloying ways, lady-of-the-night's perfume seems never to be in excess, never overripe. It lasts 2, maybe 3 nights, and then is gone until the next wave of flowers washes over the twigs. This brunfelsia is incredibly showy when flowering; it blooms profusely all at once. The flowers form in the leaf axils, elongating gradually until they open at night, slightly close, and open again. The corolla sits on a long tube, inviting the proboscis of a night-flying moth with its after-sundown scent. After 2 days, most of the flowers have aged to a creamy yellow, and they fall. Rather than pruning mine into a squat hedge, I have staked a couple of arching branches to cascade forward from the shrub bed. Behind the brunfelsia are the dinner-plate leaves of *Begonia nelumbiifolia*, and behind them, the soft and feathery fronds of the *Chamaedorea* palms. The foliage shapes nicely play against each other, and the green background allows the brunfelsia's flowers to be seen easily. From the West Indies, lady-of-the-night is in the large Solanaceae family, as are tomatoes, angel's trumpets, peppers, and eggplants. The plants like full sun and moist soil, with fertilizer every 3 months to keep the flowers flushing. I have a couple of small daughter plants from this main plant, and they have taken well to two different settings: one in the shade of the north side of the house, the other in sun just at the front of the shade house. Both have flowered.

WHEN TO PLANT

Plant at the beginning of the rainy season, late May / early June, or from March to midsummer if consistent irrigation is practical early on.

WHERE TO PLANT

Plant lady-of-the-night where she gets 5 or 6 hours of sun in the summer. This is another next-to-the-bedroom-window shrub. Place it at the southeast corner of the house, and the fragrance will be carried into the house on the prevailing breeze of summer. Enrich the soil with peat moss or compost, and keep the root zone mulched.

How to Plant

Dig a hole twice as wide but just as deep as the rootball. If roots in the container are circling, then make several 1/4-in. cuts in the rootball with a sharp knife to promote new, outward root growth. Add compost or peat moss to make up 1/3 of the backfill to enrich the planting hole. Water in backfill to eliminate air pockets. Mulch to a depth of 3 or 4 in., making sure the mulch is several inches away from the trunk of the shrub to prevent fungus.

Advice for Care

Water every few days in the dry season. Fertilize 3 times a year with a 7-3-7 in the spring and summer and a 4-6-8 right before winter to avoid pushing out new leaves. I try to apply new mulch twice a year because it wears thin every 6 months or so. When I spray liquid fertilizer on the nearby *Vanda* 'Miss Joaqium' grown on a totem, I hit this shrub at the same time. I use a 12-4-12-4 slow-release fertilizer formulated for palms on my shrubs, since both nitrogen and potassium are in slow-release form and both leach from the soil at about the same rate. The *Brunfelsia* seems to thrive on this regimen. To sow seeds, remove the skin and pulp, push seeds just beneath the surface of a 50-50 mix of peat moss and perlite, and keep moist.

Additional Information

Only rarely does a flower get pollinated, and the fruit takes many months to form. It eventually turns orange, then red, then dark.

Additional Species, Cultivars, or Varieties

Yesterday-today-and-tomorrow is a winter-flowering cousin, *Brunfelsia pauciflora*, from Brazil. The 3-in. flowers open blue-purple and fade to white, hence the name. *Brunfelsia grandiflora*, from other South American countries, blooms in the warm season, also with purple flower, but these have white centers. And *Brunfelsia australis*, from southern Brazil, is another purple-to-white bloomer.

Advice for Regional Care

Brunfelsia grows throughout Central Florida, but may be damaged by cold. Prune off damage in early spring after new growth appears as an indication of where live wood begins.

291

Ligustrum

Ligustrum japonicum

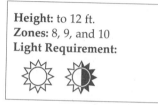

Height: to 12 ft.
Zones: 8, 9, and 10
Light Requirement:

Talk about a plant that is a backbone of the landscape industry, and you must be discussing the ligustrum. It's planted as a hedge, view barrier, accent plant, and tree. Ligustrums have large, very shiny leaves and open white blossoms in the spring. A blue berry follows in fall for extra color. Most landscapes have one or more ligustrums just because they have a durable reputation. They survive in all but the wettest soil and can live with minimal care. Ligustrums can be pruned to almost any shape or permitted to grow naturally for a slightly upright to spreading form. Another feature that most home gardeners like is its rapid growth to fill in voids and give the landscape a quick, recognizable form.

WHEN TO PLANT

Plants of ligustrums are best transplanted from one area of the landscape to another between December and February. Experienced nurserymen move the plants as burlapped specimens at any time of the year. Most plants sold at garden centers are in containers and can be added to the landscape at any time of the year. Plant in spring or early summer in South Florida.

WHERE TO PLANT

Ligustrum plants prefer a full-sun location but tolerate filtered sun where they develop a more open growth habit. A well-drained soil is best. They are very tolerant of Florida sands. Where possible, improve the planting site with organic matter before planting. Enrich a large area with compost or peat moss and manure.

HOW TO PLANT

Dig a hole that's much wider than the rootball but not deeper. Position the ligustrum plant at the same depth it was growing in the container or original planting site. It may be set a little higher above the soil level, especially in a poorly drained location. Add soil around the rootball with adequate water to make good soil-to-root contact. After planting, form a berm at the edge of the rootball so that water moves down through the root system and then out into the surrounding soil. Add a 2- to 3-in. mulch layer. No pruning is usually needed at planting time.

ADVICE FOR CARE

Once established, most shrubs grow well with minimal care, and ligustrums are no exception. They make the best growth if fed once in March, May, and September. Use a 6-6-6, 16-4-8, or similar analy- · sis fertilizer at label rates. Ligustrums are fairly drought tolerant, able to exist with natural rainfall for all but the drier times. Best growth is made with weekly watering, especially during periods of drought.

ADDITIONAL INFORMATION

All shrubs need periodic pruning to keep the plantings in bounds and to remove old and diseased portions. Ligustrums maintained as formal hedges may need pruning several times during the growing season. The tree forms need periodic pruning to keep an open habit of growth and remove lower sprouts along the trunks. Some pests that may affect the ligustrum include caterpillars, grasshoppers, and scales. Hand pick pests from the plantings, or treat them with a pesticide recommended by the University of Florida, following label instructions. Plantings that are not vigorous develop fungal leaf spots. Good care overcomes this problem.

ADDITIONAL SPECIES, CULTIVARS, OR VARIETIES

Gardeners plant the glossy privet, *Ligustrum lucidum*, which grows to 20 ft. tall as a tree in the landscape. It resembles the Japanese privet, but it's bigger. Another ligustrum is the Chinese privet, *Ligustrum sinense*, often just known by its species name. The variegated form is usually the favorite, but it often has some branches that revert to the green leaf stage and need removal. It is used in foundation plantings and as a hedge.

ADVICE FOR REGIONAL CARE

Ligustrums grow well in all but the most southern regions of the state. Care is similar in all areas.

Nandina

Nandina domestica

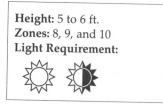

Height: 5 to 6 ft.
Zones: 8, 9, and 10
Light Requirement:

According to folklore, planting the nandina, also called heavenly bamboo, at the entrance to your home brings good luck. Its colorful berries and unique foliage add to the list of reasons to plant the shrub. As the name suggests, it resembles bamboo, producing upward growth from canelike stems. The leaves look somewhat like bamboo foliage. You may plant 1 nandina by the entrance, but nandinas are best used in clusters of 3 or more plants so that you can get the full effect of the growth habit, the fall through winter fruits, and the fall leaf color. The plants produce clusters of yellowish flowers for spring, but they may be hidden within the branches. Nandinas may be used as a shrub border, groundcover, or light view barrier. Some gardeners grow plants in containers to use on porches and patios. Depending on how much cold weather the plants endure and the variety, they may be evergreen to semievergreen in habit.

WHEN TO PLANT

Plants of the nandina are best transplanted from one area of the landscape to another between December and February. Most plants sold at garden centers are in containers and can be added to the landscape at any time of the year.

WHERE TO PLANT

Nandina plants prefer a full-sun to partial-shade location. A well-drained soil is best. The plants grow well in Florida's sandy soils. Where possible, improve the planting site with organic matter before planting to make plant care easier. Enrich a large area with compost or peat moss and manure.

HOW TO PLANT

Dig a hole that's much wider than the rootball but not deeper. Position the nandina plant at the same depth it was growing in the container or original planting site. It may be set a little higher above the soil level, especially in a poorly drained location. Add soil around the rootball with adequate water to make good soil-to-root contact. After planting, form a berm at the edge of the rootball so that water moves down through the root system and then out into the surrounding soil. Add a 2- to 3-in. mulch layer. No pruning is usually needed at planting time.

ADVICE FOR CARE

Once established, most shrubs grow well with minimal care. Nandinas exist with care given nearby shrubs and trees. They make the best growth when fed once in March, May, and September. Use a 6-6-6, 16-4-8, or similar analysis fertilizer at label rates. Nandinas can tolerate short periods of drought but grow best with weekly watering, especially during periods of drought.

ADDITIONAL INFORMATION

All shrubs need periodic pruning to keep the plantings in bounds and to remove old and diseased portions. Many of the older canes lose their leaves and grow too tall for the garden site. An annual rejuvenation pruning in late winter takes out the older canes to allow new growths to fill in from the base. One pest that may affect the nandina is the scale insect. Where needed, apply a pesticide recommended by the University of Florida, following label instructions.

ADDITIONAL SPECIES, CULTIVARS, OR VARIETIES

Several selections of nandina have been made for their growth habit and fruit color. Some tested in Florida include the variety 'Alba', with white fruits; 'Nana', growing to 2 ft. tall; 'Compacta', with a low-growing, dense habit; and 'Harbor Dwarf', a low-growing type.

ADVICE FOR REGIONAL CARE

Plantings in the cooler portions of the state are likely to show the best leaf color and exhibit the deciduous growth habit during the winter months. Protect plantings in the southern and hotter areas of the state from midday sun.

Necklace Pod

Sophora tomentosa

Height: 6 to 10 ft.
Zones: 10 and 11
Light Requirement:

This is a medium to large evergreen shrub, with silvery-green leaves and yellow flowers on racemes or stalks that appear on the ends of the new branches. With kid-soft compound leaves that are covered with silver-white hair, the necklace pod is durable, salt tolerant, and beautiful. It is a coastal plant, wandering from dune to coastal hammock and amply protected from too much sun exposure by those white hairs that reflect light. A hirsute covering is an old trick of plants exposed to too much light that could harm tender leaf tissue; bromeliads that cling to high tree branches, plants exposed to wind and salt air, and desert plants all have this one in their repertoire of survival skills. The leaves also can indicate that shade and too much water can lead to fungus and dieback. Silver plants generally are drought tolerant (the hairs also keep moisture in), and *Sophora* is no exception. Necklace pods, along with scarlet milkweeds, asters, and Spanish needle, can serve as lures to butterflies. Flowering is most satisfying in the winter and spring, but the plants may produce some flowers throughout the year. A member of the pea family, the necklace pod produces long, segmented pea pods, with each pea readily detectable, like small pearls of a necklace.

WHEN TO PLANT

Plant at the beginning of the rainy season, late May/early June.

WHERE TO PLANT

Plant in full sun, where you might be able to see the shrub from a porch or window and watch for butterflies. The necklace pods can take pruning every year in the spring to keep the long branches in check. I have a single plant that has been replanted 3 times: the first time, it was shaded in winter and nearly passed out from lack of sunshine. Then it went into a small native plot near the driveway and got unruly. Finally, last year, it was cut back to within an inch of its life and moved again—this time to the base of a slash pine. There it joins a blue-gray palmetto in a mulched area to trigger thoughts of the presuburban era.

296

HOW TO PLANT

Dig a hole twice as wide but just as deep as the rootball. If roots in the container are circling, then make several 1/4-in. cuts in the rootball with a sharp knife to promote new, outward root growth. Water in backfill to eliminate air pockets. Mulch to a depth of 3 or 4 in., making sure the mulch is several inches away from the trunk of the shrub to prevent fungus.

ADVICE FOR CARE

Keep the roots well watered while necklace pod's roots are becoming established—2 or 3 months—and then stand aside. If there are occasional caterpillars, from whence the butterflies come, remember to reach for Dipel first, or hand pick, or just allow the leaves to look ratty for a while knowing they'll recover with the next flush of leaves. Part of this plant's appeal is its attraction to beauty on a scaly wing.

ADDITIONAL INFORMATION

Necklace pod will take pruning well.

ADDITIONAL SPECIES, CULTIVARS, OR VARIETIES

Sophora sceundiflora is identified by Graf in *Tropica* as native to Texas and Mexico. Its common name is Mescal-bean.

ADVICE FOR REGIONAL CARE

In Central Florida, try growing necklace pod in a protected area, such as a sunny southeast corner. Cold or freeze damage may be pruned away in spring after new growth emerges.

Night-Blooming Jessamine

Cestrum nocturnum

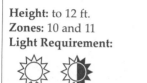

Height: to 12 ft.
Zones: 10 and 11
Light Requirement:

As the name suggests, this jessamine is a fragrant plant to enjoy during the evening hours. The greenish-white flowers are produced throughout the year, with major displays during spring and summer. They are not very noticeable but are very fragrant. Use the night-blooming jessamine, also called night cestrum, where you need a large, sprawling shrub, perhaps near a patio or along a walkway. It could also be used as a view barrier or space divider in full-sun locations. One word of warning: do not use the plant where the fragrance could be overpowering. Many gardeners avoid planting too close to bedroom windows. White fruits are produced but, like all portions of this plant, are poisonous.

WHEN TO PLANT

Plants of the night-blooming jessamine are best transplanted from one area of the landscape to another between December and February. Most plants sold at garden centers are in containers and can be added to the landscape at any time of the year. It is ideal to plant in spring or early summer in South Florida.

WHERE TO PLANT

Night-blooming jessamine plants prefer a sunny location but tolerate light shade. A well-drained soil is best. The plants grow well in Florida's sandy soils. Where possible, improve the planting site with organic matter before planting. Enrich a large area with compost or peat moss and manure.

HOW TO PLANT

Dig a hole that's much wider than the rootball but not deeper. Position the night-blooming jessamine plant at the same depth it was growing in the container or original planting site. It may be set a little higher above the soil level, especially in poorly drained locations. Add soil around the rootball with adequate water to make good soil-to-root contact. After planting, form a berm at the edge of the rootball so that water moves down through the root system and then out into the surrounding soil. Add a 2- to 3-in. mulch layer. No pruning is usually needed at planting time.

ADVICE FOR CARE

Once established, most shrubs grow well with minimal care. Night-blooming jessamine make the best growth if fed once in March, May, and September. Use a 6-6-6, 16-4-8, or similar analysis fertilizer at label rates. Plantings can tolerate short periods of drought but make the best growth if watered weekly, especially during periods of drought.

ADDITIONAL INFORMATION

All shrubs need periodic pruning to keep the plantings in bounds and to remove old and diseased portions. Since the night-blooming jessamine is a sprawling shrub, more frequent pruning is needed to remove long and lanky shoots. Some pests that may affect the night-blooming jessamine include caterpillars and grasshoppers. Hand pick pests from the plantings, or treat them with a pesticide recommended by the University of Florida, following label instructions.

ADDITIONAL SPECIES, CULTIVARS, OR VARIETIES

The species *Cestrum diurnum* opens fragrant blossoms during the day.

ADVICE FOR REGIONAL CARE

Landscape plantings of night-blooming jessamine are limited to warmer areas of Central Florida and South Florida. Plantings in Central Florida may be affected by freezing weather and need spring pruning to remove the dead or damaged shoots.

Oleander

Nerium oleander

Height: to 12 ft.
Zones: 8 through 11
Light Requirement:

Give your yard a tropical look with a Florida oleander. It is one of the showiest shrubs you can add to the landscape, in bloom from spring through fall. If you want a shrub with hot-pink, deep-red, or pure-white blossoms, then the oleander is a good choice. It can be planted as a hedge or space divider. Many gardeners plant larger oleanders to the rear of the yard to enjoy the distant color. You can plant just 1 shrub as an accent, but 3 or more provide a cluster of color. Dwarf types can be used in foundation plantings and around the patio. For all its beauty, the oleander is a poisonous plant. All portions are toxic if eaten.

When to Plant

Oleanders are best transplanted from one area of the landscape to another between December and February. Most plants sold at garden centers are in containers and can be added to the landscape at any time of the year. Plant in spring or summer in South Florida.

Where to Plant

Oleanders prefer a sunny location but can tolerate very light shade. In the reduced light they produce a more open plant. A well-drained soil is best, but they also thrive in Florida sands when they receive proper care. Where possible, improve the planting site with organic matter before planting. Enrich a large area with compost or peat moss and manure.

How to Plant

Dig a hole that's much wider than the rootball but not deeper. Position the oleander plant at the same depth it was growing in the container or original planting site. It may be set a little higher above the soil level, especially in poorly drained locations. Add soil around the rootball with adequate water to make good soil-to-root contact. After planting, form a berm at the edge of the rootball so

that water moves down through the root system and then out into the surrounding soil. Add a 2- to 3-in. mulch layer. No pruning is usually needed at planting time.

ADVICE FOR CARE

Once established, most shrubs grow well with minimal care. Oleanders can exist with the nutrients obtained from feedings of nearby trees, shrubs, and lawns. Where extra growth is needed, they can be fed once in March, May, and September. Use a 6-6-6, 16-4-8, or similar analysis fertilizer at label rates. This is a very drought tolerant plant that needs watering only to encourage growth or to withstand periods of severe drought. Normal rainfall is sufficient for most plants.

ADDITIONAL INFORMATION

All shrubs need periodic pruning to keep the plantings in bounds and to remove old and diseased portions. During some winters, Mother Nature does the pruning. Plants in cold locations may be frozen back to the ground but grow back from the base. Plants in warmer locations get tall and out of bounds. These plantings need a renewal pruning every few years. Some pests that may affect the oleander include oleander caterpillars, aphids, and scale insects. Hand pick pests from the plantings, or treat them with a pesticide recommended by the University of Florida, following the label instructions.

ADDITIONAL SPECIES, CULTIVARS, OR VARIETIES

Many selections of oleanders have been made for the landscape. Gardeners can pick a dwarf form such as Petite Salmon or Petite Pink. Also available are colorful selections, including Hardy Red, Calypso, and Mrs. Roeding.

ADVICE FOR REGIONAL CARE

More northern plantings and some in Central Florida are sure to suffer cold damage in many years. They need late winter pruning to take out the dead and allow spring growth from the base.

Plumbago

Plumbago auriculata

Height: 3 or 4 ft. **Zones:** 10 and 11 **Light Requirement:**

For many years, I dismissed plumbago. Its pale-blue flowers, though pretty enough for butterflies, were no selling point for me. Then the cobalt-blue cultivar 'Royal Cape' (or 'Imperial Blue') appeared, and I was convinced. The blue is worthy of Giotto's frescoes, Monet's pond, or Picasso's early period. It is a jubilant color and jumps out of the cloud of green behind it. South African in origin, plumbago's paler self doesn't stand up to the intensity of light that floods these latitudes. It wants to disappear in midday. Not so the new blue. And because such color is rare in landscape plants, it makes a wonderful foil for yellow, it segues beautifully from white to maroon, and it brings a little sky to earth as a mass planting, surrounded by deep-pink pentas. Although it clambers and straggles and sprawls unless pruned, it also mounds and climbs and mushrooms, and it may be just what you need at an entry gate. It is somewhat salt tolerant, though you shouldn't use it where it can catch spray. It can be made to vine. Plumbago is the larval plant of the Tropical Striped Blue butterfly.

WHEN TO PLANT

Plant at the beginning of the rainy season, late May/early June, or from March to midsummer if consistent irrigation is practical early on.

WHERE TO PLANT

Plant this in full sun. It can serve as a short shrub or even a groundcover, and would complement magenta bougainvillea, *Clerodendron quadriloculare* (with large dark-green leaves that have burgundy undersides), yellow turnera, or buttercup.

HOW TO PLANT

Dig a hole twice as wide but just as deep as the rootball. If roots in the container are circling, then make several 1/4-in. cuts in the rootball with a sharp knife to promote new, outward root growth.

Because plumbagos like fertilizer, add compost or peat moss to make up 1/3 of the backfill to enrich the planting hole. Water in backfill to eliminate air pockets. Mulch to a depth of 3 or 4 in., making sure the mulch is several inches away from the trunk of the shrub to prevent fungus.

ADVICE FOR CARE

Prune back hard at the end of winter (late February in South Florida) to encourage pretty new growth. Flowers are terminal and appear in flushes. Use slow-release fertilizer in late February or early March, in July or August, and again at the end of October or early November. Although the plant is moderately drought tolerant, water in the dry season.

ADDITIONAL INFORMATION

The South African shrub has another name: Cape leadwort.

ADDITIONAL SPECIES, CULTIVARS, OR VARIETIES

Plumbago indica is a red-flowering shrub with many of the same characteristics of the blue auriculata. It commonly is called scarlet leadwort.

ADVICE FOR REGIONAL CARE

Plumbago may be grown in Central Florida, but it will be affected by freezing weather. Prune away damage after new growth appears in early spring.

Sweet Viburnum

Viburnum odoratissimum

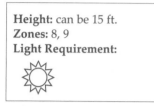

Height: can be 15 ft.
Zones: 8, 9
Light Requirement:

Need a large shrub or hedge? Chances are good that a viburnum would be just right for your landscape. This is a group of readily available and reliable shrubs for home planting. All types commonly planted in Florida have evergreen leaves and white flowers for the spring season. The largest of the landscape viburnums is the sweet viburnum *Viburnum odoratissimum*. It can be trained to become a small tree over 15 feet tall if you wish, but most gardeners plant it to become a large hedge that is kept half as wide as tall. The light-green leaves are large to over 6 in. long. The name sweet viburnum comes from its large clusters of fragrant flowers. One of the more usable species for the modern and often crowded landscape is the sandankwa viburnum, *Viburnum suspensum*. This plant stays at 4 to 6 ft. in height with very little pruning needed to keep the hedge form. The leaves are bright green and 4 to 6 in. long. No matter which viburnum you choose, just make sure it's in a spot where it has room to grow and become an attractive shrub with minimal pruning. Viburnums make good view barriers and space dividers as well as hedges. They are attractive shrubs for use in foundation plantings near large buildings and are often a home for wildlife. The wild creatures appear to enjoy the small fruits that form on most viburnums.

When to Plant

Viburnums transplanted from one area of the landscape to another are best moved between December and February. Most plants sold at garden centers are in containers and can be added to the landscape at any time of the year.

Where to Plant

Viburnum plants prefer a full-sun location but can tolerate some filtered shade. A well-drained soil is best. These plants grow well in sandy soils, but when possible, improve the planting site with organic matter before planting. Viburnum grows best in a large area enriched with compost or peat moss and manure.

HOW TO PLANT

It's best to dig a hole that's much wider than the rootball but not deeper. Position the viburnum plant at the same depth it was growing in the container or original planting site. It may also be set a little higher above the soil level, especially in a poorly drained location. Add soil around the rootball with adequate water to give good soil-to-root contact. After planting, form a berm at the edge of the rootball so that water moves down through the root system and out into the surrounding soil. Add a 2- to 3-in. mulch layer. No pruning is normally needed at planting time.

ADVICE FOR CARE

Once established, most shrubs grow well with minimal care. Viburnums should be given a feeding once in March, in June, and again in September, to encourage growth. Use a 6-6-6, 16-4-8, or similar analysis fertilizer at label rates. Most viburnums are drought tolerant, but they are usually watered about once a week, especially during periods of drought.

ADDITIONAL INFORMATION

All shrubs need periodic pruning to keep the plantings in bounds and to remove old and diseased portions. Many viburnums are sheared to form a hedge. This pruning is performed "as needed." It's best if you pick a viburnum that needs minimal pruning so as to reduce landscape work. Some pests that may affect the viburnum are thrips, scales, and white fly. These can be controlled with an oil-containing spray or another University of Florida recommended pesticide used at the label rate.

ADDITIONAL SPECIES, CULTIVARS, OR VARIETIES

Florida gardeners can plant the native Walter viburnum, *Viburnum obovatum*, with its small bright-green leaves about 1 in. in length. It forms a dense shrub and grows to 12 ft. or more. The laurestinus viburnum, *Viburnum tinus*, has pink or white flowers and grows to 6 ft.

ADVICE FOR REGIONAL CARE

Viburnums grow best in Northern and Central Florida where they receive some cool winter weather. During extremely cold winters, some species have suffered the limb damage that can be pruned away before spring growth begins.

Thryallis

Galphimia glauca

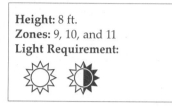

Height: 8 ft.
Zones: 9, 10, and 11
Light Requirement:

When the summer flowers start to fade, you can pop up the color with thryallis. Its bright-yellow blossoms open along a terminal spike to put the color above the foliage. The blossoms start to open from late spring through fall, but some color may occur at any time of the year in the warmer areas of the state. Thryallis makes a good natural hedge or view barrier. Establish this plant as a cluster of several shrubs for a burst of color. Use it as a backdrop for flower beds or for other spring-flowering shrubs. Keep it back from walkways; the wood is brittle and may be damaged by traffic or landscape maintenance. This evergreen shrub tolerates a frost and light freeze.

WHEN TO PLANT

Plants of thryallis are best transplanted from one area of the landscape to another between December and February. Most plants sold at garden centers are in containers and can be added to the landscape at any time of the year. Plant in spring and early summer in South Florida. Be careful during transporting and planting not to break the limbs.

WHERE TO PLANT

Thryallis plants prefer a sunny location but can survive light shade. At the lower light level they develop a more open growth habit. A well-drained soil is best. The plants grow well in sandy soils. Where possible, improve the planting site with organic matter before planting. Enrich a large area with compost or peat moss and manure.

HOW TO PLANT

Dig a hole that's much wider than the rootball but not deeper. Position the thryallis plant at the same depth as it was growing in the container or original planting site. It may be set a little higher above the soil level, especially in a poorly drained location. Add soil around the rootball with adequate water to make good soil-to-root contact. After planting, form a berm at the edge of the rootball so that water moves down through the root system and then out into the surrounding soil. Add a 2- to 3-in. mulch layer. No pruning is usually needed at planting time.

ADVICE FOR CARE

Once established, most shrubs grow well with minimal care. Thryallis can exist with feedings given nearby lawns and flower beds. For best growth, feed once in March, May, and September. Use a 6-6-6, 16-4-8, or similar analysis fertilizer at label rates. Thryallis can tolerate short periods of drought but makes the best growth with weekly watering.

ADDITIONAL INFORMATION

All shrubs need periodic pruning to keep the plantings in bounds and to remove old and diseased portions. In colder locations, gardeners can expect winter injury that needs late winter removal. The plants grow lanky with time; give them an early spring rejuvenation pruning. Some pests that may affect the thryallis include caterpillars and grasshoppers. Hand pick pests from the plantings, or treat them with a pesticide recommended by the University of Florida, following label instructions.

ADDITIONAL SPECIES, CULTIVARS, OR VARIETIES

One additional species, *Galphimia gracilis*, is planted in Florida landscapes. It resembles the common thryallis. They are often sold as the same plant.

ADVICE FOR REGIONAL CARE

Because of its cold sensitivity, the thryallis is limited to Central and South Florida. In the colder regions, give the plants a protected location, and be ready to prune in late winter.

Wax Myrtle

Myrica cerifera

Height: 15 to 25 ft.
Zones: All
Light Requirement:

Native to the entire state, wax myrtle wanders among the cocoplum, the pond apples, and the sweet bay magnolia in the estuaries and strands of the Everglades, then heads into the hammocks and meanders through the open pinelands. While the image of South Florida is that of orange trees and coconut palms, these plants are foreign born. The wax myrtle, sabal palm, and palmetto speak in a Florida dialect. Great clumps of wax myrtle can be seen from many a highway, which is how we most often see landscapes today, and in winter, it often gives a brownish green color to otherwise gray-brown settings. It is twiggy and dense, but can be more open growing in light shade. It is a wonderful wildlife plant, a fine cover for wrens and warblers, utilized for nesting and perching by smaller birds, and its berries are fed upon in autumn by the migrants heading south. Flowers are tiny and grow on catkins, or small spikes. The female flowers are green; male flowers are greenish yellow. For those who want privacy, wax myrtles can grow into screens. Yet they can also be shaped into hedges. The plant can send up root suckers, but the aroma is so pleasant and uplifting that it outweighs the troublesome suckering. I've planted a wax myrtle in the very poor, rocky soil in Dade County and have not had a problem with root suckers, which may indicate that the plant at 6 years doesn't sucker yet or that poor soil doesn't encourage it. P. B. Tomlinson in *The Biology of Trees Native to Tropical Florida* says the wax myrtle in South Florida often forms a small tree. The berries are covered with a grayish waxy substance once made into candles and soap.

WHEN TO PLANT

Plant at the beginning of the rainy season, late May / early June, or from March to midsummer if consistent irrigation is practical early on.

WHERE TO PLANT

Plant it wherever your heart desires. This is a supremely versatile plant.

HOW TO PLANT

Dig a hole twice as wide but just as deep as the rootball. If roots in the container are circling, then make several 1/4-in. cuts in the rootball with a sharp knife to promote new, outward root growth. Water in backfill to eliminate air pockets. Mulch to a depth of 3 or 4 in., making sure the mulch is several inches away from the trunk of the shrub to prevent fungus.

ADVICE FOR CARE

Occasional pruning and 6-6-6 fertilizer with micronutrients in spring and fall are about the only things needed for the hardy wax myrtle after it is established. It's an excellent plant for Xeriscape, low-maintenance, and native landscapes.

ADDITIONAL INFORMATION

The wax myrtle is dioecious, so if you have a male plant, you won't have berries.

ADDITIONAL SPECIES, CULTIVARS, AND VARIETIES

Myrica heterophylla is green bayberry and *M. inodora* is an odorless bayberry.

ADVICE FOR REGIONAL CARE

Care is similar throughout Florida.

Wild Coffee

Psychotria nervosa

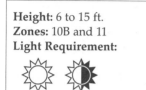

Height: 6 to 15 ft.
Zones: 10B and 11
Light Requirement:

When finely grown, this is one of South Florida's loveliest shrubs. The leaf texture and shine are positive additions to any garden, while the plant is especially useful in native gardens. The specific name, nervosa, means "well-developed nerves," which we take to mean leaf veins. It doesn't have anything to do with nerve jangle from drinking coffee. If at first, native shrubs confuse you—as they do everyone on first encounter—this is one you can immediately identify and use as a stepping-stone along the path of taxonomic skills in the woods. The shrub stretches out and becomes lanky in the shade, but stays compact in sun. High or partial shade is ideal. Seeds of the *Psychotria* can take up to 6 months to germinate, yet you will find seedlings here and there in your native plant garden. If you want to propagate wild coffee for your own use, you can germinate the seeds and transplant them after the second set of true leaves form. Keep seedlings in partial shade at first, and after about a month move them into sun. Wild coffee is related to firebush, and the shrubs are a nice complement for each other. The firebush is bigger and a faster grower, and it will take more pruning. Wild coffee, beautyberry, and wax myrtle are 3 excellent bird-attracting native shrubs. Blend in a necklace pod shrub, add a gumbo limbo, a paradise tree, and a pigeon plum, and you have a wonderful, home-grown hammock. And the wildlife will thank you for it.

When to Plant

Plant at the beginning of the rainy season, late May / early June, or from March to midsummer if consistent irrigation is practical early on.

Where to Plant

Use as part of a mixed border of native plants, as understory shrubs in a hammock planting, or as an informal hedge. Plant in partial shade to full sun.

How to Plant

Dig a hole just as deep but 1 ft. wider than the rootball (2 to 3 times as wide in rocky ground). If roots in the container are circling, then make several 1/4-in. cuts in the rootball with a sharp knife to promote new, outward root growth. Water in backfill to eliminate air pockets. Build a saucerlike basin of soil around the edge of the planting area to retain water. Mulch to a depth of 3 or 4 in., making sure the mulch is several inches away from the trunk of the shrub to prevent fungus.

Advice for Care

Keep the root zone moist until the shrub is established, then water during periods of drought. Coffee wilts when thirsty. Use a 6-6-6 or 7-3-7 fertilizer twice yearly, in spring and fall, for these plants to look their best.

Additional Information

Wild coffee takes well to pruning, but not shearing. Pruning in spring will make a fuller shrub; pruning done in summer, after renewal growth has flushed, serves to shape a shrub.

Additional Species, Cultivars, or Varieties

Psychotria ligustrifolia is Bahama wild coffee, with smaller leaves resembling ligustrum. In addition to the Bahamas, this coffee grows in the Florida Keys. *Psychotria sulzneri* is soft-leaved wild coffee. The leaves have a slight velvet texture and are gray-green.

Advice for Regional Care

This plant is recommended for use in South Florida. Wild coffee is not a landscape plant for Central or North Florida.

CHAPTER ELEVEN

Trees

*A*SOUTHERN LIVE OAK MAY LIVE FOR 200 OR 300 OR MORE YEARS. Its massive branches can stretch horizontally, if allowed, so that the canopy is wider than the tree is tall. Its furrowed bark and leathery leaves support millions of living creatures, smaller than we can see, and a good many large enough for us to discern: lichens, mosses, liverworts, a couple of squirrel nests, gnats, aphids, hairstreak larvae, germinating seeds of bromeliads, mats of resurrection fern and whisk fern, an ant highway, and a well-worn path of raccoons that teeter from topmost branches and watch the goings-on below. A whole world lives in this one organism, and on, around, and under it, while it, too, thickens, stretches, and lengthens through complex metabolic activities.

It pulls water from the ground at the rate of hundreds of gallons a day, and it takes in carbon dioxide from the air and releases oxygen. The mycorrhizae attached to its roots are probably connected to other trees around it, like the invisible strings of matter in the universe, linking and interacting with other trees. Dissolved minerals flow into the vascular tissue, up and out to the limbs and leaves. The machinery to produce the leaves and cause them to fall at the right time, to produce flowers and acorns in their course, is hidden in the smallest bits of material within these cells, cells that constantly are being born and constantly dying. The cellulose of the cells is thicker on the tops of branches to act like muscles, allowing the tree to bear the great weight. When a branch is not needed any

longer, tissue around the inside of the branch connection isolates
that section of trunk as a guard against disease, while on the outside, a callus is formed to seal over the wound.

So trees are more than the sum of their parts; they are living and
breathing entities that support, protect, feed, shelter, and shade
other living and breathing entities—including you. And while
they're at it, they adapt, reproduce, evolve, so that they, like the rest
of us, can survive.

Florida has an enormous number of native trees, which have
adapted and evolved to suit the conditions in which they find themselves, from mangroves that grow in salt water to scrub oaks that
make do in arid and infertile sands.

Some of these natives are North Florida residents only and
don't venture into the warmer parts of the state, and vice versa.
Dogwood, sweetgum, black gum, sycamore, and linden stay away
from the likes of gumbo limbo, fiddlewood, and sea grape. A hand-
ful of temperate trees venture south, including red maple, persim-
mon, wax myrtle, and live oak.

In the southern tip of the peninsula and the Florida Keys, tropical
trees of the West Indies such as West Indies mahogany, lignum vitae,
and wild tamarind are found in sun-dappled forests and hammocks.

As you plan your garden, think architecturally about trees and
the way they can enhance your home by framing it, tying it visually
into its setting, providing the background against which other
vignettes may be composed. When flowering or changing color,
trees themselves are living canvases.

Chapter Eleven

Be sure you know the mature size of trees you select for your home so that you can locate them properly in the right soils and drainage conditions, in ways that will cool and shade the house but won't threaten it in storms or invade the water pipes or the drain field. If a breathtaking flowering tree will be too large for your yard when it is mature, then you may want to find a shrub with the same color that will serve you better.

Look up when selecting a planting site. Are there power lines that will result in years of hard pruning for the tree you have in mind? If so, select a smaller tree. Before you begin digging, call your local utilities company to come out and check the site for underground pipes or cables.

If you are planning to plant on a swale, remember it is public property. Contact your local building and codes department for restrictions.

If planting your own trees, you most likely will buy them in containers. Large, field-grown trees should be transplanted by professionals with equipment such as backhoes that can more easily move the enormous rootballs.

When buying a containerized tree, slip the container off the rootball, and look at the root system. Roots should be white and healthy, not soggy or brownish-black. They should fill the container, but not poke out the bottom drain holes or circle the inside of the pot. If roots creep up and over others, they may effectively girdle the tree, preventing the flow of water and nutrients between roots and leaves as the tree enlarges.

Chapter Eleven

To ensure survival of the transplant, water daily for 1 to 4 weeks; every other day for the next 2 weeks; twice a week for the next 4 to 6 weeks; weekly thereafter until the tree has been in the ground for the first year's growing season. Planting at the beginning of the rainy season may lessen the need for manual irrigation. The roots should not dry during the first growing season; they grow inches every day and often many yards every year.

Begin your garden with the trees, and you will begin on sure footing.

Avocado

Persea americana

Height: to 20 ft.
Zones: 10, 11
Light Requirement:

Avocado, a pretty tree, offers tasty fruits that can be eaten fresh with a little salad dressing or used in salad dishes. Some older folks tell of war times when they buttered bread with advocados, which are high in oils. Many a gardener got a start by growing avocados from a fruit bought at a grocery store. The large seed sprouted over a glass of water, and the gardener was on the way to growing a tree. These self-started seeds, though fun to grow, don't always result in the best varieties, and gardeners are encouraged to obtain a grafted tree. There are many varieties to choose from, each with different characteristics. Some produce green fruits, some purple fruits, and some produce fruits that are especially large. Those with Mexican parentage have the highest degree of cold tolerance, occasionally surviving freezing weather. Even if you don't want the fruit of an avocado, it is a good tree for providing shade and creating framing for the home. Most are planted to the rear or side of the property so the fruits that fall won't make too much of a mess.

WHEN TO PLANT

Trees transplant best during the dormant time of the year, normally between December and February. Most avocado trees are available in containers at local garden centers and can be added to the landscape at any time of the year.

WHERE TO PLANT

Give avocados a full-sun location. It's best to position this tree at least 15 to 20 ft. from buildings, sidewalks, and streets. Provide a site without overhead wires and away from drain fields. Avocado trees grow best in a well-drained soil; wet soils may lead to root rot problems.

HOW TO PLANT

Avocado plants grow well in sandy Florida soils. You can reduce the required care by enriching most planting sites with organic matter. Before planting trees, you have to improve a large area with compost or peat moss and manure. Prepare a hole that's about 2 times wider than the rootball but no deeper. Position the avocado tree in the hole at the same depth it was growing in the field or container. Add soil and sufficient water to give good soil-to-root contact. After planting, create a berm of soil around the edge of the rootball to act as a basin to hold irrigation water; then add a 2- to 3-in. mulch layer.

ADVICE FOR CARE

After planting, keep the avocado tree moist. Some growers like to water every day for the first few weeks, then gradually taper off to watering on an "as needed" basis. The tree is ready for a first feeding 4 to 6 weeks after planting. Continue feeding new trees every other month, March through September. Established trees can be given light feedings in February, April, June, and September with an avocado-type fertilizer. Established avocado trees require watering only during periods of severe drought—but for best production, water weekly.

ADDITIONAL INFORMATION

An avocado tree needs pruning to keep a straight trunk and develop even branching. Most pruning is performed after harvest. Pests that commonly affect avocado include lace bugs, scales, caterpillars, and grasshoppers. When needed, apply a control recommended by the University of Florida, following label instructions.

ADDITIONAL SPECIES, CULTIVARS, OR VARIETIES

Many avocado varieties have been developed for Florida planting. Some with the most cold resistance are Brogdon, Gainesville, Lula, Mexicola, Taylor, Tonnage, and Winter Mexican. Other good varieties for warmer locations are Booth 7, Choquette, Hall, Monroe, Pollock, Ruehle, Simmonds, and Waldin.

ADVICE FOR REGIONAL CARE

Avocados grow well in South Florida. Plant avacados in the spring or at the beginning of the rainy season, late May or early June. In hurricane-prone South Florida, keep avocados pruned because the wood breaks readily in storms. An appropriate fertilizer for fruit trees in South Florida is 8-3-9 or 8-2-10 with an additional three percent magnesium and micronutrients. Residents of Central Florida must choose the cold-resistant varieties, though some years even these will suffer damage. When cold does affect the trees, later winter pruning is needed.

Bald Cypress

Taxodium distichum

Height: can be 100 ft.
Zones: 8, 9, 10, 11
Light Requirement:

One of Florida's prettiest trees is the native bald cypress. These are the large trees that grow right into the water and can be seen at the edge of many neighborhood lakes. One intriguing feature is their trunklike limbless growths that are just a foot or two high—residents call these "knees." When the trees grow near the water, the knees help provide air to the roots. Most residents don't realize that the bald cypress is just as happy growing in sandy soils with limited amounts of water as it is growing in water. Under the drier conditions, they don't develop their knees. Bald cypress trees grow quite large, often over 100 ft. tall; they are best used to frame the house and property. The needlelike leaves have a feathery appearance, giving a light airy feeling to the landscape. Throughout the summer the leaves are bright green. During the fall they turn a coppery color and drop from the trees. Bald cypress can be used where large trees are needed for shade and where there is room for street trees.

WHEN TO PLANT

Trees transplant well during the dormant time of the year, normally between December and February. Most bald cypress are available in containers at local garden centers and can be added to the landscape at any time of the year, though the cooler and more dormant times are best for planting.

WHERE TO PLANT

Give the bald cypress a full-sun location. It's best to position this tree at least 15 to 20 ft. from buildings, sidewalks, and streets. Provide a site without overhead wires and away from drain fields. Bald cypress is one of the few Florida trees that can grow in wet or dry soils. Many are seen growing right in the lake, though they are best planted near the lake's edge.

How to Plant

There is no need to give bald cypress special soil preparation at planting time. Just open up the hole and add the tree at the same depth it was growing in the container. Add soil and sufficient water to give good soil-to-root contact. If planted in a dry area, create a berm of soil around the edge of the rootball to act as a basin to hold irrigation water. Then add a 2- to 3-inch mulch layer. When planted in wet areas, the trees establish quicker if the rootballs are not completely submerged in water. But even those planted in water can grow to be normal trees.

Advice for Care

Keep the bald cypress trees planted in the drier areas moist. Some growers like to water every day for the first few weeks then gradually taper off to watering as needed. Trees planted out of the water are ready for their first feeding 4 to 6 weeks after planting. Continue the feedings in March and in June for the first 2 to 3 years. Trees along the lakes and in water do not need special feedings. Established bald cypress trees growing out of the wet areas need watering only during periods of severe drought.

Additional Information

Bald cypress trees may need pruning to keep a straight trunk and to develop even branching around the trunk. Most pruning is performed during the winter months. Caterpillars may affect the bald cypress. They are seldom a major problem, but if needed, the natural Bacillus thuringiensis insecticide can be applied as instructed on the label. Where other pests are noted, check with the Cooperative Extension Service for a University of Florida recommended control.

Additional Species, Cultivars, or Varieties

One additional species, the pond cypress *Taxodium ascendens*, is often found growing near lakes. It's similar to the bald cypress, but its needles are more appressed to the stems. It is sometimes available at garden centers and native plant nurseries.

Advice for Regional Care

Bald cypress grows throughout the state of Florida. It needs similar care in all areas.

Black Olive

Bucida buceras

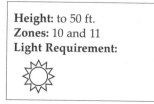

Height: to 50 ft.
Zones: 10 and 11
Light Requirement:

A native of Central America and the West Indies, the black olive is a tree for large yards or for use as a street tree. A moderately fast-growing tree, it has dark-gray bark, simple leaves, and zigzagged branches. If you look carefully at the crown, you can see that it grows in tiers, like its relative the tropical almond. Because of their good qualities, black olives were planted with much too liberal a hand a couple of decades ago, and they fell to the bottom of the tree lover's list because they were overused. That doesn't diminish their good qualities; it simply means a bigger palette of trees ought to be used in the landscape. The crown of a mature black olive is a huge thing, and home owners tend to underestimate its size. Therefore, many black olives are hat-racked (limbs cut back to stubs). This causes massive resprouting and results in an extra-dense canopy that is vulnerable to wind-toss. Remember the trees downed by Hurricane Andrew. When selected for the right place and maintained properly, the black olive is a fine tree, resistant to wind and tolerant of salt breezes. It grows well on rocky soil. Black olives drop leaves and replace them throughout the year, so the tree is evergreen. The flowers are tiny, appearing in April. Older reference books recommend the black olive for a windbreak and seaside planting.

When to Plant

Plant in the spring, at the beginning of the rainy season, or until midsummer. The end of May through early June is best to take advantage of the rainy season that will help keep the rootball moist during establishment.

Where to Plant

Plant in a large area so that it can develop without being cut back severely. It is adaptable to many situations. Eastern or western locations ought to be considered to help reduce heat buildup in the walls of concrete block houses, thus saving on your energy bills.

How to Plant

Dig a hole as deep as and 2 to 3 times as wide as the rootball. Remove the container from the rootball, and position the tree in the planting hole. If you enrich the soil, use not more than $1/3$ peat, compost, or aged manure to $2/3$ of the backfill. Water in the soil as you fill the planting hole to eliminate air pockets that kill roots. Mulch, keeping mulch 2 or 3 in. away from the trunk to avoid disease.

Advice for Care

Keep the rootball moist until the tree is established—which means until the growth rate of the new tree is that of a mature tree. It takes 3 to 4 months per inch of trunk diameter for a tree to become established, and during that time, the rootball needs to be moist. Your job is to water daily for 1 month to 3 months, then gradually taper off to every other day, then every third day. Fertilize 3 months after planting, using a 6-6-6 or another balanced fertilizer with micronutrients. Young trees may be fertilized 3 times a year, in late February/early March, June/July, and late October/early November. In alkaline soil, which has high amounts of phosphorus which ties up micronutrients, you may want to use a 7-3-7 or 12-4-12-4 for long-term fertilizing needs. Once mature, the black olive needs very little attention. If you fertilize your lawn, that may well be enough to keep your mature trees supplied with nutrients. Prune dead wood, crossing branches, and water sprouts. Consult an arborist on crown shaping before you prune to shape the tree.

Additional Information

Some black olives develop long spiraling fruit as a result of a kind of gall from mites.

Additional Species, Cultivars, or Varieties

Bucida spinosa, a native of the Bahamas, is a small Oriental-looking tree that is often used as a bonsai subject.

Advice for Regional Care

Plant in a protected area or southern exposure outside southern Florida because the black olive can be cold sensitive.

Bottlebrush

Callistemon rigidus

Other Names: *Callistemon viminalis* Weeping Bottlebrush
Height: to 15 ft.
Zones: 9, 10, 11
Light Requirement:

Bottlebrush trees add a tropical look to the landscape. The flowers cluster along the ends of the stems, resembling a red bottlebrush. This is a good accent plant for an area near the entrance, off the patio, or at the end of a view. Where there is room, consider clustering several together for a burst of spring color. The plants continue to produce sporadic flowers throughout most of the year. Many gardeners have found the bottlebrush to be a good space divider, as the trees are evergreen and keep their branches near the ground. They can be grown as an unclipped hedge and used as a view barrier.

WHEN TO PLANT

The trees transplant best during the dormant time of the year, normally between December and February. Most bottlebrush plants are available in containers at local garden centers. Though they can be added to the landscape at any time of the year, the cooler and more dormant times are best.

WHERE TO PLANT

Give bottlebrush a sunny location. It's best to position this tree at least 10 to 15 ft. from buildings, sidewalks, and streets, but it's not abnormal to find them just a little closer. This is a good small tree to plant under overhead wires without having to worry about the trees growing too tall. Plant bottlebrush away from drain fields. These trees grow best in a well-drained soil.

HOW TO PLANT

Bottlebrush grows well in sandy Florida soils. You can reduce the amount of care required by enriching most planting sites with organic matter. When planting trees, even small ones, you have to improve a large area with compost or peat moss and manure. Open a hole that's about 2 times wider than the rootball but no deeper. Position the bottlebrush tree in the hole at the same depth it was

growing in the field or container. Add soil and sufficient water to give good soil-to-root contact. After planting, create a berm of soil around the edge of the rootball to act as a basin to hold irrigation water, and add a 2- to 3-inch mulch layer.

ADVICE FOR CARE
After planting, keep the bottlebrush tree moist. Some growers like to water every day for the first few weeks, then gradually taper off to watering as needed. This tree is ready for a first feeding 4 to 6 weeks after planting. Continue the feedings, once in March and once in June, for the first 2 to 3 years. Established bottlebrush trees need watering only during periods of severe drought.

ADDITIONAL INFORMATION
Bottlebrush trees are usually grown with several trunks that branch out from the base starting a few feet from the ground. They may need pruning to help them develop an even branching habit. Most pruning is performed during late spring after the major bloom. It usually consists of removing limbs that interfere with traffic or plant care. Pests are few, but one that can affect the bottlebrush is nematodes. Before adding nursery-grown plants to the landscape, plant them in a nematode-free soil. No control exists for nematode-affected trees.

ADDITIONAL SPECIES, CULTIVARS, OR VARIETIES
There are numerous varieties of bottlebrush available for home plantings. One species, *Callistemon citrinus*, resembles the species *Callistemon rigidus*. The main difference is a shorter broader leaf that has a citrus smell when crushed. Species *Callistemon viminalis* is also a favorite and has a weeping growth habit. Some varieties of bottlebrush have flowers that are a deeper red than the standard species. There are also bottlebrush trees that have green-and-violet flowers.

ADVICE FOR REGIONAL CARE
Bottlebrush grows well throughout the Central and Southern parts of Florida. In Central Florida, give the plantings a warm location. They may suffer cold damage during some winters and may need pruning before spring growth begins. In South Florida, plant at the beginning of the rainy season. Bottlebrushes thrive with regular water and fertilizer in South Florida conditions. Occasionally they are prone to witches' broom—which is the profusion of twigs. Witches' brooms often are caused by fungi or mites. Prune off the affected area.

Crape Myrtle

Lagerstroemia indica

Height: 15 to 20 ft.
Zones: 8, 9, 10
Light Requirement:

Crape myrtles were imported into the Northern states during the mid-1700s, but luckily, it was too cold for good growth, and plant enthusiasts brought them South. They flourish here and have become one of the basic small trees that can be found in just about every landscape. They so closely resemble the lilacs left behind in the North that they became known as the "lilac of the South." Crape myrtles provide year-round interest that few landscapes can be without. It's a great accent, giving clusters of colorful flowers beginning in May and lasting through September. In fall, it provides colorful foliage that turns from yellow to orange. In winter, you will see an attractive bark that ranges from tan to cinnamon depending on the variety. Use crape myrtles as small trees to frame the house or to line the streets, and plant a crape myrtle near an entrance or off a patio. Where possible, it's best to cluster 3 or more together for a impressive display of summer color. The plants are also good to use at the end of a vista to create an attractive accent.

WHEN TO PLANT

Trees transplant best during the dormant time of the year, normally between December and February. Most crape myrtles are available in containers at local garden centers and can be added to the landscape at any time of the year.

WHERE TO PLANT

Give crape myrtles a sunny location. It's best to position this tree at least 15 to 20 ft. from buildings, sidewalks, and streets, but many are planted a bit closer. This is one plant that can be set under overhead wires without having to worry about it growing too tall. It should be planted away from drain fields. Crape myrtles grow best in a well-drained soil.

HOW TO PLANT

Crape myrtles take to our sandy Florida soils. You can reduce the amount of care needed by enriching most planting sites with organic matter. When planting trees, you must improve a large area with compost or peat moss and manure. Open a hole that's about 2 times wider than the rootball but no deeper. Position the crape myrtle tree in the hole at the same depth it was growing in the field or container. Add soil and sufficient water to give good soil-to-root contact. After planting, create a berm of soil around the edge of the rootball to act as a basin to hold irrigation water and add a 2- to 3-inch mulch layer.

ADVICE FOR CARE

Keep the crape myrtle tree moist. Some growers like to water every day for the first few weeks, then gradually taper off to watering as needed. Continue the feedings, once in March and once in June, for the first 2 to 3 years. Trees along the lakes and in water do not need special feedings. Established crape myrtle trees require watering only during periods of severe drought, though they do flower best when given weekly waterings.

ADDITIONAL INFORMATION

Crape myrtle trees need pruning to keep a straight trunk and to develop even branching around the trunk. Many, however, are grown with multiple trunks from the ground. Some pruning is needed to restrict the trunks to between 5 and 7. Most pruning is performed during the late winter season. Please do not remove stems larger than pencil-sized in diameter. Pests that commonly affect crape myrtle trees include aphids and white flies. When a control is needed, apply an oil, soap, or other insect spray recommended by the University of Florida, following the label instructions.

ADDITIONAL SPECIES, CULTIVARS, OR VARIETIES

Numerous hybrids of the common crape myrtle have been developed for landscape use. Some that are resistant to the common disease powdery mildew are named after American Indian tribes, including Miami, Muskogee, Natchez, and Tuscarora. There are also many smaller crape myrtles that can be used as shrubs in the home landscape. One additional species, *Lagerstroemia speciosa*, has extra-large flower clusters. Known as the queen's crape myrtle, it grows only in South Florida.

ADVICE FOR REGIONAL CARE

The standard crape myrtle grows best in North and Central Florida. South Florida residents should select mildew-resistant varieties to ensure good flowering.

Geiger Tree

Cordia sebestena

Height: 25 ft.
Zones: 10 and 11
Light Requirement:

One of the few flowering trees native to South Florida and the Florida Keys, the Geiger tree was said to be named by John J. Audubon for boat pilot and wrecker John Geiger from Key West. Audubon stayed at Geiger's house when he visited the island to paint tropical birds—and painted white-crowned pigeons on a branch of a Geiger. Two Geiger trees at what is now the Audubon House in Key West are said to be more than 100 years old. The trees were introduced to Key West from Cuba in the 1820s. The Geiger's leaves have the texture of sandpaper, and the crepe-textured flowers are bold orange, appearing throughout the year. Hummingbirds, such as the rare Bahama Woodstar, are attracted to the bright flowers. It's a tough little tree that is salt tolerant and drought tolerant, but not cold tolerant. Leaves—particularly those on young trees—will turn brown when temperatures hit the low 40s to upper 30s. In a freeze, the tree will die back to the ground but resprout from the roots.

WHEN TO PLANT
Plant at the beginning of the rainy season (end of May or early June), throughout early and midsummer.

WHERE TO PLANT
Plant in full sun in a well-draining or dry area, perhaps with other native trees on the perimeter of the yard where irrigation doesn't reach. It may be planted with sea grape and seven-year-apple for a natural-looking setting along the coasts, or simply honored by a place of its own.

HOW TO PLANT
When transplanting from a pot, dig a hole 3 times as wide as the rootball and as deep. Remove the container from the rootball; situate the tree in the planting hole so that the top of the rootball is even with the soil surface. Fill in with soil from the planting hole. Use a

hose to water in the soil as you fill the hole to remove any air pockets. Mulch to a depth of 3 to 4 in., being careful to keep mulch from getting next to the tree's trunk to avoid disease.

ADVICE FOR CARE
Once established, this hardy tree needs little more than occasional irrigation in the dry season and fertilizer once or twice a year, in spring and fall. The Geiger beetle can be a nuisance. A metallic green-and-blue beetle that menaces the trees in the spring, it can cause defoliation. Adults eat the leaves, and larvae damage roots. Use Sevin or Rotenone on the larvae. A single Geiger is less likely to attract beetles than several in close proximity.

ADDITIONAL INFORMATION
Early South Florida settlers are said to have used the tough leaves to scrub pots and polish wood. The fruit of the Geiger, about the size of a big macadamia nut, is white when ripe and somewhat fragrant. I have germinated a few, but it takes many months, and I have found the roots to be scant. The seedlings wilt readily and seem to require extra protection.

ADDITIONAL SPECIES, CULTIVARS, OR VARIETIES
Cordia boissieri is a cold-tolerant and white-flowering relative from Texas that is a beautiful year-round bloomer. It is a pretty tree with a round canopy. Cold doesn't faze it but, on the contrary, seems to jolt it into producing more flowers. Some landscape designers and architects favor this over the orange-flowering Geiger. It, too, is drought tolerant but not as salt tolerant as the Geiger. *Cordia lutea* is a yellow-flowering version, smallest of the three cordias.

ADVICE FOR REGIONAL CARE
Used away from the water in South Florida, the Geiger will need some winter protection, such as a windbreak of trees or a cozy southeast corner. Not appropriate for Central or North Florida.

TREES

Grapefruit

Citrus × paradisi

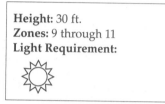

Height: 30 ft.
Zones: 9 through 11
Light Requirement:

A chief benefit of living in Florida is picking a sweet, plump, juicy grapefruit for breakfast from a tree in the backyard. Grapefruit trees are larger than most other citrus except sweet oranges, and their fruit is larger, too, though not nearly so big as the parent pommelo or pummelo (which can measure 12 in. in diameter). Introduced into Florida in the early 19th century, the grapefruit probably developed in the West Indies. The pommelo, originally from Malaysia and Indonesia, was carried to Spain by the Arabs and to the West Indies from there in the 17th century. Many varieties come true to seed, but some don't. That means that often what you plant is what you will get—but sometimes not. Grapefruit from seed may take 6 to 10 or more years to bear fruit. Grapefruit demand good drainage and require fertilizers with extra magnesium, but they repay your efforts. Grapefruit may begin ripening in November or December and continue to hold their fruit through winter.

When to Plant

The best time to plant is at the beginning of the rainy season (end of May or early June), throughout early and midsummer. However, you may plant year-round.

Where to Plant

Use in a sunny location that has excellent drainage. Grapefruit trees, because of their dark-green leaves and medium height, are good for framing your house and garden because more colorful plants will show up well against them.

How to Plant

When transplanting from a pot, dig a hole 2 to 3 times as wide as the rootball and just as deep. Remove the container from the rootball; situate the tree in the planting hole so that the top of the rootball is even with the soil surface. Use a hose to water in the soil as you fill the hole to remove any air pockets. Keep mulch away from the trunk, and mulch lightly.

ADVICE FOR CARE

Use a citrus fertilizer, such as 8-2-10-3, 3 times a year for bearing trees, and water weekly in periods of drought. Keep grass from growing beneath the trees. Sucking insects, such as aphids, mealy-bugs, and whiteflies, are attracted to new leaves and can cause curling. Insecticidal soap, or 2 tablespoons liquid detergent in a gallon of water, can be used against sucking pests. Sooty mold on citrus occurs when insects on the undersides of leaves excrete a honeydew that sticks to the leaves beneath them, and mold grows on the honeydew. Soapy water can help remove the mold. Leaf miners are a current pest. They are larvae of tiny moths that develop from eggs laid in the leaves. The larvae eat their way out of the leaf by tunneling just beneath the surface.

ADDITIONAL INFORMATION

Giant swallowtail butterflies lay eggs on citrus, and caterpillars eat the leaves. Prune dead wood from crowns, but little other pruning is needed.

ADDITIONAL SPECIES, CULTIVARS, OR VARIETIES

'Marsh', 'Redblush' (the new name for 'Ruby'), 'Thomson', 'Duncan', and 'Flame' are some of the cultivars available.

ADVICE FOR REGIONAL CARE

Grapefruit trees require similar care throughout Central Florida.

Gumbo Limbo

Bursera simaruba

Height: to 50 ft. or more **Zones:** 10B and 11 **Light Requirement:**

From the coastal hammocks of South Florida and the West Indies, the gumbo limbo is instantly recognizable by its red to silver-red and peeling bark. Park and preserve guides will tell you it is nicknamed the tourist tree for its red, flaking skin, but that name has been relegated to the fable file and isn't really used. An older tree can develop remarkable girth, with heavy branches and a spare canopy. Its shade is more or less mottled and shifting. In late winter, the gumbo begins to lose leaves, and new growth can begin in late February or March. It flowers in the early spring, but don't look for a show; the flowers are but 3/16 in. in diameter. Fruit, which develop over summer, are noisily appreciated by mockingbirds, vireos, and naturalized parrots. The dingy purple-wing, a rare butterfly, uses it as larval food. The gumbo has been put to good use over the years. It is said the Indians, presumably the Miccosukees of South Florida, used the sticky resinous sap as a bird trap, spreading it on branches. When birds were unable to fly away, they were caught and caged, and used to entertain cigar makers in Key West and Cuba. The sap also once was boiled into a gum and used to make varnish or glue for canoes; the leaves were used to make tea and remedies for snake bites.

WHEN TO PLANT
Plant at the beginning of the rainy season (end of May or early June), throughout early and midsummer.

WHERE TO PLANT
Plant in sun or light shade; choose a spot with good drainage.

HOW TO PLANT
The trees can be started from branch cuttings. The planting hole should be 12 to 18 in. deep, and the cutting should be watered faithfully until leaves begin to emerge, which can take several weeks. It

330

pays to water the entire branch as well as the root zone. Forestry professors from the University of Florida found that a greater number of gumbos from cuttings were thrown over in Hurricane Andrew than those that grew from seed.

ADVICE FOR CARE

Once established, the gumbo limbo needs little care. Water in periods of drought; keep mulched. The tree is cold sensitive and will drop leaves after cold snaps.

ADDITIONAL INFORMATION

Gumbo limbos have some salt tolerance since they are native to coastal areas.

ADDITIONAL SPECIES, CULTIVARS, OR VARIETIES

Tomlinson in *The Biology of Trees Native to Tropical Florida* says two other species are from the southwestern United States, but *Bursera* is the only New World genus in the family.

ADVICE FOR REGIONAL CARE

Gumbo limbos are recommended for use in South Florida. This is not a tree for use in Central and North Florida.

Lignum Vitae

Guaiacum sanctum

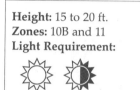

Height: 15 to 20 ft.
Zones: 10B and 11
Light Requirement:

Slow growing, with extremely hard wood and black heartwood, the lignum vitae is a tree loved in Florida and throughout the West Indies. Contemporary wood turners use the wood for bowls and cups, though the tree is endangered and wood is hard to come by. Early after the discovery of the New World by Europeans, the wood was taken to Europe, where its resin was said to cure syphilis, among other diseases. The tree has a rich history, not only because of medicinal uses of the sap for arthritis, rheumatism, and skin diseases, but also because the wood itself is so heavy it will not float and it has been employed in boat and even submarine construction. The United States Navy harvested trees from the Florida Keys, where it naturally occurs in Florida, and so few are left today that they are endangered. Lignum Vitae Key is a state botanical preserve and a protected site. The name, tree of life, no doubt stems from its medicinal qualities, but it also has been called holy wood (*sanctum* of its botanical name means "holy"). It grows throughout the Caribbean. On Puerto Rico, it mingles with gumbo limbo on the arid western side of the island. It is the national tree of the Bahamas.

WHEN TO PLANT

Plant at the beginning of the rainy season (end of May or early June), throughout early and midsummer.

WHERE TO PLANT

Plant this where the small flowers can be seen by guests entering the house, near a patio, or keep in a large pot for years. Though extremely slow, lignum vitae can produce considerable canopy if not shaped. Plant in full sun in a spot with excellent drainage.

HOW TO PLANT

When transplanting from a pot, dig a hole 2 to 3 times as wide and just as deep as the rootball. Remove the container from the rootball; situate the tree in the planting hole so that the top of the rootball is even with the soil surface. Backfill with soil from the planting hole. Use a hose to water in the soil as you fill the hole to remove any air pockets. Mulch.

ADVICE FOR CARE

Make sure you keep the rootball moist after planting. The Lignum Vitae Conservation Project of the Key West Garden Club, which seeks to reintroduce the tree to the island, suggests 20-20-20 at half strength weekly for seedlings; use slow-release fertilizer every 3 to 4 months for larger trees. Transplanting is tricky. Root prune at least a month ahead in the rainy season; take the taproot with the rootball if possible; water daily, not only root zone but wood as well. Leaves will drop with transplant shock, but new ones will emerge. A lignum vitae I had transplanted last year dropped its leaves and scared me to death, but with twice daily waterings, it survived.

ADDITIONAL INFORMATION

One of the field characteristics used to recognize this tree — aside from its location — is the little point on the tip of the leaflets on the compound leaves.

ADDITIONAL SPECIES, CULTIVARS, OR VARIETIES

Guaiacum officinale.

ADVICE FOR REGIONAL CARE

This tree is recommended for use in South Florida only.

333

Live Oak

Quercus virginiana

Height: 50 or more ft.
Zones: All
Light Requirement:

Strong, long-lived, and beautiful, the live oak in Florida is a native plant highly prized as a shade tree or street tree. A single, mature live oak in a front yard may be ornament enough for the yard, as bromeliads will eventually germinate on its massive horizontal limbs, lichens will color its furrowed bark, and its branches may spread many yards across. Several aged live oaks are famous in Florida. Fort Lauderdale's Birch State Park boasts a 400-year-old specimen called the Grandfather Oak beneath which John Birch signed the papers deeding the property to the state. Various wounds have been treated over the decades with tin or tar, yet it persists. The Treaty Live Oak in Jacksonville is more than 200 years old, and legend has it that many treaties with Indians were signed beneath it. Although it lost much of its canopy in Hurricane Andrew, a huge tree at the Charles Deering Estate in South Dade County still sits atop a prehistoric Tequesta Indian burial site. The trunk is nearly 4$\frac{1}{2}$ ft. in circumference. When allowed to grow naturally, live oaks are magnificent trees, with great horizontal branches that can stretch twice as wide as the trees are tall. Orlando's Lake Eola Park, near the historic downtown section, is graced with some wonderful oaks whose branches lazily stretch and curve just above the ground. Once the trees were thought to be slow growing, but gardeners have found that fertilizer, water, and mulch can bring much faster results than benign neglect. Leathery, simple leaves are toothed when young and gray-green on the undersides. Young trees can be twiggy. As the crown grows, lower limbs die and drop. Oaks drop their leaves over a couple of weeks in February/March before new leaves flush.

WHEN TO PLANT

In more northern parts of the state, live oaks are planted in the dormant season. In the 1930s, the Florida legislature declared the state's arbor day to be in January since that was the best time to plant oaks. In South Florida, plant any time, but the best time remains the beginning of the rainy season (end of May or early June), throughout early and midsummer.

WHERE TO PLANT
Plant in sun, in a wide range of soils.

HOW TO PLANT
When transplanting from a pot, dig a hole as deep and 3 times as wide as the rootball. Remove the container from the rootball; situate the oak in the planting hole so the top of the rootball is even with the soil surface. Fill in with soil from the planting hole. Use a hose to water in the soil to remove any air pockets that might kill feeder roots. Mulch to a depth of 3 to 4 in., being careful not to pack the mulch next to the tree's trunk in order to avoid disease.

ADVICE FOR CARE
Once the tree is established, little care is necessary. The large crown may require fine pruning to remove deadwood, but oaks usually don't need hard pruning.

ADDITIONAL INFORMATION
Young oaks send up multitudes of root suckers if the soil around the root zone is disturbed. Mulch or plant with groundcover such as ferns that have shallow surface roots. Shade from oaks is ideal for nursing sick plants back to health and for protecting an herb garden in winter. In 1799, the U.S. Congress set aside 350 acres of live oaks in Florida because the wood was so valuable in ship building.

ADDITIONAL SPECIES, CULTIVARS, OR VARIETIES
Quercus laurifolia, the laurel oak, occasionally grows into the northern Everglades of South Florida. A taller (to 100 ft.), shorter-lived tree, it can drop limbs because of weak wood.

Lychee

Litchi chinensis

Height: to 40 ft.
Zones: 10, 11
Light Requirement:

This is a fine tree for the warmer locations of Florida with a fringe benefit: an edible fruit. The trees have a naturally spreading growth habit with branches that sweep down to the ground. The leaves are a very deep green and are shiny, sure to catch attention. New growth is especially attractive, being red at first then turning green. Plantings make a nice shade tree for any area of the landscape. You may want to use them to border the home site and reap the benefits of some late spring through summer fruits. Peel the fruit, and you will find the edible portion is a white pulp that surrounds a large brown seed. The fruits are sweet and slightly acid.

WHEN TO PLANT

Trees transplant best during the dormant time of the year, normally between December and February. Most lychee trees are available in containers at local garden centers and can be added to the landscape at any time of the year.

WHERE TO PLANT

Give lychee trees a sunny location. It's best to position this tree at least 15 to 20 ft. from buildings, sidewalks, and streets. Provide a site without overhead wires and away from drain fields. Lychee trees grow best in a well-drained acid soil. Many are grown in the alkaline soils of South Florida and given special foliar feedings to provide the minor nutrients.

HOW TO PLANT

Lychee trees grow well in sandy Florida soils. You can reduce the amount of care required by enriching most planting sites with organic matter. When planting trees, you have to improve a large area with compost or peat moss and manure. Open a hole that's about 2 times wider than the rootball but no deeper. Position the lychee tree in the hole at the same depth it was growing in the field or container. Add soil and sufficient water to give good soil-to-root contact. Create a berm of soil around the edge of the rootball to act as a basin to hold irrigation water, and add a 2- to 3-inch mulch layer.

TREES

ADVICE FOR CARE

Keep the lychee tree moist. Some growers like to water every day for the first few weeks, then gradually taper off to watering as needed. The tree is ready for a first feeding 4 to 6 weeks after planting. Continue the feedings every other month through September for the first year. Then provide feedings once in March, May, and early October, using a 6-6-6 or fruit tree product. Established lychee trees need watering only during periods of severe drought, but for best fruit production, water at least weekly.

ADDITIONAL INFORMATION

Lychee trees need pruning to keep a straight trunk and to develop even branching around the trunk. Most pruning is performed during late winter. A pest that may affect lychee trees is the scale insect. When needed, apply a fruit tree spray recommended by the University of Florida, following label instructions.

ADDITIONAL SPECIES, CULTIVARS, OR VARIETIES

Numerous varieties of lychee trees have been selected for planting, mainly to give improved fruit production. Some recommended varieties are Bengal, Brewster, Hanging Green, Kwai Mi, Sweet Cliff, and Yellow Red.

ADVICE FOR REGIONAL CARE

Lychee plantings are restricted to South Florida and some very warm areas along the coast of Central Florida. In the limestone soils of South Florida, minor nutrient soil sprays applied to foliage and allowed to drip on top of root zone are usually needed 2 to 3 times a year to prevent deficiencies.

Mahogany

Swietenia mahagoni

Height: to 50 ft.
Zones: 10, 11
Light Requirement:

Once a major source of timber, the native Florida mahogany is now used mainly as a good landscape tree for the warmer climates. It's an upright growing tree with a rounded crown that gardeners like to use for shade, to plant streetside, or to frame the home. This is one tree under which grass can be grown, as it provides only light shade, letting through the filtered sun. It's a tree with good salt tolerance, so it's suitable for planting in coastal landscapes. One particular feature that's really appreciated is the mahogany's resistance to storms. The shape of the tree appears to make it wind resistent, and the wood is tough. Even though some small branches and leaves may be blown from the trees by high winds, they quickly grow back. The leaves are persistent into the fall and winter months; in the spring, they quickly drop from the tree and new growth begins. The flowers are insignificant, and the tree produces a brown pod that's suspended from a string-like stem.

WHEN TO PLANT

Trees transplant best during the dormant time of the year, normally between December and February. Most mahogany trees are available in containers at local garden centers and can be added to the landscape at any time of the year, though the cooler and more dormant times are best for planting.

WHERE TO PLANT

Give the mahogany a full-sun location for best growth, but it does tolerate some light shade. It's best to position this tree at least 15 to 20 ft. from buildings, sidewalks, and streets. It is suggested that street trees be given a 25- to 30-ft. spacing. Provide a site without overhead wires and away from drain fields. Mahogany trees grow best in a well-drained acid or alkaline soils.

HOW TO PLANT

Mahogany trees grow well in sandy Florida soils. You can reduce the amount of care required by enriching most planting sites with organic matter. When planting a tree, you should improve a large area with compost or peat moss and manure. Open a hole that's about 2 times wider than the rootball but no deeper. Position the mahogany tree in the hole at the same depth it was growing in the field or container. Add soil and sufficient water to give good soil-to-root contact. Create a berm of soil around the edge of the rootball to act as a basin to hold irrigation water, and add a 2- to 3-inch mulch layer.

ADVICE FOR CARE

Keep the mahogany tree moist. Some growers like to water every day for the first few weeks, then gradually taper off to watering as needed. The tree is ready for a first feeding 4 to 6 weeks after planting. Continue the feedings, once in March and once in June, for the first 2 to 3 years. Established mahogany trees are drought tolerant and need watering only during periods of severe drought. They do not need additional feedings after the first few years, as they receive the nutrients they need for growth from fertilizer applications to nearby turf and shrub plantings.

ADDITIONAL INFORMATION

Mahogany trees need pruning to keep a straight trunk and to develop even branching around the trunk. Most pruning is performed during the winter months, but an occasional trimming to remove a branch or two can be performed at any time. Pests that commonly affect mahogany trees include caterpillars and borers. When needed, a Bacillus thuringiensis caterpillar control, a borer spray available from garden centers, or other University of Florida recommended controls can be applied, following label instructions.

ADDITIONAL SPECIES, CULTIVARS, OR VARIETIES

The native mahogany is the only species used in the Florida landscape. Another Central and South American relative, *S. macrophylla*, is used for timber, growing too tall for the landscape.

ADVICE FOR REGIONAL CARE

The mahogany is cold sensitive and restricted to use in South Florida in frost- and freeze-free locations. In South Florida, the mahogany is considered semi-deciduous because it drops leaves in spring before flushing out new leaves. Planting is done when leaves are beginning to drop.

Mango

Mangifera indica

Height: 30 to 50 ft.
Zones: 10B and 11
Light Requirement:

One of South Florida's most treasured and delicious fruits, mangos are neighborhood friendly, making great shade and climbing trees as well as fruit trees, and can be long-lived. One of the oldest in the United States is in West Palm Beach. It was sent to Dr. Eldridge Gale, a retired horticulture professor from Kansas State Agriculture College, by David Fairchild, his student. Fairchild founded the plant and seed introduction program of the United States Department of Agriculture, and he had several of the mulgobas sent to Gale from India, where the trees are thought to have originated. A seedling of this tree, planted in 1902 by Capt. John Haden in Coconut Grove, produced the Haden mango, which launched the mango industry in Florida. Two of the original Hadens still stand in the Grove. Big trees, mangoes have broad to round crowns, depending on the cultivar. They are messy, dropping fruit and leaves, and should be placed where such things are not a problem. Trees should be grafted to come true to seed. Flowers may appear in December, and the tree may flower more than once. Fruit, again depending on type and cultivar, mature from May to September.

WHEN TO PLANT
Plant at the beginning of the rainy season (end of May or early June), throughout early and midsummer.

WHERE TO PLANT
Plant in a sunny location at least 30 ft. from the house.

HOW TO PLANT
When transplanting from a pot, dig a hole 2 to 3 times as wide as the rootball and just as deep. Remove the container from the rootball; situate the tree in the planting hole so that the top of the rootball is even with the soil surface. Add organic soil amendments so the peat moss, compost, or aged manure do not exceed 1/3 of the backfill. Use a hose to water in the soil as you fill the hole to remove any air pockets.

ADVICE FOR CARE

Newly planted trees need faithful irrigation so that the root zone stays moist but not wet. Bearing trees should be watered periodically when fruit is developing (often during the end of the dry season) to increase fruit size. Fertilizers such as 6-6-6 or 10-10-10 with additional 3 or 4 percent magnesium are good for juvenile trees; 8-3-9-3 or 8-2-10-3 is best for bearing trees. Use 1 lb. for each inch of trunk diameter measured 1 ft. above the ground. Apply micronutrient sprays about 3 times a year in rocky soil, and use an iron drench once a year.

ADDITIONAL INFORMATION

Many mangos are susceptible to anthracnose, a fungus that attacks leaves, twigs, and fruit. Often no harm is done to the fruit, although the skin may have tearstains running from the stem down the sides. Commercial growers spray frequently; home owners don't have to unless the fungus is severe.

ADDITIONAL SPECIES, CULTIVARS, AND VARIETIES

According to Tomlinson in *The Biology of Trees Native to Tropical Florida*, there are about 40 species in the genus *Mangifera*. In Florida, where high humidity and rainfall are likely to spread fungal spores quickly, it is best to plant cultivars that are resistant to anthracnose. Such cultivars include: Earlygold, Florigon, Saigon, Edward, Glenn, Carrie, Van Dyke, Tommy Atkins, and Keitt. New cultivars are always being introduced. Many are sold at the mango celebration in midsummer at Fairchild Tropical Garden.

ADVICE FOR REGIONAL CARE

Smaller varieties, such as Carrie, can be grown in protected areas in Central Florida.

Orange Tree

Citrus sinensis

Height: to 30 ft.
Zones: 9 to 11
Light Requirement:

Your mother was right. There is no better way to get your Vitamin C than by drinking orange juice. And Florida oranges are famous the world over—even though the fruit originated in China. Columbus introduced the orange to Haiti on his second voyage in 1493. The orange moved to Florida in the 16th century. Most Miamians know the oft-told tale of Julia Tuttle, the mother of Miami, who sent Henry Flagler a flowering twig from an orange tree in winter in order to persuade him to bring his railroad south. When growing citrus in your backyard, good drainage and root stocks are two big considerations. If you live in areas where new neighborhoods have been created on fill, you may have to plant citrus (and other non-wetland trees) on mounds if drainage is poor. Citrus cannot endure wet feet. Rootstock is selected to assure trueness to type and to overcome poor performance on certain soils. Oranges have been grafted on sour orange rootstock, but the occurrence of a viral disease called tristeza is knocking out that stock in Florida. The disease is spread by the brown citrus aphid.

WHEN TO PLANT

Plant at the beginning of the rainy season (end of May or early June), throughout early and midsummer. May be planted year-round.

WHERE TO PLANT

Plant in a sunny location with good drainage. If you live inland, a southern location will help protect citrus from north and northwest winds.

HOW TO PLANT

When transplanting from a pot, dig a hole as deep as the rootball and 2 to 3 times as wide. Remove the container from the rootball; situate the tree in the planting hole so the top of the rootball is even with the soil surface. To the planting hole or backfill add no more than $1/3$ organic material, such as peat moss, compost, or aged manure. Keep the rootball intact when planting, and use a hose to wash in the soil as you fill the hole.

ADVICE FOR CARE

Use regular 6-6-6 fertilizer in frequent, small amounts the first year (4 or 5 times during the growing season, from June through October). Start with $1/2$ lb. and increase the amount so you apply $1 1/2$ lb. for the last application. Fertilize 4 times the second year. The third year, switch to a fruit tree fertilizer such as 8-2-10-3 and reduce the applications to 3. In alkaline soil, foliar sprays of micronutrients 3 times a year are helpful. Whiteflies on the undersides of the leaves excrete honeydew, a host to sooty mold. If leaves turn black, examine the undersides for insects and treat with insecticidal soap or 2 tablespoons liquid detergent in a gallon of water applied with hose-end sprayer.

ADDITIONAL INFORMATION

If it rains heavily while fruit is developing, the skin can split because pulp develops faster than skin. If the tree receives too little moisture, the pulp is dry and grainy. Very young fruit may produce dry pulp. Remove the first fruit to keep from stressing the tree. Little pruning is necessary except to shape and remove deadwood. To test whether to pick the fruit, pick one and taste it. Don't wait for it to turn orange. The giant swallowtail butterfly lays her eggs on citrus leaves, and the caterpillar is called the orange-dog caterpillar.

ADDITIONAL SPECIES, CULTIVARS, OR VARIETIES

Hamlin and navel oranges begin ripening in October; pineapple oranges in December; temple oranges in January; Valencia in March. Dancy tangerines ripen in winter; honey tangerines are later, beginning in February. Among the newest varieties is ambersweet orange, a combination of grapefruit, orange, and tangerine.

ADVICE FOR REGIONAL CARE

Orange trees suffer from freezing weather in Central Florida; prune back in spring afterwards.

Pigeon Plum

Coccoloba diversifolia

Height: 30 to 50 ft.
Zones: 9 through 11
Light Requirement:

As the fall migration of birds funnels down through Florida and the Florida Keys, the pigeon plum's fruits are ripe and ready. When the white-crowned pigeons winter in the Keys, they include this in their foraging. And if any fruits at all are left, raccoons will clean the plate. There are male and female trees, so you might want to wait until spring when the trees flower to purchase one if you have a preference. A tree beneficial to the creatures around it, pigeon plum is plentiful in the coastal hammocks, from the center of the state to the Keys. And increasingly, it is being used in landscaping. Its dense, columnar crown and pretty bark make it useful for street planting as well as for framing a house, even in a formal design. In hammocks, pigeon plums can be tall and slender, competing with other trees in shade for a place in the sun. In sun, the crown is denser, more compact. The simple, bright-green leaves are generally large when the tree is young and reduced in size when it is older. With the appearance of flowers, in March or thereabouts, comes the first flush of new leaves. A second follows later in spring. Fallen leaves turn distinctively golden on the forest floor or in your backyard lawn or mulch. Wild coffee, fire bush, beautyberry, paradise tree, and gumbo limbo would make good companions in a native planting and would assuredly be a magnet for birds.

WHEN TO PLANT

Plant at the beginning of the rainy season, end of May or early June.

WHERE TO PLANT

Plant in sun or shade, with natives or even in formal settings. The pigeon plum is used to harsh conditions; it takes wind and drought well.

How to Plant

Dig a hole as deep as the rootball and 2 to 3 times as wide. Remove the container from the rootball, and position the tree in the planting hole. If you enrich the soil, use not more than 1/3 peat, compost, or aged manure to 2/3 of the backfill. Water in the soil as you fill the planting hole to eliminate air pockets that kill roots. Mulch, keeping mulch 2 or 3 in. away from the trunk to avoid disease.

Advice for Care

Water and fertilize consistently when the tree is young to help it get a good start in life. What's a mother for? When your pigeon plum is a few years old, you can let go of the reins.

Additional Information

Pigeon plum grows throughout the Bahamas and the Antilles, and in Florida from Monroe and Dade Counties into Broward and Lee.

Additional Species, Cultivars, or Varieties

The sea grape, *Coccoloba uvifera*, is also a related native. It is a shorter, stouter tree with leaves that can be nearly round. Like the pigeon plum, there are male and female trees. The fruit is edible and often made into jelly. Sea grapes can be readily pruned into wonderful sculptural forms or even hedged. Highly salt tolerant, they tend to be quite wide. Old leaves turn yellow to orange to dark red before falling, especially after extreme cold.

Advice for Regional Care

Use this tree in coastal areas of Central Florida. Care is similar. It is not for use in North Florida.

Red Maple

Acer rubrum

> **Height:** to more than 40 ft.
> **Zones:** 10A and 10B
> **Light Requirement:**
>
>

A swamp dweller at heart, red maple doesn't grow with its feet in deep water, like cypress and pond apples. But it can be found nearby and in slightly drier areas with cabbage and royal palms or in hydric or periodically wet hammocks with acid soils. This should tell you that red maples like low-lying swales or backyards, and they have a low tolerance for drought. At the southern end of its range, the red maple is var. *trilobum*, with 3 pointy leaf lobes edged in teeth to distinguish it. It does not venture into the tropical Florida Keys. In addition to its red fall color, the leaves have leaf stems or petioles that are red, as are its flowers that appear in December and January. Male trees are described as being redder than females by John Eastman in *The Book of Swamps and Bogs*. The females, he writes, are more orange-yellow. Eastman also says red maples reproduce from seed more often when they grow in moist soil and by suckers in drier soil. The leaves are fed upon by a variety of living organisms, from white-tailed deer to a host of moth larvae—read caterpillars—and the seeds are enjoyed by wildlife.

When to Plant

Plant at the beginning of the rainy season (end of May or early June), throughout early and midsummer. In South Florida's natural areas, the seeds germinate in the dry season and shoot up before rains return and flood the swamps.

Where to Plant

Plant in full sun in a low-lying, wet area. Trees thrive better in sandy soil than rocky soil, although mulch can help them adapt. In sandy soil, they can be used to frame a house or garden, or they can be shade trees or even specimen trees.

How to Plant

When transplanting from a pot, dig a hole 2 to 3 times as wide as the rootball and just as deep. Remove the container from the rootball; situate the tree in the planting hole so that the top of the

346

rootball is even with the soil surface. Add 1/3 as much organic material to the planting soil from the planting hole. Use a hose to water in the soil as you fill the hole to remove any air pockets. Mulch.

ADVICE FOR CARE
Shallow-rooted, red maples also have brittle wood and can break in storms. Look for trees with a single leader to prevent splitting. If you have a lake front or wet area, use red maple with cabbage (sabal) palms, leather fern, dahoon holly, willow, and elderberry. Little care is required if the tree is properly located.

ADDITIONAL INFORMATION
Flowers tend to be male or female on the same tree, but sometimes they occur on different trees. Fruits develop quickly after December flowering and may be ripe by January or February before new leaves appear. Fruits are winged samaras that flutter to the ground like little helicopter blades.

ADDITIONAL SPECIES, CULTIVARS, OR VARIETIES
Acer rubrum var. *trilobum* is the South Florida form, with three lobes near the apex of the leaf and an underside that is usually covered with fine hairs. It wanders over into Texas as well. Silver maple, *Acer saccharinum*, occurs in North Florida.

ADVICE FOR REGIONAL CARE
Use other maple species or varieties in Central and North Florida.

Redberry Stopper

Eugenia confusa

Height: 20 to 30 ft.
Zones: 10B and 11
Light Requirement:

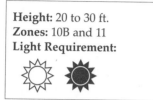

A long, recognizable "drip-tip" on shiny leaves is your key to identifying this stopper, one of a number of small, understory hammock trees native to South Florida. A drip-tip is an elongated, pointy apex of the leaf that allows raindrops to drip from the surface—a characteristic of many tropical trees found in areas of high rainfall. The redberry stopper resembles Surinam cherry, its cousin. Stoppers—the name comes from their use as decoctions to stop diarrhea—are the understudies of the big hammock stars. They populate the space between the pigeon plums and the shrubs, between the gumbo limbo and the strangler figs and the wild coffee. They are second fiddles, but useful ones and extraordinarily adaptable to the tune being played—ideal for zero lot line or townhouse gardens in the southernmost part of the peninsula or the Keys. Redberry is not a common tree, but it should be planted much more widely instead of cheaper, faster growing species. True, it is slow growing, but that's what makes it so durable and dependable. If you expect it to stay small for a long time, you'll be surprised when one day you find it looking down at you. The leaves are extraordinarily pretty. They are glossy and dark green, small, and distinct. Flowers are what horticulturists often call insignificant. You won't notice them unless you set about to find them—so look in the summer and fall.

WHEN TO PLANT

Plant at the beginning of the rainy season (end of May or early June), throughout early and midsummer.

WHERE TO PLANT

Plant in high shade or full sun. Understory trees tolerate the shade of the hammock. Adapted to rocky soil, this is a wonderful tree for small gardens and patios, or with a group of natives.

How to Plant

When transplanting from a pot, dig a hole 2 to 3 times as wide as the rootball and just as deep. Remove the container from the rootball; situate the tree in the planting hole so that the top of the rootball is even with the soil surface. Use a hose to water in the soil as you fill the hole to remove any air pockets. Mulch.

Advice for Care

After the redberry has become established, it requires little fussing over. Mulching will mediate soil moisture and temperature, which are somewhat mediated inside a hammock by virtue of the overstory trees. It needs fertilizer in moderate amounts—the leaves will complain when the tree is hungry, turning a little yellow.

Additional Information

Plentiful red fruit make this a good bird-attracting tree.

Additional Species, Cultivars, or Varieties

Eugenia rhombia, the red stopper, one of Florida's rarest native trees, is found in the Florida Keys. Its pointed leaves are less distinctive and it has gray bark. *Eugenia foetida*, the Spanish stopper, has blunt leaves at the ends of small branches, and fruit grows along the branches; *Myrcianthes fragrans* is Simpson stopper, with flaking bark.

Advice for Regional Care

Redberry stopper is recommended for use in South Florida. It is not recommended for use in Central or North Florida.

Royal Poinciana

Delonix regia

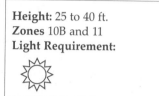

Height: 25 to 40 ft.
Zones 10B and 11
Light Requirement:

No other tree causes so much excitement that it has its own annual fiesta in Miami. A cascading canopy that is supported by fat, yet languid, limbs on a stout trunk, the Madagascar native (called *tamahbus* in its homeland) is a cosmopolitan citizen of the pantropical world. Doubly compound leaves—called bipinnate—have a ferny look to them. Messy, with aggressive roots, it expiates its sins every May/June with transporting color. The flowers have five petals: four spatulate petals of a solid color and a fifth called the standard, which is upright yellow or white with flecks of crimson. When the poincianas are in bloom, every street or park they grace is lifted out of the ordinary to become dazzling. The tree is called flamboyant in the Caribbean, and indeed it is. The canopies shimmer beneath clouds of cerise, scarlet, blood red . . . After enormous initial show, flowers linger here and there throughout the summer. Often but not always deciduous, the tree's aggressive roots and foot-long pods create a grass cutter's nightmare. An intriguing detail about the tree is the way the bark resembles loose skin where limbs attach to the trunk.

WHEN TO PLANT

Plant at the beginning of the rainy season (end of May or early June), throughout early and midsummer.

WHERE TO PLANT

Plant in a large, open space in full sun. This tree is really too large for a small yard. Roots will uplift asphalt. Limbs are brittle. Seedlings germinate readily.

HOW TO PLANT

If planting from seed, nick the hard shell and soak in water. When the seed has doubled in size, plant in 50-50 peat and perlite. When transplanting from a pot, dig a hole 2 to 3 times as wide as the rootball and just as deep. Remove the container from the rootball; situate the tree in the planting hole so that the top of the rootball is even with the soil surface. Add 1/3 as much organic material to the planting soil from the planting hole. Use a hose to water in the soil as you fill the hole to remove any air pockets. Mulch. Stand back.

ADVICE FOR CARE

Prune out deadwood. On rocky soils, trunks develop some buttressing and roots rise to the surface. Groundcovers are better suited beneath this tree than grass, and tall groundcovers at that because the roots can rest several inches above the soil surface.

ADDITIONAL SPECIES, CULTIVARS, OR VARIETIES

A yellow form exists and is planted sparingly in Dade County.

ADVICE FOR REGIONAL CARE

Royal poinciana is recommended for use in South Florida. It is not a tree for Central or North Florida.

Satinleaf

Chrysophyllum oliviforme

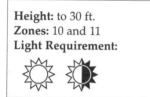

Height: to 30 ft.
Zones: 10 and 11
Light Requirement:

Few other trees have leaves as beautiful as those of the satinleaf. When they dance in the wind and show the backs of their hunter green leaves, covered with bronze or copper hairs, they are the Fred Astaire of trees, all dazzle and grace in movement and light. The crowns are erect, and in shade they will zoom to the light, squeezing through the smallest spaces to reach it. The branches tend to come out on one side. When you plant it, notice that direction so you don't end up replanting the tree later. (*Pseudophoenix sargentii*, the buccaneer palm, does this, too, but eventually its crown becomes rounded.) Some of the branches are long, arching, and unbranched—particularly in shade. But the trees can be cut back and even sheared into a hedge if that's your heart's desire. Fruits of the satinleaf are, as the species name suggests, like dark-purple olives. Birds and mammals appreciate them more than do most bipeds. This is a good tree to use in a hammock planting along the lower Florida coasts because it is cold sensitive. When planted among other plants, it is afforded some protection it wouldn't receive as a specimen. Its pretty looks can add a bit of color to a native area, because of the copper-colored undersides of the leaves, and later when they turn bright-red with age.

WHEN TO PLANT

Plant in late May or early June, at the beginning of the rainy season.

WHERE TO PLANT

Plant in a grouping of native trees or in a perimeter planting. The tree is drought tolerant, and once established doesn't require irrigation.

HOW TO PLANT

Dig a hole 2 to 3 times as wide and just as deep as the rootball. Remove the container from the rootball, and position the tree in the planting hole. If you enrich the soil, use not more than 1/3 peat, compost, or aged manure to 2/3 of the backfill. Water in the soil as you fill the planting hole to eliminate air pockets that kill roots. Mulch, keeping mulch 2 or 3 in. away from the trunk to avoid disease.

ADVICE FOR CARE
Keep roots moist throughout the first growing season. Fertilize with 6-6-6 or a slow-release balanced fertilizer according to package directions. Once the tree becomes a large specimen, mulching consistently should be ample care.

ADDITIONAL INFORMATION
Seedlings may proliferate around the base and can be dug at any time.

ADDITIONAL SPECIES, CULTIVARS, OR VARIETIES
Equally pretty is a relative with larger leaves and edible fruit. This is the caimito, *Chrysophyllum cainito*. In the West Indies, it is a "dooryard" fruit, with sweet, granular flesh.

ADVICE FOR REGIONAL CARE
Plant along the coasts up to the center of Florida; it will freeze back when unprotected.

Sea Grape

Coccoloba uvifera

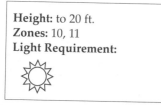

Height: to 20 ft.
Zones: 10, 11
Light Requirement:

Gardeners in warmer locations throughout Florida should plant the sea grape, if for no other reason than its exotic look. Even in the cooler spots, a protected site can be chosen and the plants given protection from cold so that the gardener may enjoy the tree's unique growth habit. The leaves catch the eye—they are circular in shape and grow to 8 in. in diameter. Each leaf has red veins, and the entire leaf turns red before dropping. This is a plant for the patio garden that's sure to start conversations. Sea grapes can be used to soften large walls and are often planted to frame buildings. They can be espaliered against walls and used as hedges. This is a small, broad, spreading tree with a very open branching habit. Gardeners along the coast appreciate the sea grape because it's quite salt tolerant, growing down to the beaches. A little bonus feature is the clusters of purple fruits that are produced throughout the year in the warmer locations. These are edible and often made into jelly.

WHEN TO PLANT

Trees transplant best during the dormant time of the year, normally between December and February. Most sea grapes are available in containers at local garden centers and can be added to the landscape at any time of the year, though the cooler and more dormant times are best for planting; spring and early summer in South Florida.

WHERE TO PLANT

Give sea grapes a full-sun location. It's best to position this tree at least 5 to 10 ft. from buildings, sidewalks, and streets. Since the sea grape is a small tree, it can be used in sites with overhead wires. Sea grapes grow best in a well-drained soil and are very tolerant of salt exposures, making them ideal for seaside plantings.

HOW TO PLANT

Sea grape grows well in sandy Florida soils. Reduce the amount of care required by enriching most planting sites with organic matter. When planting a tree, you should improve a large area with compost or peat moss and manure. Open a hole that's about 2 times wider than the rootball but no deeper. Position the sea grape in the hole at the same depth it was growing in the field or container. Add soil and sufficient water to give good soil-to-root contact. Create a berm of soil around the edge of the rootball to act as a basin to hold irrigation water, and add a 2- to 3-inch mulch layer.

ADVICE FOR CARE

Keep the sea grape tree moist. Some growers like to water every day for the first few weeks, then gradually taper off to watering as needed. The tree is ready for a first feeding 4 to 6 weeks after planting. Continue the feedings, once in March and once in June, for the first 2 to 3 years. Established sea grape trees are drought tolerant and need watering only during periods of severe drought. They do not need additional feedings after the first few years, as they receive the nutrients they need for growth from fertilizer applications to nearby turf and shrub plantings.

ADDITIONAL INFORMATION

Sea grape trees need pruning to keep a straight trunk and to develop even branching around the trunk. Most pruning is performed during winter months. A boring insect can cause damage to sea grape stems but seldom needs control. Where stems are affected they are best pruned from the trees.

ADDITIONAL SPECIES, CULTIVARS, OR VARIETIES

Gardeners should consider planting the pigeon plum *Coccoloba diversifolia* a small native tree to 40 ft. tall. Its leaves are oval to somewhat variable in shape and it produces a reddish fruit. It can be used to frame homes, in street plantings and as a featured plant near the patio. The big leaf sea grape *Coccoloba pubescens* is sometimes planted in the landscape or a container for its 3-foot-diameter foliage.

ADVICE FOR REGIONAL CARE

All sea grapes and their relatives are cold sensitive, limiting most culture to South Florida and the coastal areas of Central Florida. Inland plantings of Central Florida usually need winter protection and are often planted in containers to bring indoors during freezing weather. In South Florida, trees in homeowners' yards are best planted in spring (if you plan to water consistently) or at the start of the rainy season to take advantage of "free" irrigation. Sea grape may take two to three years to produce a good root system before it really takes off.

355

Slash Pine

Pinus elliottii

Height: to 100 ft.
Zones: 8, 9, 10
Light Requirement:

Gardeners relocating to Florida are often surprised to find very few good pines for landscape use. Most are finicky about their care and just don't offer the versatility found with Northern species. The slash pine is a tall tree that can grow to 100 ft., but is usually a bit smaller in home landscapes. Once established it grows quite rapidly, providing light shade. Gardeners often like to cluster several of the trees together to create a park-like atmosphere under which to set tables and have family gatherings. They can also be used to frame the home and added to the sides of the property where tall open trees are needed. Many gardeners also like to gather the cones for use in home crafts and holiday arrangements.

WHEN TO PLANT

Trees transplant best during the dormant time of the year between December and February. Slash pines are available as seedlings during the winter months but most plants for home use are available in containers at local garden centers and can be added to the landscape at any time of the year. Still the cooler and more dormant times are best for planting and establishing the root system.

WHERE TO PLANT

Give slash pines a sunny location. It's best to position this tree at least 15 to 20 ft. from buildings, sidewalks, and streets. Provide a site without overhead wires and away from drain fields. Slash pines grow best in well-drained acid soils and in naturalistic areas that receive limited feedings and waterings.

HOW TO PLANT

Slash pines grow well in sandy Florida soils. Open a hole that's about 2 times wider than the rootball but no deeper. Position the slash pine tree in the hole at the same depth it was growing in the field or container. Add soil and sufficient water to give good soil-to-root contact. After planting, create a berm of soil around the edge of the rootball to act as a basin to hold irrigation water, and add a 2- to

3-inch mulch layer. Pine needles are usually best.

ADVICE FOR CARE

Keep the slash pine trees moist. Some growers like to water every day for the first few weeks, then gradually taper off to watering as needed. The tree is ready for a first feeding 4 to 6 weeks after planting. Continue the feedings, once in March and once in June, for the first 2 to 3 years. Established slash pine trees need watering only during periods of severe drought. In fact, too frequent watering of established trees can cause decline. And once established, eliminate feedings, as they receive the nutrients they need for growth from fertilizer applications to nearby turf and shrub plantings. Excessive feedings can cause decline.

ADDITIONAL INFORMATION

Slash pine trees need little pruning except to remove limbs that might be in the way. When needed, the pruning is performed during winter months. Pests that commonly affect slash pine trees include caterpillars and borers. Borer damage is best prevented by keeping construction equipment away from the trees and preventing digging within the root zone. When caterpillars are a problem, use a University of Florida recommended control, following label instructions.

ADDITIONAL SPECIES, CULTIVARS, OR VARIETIES

A number of additional pines may be considered for the Florida landscape, including the sand pine, *Pinus clausa*, and the spruce pine, *Pinus glabra*. Both grow to about 40 ft. and have a denser growth habit. Some additional pines to consider are the longleaf pine, loblolly pine, Japanese black pine, and Virginia pine, but not in South Florida.

ADVICE FOR REGIONAL CARE

Pines grow well throughout most of Northern and Central Florida. South Florida selections are limited to the slash, sand, longleaf, and loblolly pines. The slash pine native to South Florida is *Pinus elliottii* var. *densa*. Its wood is especially hard, hence the varietal name. It is used to growing on rocky soils and the planting soil should not be amended. Plant any time, but if planted March through early June, roots develop quickly. Mulch with pine needles. Take care not to drive over pine roots or run heavy equipment over roots as they are sensitive to damage.

Sweetbay

Magnolia virginiana

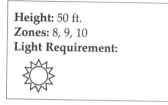

Height: 50 ft.
Zones: 8, 9, 10
Light Requirement:

Gardeners with damp to wet areas are always in a quandary about what to plant. One answer is the sweetbay, which is a native magnolia. It needs a moist soil to develop into an attractive upright tree of about 50 ft. tall. When young, the tree grows with evenly spaced branches and a rounded crown. As this magnolia grows older, it takes on an irregular shape. Gardeners should consider the sweetbay for use anywhere a reliable flowering tree is needed. In damp areas, use it to frame a home, as a street tree, or clustered with other plantings along the property line. It's a great tree for naturalistic plantings with other wetland trees and shrubs. Sweetbays take their name from the fragrant cream-colored blossoms that open during the spring season. They are followed by conelike fruits that produce red seeds for fall.

WHEN TO PLANT

Trees transplant best during the dormant time of the year, normally between December and February. Most sweetbays are available in containers at local garden centers or native plant nurseries, and they can be added to the landscape at any time of the year—though the cooler and more dormant times are best for planting, such as spring and early summer in South Florida.

WHERE TO PLANT

Give sweetbay trees a full-sun to lightly shaded location. It's best to position this tree at least 15 to 20 ft. from buildings, sidewalks, and streets. Provide a site without overhead wires and away from drain fields. Sweetbays grow best in moist, fertile soils. They can tolerate a wet soil with poorer drainage.

HOW TO PLANT

Sweetbays grow well in sandy Florida soils if provided with adequate water. You can reduce the amount of care required and provide extra water retention by enriching the planting sites with organic matter. When planting a tree, improve a large area with compost or peat moss and manure. Open a hole that's about 2 times wider than the rootball but no deeper. Position the sweetbay tree in the hole at the same depth it was growing in the field or container. Add soil and sufficient water to give good soil-to-root contact. After planting, create a berm of soil around the edge of the rootball to act as a basin to hold irrigation water, and add a 2- to 3-inch mulch layer.

ADVICE FOR CARE
Keep the sweetbay tree moist. Some growers like to water every day for the first few weeks, then gradually taper off to watering as needed. The tree is ready for a first feeding 4 to 6 weeks after planting. Continue the feedings, once in March and once in June, for the first 2 to 3 years. Established sweetbay trees should not be allow to dry—water whenever the soil starts to dry to the touch. They do not need extra feedings after the first few years, as decomposing mulches and fertilizer supplied to nearby plantings provide the nutrients needed for growth.

ADDITIONAL INFORMATION
Sweetbay trees need pruning to keep a straight trunk and to develop even branching around the trunk. Most pruning is performed during late winter. Pests that commonly affect sweetbay trees are scales and borers. Control scales with an oil spray. Control borers with a borer spray available from garden centers, or use other University of Florida recommended controls, following label instructions.

ADDITIONAL SPECIES, CULTIVARS, OR VARIETIES
One of the most popular magnolias for Florida is the Southern magnolia, *Magnolia grandiflora*. It grows to 70 ft. tall in all soil types and opens fragrant and quite-large white blossoms for spring. Another magnolia for the Northern and Upper Central Florida landscape is the saucer magnolia, *Magnolia × soulangiana*. It grows to about 25 ft. tall and has pink-and-cream-colored blossoms in late winter.

ADVICE FOR REGIONAL CARE
Magnolias grow best in Northern Florida, Central Florida, and upper portions of South Florida (they don't grow in the Keys.)

Sweet Gum

Liquidambar styraciflua

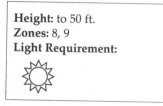

Height: to 50 ft.
Zones: 8, 9
Light Requirement:

Most gardeners cannot say enough good things about the sweet gum. It's one of the truly reliable native trees that has a good shape and won't get too tall for the average landscape. The trees are upright and pyramidal in habit, growing to about 50 ft. tall in most Florida landscapes. The shape of the leaf with its 5 to 7 lobes gives it a starlike appearance. Due to its leaf shape, the sweet gum is sometimes confused with the red maple, which has a 3-lobed leaf. Use the sweet gum for a shade tree or plant it to frame the house, using several specimens. It can also be used along the edge of the property for a large space divider with underplantings of shade-loving shrubs. Many communities like to use the sweet gum as a street tree. As the limbs grow older, they often produce a corky ridge. Don't get alarmed, this is not a scale insect, and the growths are normal. Mature sweet gums produce a seed ball with prickles that can hurt bare feet. Most homecrafters save the gumballs for dried arrangements and holiday decorations.

When to Plant

Trees transplant best during the dormant time of the year, normally between December and February. Most sweet gums are available in containers at local garden centers. These can be added to the landscape at any time of the year, though the cooler and more dormant times are best for planting.

Where to Plant

Give sweet gums a full-sun to slightly shady location. It's best to position this tree at least 15 to 20 ft. from buildings, sidewalks, and streets. Provide a site without overhead wires and away from drain fields. Sweet gums grow best in a well-drained soil.

How to Plant

Sweet gums grow well in sandy Florida soils. You can reduce the amount of care required by enriching most planting sites with organic matter. When planting a tree, improve a large area with compost or peat moss and manure. Open a hole that's about 2 times wider than the rootball but no deeper. Position the sweet gum tree in the hole at the same depth it was growing in the field or container. Add soil and sufficient water to give good soil-to-root contact. After planting, create a berm of soil around the edge of the rootball to act as a basin to hold irrigation water, and add a 2- to 3-inch mulch layer.

ADVICE FOR CARE

Keep the sweet gum tree moist. Some growers like to water every day for the first few weeks, then gradually taper off to watering as needed. The tree is ready for a first feeding 4 to 6 weeks after planting. Continue the feedings, once in March and once in June, for the first 2 to 3 years. Established sweet gum trees are very drought tolerant and need watering only during periods of severe drought. They do not need additional feedings. Sweet gum trees obtain needed nutrients from decomposing mulch layers and feedings given to nearby plantings.

ADDITIONAL INFORMATION

Sweet gum trees need pruning to keep a straight trunk and to develop even branching around the trunk. Most pruning is performed during late winter before spring growth begins. Pests that commonly affect sweet gum trees include caterpillars and thrips. Use the Bacillus thuringiensis caterpillar control, an oil spray, or other University of Florida recommended control, following label instructions.

ADDITIONAL SPECIES, CULTIVARS, OR VARIETIES

A number of native sweet gum varieties have been selected for landscape plantings, including Festival, a columnar form; Moraine, with reddish fall foliage; Purple Majesty, with good fall color; and Variegata, with green-and-cream-colored foliage. Gardeners can also grow the Formosan gum, *Liquidambar formosana*. It has a 3- to 5-lobed leaf and grows to 60 ft. tall. The Oriental sweet gum, *Liquidambar orientalis*, has a 5-lobed leaf and grows to 25 ft. tall in the home landscape. *Liquidambar styraciflua rotundiloba* is narrow, pyramidal shaped with rounded leaf points and no seed pods.

ADVICE FOR REGIONAL CARE

All sweet gums grow well through Northern Florida down to the uppermost portions of Southern Florida.

Tabebuia

Tabebuia caraiba

Height: 25 to 40 ft.
Zones: 10, 11
Light Requirement:

There is much confusion over the flowered tabebuias growing in Florida, and no wonder! There are more than 100 species of this tree, and up to half of them have been introduced to Florida. At least two tabebuias with yellow flowers are commonly grown in home landscapes. *Tabebuia caraiba* or silver tabebuia grows mainly in South Florida, and *Tabebuia chrysotricha* or golden trumpet tree grows from Central Florida southward. Most likely the regional differences are a result of where the trees were first introduced and minor differences in cold hardiness. Both are showstoppers with bright yellow flowers produced during the early spring months. The flowering period lasts for up to a month and the fading blossoms drop to the ground to produce a yellow carpet that extends the enjoyment. Tabebuias make the ideal accent tree, growing between 25 and 40 ft. tall and developing an open, rounded growth habit. They hold their leaves through the winter and drop them just before the flowers appear. Use them anywhere a colorful small tree is needed, including the entrance to a home, off a patio, or near attractive garden features. After flowering they produce long pods which gardeners often like to save to germinate the seeds. The seeds must be sown immediately after the pods crack open to get good germination.

When to Plant

Most tabebuias are available in containers at local garden centers. These can be added to the landscape at any time of the year, though spring and early summer are best in South Florida.

Where to Plant

Give tabebuias a sunny location. It's best to position this tree at least 10 to 15 ft. from buildings, sidewalks, and streets. Provide a site without overhead wires and away from drain fields. Tabebuias grow best in a well-drained soil.

How to Plant

Tabebuias grow well in sandy soils. You can reduce the amount of care required by enriching most planting sites with organic matter. When planting a tree, improve a large area with compost or peat moss and manure. Open a hole that's about 2 times wider than the rootball but no deeper. Position the tabebuia tree in the hole at the same depth it was growing in the field or container. Add soil and sufficient water to give good soil-to-root contact. After planting, create a berm of soil around the edge of the rootball to act as a basin to hold irrigation water, and add a 2- to 3-inch mulch layer.

ADVICE FOR CARE

Keep the tabebuia tree moist. Some growers like to water every day for the first few weeks, then gradually taper off to watering as needed. The tree is ready for a first feeding 4 to 6 weeks after planting. Continue the feedings, once in March and once in June, for the first 2 to 3 years. Established tabebuia trees are drought tolerant and need watering only during periods of severe drought. They do not need special feedings after the first few years of growth.

ADDITIONAL INFORMATION

Very few pests affect the tabebuias. Occasional beetles and grasshoppers may affect the trees, but they cause minor damage and no control is usually needed.

ADDITIONAL SPECIES, CULTIVARS, OR VARIETIES

Some additional yellow-flowering tabebuias may be found in Central and South Florida. These include *Tabebuia chrysantha* and *Tabebuia umbellata*. Each grows between 15 and 25 ft. tall and produces colorful flower clusters for spring. *Tabebeui caraiba* is prized for its curving or gnarled-looking trunks—which make good growing surfaces for air plants such as orchids and bromeliads.

ADVICE FOR REGIONAL CARE

The northern limit for tabebuias is mid-Central Florida. In this upper region, the trees need the warmest location in the landscape. Areas near a lake are best, as they remain a few degrees above the coldest winter temperatures. If frozen the trees do grow back, but they need training to keep one central trunk. In South Florida tabebuias may be planted late February through June for root growth in spring. If they are planted at the beginning of the rainy season less irrigation is required. Little pruning is done on *T. caraiba* or *T. chrysotricha* as trees are prized for their crooked trunks. However, trees should be pruned to remove crossed or dead limbs after flowering has finished.

Tabebuia Ipe

Tabebuia impetiginosa

Height: approx. 25 ft.
Zones: 10, 11
Light Requirement:

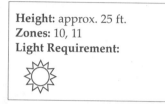

Create some springtime excitement by planting a pink tabebuia. One of the most popular is simply know as Ipe, a shortening of the species name. In late winter, the leaves suddenly drop. As the days begin to warm, the trumpetlike pink blossoms begin a month-long display. As the flowers begin to fade, they drop to the ground to create a carpet of color. The tree grows to about 25 ft. and has a upright to rounded growth habit. Use Ipe wherever color is needed at an entrance, off a patio, or along the walkway. This is also a good shade tree under which gardeners like to plant smaller shrubs and groundcovers.

WHEN TO PLANT

Most tabebuias are available in containers at local garden centers. They can be added to the landscape at any time of the year, though spring and early summer are best for planting.

WHERE TO PLANT

Give tabebuias a sunny location. It's best to position this tree at least 10 to 15 ft. from buildings, sidewalks, and streets. Provide a site without overhead wires and away from drain fields. Tabebuias grow best in a well-drained soil.

HOW TO PLANT

Tabebuias grow well in sandy soils. You can reduce the amount of care required by enriching most planting sites with organic matter. When planting a tree, improve a large area with compost or peat moss and manure. Open a hole that's about 2 times wider than the rootball but no deeper. Position the tabebuia tree in the hole at the same depth it was growing in the field or container. Add soil and sufficient water to give good soil-to-root contact. After planting, create a berm of soil around the edge of the rootball to act as a basin to hold irrigation water, and add a 2- to 3-inch mulch layer.

ADVICE FOR CARE

Keep the tabebuia tree moist. Some growers like to water every day for the first few weeks, then gradually taper off to watering as needed. The tree is ready for a first feeding 4 to 6 weeks after planting. Continue the feedings, once in March and once in June, for the first 2 to 3 years. Established tabebuia trees are drought tolerant and need watering only during periods of severe drought. They do not need special feedings after the first few years of growth, as the mature trees can obtain needed nutrients from mulches and feedings given to nearby plantings.

ADDITIONAL INFORMATION

Tabebuia trees need pruning to keep a straight trunk and to develop even branching around the trunk. Most pruning is performed during late spring after flowering is complete. Very few pests affect the tabebuias. Occasional beetles and grasshoppers may affect the trees, but they cause minor damage and no control is usually needed.

ADDITIONAL SPECIES, CULTIVARS, OR VARIETIES

Some additional pink-flowering tabebuias may be found in Central and South Florida. These include *Tabebuia heterophylla*, the pink trumpet tree; *Tabebuia pentaphylla*, the pink tabebuia; and *Tabebuia rosea*, the rosy trumpet tree. Each grows between 25 and 40 ft. tall and produces colorful pink flower clusters for spring. *Tabebuia caraiba* and *Tabebeuia chrysotricha* are good yellow flowering selections.

ADVICE FOR REGIONAL CARE

The tabebuia is generally better suited to growing in lower Florida. Ipe appears to be one of the more hardy pink types. During cold winter the flowers may be damaged, but the limbs are left unaffected. When more sensitive tabebuias are planted, they may be more severely damaged, some even frozen to the ground. These trees usually grow back, but they need training to keep one central trunk. In South Florida, tabebuias seldom need pruning except for deadwood or crossed limbs.

Tangerine

Citrus reticulata

Height: approx. 25 ft.
Zones: 9, 10, 11
Light Requirement:

Perhaps one of your first experiences with the tangerine came a Christmastime when a visiting Santa gave away the bright orange-colored fruits. This fruit was probably the Dancy tangerine found in a Florida grove in 1867. It has very loose skin and ripens just in time for the holidays. Other good tangerine varieties include the Robinson that ripens in October and the Sunburst, ripening in November. All tangerine trees grow to about 25 ft. tall and have a rounded growth habit. Besides producing the tasty fruits, they can be used as small shade trees and view barriers. They also produce some of the sweetest flowers for the landscape during late winter and give lots of ornamental color when the fruits start to ripen during the fall and winter months.

When to Plant

Trees transplant best during the dormant time of the year, normally between December and February in Central Florida. Some tangerine trees are marketed bareroot, but most are available in containers at local garden centers. They can be added to the landscape at any time of the year, though the cooler and more dormant times are best to start the root growth.

Where to Plant

Give tangerine trees a sunny location. It's best to position this tree at least 15 to 20 ft. from buildings, sidewalks, and streets. Provide a site without overhead wires and away from drain fields. Tangerine trees grow best in a well-drained soil.

How to Plant

Tangerine trees grow well in sandy Florida soils without added soil amendments. Some gardeners do like to enrich the planting sites with organic matter. When planting a tree, improve a large area with compost or peat moss and manure. Open a hole that's about 2 times wider than the rootball but no deeper. Position the tangerine tree in the hole at the same depth it was growing in the field or container.

Add soil and sufficient water to give good soil-to-root contact. After planting, create a berm of soil around the edge of the rootball to act as a basin to hold irrigation water. Do not add mulch to citrus trees. In fact, most growers like to keep a 2- to 3-ft. area surrounding the trunk free of all vegetation and mulch to prevent a foot rot disease.

ADVICE FOR CARE

Keep the tangerine tree moist. Some growers like to water every day for the first few weeks, then gradually taper off to watering as needed. The tree is ready for a first feeding 4 to 6 weeks after planting. Continue the feedings every 6 to 8 weeks, March through September, for the first 2 to 3 years. Established tangerine trees need watering once or twice a week to ensure adequate moisture needed for good fruit production. They also need a light feeding once in March, May, August, and October to give good growth and fruit production. In South Florida use citrus fertilizer: 8-3-9-3.

ADDITIONAL INFORMATION

Tangerine trees need very little pruning except to remove lower limbs that may be in the way of maintenance and to remove errant limbs. Most pruning is performed during February before new growth begins. Pests that commonly affect tangerine trees include aphids, white fly, and caterpillars. Control caterpillars by hand picking or by applying the Bacillus thuringiensis spray as needed. Aphids and white fly can be controlled with an oil spray or other University of Florida recommended control, following label instructions.

ADDITIONAL SPECIES, CULTIVARS, OR VARIETIES

Within this genus is another great mandarin fruit, the Satsuma. It is extremely cold hardy, often growing in North Florida. The fruits ripen in September and have a sweet taste. The tangerine is also one of the parents of the tangelos that home gardeners enjoy.

ADVICE FOR REGIONAL CARE

Citrus trees grow well in most of Central Florida and southward. They sometimes suffer cold damage in Central Florida and need rejuvenation pruning to remove the dead wood. When extremely cold weather is expected, gardeners can mound soil up around the trunks to protect the grafted portions from freezing. Bareroot trees are not planted in South Florida's rocky soils. Plant from containers in early summer.

CHAPTER TWELVE

Tropical Plants

$\mathcal{L}$ ONG AGO WE CALLED THE TROPICS "THE TORRID ZONE." Perhaps we should go back to that name to once again bring a sense of urgency to what we now discuss so dispassionately, given the wholesale destruction underway there.

If we knew more about the tropics, this sense of danger to the tropical natural world might be more real to us. Because so much of life exists in the tropics, our concern needs to manifest itself before all life is threatened.

If we look closely at tropical plants, we can allow them to serve as gateways to our understanding of larger tropical ecosystems. They will lead us not to one vast, oppressively hot place, but to a whole galaxy of niches, from the tops of enormous, 200-ft. trees to the diminutive and mostly unknown world of fungi. The stories of tropical plants are tales of adaptation, exploitation, temptation, seduction, and unlikely triumph in a climate that promotes ceaseless competition for life itself.

Start with the story of a vine that begins its life on the forest floor where it seeks not light at germination but darkness. For darkness means shadow, and shadow in all likelihood means a tree trunk. Once there, a small leaf emerges and flattens itself against the damp bark of the buttressing root, itself an architectural wonder. The next leaf is thrust over the top of the first, slightly higher on the tree, until eventually, the vine has worked its way into the upper canopy. There, it can quit making these tiny, clinging-for-dear-life leaves. There, it can detect more light and more air, and so it begins growing bigger leaves, better able to take in the sun, to bask in the rain, to reach out from the trunk and wobble in the wind, vigorous and, yes, victorious.

Or repeat the story of the strangler fig that is deposited as a seed in the crotch of an unsuspecting tree. Tell how it germinates and sends down a single root, long and thin but for a corklike covering. Then it produces another root, then another, and wraps them around the trunk of the tree that is its host. Its leafy shoots squirm and wedge their way through the canopy of the host until they can produce carbohydrates at a good clip in order to swell the roots and strengthen them. And eventually, the perch becomes the victim, the fig the strangler, not literally strangling its host but suffocating it, stealing its sunlight and its place in the forest.

Orchids, on the other hand, do not attack their hosts, but coexist with them. Dustlike seeds find the fungus-rich compost that collects on a tree branch, and they germinate, uniting with the fungus in a relationship that provides food for the seed and a home for the fungus. Then, residing in a peculiar elevation, the plant has figured out a way to signal pollinators to find it.

One of them creates flowers with the exact scent that a male euglossine bee uses to attract a female bee, and it disperses the scent, molecule by molecule, to bring in the bee. Once there, the bee wedges himself inside the flower to secure packets of the perfume for himself, and in the process he triggers the latch of the pollinia (the tiny golden orbs of male pollen produced by the flower); they stick to him as he backs out to fly away. Greedy for more, the bee visits another flower. Only this time, the pollinia become attached to the sticky female stigma, and the orchid is pollinated.

Chapter Twelve

Other orchids create bee lookalike flowers, so the male bees believe they have spotted a female bee. The disguise works.

These stories are endlessly intriguing. They turn the tropics from simple forests to living organisms, flirting, tempting, copulating, reproducing, and communicating in ways that are stunning to behold—once you have the Rosetta stone of understanding.

Additionally, these plants are super resourceful because of the competition with other plants for space, light, air, water, and reproductive success. They have devised all kinds of strategies for surviving: they climb; they soar; they perch; they strangle; they jump into the light at the first opportunity. You would too, if your life depended on it. And in the process, they have become glorious garden specimens.

The orchid and the vine are just two examples of plants useful in Florida gardens. Add to them gingers, which attract their pollinators with flower spikes of brilliant color; bromeliads that store water in their vaselike rosettes; herbaceous low-lying plants that have leaf cells to catch light or special coloring to better utilize the light available or holes to keep from tearing or drip tips to let the rain run off . . . these plants are the dressing for subtropical gardens, the pin on the lapel, the brooch at the throat.

Many require extra care, particularly from the center of Florida northward. Like human Floridians, they get cold quickly and need protection in what is inclement to them. Like human Floridians, they may be sensitive to light, and so prefer the protection of shade. Like human Floridians, they like their daily shower but don't want to sit in a bath for long or they'll wrinkle. It just takes common sense, when you think about it.

Chapter Twelve

Most of the plants in this section thrive best in South Florida gardens if planted outdoors. Many will also do well outside in other areas of Florida during the summer. In pots, they can easily be moved back and forth, provided there is adequate humidity indoors.

Don't be afraid to try them. They bring wonderful foliage patterns and colors, beautiful flowers, and an intriguing way of life with them. And they tell stories that you can repeat to your friends.

Aglaonema

Aglaonema cultivars

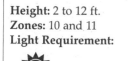

Height: 2 to 12 ft.
Zones: 10 and 11
Light Requirement:

Sometimes called "Chinese Evergreen," the aglaonema is an often-overlooked resident of the shady tropical garden. The gift it brings to a garden is its ability to transform shadows, enliven dark spots, and add interest where there might otherwise be mulch. Pewter or silver patterns against dark-green leaf blades are the hallmark of this plant that is found naturally in China, Southeast Asia, Malaysia, and the Philippines. Many of them have been collected from the Philippines by Florida plantsman Frank Brown, and many more have been hybridized, so some plants have several shades of green and silver in them. Like peace lilies, aglaonemas now come in any pattern or shade you would care to name. Many years ago, when Nat DeLeon was the horticulturist at Parrot Jungle, a historic tourist attraction in Miami, he hybridized and planted numerous aglaonema cultivars beneath the heliconias and the philodendrons that luxuriated along the garden pathways. When you looked down, you saw the beautiful leaves were looking back. Today, the plants may be more successful as ornamental foliage plants for malls and hotels than as garden denizens. Somewhat cold sensitive, they nevertheless can be protected by the leafy fellows above. In temperatures in the 30s, newspaper can be used as blankets to stave off damage. As potted plants that can move in or out in cold weather, they can readily beautify a patio or townhouse garden.

WHEN TO PLANT
Plant in the late spring or early summer.

WHERE TO PLANT
Aglaonemas will show off in strategic areas of the garden, next to a path, or in raised beds. They prefer shade, although morning sun or flecks throughout the day are fine. Aglaonemas thrive in 75 percent shade and well-drained soil. They grow well in a basic peat-perlite mix, or peat-perlite-pine bark with crushed limestone. Any variation

on this theme will do. If planting them in beds beneath trees, use a good potting mix throughout the bed with pine bark soil conditioner or another additive such as perlite.

How to Plant
Dig a hole a little larger than the size of the container. Carefully remove the pot from the rootball, place the aglaonema in the planting hole, and backfill. Mulch.

Advice for Care
Water well, and let the soil become medium-dry before watering again. Using a 20-20-20 soluble fertilizer at half strength every 2 weeks means tender loving care for these plants. A 30-10-10 or a slow-release fertilizer formulated for foliage plants also works. Protect plants from cold. Watch for mites in dry weather; mealybugs may be a problem if you bring them inside during winter.

Additional Information
Little spathes and spadices—the protective leaves and flower stalks of the aroid family—develop in the axils of the leaves, and bright red or yellow fruits form on small flower stalks.

Additional Species, Cultivars, or Varieties
Several species have been used to hybridize garden center aglaonemas, including *Aglaonema commutatum, A. pictum* (a smaller form in silver, lime, and dark green), *A. costatum, A. oblongifolium curtisii*, and a plain green *A. modestum*.

Advice for Regional Care
Use these low-light plants indoors as houseplants in colder areas of the state.

Anthurium

Anthurium spp.

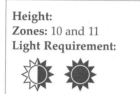

Height:
Zones: 10 and 11
Light Requirement:

Anthuriums are either terrestrial or epiphytic plants with colorful or dramatic leaves. Flowers are characteristic of the aroid family and consist of a stalk called a spadix surrounded by a specialized leaf called a spathe. *Anthurium andraeanum* is the "flamingo flower" that is grown in Hawaii by the millions and sold by florists and street vendors for tropical flower arrangements. The red spathe looks like a patent leather heart, and the column of minute flowers, the spadix, can be white or pink. The plants don't grow as well in Florida as some other anthuriums, but a wide range of others is suitable. Although the flowers may not be as attractive as the flamingo flower, the velvet-leaved anthuriums are seductively beautiful. Their leaves are gorgeous. *A. crystallinum*, *A. magnifica*, and *A. clarinervium*, each of which has white veins against dark, velvety green with slightly different veination and size, are as splendid in the tropical leaf department as Gauguin in the tropical art department. One of the biggest-selling plants in the foliage business is *Anthurium* 'Lady Jane', first produced in 1984 by Florida nurseryman Ray Oglesby and named for his wife. The heart-shaped leaves are tough and shiny, and the spathes are sweetly pink. Oglesby's lab produces about 5 million of these identical plants annually from tissue culture, and they become houseplants. But they shouldn't be relegated to the indoors alone because anthuriums are wonderful outdoors in the right light and soil, and this one, planted in a big pot, can take all kinds of weather. Besides the anthuriums famed for flower or leaf, there are the bird's-nest types, which refuse to be relegated to the back bench of the shade house. In fact, they can be so large, they seem to be in danger of suffocation when made to stay inside. Beneath trees, the rosette of long leaves of *A. salvinae* becomes several feet long and 1 ft. or more wide. One tough anthurium that I've grown for more than 15 years is *A. bakeri*, or a narrow, strap-leaf anthurium. Its leaves are 2 in. wide, velvet to the touch, and droop several feet from a central stem. This one, like many anthuriums, can endure cold weather.

WHEN TO PLANT

Plant when seed ripens, or in spring or early summer if transplanting from a container. The bird's-nest anthuriums tend to grow straight up on a fat column of roots. To transplant, slice off a reasonable clump with roots and relocate.

WHERE TO PLANT

Plant in shady beds with other tropicals, in pots, or as specimens throughout the garden.

HOW TO PLANT

For aroids in clay pots, allow for drainage by using peat moss, perlite, and another ingredient in equal parts. The other ingredient may be pine bark, cypress mulch, or orchid mix.

ADVICE FOR CARE

If using terra-cotta, check the moisture levels closely. Soil in clay dries faster because the pot is porous. In windy weather, you may water daily if you grow these in pots. In the ground, they require watering less often, depending on location. 'Lady Jane' types allow their leaves to lower instead of holding them straight up when the plants are thirsty. Anthuriums do well with slow-release fertilizer, supplemented with occasional foliar sprays of 20-20-20. My strap-leaf anthurium receives only 20-20-20 when I fertilize the orchids, which is twice monthly in the growing season and monthly in winter.

ADDITIONAL INFORMATION

The velvet surface of some *Anthurium* leaves is due to the shapes of the epidermal cells, which are hemispherical (not flat, as is the rule) and reflect light at many angles.

ADVICE FOR REGIONAL CARE

Anthuriums may be used as summer flowers in Central and North Florida or grown in containers.

Banana

Musa × paradisica

Height: 5 to 20 ft.
Zones: 10 and 11
Light Requirement:

The banana is a popular backyard fruit in South Florida. Bananas themselves are nearly universally loved, and the plants are evocative of the tropics, with oblong, smooth leaves on succulent stems. Just about anywhere you travel in the tropics you will find them, for they have been cultivated and carried worldwide by that wanderer, man. Wild bananas still grow in Indonesia and Malaysia, which are thought to be centers of origin. In Hawaiian legend, the ubiquitous banana is said to have been brought to the islands by the brother of Pele, goddess of volcanoes, according to Marie Neal in her book *In Gardens of Hawaii*. Until the 19th Century, it was one of the many foods that Hawaiian women were forbidden to eat. And Hawaiian folklore asserts that dreaming of bananas brings bad luck. The fruit we eat is sterile: the little dots in the center are vestiges of seeds. We plant bananas from corms, or underground stems, which sucker after each new growth has bloomed and fruited. The fruit take anywhere from 12 to 18 months to form and develop. Male flowers normally form at the end of the stem, females closest to the top of the stalk. Once formed, the fruit may take 2 to 3 months to mature. When the ridges on the individual fruit round out, bananas can be picked and tied up in a garage or carport to ripen. If you leave the bunches on the plant, the skins will split. Dwarf Cavendish is a banana suitable for South Florida. More than 500 cultivars of bananas exist today, and you can find fruit that range from finger length to 1 ft. or more. *The Complete Book of Bananas* by W. O. Lessard is an excellent guide for growing bananas in Florida.

WHEN TO PLANT

Plant at the beginning of the rainy season to allow the banana plenty of growing time before winter.

WHERE TO PLANT

Choose an area where the plant will be protected from winds. The large leaves can be shredded in high winds, and plants with fruit can be toppled. Bananas like plenty of water, so put your stand where you easily can irrigate it, but not in a low spot where water will stand because the underground stem will rot.

How to Plant

Dig a hole 2 or 3 ft. across by about 2 ft. deep, and enrich it with aged compost or potting soil. South Florida's banana expert Bill Lessard cautions against using manure or peat moss in the planting hole because such material holds too much moisture and breeds fungi. Place the corm in the hole to a depth of 8 in., with its white roots on the bottom, then backfill. Mulch only after the plant has become established and is pushing out a new leaf.

Advice for Care

When new leaves begin growing, water daily. Young plants need small but frequent applications of fertilizer. Apply 1 lb. every 2 months, increasing the amount until you apply 5 or 6 lb. by the time the plant begins to flower 10 to 15 months later. Use a 6-6-6 fertilizer initially, then switch to 9-3-27 or another high-potassium fertilizer to ensure many large fruit. Manganese and zinc can be applied as a foliar spray.

Additional Information

If leaves begin to flag, and your cultural program is good, you may be seeing nematode infestation, sigatoka, or Panama disease. Nematodes are microscopic worms that infest the roots, interrupting the flow of water and nutrients to the plant. Keeping the plants healthy and well mulched reduces the nematode population. Sigatoka is a fungal disease that causes leaf spotting and eventually death of leaves. Panama disease is a fungal disease that infects the stems, causing them to turn oily black, and it is spread by spores or contaminated tools.

Additional Species, Cultivars, or Varieties

Musa coccinea is an ornamental banana grown not for the fruit but for the beautiful maroon-and-green leaves and red bananas.

Advice for Regional Care

Bananas can tolerate cold weather but should be covered with a cloth over poles, like a tepee, when frost or freezing is expected. Freezes can take them back to the ground, but usually they will resprout.

Bromeliad

Aechmea

Other Names: *Billbergia, Guzmania, Neoregelia, Vriesea*
Height: few in. to several ft.
Zones: 10 and 11
Light Requirement: depending on genus/species

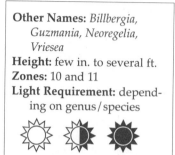

Bromeliads are all-around performers, bringing tropical color and an architecturally interesting shape to a subtropical setting. They can grow in trees or under them, on rocks or in mulch, in sun or shade, as accents or mass plantings. Their often brilliant colors—particularly before flowering—render many of them extroverts in a garden, while some produce astounding inflorescences (flower stalks that emerge from the center of the vase) that last many months before fading. In Florida, a group of native bromeliads in the *Tillandsia* family grows in cypress domes, hammocks, and pinelands. A coating of minute gray hairs protects tillandsias in sunny treetops; their flower stalks form little tongues of flame (some of them, admittedly, pink). Deep in the shadier swamp, the thinner-leaved *Guzmania* species cluster on the pond apple and pop ash trees, along with orchids, ferns, and peperomia. The cup that forms inside the vase of bromeliad leaves holds water, and in areas with distinct dry seasons, these often are the refuge for frogs and a whole universe of microscopic living things. The poison arrow frog of the Central American tropics is known to carry eggs to the cups of bromeliads, where the tadpoles hatch. The tiny mother frog lays a single infertile egg in the cup to provide food for her offspring. In some genera, such as *Neoregelia*, the flowers occur within the cup. The *Neo*'s inner leaves turn a brilliant color before the plant flowers, as if overjoyed about the coming event. In other genera, *Aechmea* and *Vriesea* for instance, the stalks of flowers rise several feet out of the center, and some even branch like small trees. *Aechmea* species have spines on the edges of the leaves, and working with them is a literal pain. Beekeeper gloves—with leather hands and canvas sleeves—prevent scratches and wounds. *Aechmea blanchetiana*, in my front yard, is exposed to full sun, and the leaves are a glowing copper; those of the same species in the shade have apple-green leaves. *A. mexicana* takes on a red color in sun. *V. regina*, a light green, has a 4-ft. inflorescence that can branch impressively; *V. gigantea* is a beautiful

blue-green with fine green lines throughout. As a general rule, plants with thin leaves require shade; those with thick, tough, silvery leaves can take sun.

WHEN TO PLANT

Plant any time, particularly if putting them in trees. If you wish to remove a pup from a mother plant, wait until the pup is $1/3$ the size of the mother, then cut away close to the stem.

WHERE TO PLANT

Plant in beds beneath the canopy of a shade tree, such as a live oak; use large bromeliads as accents.

HOW TO PLANT

Plant in rock or mulch. Orchid mix is wonderful for bromeliads grown in terra-cotta pots, or equal parts peat, perlite, and bark.

ADVICE FOR CARE

Keep the cups filled with water; fertilize at $1/4$ strength every 2 weeks. Fertilize less often or at decreased strength for banded, spotted, or colorful leaves, if at all, or color/spotting can disappear. When the plant produces off-shoots called pups, and a pup is $1/3$ the size of the mother plant, carefully remove it with secateurs, and pot or plant.

ADDITIONAL INFORMATION

If the water in bromeliad cups is allowed to stagnate, mosquito larvae can take up residence and make life miserable when they hatch. Use a home or garden spray, or flush the cups with the hose every couple of days.

ADDITIONAL SPECIES, CULTIVARS, OR VARIETIES

A. fasciata is the well-known silver vase bromeliad with a deep-pink inflorescence (a spineless form has been developed by Florida breeder Nat DeLeon).

ADVICE FOR REGIONAL CARE

Bromeliads often are grown outdoors in Central and North Florida, but they must be removed from their beds or protected with covers during freezing weather.

Costus

Costus barbatus

Other Name: Spiral Ginger
Height: 3 to 6 ft.
Zones: 10B, 11
Light Requirement:

The first thing you do to fall in love with this plant is to feel the undersides of the leaves, which are as soft as down. Otherwise you might think that young plants are rather awkward looking. The stems are slender and tend to snake and sway like boas being charmed. At the ends of the stems, red and waxy conelike structures gradually form, growing to a few inches in length, making the stalk top-heavy so that it snakes and sways even more. Then one at a time, bright-yellow flowers worm their way out between bracts, and from this time forward, the plants become interesting and eye-catching in the garden. The crepe ginger, *C. speciosus*, is a bigger plant than spiral ginger; it grows to about 9 ft. Its leaves are darker green, and it has a fatter, more compact cone from which lovely and fairly large white flowers appear. The interior of the flower's throat is yellow. Spiral gingers look quite wonderful in the summer rainy season, but they tend to look haggard in winter. After 2 years of growth, they can be made to look handsome again by thinning the clumps. Like many other tropical plants, they look best when they're among friends and relatives. The plant shapes and fairly large leaves, when surrounded by heliconias and monsteras, palms and bird's-nest anthuriums, make a wonderfully harmonious, if exuberant, picture in the light shade of high oaks. Clumps can be divided for transplanting in the spring, or pieces of stem can be placed horizontally on moistened peat-perlite.

WHEN TO PLANT
Plant in the spring when the new growth begins, so the stems have plenty of time to mature and develop terminal flowers.

WHERE TO PLANT
Choose an area of high, light shade and organic soil where plants can clump and spread.

380

How to Plant

Planting holes for costus, gingers, and other herbaceous tropicals don't have to go to China, but can be several inches deep. The plants are shallow rooted, spreading on underground stems beneath the surface.

Advice for Care

If you mulch to keep the soil moist around the plants and keep them well fertilized, they are happy campers. Costus and other members of the ginger family grow best when well nourished, and the use of slow-release fertilizer will keep a steady supply of nutrients at the disposal of the plants over the growing season. Once the stems have flowered and the bracts have faded, you can cut out the parent stem. Or do a good housekeeping every 2 years. Like heliconias, costus can be dug and their planting beds freshened with compost if you are a conscientious gardener or need to work off some energy.

Additional Information

Costus are related to gingers, bananas, and birds-of-paradise.

Additional Species, Cultivars, or Varieties

Other plant possibilities include *Costus curvibracteata* 'Orange Tulip', *C. erothrophyllus*, *C. speciosa variegatus*, and *C. stenophyllus*.

Advice for Regional Care

Grow costus trees in protected areas in summer or in containers.

Dracaena

Dracaena fragrans

Other Name: *Dracaena marginata*
Height: 20 ft.
Zones: 10B and 11
Light Requirement:

There are approximately 150 species of *Dracaena*, many of which are used as ornamental interior plants because they can live in low light where they tend to stay at much the same size for years—if they can survive house dust. *Dracaena fragrans*, the corn plant, is from tropical Africa. Its yellowish flowers are sweetly fragrant at night, growing terminally in winter. The flowers form round clusters and fall like tassels over the top of the cornlike leaves. In tropical countries, cuttings of this *Dracaena* are often sawed to roughly the same length and planted in long rows as fences, with leaves sprouting from the tops. In full sun, the leaves are yellowish and washed out, but in shade, these handmade fences have a rough-hewn charm. Plants with such strong architectural character can be effective vertical elements in tight spaces, by entrances, or in background plantings. If they grow long enough and tall enough, the top-heavy limbs will bend over, and buds will break along the curve, so the plant eventually forms an interesting and complex substance. *Dracaena fragrans* 'Massangeana' is a variety with a bold golden stripe down the center of the leaf. It needs more light than the plain-leaved corn plant. *Dracaena marginata* is a close relative, with a skinnier trunk and thinner leaves edged in red. Others cultivars have lime-green stripes on them. These, too, are useful in the right place, such as a narrow strip of ground edging a porch. Long branches tend to be whippy, but often form curves or half-loops or S-shapes. If you cut off the top of a long branch, new buds will pop and new heads of leaves form; in this way, you can readily shape the plant—in addition to being able to root the top. Several plants used together are effective. When old, the bases have considerable character.

When to Plant

Plant in the spring to take advantage of the rainy season's natural irrigation. Cuttings are rooted best in spring, but can be made any time.

WHERE TO PLANT
Select areas calling for vertical lines. The plants like a shady area, and they prefer an acid soil. Alkaline soil causes yellowing.

HOW TO PLANT
Dig a hole slightly larger than the rootball, and add compost or some organic matter to enrich it, but only enough to make it 1/3 of the backfill. Mulch the root zone.

ADVICE FOR CARE
Dracaenas are not fussy about their care, but like fertilizer and shade to stay a rich green. Drainage is required; the plants can stay fairly dry for long periods and do well despite neglect. Fertilize them along with the rest of the landscape plants in the spring, summer, and fall. The more care they receive, the better they look.

ADDITIONAL INFORMATION
As houseplants, they are rugged and widely used. They are often planted in atriums.

ADDITIONAL SPECIES, CULTIVARS, OR VARIETIES
Dracaena reflexa, which also is called *Pleomele reflexa*, is a pretty relative with whorls of leaves all along the stems to the ground. There is an attractive form called 'Song of India' with cream-and-green variegated leaves.

ADVICE FOR REGIONAL CARE
Grow these tropical plants in containers, and protect them from temperatures below 40 degrees Fahrenheit in Central and North Florida.

Elephant Ear

Alocasia spp.

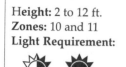

Height: 2 to 12 ft.
Zones: 10 and 11
Light Requirement:

Much of tropical gardening is about dramatic size and shape. Drama, after all, is a legitimate element of a garden when played well. Rising from a host of smaller green leaves, elephant ears are as theatrical as *Twelfth Night*. These enormous leaves that feel like calfskin proclaim that a bold gardener lives here. *Alocasia macrorrhiza* is the best known of the group, with leaves that can reach 2 ft. long held on beefy stems. The leaves are lightly scalloped, and the blade surface between the veins is slightly puckered around the edges. *Alocasia macrorrhiza* 'Variegata' is a green-and-white version that is truly spectacular. Smaller, but just as grand are two of my favorite garden plants: *Alocasia cuprea* and *Alocasia × amazonica*. The first has a pewter-and-dark-green upper leaf surface with a maroon underside. When seen from the back, individual leaves seem outlined in white. The veins are prominent, and the darker coloration on top follows the veination, giving the leaf a quilted look. *Alocasia × amazonica* is a hunter green with silver veins and scalloped edges. A single planting of this can be dazzling. I have one tucked among other tropicals—bird's-nest anthuriums, elkhorn fern, *Anthurium clarinervium*, costus, and philodendrons—and it provides the visual punch for the group. I find these leaves are strong and arresting, and they play against each other better than they suit the company of smaller-leaved woody plants such as hibiscus, ligustrum, or Surinam cherry. A parent of amazonica is *A. sanderiana*, with a skinnier leaf that is much more deeply indented. *A. lowii grandis* has the same combination of deep-green-and-silver veination, but is a plumper elephant-ear shape.

WHEN TO PLANT
Plant in the late spring or early summer.

WHERE TO PLANT
Plant them in the center of a tropical grouping, in a corner, or toward the back of a garden, so the dramatic effect can be given a visual context. Some are quite attractive in terra-cotta pots; a well-

draining soil mix is needed. Some elephant ears can take more sun than other kinds of alocasias, but they may bleach out when in sun all day.

How to Plant
Fill a bed with equal parts potting soil, pine bark mulch, and perlite. Dig a hole a little larger than the size of the container in which you buy the plant. Carefully remove the pot from the rootball, place the plant in the planting hole, and backfill. Mulch.

Advice for Care
Water twice a week if it does not rain. Use a slow-release fertilizer (such as 18-6-8) 2 to 3 times a year in the garden; once in the spring if plants are in pots. Supplement with a foliar spray of 20-20-20 or 30-10-10 to bolster their nutrient supply. If you see yellowing of leaves, use a micronutrient foliar spray or fish emulsion with a spreader sticker or a few drops of liquid Ivory.

Additional Information
The International Aroid Society publishes *Aroideana*, a journal of articles spanning hobbyist to scientific interests. Write Amy Donovan, 9350 SW 24th Street, Miami, Florida 33165 for journal information.

Additional Species, Cultivars, or Varieties
Many enormous hybrids have been made in South Florida. The International Aroid Society, which has an annual show, is a good source for plants not found in commercial nurseries.

Advice for Regional Care
These plants will be damaged by cold in northern regions of the state. Prune away damaged leaves in the early spring, or use as container plants.

Fern

Adiantum spp.

Other Names: *Davallia* spp., *Nephrolepis* spp., *Platycerium* spp., *Polypodium* spp.
Height: from 6 in. to 3 ft.
Zones: 7 through 11
Light Requirement:

For some reason, ferns maintain a Victorian aura in my imagination, perhaps because of the ubiquity of Boston ferns in photographs of Victorian interiors or perhaps because of their frilly fussiness. Of course, ferns could just as easily be associated with pterodactyls or solution holes or Douglas fir, and that would be somewhat true as well. Ferns are as widespread and diverse, as ancient and current as the temperate ginkos and the tropical cycads. With such history, little wonder they have so many splendid forms. In South Florida, hammocks and solution holes both claim native ferns: the sword fern and the maidenhair. The first is a pinnate, upright, pretty, and bright green, *Nephrolepis biserrata*. The second, *Adiantum tenerum*, is a delicate black-stemmed plant with medium-sized wedge to deltoid leaflets. On the rain forest trees of Madagascar, New Guinea, Australia, and the Polynesian islands are the staghorn ferns, with round basal, or sterile, fronds hiding the delicate roots and erect, forked fronds that resemble horns and carry the spore cases, hence are called fertile fronds. *Platycerium* is the genus; the staghorn most commonly grown is *P. bifurcatum*. Strap ferns in the swamps and hammocks are *Polypodium phyllitidis*, and they grow on logs or on the forest floor. On the limbs of oaks are amazing little ferns called resurrection ferns, *Polypodium polypodioides*. When well soaked with rain, the serrated fronds are green and upright; when dry, they curl and turn brown. In between are whole garden centers full of species that have the two-stage life cycle, the ceaseless need for water to complete that cycle, the good luck to find it. In our gardens, they run over rocks, across mulch, over tree limbs; pop up unheeded in orchid baskets; take over the shrub beds; disguise the roots of the poinciana; and absorb the leaves of the live oak. They bring grace to everything they do.

WHEN TO PLANT

Plant in the rainy, warm season; some go dormant or semidormant in winter.

WHERE TO PLANT

It depends on the fern. Maidenhair will perform miracles on rocks around a waterfall as long as it's shady. The rabbit's and other footed ferns can dress up a tree, while the staghorns most often are seen hanging by a chain (but attached to a board) in a live oak or a mango.

HOW TO PLANT

Good drainage is a must, and attaching ferns to trees or planting in mulch is ideal. Maidenhair ferns can easily be grown in pots, so you can place the pots where you want them in the garden. Crushed rock or large limestone rocks suit the maidenhairs, which are fond of alkaline conditions. Boston-like sword ferns will grow in any mulch. Resurrection ferns are tricky to get started, and I have found that pieces of bark that fall from old oak trees with the ferns embedded in them are easily wired onto other trees so the rhizomes can crawl at their own pace. The staghorns are often planted on mounds of sphagnum moss wired onto wooden plaques, then hung in trees.

ADVICE FOR CARE

Tender roots of ferns can be burned easily by pellet or granular fertilizer. Water-soluble 20-20-20 is usually successful. Organic fertilizer, such as fish emulsion, may be best. Fertilize monthly, every 2 weeks, or every time you water, but at $1/2$ strength or less.

ADDITIONAL INFORMATION

Footed ferns can be cut back to the rhizomes in the spring to produce a revitalized plant. Some will drop their leaves before producing new fronds in the spring. When temperatures drop into the 40s, many ferns need protection. *Adiantum tenerum* can take short periods of cold, while davallias may drop their leaves. The sword ferns and the resurrection ferns don't mind cold, but will be killed to the rhizomes in freezes. And staghorns, since they are usually under a tree canopy, are somewhat protected except during freezing weather. Then, because many are too big to bring inside, wrap a blanket or sheet around the fern to get it through the night.

ADDITIONAL SPECIES, CULTIVARS, OR VARIETIES

An enormous number of ferns, including tree ferns, can be grown in Florida

ADVICE FOR REGIONAL CARE

Ferns grown beneath trees will be naturally protected in cold weather, but require covers when a freeze is forecast.

Ginger

Alpinia spp.

Height: to 25 ft.
Zones: 10B and 11
Light Requirement:

The nice thing about red ginger, *Alpinia purpurata*, is its bald-faced "come hither" brilliance. The foliage is pretty in a tropical sort of way, making a full and lush green backdrop, but in truth there are far more exciting leaves in the tropics. The flowers are lovely, and seen together with the leaves that help them pop out visually, they are extremely photogenic. Originating in the Pacific islands, red ginger is grown in many Hawaiian gardens, and it has worked its way east to become a favorite garden subject in Florida. It is easy to care for, with water and sun being the main requirements. While red ginger prefers organic soil, it can do quite well in alkaline Florida soil with some organic matter in the planting hole and mulch on the surface. If conditions are right—high humidity and good soil moisture—baby plantlets will germinate in the bracts of the old ginger flowers. The heads eventually fall to earth, and some of them may take root. A popular pink ginger is a nice contrast to the ruby red. Shell ginger, *Alpinia zerumbet*, produces an entirely different show. Porcelainlike flower buds dangle from long terminal stems, and flowers open a few at a time to show a corolla or fused petals; the throat is yellow with red stripes. The plants can form large and quite massive clumps, and the racemes (the cluster of flowers) are big and showy. A less frequently grown but stunning ginger is torch ginger, *Nicolaia elatior*. The flowers are produced on their own stalks that emerge near the base of the leafy stem. The hot-pink to red bracts form a protealike cone. Another so-called ginger is *Tapeinochilus ananassae*, or the Indonesian ginger. It, too, sends up flower stalks with bracts shaped like the curved parts of pitchers over which your lemonade is poured. Instead of lemonade, however, yellow flowers poke out. This one is more closely related to *Costus* than *Alpinia*. There are about 1000 species of gingers (counting the weird and famous), but new ones are being discovered all the time. In 1996, for instance, several gingers new to science were collected in Borneo and were donated to Fairchild Tropical Garden by Hawaiian resident John Mood, Jr., who has been collecting and identifying gingers for nearly a decade.

WHEN TO PLANT
Plant at the beginning of the rainy season to midsummer.

WHERE TO PLANT
Choose a location in full sun to high shade, allowing the plants room to grow.

HOW TO PLANT
Enrich soil to a depth of 8 or 10 in., and slip the container from the rootball. Keep the rootball at the same level in the ground as it was growing in the container. Water in the backfill, and mulch.

ADVICE FOR CARE
Alpinias accept many conditions, but like to be well fertilized. Use 7-3-7 with micronutrients, or 6-6-6, around the planting area. The plants are fast growers.

ADDITIONAL INFORMATION
Red and pink gingers are popular as cut flowers, and you will find them in arrangements with birds-of-paradise, ornamental bananas, heliconias, perhaps a pitcher plant or two, with large tropical leaves such as palm, cycad, or caladiums.

ADDITIONAL SPECIES, CULTIVARS, OR VARIETIES
Many cultivars are to be found, as well as relatives such as *Curcumas*, which are deciduous but enticingly beautiful, calatheas, globbas, and cannas.

ADVICE FOR REGIONAL CARE
Use these tropicals in containers in Central and North Florida, protected from chilling winds.

Ginger Lily

Hedychium coronarium

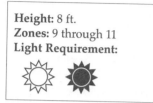

Height: 8 ft.
Zones: 9 through 11
Light Requirement:

If you like your perfume sweet, *Hedychium coronarium*, the ginger lily, or white butterfly ginger, is for you. Few other plants are as redolent as this mariposa, the national flower of Cuba. Originally from India and Indonesia, it traveled to Hawaii, where it remains popular for use in leis. Its flowers, like those of its cousins *Zingiber* and *Globba*, are evolutionarily more advanced than other members of the giant ginger family. That means it has reduced some flower parts. Others in the ginger family have more numerous flower parts and are considered by some experts to have evolved first. The flowers are kept inside green bracts, and each bract allows only one flower to open at a time. The flowers themselves aren't long lasting, but the blooming period lasts several weeks. A strategy in planting hedychium is to locate it by an entrance where you can take in the aroma as you pass. A garden walk, through palms and pandanus, around crotons or spathiphyllums, might also include several white ginger lilies, where white flowers will light up the shadows. Other flower colors are becoming more available as hybridizers are working to produce larger flowers on them. The yellow-flowered *H. gardnerianum* is known as the Kahili ginger. Kahili has bright-red stamens that play against yellow petals. *H. rafillii* is a hybrid made more than 50 years ago. It grows to 8 or 10 ft. and has orange flowers and red stamens.

WHEN TO PLANT

Plant in the early spring while the plants are less active or near dormant.

WHERE TO PLANT

Choose a sunny or a shady area large enough to accommodate its tendency to spread.

How to Plant

Like other gingers, this one grows on a rhizome and is fairly close to the surface. David Bar-Zvi, horticulturist at Fairchild Tropical Garden and the author of *Tropical Gardening*, recommends planting the rhizome twice as deep as it is thick.

Advice for Care

Hedychiums are assertive growers and love moist soils. Shaded locations promote more rapid growth than sun. Mulch is essential to provide the right soil conditions. Fertilize when new growth starts after planting and lightly in midsummer to keep them growing well.

Additional Species, Cultivars, or Varieties

H. flavescens is a species from India, with creamy-yellow flowers, while *H. coccineum*, from Burma and Sri Lanka, is the species called the scarlet ginger lily for its scarlet flowers with pink stamens. Hedychiums are tolerant of cold because they come from high altitudes, several from the Himalayas.

Advice for Regional Care

These plants can be grown in containers for use on patios and around pools in Central and North Florida. Freezing weather will kill them to the ground, but they may resprout from underground stems if the ground itself has not frozen.

Heliconias

Heliconia spp.

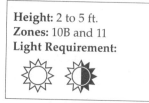

Height: 2 to 5 ft.
Zones: 10B and 11
Light Requirement:

These fascinating plants have become important tropical plants for Florida gardens as more of them have been introduced and gardeners have become acquainted with the enormous array of colorful forms and cultivars. Fueling the popularity of tropical plants is the apparently unstoppable rain forest destruction, which is sending researchers scrambling ahead of chain saws to explore, identify, and collect plants before they disappear. Growing on the light edges of lowland rainforests, beside streambanks, or in the light gaps left by fallen trees, heliconias attract their pollinators with lightning bolts of vibrant colors. Most of the plants are from the New World tropics, where they are pollinated by hummingbirds who have no sense of smell but who search by sight through the masses of green to find nectar-bearing flowers. A group of these plants occurs in the Pacific, where nectar-eating bats have the pollination honors. Here the colors may be less electric, as bats can use two senses to find them. Related to bananas, heliconias have fewer and more graceful leaves than bananas, and they are less robust in their stature. Like bananas, they grow on underground rhizomes or stems, and they can grow into large stands if left unchecked. Lovers of water, they nonetheless require good drainage so their underground parts don't rot. As cut flowers heliconias are magnificient, either by themselves with foliage or combined with gingers, birds-of-paradise, caladium leaves, and curcumas. Remember to dispose of the liquid that collects in the flower bracts before bringing them inside. Cultivars that do especially well in South Florida are those found in the Caribbean, *Heliconia bihai* and *H. caraibe*, their naturally occurring hybrids, as well as some forms of *H. stricta*, *H. latispatha*, and *H. rostrata* (an old-timer that has been grown for decades here).

WHEN TO PLANT
Plant the beginning of the rainy season or throughout the summer months.

WHERE TO PLANT

Use heliconias in shady areas which afford the plants protection from cold and wind. *H. stricta* and *H. chartacea* (cv. Sexy Pink) are apt to lose leaves to cold and cold winds. If protected by windbreaks or planted on the south side of the garden, heliconias suffer fewer setbacks in cold winters.

HOW TO PLANT

Dig a hole twice the size of the rhizome or rootball (if in container), and enrich it with peat moss and pine bark mulch. Backfill and mulch to mediate soil moisture.

ADVICE FOR CARE

Heliconias have big appetites. I have found that slow-release 18-18-18 combined with periodic foliar sprays of micronutrients keep them performing well. When they are hungry, their leaves quickly begin to yellow. Whenever I am fertilizing orchids, I also spray 20-20-20 on the leaves of the heliconias. Water daily or every other day, especially in the summer if it doesn't rain. Large clumps of *H. caribaea* × *H. bihai* cv. 'Jacquinii', which is an excellent grower, should be watered weekly in the winter or dry season, depending on location. (Heliconias exposed to wind and sun will require more water, as wind will pull water from the plants.)

ADDITIONAL INFORMATION

When heliconias produce their flower stalks, you may want to trim away from leaves to allow the colors to show. The flowers are terminal, and the stalk will die back after flowering, so saving leaves at this point is not necessary. In clumps or large circles, the outer, newer stems may lean. Staking from within is one way to better manage the look of the plants and allow the flower to show.

ADDITIONAL SPECIES, CULTIVARS, OR VARIETIES

Heliconia orthotricha, a Central and South American heliconia, has bracts covered with hairs; *H. stricta* is a small (2 to 6 ft.) species with maroon undersides on the leaves . . . cultivars and color forms number in the hundreds.

ADVICE FOR REGIONAL CARE

Select dwarf varieties and use them in containers, away from windy locations, in Central and North Florida. Bring them inside for winter, or move to an atrium if you have one.

393

Mussaenda

Mussaenda philippica

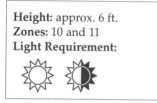

Height: approx. 6 ft.
Zones: 10 and 11
Light Requirement:

When early morning sunrises are pastel, with the softest peach light on the clouds gradually turning to pink, and the sky's deep blue dissipates into robin's-egg—that's when the tropical of subtropical seems most at hand. Those same soft colors can be found covering the landscape when mussaendas are allowed to wander the grounds. While several mussaendas can be found in tropical environs from New Guinea to Africa, the *philippica* species is from the Philippines—easy enough to remember. The sepals are all enlarged and fluffy, so the pink never fails to conjure up visions of cotton candy. This is not a shrub to be given the everyday duty of running alongside a fence or around a property line. It's lusciousness is best taken in smaller doses, and its cold-tenderness makes it vulnerable to damage below 45 degrees Fahrenheit. But it is a plant that might serve as an extraordinary accent by the front door, or a patio highlight in a confidently large container. There are single and double forms, so the froth can be as frothy as you wish. Legginess is a problem, and R.E. Holttum and Ivan Enoch in *Gardening in the Tropics* suggest planting mussaendas in a mixed border so shorter shrubs can conceal the trunks. Hard pruning is necessary because of the tendency to stretch and straggle.

WHEN TO PLANT
Plant at the beginning of the rainy season through midsummer.

WHERE TO PLANT
Locate in full sun for best color, or in high, light shade.

HOW TO PLANT
Dig a hole as deep and twice as wide as the rootball of the plant in a container. Add organic material, such as compost, peat moss, or aged manure. Carefully remove the container from the plant, and slip the shrub into the planting hole. Water in the soil and backfill. Mulch, being careful to keep mulch a couple of inches away from the trunk.

Advice for Care

Fertilize with an acid-forming or gardenia/ixora fertilizer. The flowers are formed on the ends of the branches, so pruning in spring will encourage more branches to form. If the shrubs grow too large, cut back quite hard. Fungal leaf spot can affect some plants; the pink is hardier than the salmon.

Additional Information

The shrubs flower throughout warm months.

Additional Species, Cultivars, or Varieties

'Dona Aurora' has white sepals; other Dona cultivars are pink. *Mussaenda erythrophylla* is an African species with blood-red sepals. (Erythro means red, phylla is leaf.) The flower is creamy with a red eye. *Mussaenda glabra* is yellow with a single cream-colored sepal.

Advice for Regional Care

You will have to grow these plants in containers in Central and North Florida.

Peace Lily

Spathiphyllum spp.

Height: 12 in. to 4 or more ft.
Zones: 10B and 11
Light Requirement:

One of the chief attributes of white flowers is their visibility in low light. And like a lighthouse in fog, the spathe of the peace lily is a small beacon in shadowy places. Today's cultivars have been developed to endure the ordeals of indoor abuse: they hold up well in low humidity, they hang on if not religiously watered, and they flower despite it all. Take the same plants outside, and they can flourish in medium to deep shade in well-drained soil. I'm always of two minds about the looks of these plants: that they are, by virtue of their upright flower stalks, rather formal in demeanor, given to proper behavior, perhaps rather British; or, often peering over their leaves as they do, that they're somewhat impish, just looking for a chance to spring out of there. Like so many other rain forest plants, the *Spathiphyllum* likes water but good drainage. If you have ever hiked in wet tropical forests, where the roots of trees lie at the surface and the mud is as slippery as a sheet of ice, you can get an idea of what it's like to grow there. The rain rushes down, then rushes away, leaving you to drip and sweat as the sun returns. Humidity is high; temperatures are warm; soil is thin and poor. So much vegetation means constantly dropping leaves are constantly being decomposed for release of nutrients. Reproducing those conditions outside the tropics is only a daydream, but Florida comes close with its rainy season and high humidity. You, the gardener, can provide the frequent watering and the quick drying time and the supply of nutrients. In my garden, my *Spathiphyllum* rubs shoulders with bird's-nest anthuriums and philodendrons in a cozy microclimate beneath the avocado tree. It produces its "flowers" in the warmer months and has yet to croak in cold down into the 30s because it is protected by larger-leaved companions. Costus, palms, coleus, ferns, anthuriums, and bromeliads also grow in this little pseudotropical garden, which I water daily and provide with slow-release fertilizer as well as fertilizer in the form of foliar spray.

When to Plant
Plant at the beginning of the rainy season through midsummer.

Where to Plant
Choose a shady location with some protection against cold and well-draining soil.

How to Plant
Use slow-release fertilizer for foliage plants to keep a supply of nutrients available to the plants throughout the growing season.

Advice for Care
Water daily or every other day, depending on conditions.

Additional Information
By containing the tropical plants in a confined and protected area, water use can be reduced.

Additional Species, Cultivars, or Varieties
Spathiphyllum 'Clevelandii' is a large and quite beautiful plant, with deeply veined dark leaves. Any size to suit your need can be found.

Advice for Regional Care
Potted plants can be moved outside in the summer to shaded patios or pool areas. You also may use *Spathiphyllum* as a temporary groundcover during the summer in Central and North Florida.

Peperomia

Peperomia spp.

Height: 1 to 1½ ft. if upright
Zones: 10 and 11
Light Requirement:

Were you to venture into the Big Cypress Swamp, wade through the sloughs of the Fakahatchee Strand, or watch nature from the distinctly dry vantage of the boardwalk at Corkscrew Swamp Sanctuary near Naples, you would find native peperomias. They love to loll about on fallen logs, sharing the ride with ferns and perhaps some orchids. And were you to wander into a garden center, you no doubt would find them among the houseplants and dish gardens. Choose the first; you'll have an excellent adventure. Were you to chow down on a big breakfast before that adventure and you prefer your sunny-side-up eggs with salt and pepper, the pepper, you should know, is from a relative of the 5 kinds of peperomias you can see in Florida's wilds. Piperaceae is the family, and it includes everything from commercial pepper to trees, with a long list of approximately 500 relatives scattered around the tropical world. In your garden, peperomias can easily serve as groundcovers, potted plants for the patio or waterfalls, fillers in the crags of shaded rocks around your pond, or roamers among the mulch in your hammock. The plants have not been wildly popular in recent years, but they are steady, shoulder-to-the-wheel plants. Those in my garden have round leaves and medium-green color. They have been transplanted to 3 locations over the years and like it best on the north side of the house, sneaking out from beneath the *Monstera* and the *Chamaedorea* palms. The first location was too sunny, the second was too shady, but this is just right. A key ingredient to the successful culture of peperomias in the garden is mulch to keep the soil evenly moist.

WHEN TO PLANT

Plant in spring or any time during summer.

WHERE TO PLANT

Select a shady, well-draining area, which nonetheless can retain moisture. If you think about an old log, you can visualize the way water runs off, but moisture is kept in the decomposing bark and detritus.

How to Plant

As a groundcover, plants may be spaced quite close or farther apart, depending on the leaf size. Plants will spread, though loosely. Some plants will clump up or mound slightly.

Advice for Care

Fertilize with a 7-3-7 granular fertilizer containing micronutrients 2 or 3 times a year; less often if you use mulch; and less often if you fertilize plants around which the peperomias grow.

Additional Information

You can multiply your groundcover easily from cuttings taken in the spring. Root them in a moist 50-50 mix of peat moss and perlite, and keep them shady until roots have begun. Or plant cuttings directly into the bed, and keep well irrigated until the plants are growing well.

Additional Species, Cultivars, or Varieties

Peperomia caperata 'Red Ripple' has beautiful burgundy-green and quilted leaves. It can take more sun than others.

Advice for Regional Care

These plants are too tender for widespread use in North and Central Florida, unless they are grown in containers.

Philodendron

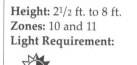

Height: 2¹/₂ ft. to 8 ft.
Zones: 10 and 11
Light Requirement:

To import the feel of the tropics, try a philodendron. Displaying big to giant leaves with plain to ruffled and lobed edges, these plants from the American tropics can be suggestively exotic, bringing the hallmark of a tropical garden to your door with little expense on your part—except to occasionally get out the machete and, as the Queen of Hearts ordered, off with its head. *Philodendron selloum*, with its deeply lobed leaves, may be the best known for the garden. It can form a spreading mound and serve as a cross between a shrub and a groundcover. Eventually, a selloum can have an upright trunk beneath the head of terminal leaves. Should the plant reach a tree, it can shinny up it and send down its aerial roots in no time at all. *Philodendron × evansii* is a cross between *P. selloum* and *P. speciosum*. It makes a giant cluster of impressive leaves, rather undulating on the edges and lobed as well. *Philodendron williamsii* is a narrow-leaved species; the top of the leaf is hastate, meaning it's like a heart with pointed instead of rounded top lobes. *Williamsii* is called "Espiritu Santo" in Brazil. *Philodendron gloriosum* has a velvet finish with white veins, while *Philodendron × magnificum* has the same look with a slick finish. Gloriosum spreads rather slowly compared to most philodendrons.

WHEN TO PLANT
Plant any time during the warm season.

WHERE TO PLANT
Plant them wherever you wish.

HOW TO PLANT
A huge planting hole is not necessary. If you buy a philodendron in a container, make the planting hole as big as the rootball. If you take home a cutting from a friend's garden, you may be able to set it down in shade and let it go. It is advisable to cover the roots with a layer of mulch and water daily until the cutting roots or sends out a

new leaf. I've had good luck with pieces of climbing types that I've set against trees or a fence so that they have some support.

ADVICE FOR CARE
Slow-release fertilizer will get the cutting or transplant started and is good for self-heading types that don't crawl up trees. Vining philodendrons can be sprayed with 20-20-20 combined with a spreader sticker (to help the fertilizer stay on the leaf long enough to be absorbed) or with a teaspoon of liquid detergent, which will also serve as a spreader sticker. Many philodendrons are cold tolerant.

ADDITIONAL INFORMATION
A characteristic of many philodendrons is that they have one kind of leaf when small and reclining innocently at the base of a tree. But as plants grow, the leaves enlarge and turn into sun-harvesting machines in the treetops where sunlight is more available. The long, corky, aerial roots that hang from philodendrons when they reach the canopy somehow seem to make the garden more tropical.

ADDITIONAL SPECIES, CULTIVARS, OR VARIETIES
Wine-colored philodendrons are among the many patented cultivars available. Heart-leaf philodendron is grown by the millions for containers; it also comes in a variegated form.

ADVICE FOR REGIONAL CARE
Philodendrons can withstand some cold, but not freezing weather. Gardeners in Central and North Florida can best utilize them as container plants.

Ti Plant

Cordyline terminalis

Height: varies, many 4 ft.
Zones: 10B and 11
Light Requirement:

If you were to dip feather dusters in a can of paint and insert them in the ground, feathers-up, you would have a good idea of what a ti plant loooks like. A sunburst of red wine coloration in the garden has long been the ti plant's contribution, but with extensive hybridization, color can now be copper, green, fuchsia, yellow, cream, and any and all combinations of these. This Southeast Asian native has found its greatest admirers in Hawaii, where gardeners are exuberant users of the color red. To the tourist's eye, it sometimes appears that these island gardeners don't really care how the red is used, just so it is used: often in rows, sometimes in groups, and from time to time as the perfect grace note in a tropical landscape. Floridian B. Frank Brown devoted a whole book to the subject in 1994, called *The Cordyline, King of Tropical Foliage.* In his book Brown admits that the plants are often "so showy, they are called gaudy . . ." Be warned that restraint may be the better part of valor when planting them. Brown includes his own Valkaria garden among a listing of great cordyline collections, along with nurseries in Thailand, the Philippines, Hawaii, Granada, Texas, and Suriname. An affable man, Brown is as exuberant about ti plants as he once was about aglaonemas, which he collected and described years ago. He describes new cultivars from Thailand as "awesome." In his book can be found dozens of photos of the latest colors and leaf-shapes, from miniature to giant. Many new cultivars are entering the Florida market, and nurseries that specialize in tropicals will have them. Color combinations are exciting, and leaves range from ribbonlike to as fat and round as your overfed cat. The colors can be glorious, and temptation lurks. Garish, of course, is in the eye of the beholder. And yet, one of the best uses of ti that I've seen mixed several wine/maroon tis with the shrub *Clerodendron quadrilocular* which has maroon undersides on its leaves; pink pentas; and pink porterweed.

WHEN TO PLANT
Plant at the beginning of the rainy season through midsummer.

402

WHERE TO PLANT
Plant in what is best described as high shade—akin to that beneath an oak, where light is bright without being direct. Ti plants can sunburn in summer in direct sun, but they can gradually peter out in too much shade.

HOW TO PLANT
Dig a hole larger than the rootball, add some peat moss or compost to enrich it (no more than 1/3 the total backfill should be organic), and water in the soil as you backfill the planting hole.

ADVICE FOR CARE
Ti plants grow well in the rainy heat of summer, but their best color comes in fall and winter, when you ease off supplying so much water. They like to dry slightly in the dry season. Too much light and too much fertilizer can bleach the foliage. Organic fertilizer, such as compost or fish emulsion, is the gentlest, but slow-release is fine. Brown recommends a high-nitrogen (10-5-5 or 30-10-10) for summer months, switching to a high-potassium (4-6-8 or 6-12-20) in fall to ready plants for winter.

ADDITIONAL INFORMATION
Ti plant leaves often show up in tropical flower arrangements for a splash of color. Miniature ti plants were developed in Hawaii in the 1950s, and these are frequently seen in dish gardens.

ADDITIONAL SPECIES, CULTIVARS, OR VARIETIES
Brown, whose garden is near Melbourne and open to the public on the first two weekends of June, July, August, and September, recommends the cultivar Kilimanjaro for Florida. New and beautiful cultivars include 'Iris Bannochie', a tricolored ti with cream, red and green; 'Peter Buck' with orange suffused through the red; 'Little Rose' with older green leaves edged in red and new pink and red leaves; 'Hawaiian Flag', which is a cream and red combination; 'Yellow Bird', with butter yellow new leaves that take on some green coloration with age.

ADVICE FOR REGIONAL CARE
These are tender plants that are suitable for container culture in Central and North Florida.

Traveler's Tree

Ravenala madagascariensis

Other Name: Traveler's Plant
Height: to 40 ft.
Zones: 10 and 11
Light Requirement:

Like those of heliconia, the seeds of the traveler's palm are bright blue. When they form, they lie deep in old boat-shaped bracts between towering leaf stems. Chances are good that unless you get a ladder and cut the inflorescence, you won't see them. But know they are there. Also know this: small primates called lemurs pollinate them in the wilds of Madagascar where they are native and where, like the other native plants and animals of that much beleaguered island, they face the prospect of being edged off the planet any day now. As a landscape plant, the traveler's palm is most glorious when it is young, since that is when its remarkable head of leaves is closer to eye level. The leaves are held on a single plane, like the cards held in a bridge hand or those old-fashioned hand-held fans once given out by funeral homes. The display is a stunning bit of geometry, akin to the three-sided placement of fronds by the triangle palms, also from Madagascar. As garden specimens, these are truly impressive. And truly impressive doesn't readily belong on a 50- by 75-ft. lot, because it can overpower the rest of the garden as well as the house. A single plant, however, grown next to a chimney or a two-story dwelling in a larger setting may be just what the plant doctor ordered. Suckers sometimes form at the base, and in smaller areas, it may be wise to remove them. The flower of the traveler's plant forms in boat-shaped bracts—really over-sized versions of some upright heliconia flower stalks. These large bracts fill with water when it rains. The common name came into being because these little cisterns could be a source of water to a weary traveler (though, if anything like heliconia bracts, whole worlds of waterborne fauna and flora live there, too).

WHEN TO PLANT
Plant at the beginning of the rainy season to midsummer.

WHERE TO PLANT
Plant in full sun or high, light shade, in a space large enough to accommodate the large head of leaves.

HOW TO PLANT

Prepare a planting hole as deep and twice as wide as the rootball, and enrich with 1/3 compost before backfilling. Water in backfill to collapse air pockets. Mulch.

ADVICE FOR CARE

Use a slow-release fertilizer, either balanced, such as 18-18-18, or high-nitrogen high-potassium in the summer growing season, such as a 7-3-7 or 12-4-12-4 palm fertilizer.

ADDITIONAL INFORMATION

The large leaves may become tattered in wind. When they look ratty, remove the outermost leaves. Some that survived in the fringes of Hurricane Andrew in 1992 were pruned more severely toward the center. They eventually regrew a crown. Because they grow at about 3000 feet in Madagascar, these plants can take a little more cold than other tropicals.

ADDITIONAL SPECIES, CULTIVARS, OR VARIETIES

No other species. Related to bird-of-paradise and *Phenakospernum*.

ADVICE FOR REGIONAL CARE

Not suitable for Central and North Florida.

$\mathscr{M}$OST HOMEOWNERS TAKE PRIDE IN GROWING A HEALTHY GREEN LAWN. While they may complain about mowing the grass, they are usually happy to tell others what they do to fight off bugs and keep the turf thick. A lawn is an all-American bragging topic for most weekend gardeners.

The home turf is also a playground, supporting family football games, inviting croquet, or simply being the spot to tumble with a family pet. Many gardeners simply appreciate the open space created by turf.

A number of homeowners may not realize it, but their lawns are also producing oxygen, holding the soil in place, and helping moisture percolate down through the ground to replenish the fresh-water supply.

Not everyone wants a large lawn. The latest trend is to grow only the grass one really needs and intends to care for. After all, there is work involved!

The best lawns grow in full-sun locations. Some Florida turf varieties, mainly some of the St. Augustines, tolerate light shade. But in general, the less shade the better. Many cultural problems can be eliminated by planting grass only where it gets a full day of sunshine.

It's also best to keep lawns away from trees that cast heavy shade. Not only are light levels too low under most of the canopy, the turf also has to compete with tree roots. It is better to leave these areas for more shade-tolerant and vigorous groundcovers.

Chapter Thirteen

Most Florida soils are suitable for growing turf. Soils rich in organic matter or clay hold more moisture than sandy soils, but both are capable of growing a great lawn. Avoid low areas that may accumulate water and hold it for more than a few hours. Such wet locations encourage shallow root systems and disease problems.

All turf sites should have the proper soil pH. Most grasses like a slightly acidic to nearly neutral soil. A soil in the 5.5 to 7.5 pH range is generally ideal. Only Bahia turf benefits from keeping the soil in the acid range of pH 5.5 to 6.5. In this acidic soil, extra iron is available for growing turf—Bahia seems to need this iron more than other grasses. Soil acidity can be adjusted by following soil test recommendations. In Florida, dolomitic lime is usually used to raise the soil pH, soil sulfur to lower it. Follow information from the test recommendations to properly change the acidity.

It may be impossible to make a permanent change in acidity in the very alkaline soils of South Florida, and in pockets of organic soils throughout the state. If the soil pH cannot be changed, gardeners should grow the turf type best suited to the area. And be prepared to periodically add minor nutrients that might be depleted by the extremes in acidity levels.

Starting a new lawn is similar to filling bare spots in older turf. First, remove debris and weedy growths. Unwanted vegetation can be dug out or killed with a non-selective herbicide. Choose a product that permits planting the turf immediately after the weeds decline. Once the weeds are removed, the soil is tilled. This is the time to incorporate lime or sulfur if needed. Some gardeners also like to incorporate organic matter, including aged manure, into sandy soils.

Adding organic matter is beneficial, but usually only practical when dealing with small sites. While the matter is present, it does help hold moisture and provide some nutrients for beginning turf growth, but it quickly breaks down and leaves mainly the original sandy soil. After tilling, smooth out the ground to establish a uniform planting surface as final preparation for planting. This can be performed with a rake or a drag.

All grasses can be installed as sod. This creates an instant lawn, but is also the most expensive way to establish turf. With some grasses, seed or plugs may also be utilized.

Seeding a lawn should be performed during the warmer months of March through September, when the grass makes quick growth. In Florida, Bahia is usually the only grass that is seeded to start the home lawn. It gives the best germination with minimal care. Some Bermuda, centipede, and zoysia varieties can also be seeded. For each area of the lawn, divide the amount of seed needed in half. Move back and forth across the lawn, spreading the first portion. Then move across the lawn in a perpendicular direction and spread the remaining seed. Rake the lawn to cover the seed. Bahia seed germinates best if covered with soil 1/4 to 1/2 inch deep. Seeded lawns need frequent watering. Water daily to keep the surface of the soil wet until the grass begins to sprout. As the roots spread out into the surrounding soil, watering can be reduced to "as needed."

Plugs of grass—well-established sections of grass 2 to 4 inches square—can be used to establish all but the Bahia turf for home lawns. Some gardeners simply kill out the existing weeds and old grass, then insert the plugs into the ground. Good lawns can be established this way, but they appear to fill in more slowly than when the ground is cleared before planting.

Add the plugs to moist soil. Most are spaced 6 to 12 inches apart. The closer the spacing, the quicker the grass fills in to establish the lawn.

Some people like to add a slow-release fertilizer to the planting hole. It may be beneficial, but it is also time-consuming. A good feeding shortly after plugging seems to give a similar response.

Keep the planted area moist and the plugs will begin to grow rapidly. After 2 to 3 weeks of growth, gardeners may apply a fertilizer to encourage the grass to form the lawn.

All turf types can be established by sod, which gives an instant lawn and helps shut out weeds that may grow among seeded and plugged turf.

Most sod is sold in rectangular portions. It can be purchased by the piece or on a pallet. A pallet of sod may contain 400 to 500 square feet, so ask about the quantity before you buy.

Have the soil prepared and damp when the sod arrives. If for some reason the sod cannot be immediately installed, keep it in a shady location. Sod that sits on the pallet for longer than forty-eight hours quickly declines. Install the sod by laying the pieces next to each other, abutting the edges. Cut sections to fill in any small spaces. After the sod is laid, water the turf thoroughly. A good rule to follow to keep the sod moist is to water every day for the first week. The second week, water every other day, and the third week every third day. After 3 weeks, water only as needed to keep the turf from wilting.

Gardeners should note that sod laid in the shade needs less water than sunny locations. Too much water, especially during hot and humid weather, can cause the turf to rot and the soil will be lost.

After the sod has been growing for 3 to 4 weeks, the first application of a lawn fertilizer can be administered. After this initial feeding, assume a normal care program.

Chapter Thirteen

Home lawns do demand one thing: frequent mowing during the warmer months. From March through October, most lawns need cutting at least once a week. During the cooler months, cutting may not be necessary at all in North Florida, and just every other week or so in Central and South Florida. Every grass type has its own cutting height which ranges from 1/2 inch for Bermudagrass to 4 inches for St. Augustinegrass. The general rule is to remove no more than one-third of the grass blade at any one time. This keeps the grass from being burned after too close a mowing. Another good mowing tip is to keep a sharp blade and mow in different directions across the lawn at each cutting.

Home lawns depend on soil moisture. But don't provide the turf with more than it really needs. Allowing the turf to dry out just a little between waterings forces the grass to grow a deeper root system. Avoid the everyday watering schedule. It encourages a shallow root system, makes the grass grow too lush, favors diseases, and pops up the weeds. Surprisingly, most lawns can go 4 days to more than a week without a watering.

Let the grass tell you when it needs water. Wait until spots in the lawn just start to wilt. You can tell when the turf is reaching this stage as the leaf blades start to curl and turn grayish green. When several spots show these signs, give the entire lawn a good soaking.

Water the lawn until the soil moisture is replenished. Most gardeners try to add 1/2 to one inch of water at each irrigation.

A bright-green lawn grows from proper feedings, but don't give it too much. The result of overfeeding is a lush lawn that pests love. Too much growth also encourages an organic layer to form under the turf that harbors pests and impedes water movement into the ground.

Chapter Thirteen

Throughout most of Florida, two complete feedings a year are usually adequate for Bahia and St. Augustinegrass—once in March and again in September. Centipede can grow fine with a single feeding and both Bermuda and zoysia grasses will need extra feedings.

Use a fertilizer with a 4-1-2 ratio of major nutrients. This is the proportional amount of nitrogen, phosphorus, and potassium found in the product. A 16-4-8, 12-4-8, 15-5-10, or even a 10-10-10 is quite suitable for feeding the home turf.

During the summer months when lawns use nutrients faster than other times of the year, some iron may be applied to regreen the turf. Also, an extra feeding or two may be needed in South Florida.

Many pests affect lawns. Sod webworms and chinch bugs love St. Augustinegrass, and mole crickets feed in Bahia. Bermuda attracts a wide variety of insects. Other turf types have certain pests as well. Learn the insects of your grass, then inspect the grass regularly and treat when needed.

Diseases are a less frequent problem, but all grasses have a few. With a good cultural program, diseases are kept to a minimum. Grass that is under stress, in too much shade, or planted in areas with poor air movement is likely to have disease problems. Consult the local Extension Service office when a disease is suspected.

Finally, all lawns get a few weeds. Again, good cultural conditions help prevent weeds. Digging or spot-killing the weeds when first noted is also a good quick control. When there are too many weeds, a herbicide may help. First get the weeds identified, and then locate a herbicide that can be applied to your turf type and provide the control needed. Always follow instructions carefully to prevent damage to your lawn.

Bahiagrass

Paspalum notatum

Height: mow to 3 to 4 in.
Zones: 8, 9, 10, 11
Light Requirement:

Gardeners who want a good-looking lawn with minimal care should plant Bahiagrass. It's one of Florida's most drought-tolerant turf types, tough enough to support the backyard football game. Bahia has become the multipurpose turf used for home lawns, athletic fields, parks, and roadsides. It has the advantage of growing well from seed, and is also easy to establish as sod. There are two major varieties. Argentine has a wider-leaf blade with the smallest number of seed heads and resists yellowing during the spring season. Pensacola Bahiagrass produces a narrow blade and is the least expensive to start from seed, but it does have a tendency to yellow during spring and produces an abundance of tall seed heads.

WHEN TO PLANT

Bahiagrass is best established during the warmer months of March through early September. Grass started too late in the season makes slow growth and is susceptible to cold damage that may cause decline. Seed sown during the cooler months usually remains dormant in the ground but does germinate when temperatures are consistently above 70 degrees Fahrenheit.

WHERE TO PLANT

Plant Bahiagrass in sunny locations. It can tolerate the filtered shade of pine and similar open trees, but keep it out from under dense oaks and the northern sides of buildings. All varieties prefer an acid soil. Have the soil pH tested and, where possible, adjust to a level between 5.5 and 6.5 before planting. If a pH change cannot be made, supply extra iron to prevent yellowing.

HOW TO PLANT

Bahia is one grass that can be successfully established by seed in the home landscape. Make sure the soil is free of perennial weeds and till deeply to bury as many seeds as possible. Sow 7 to 10 lb. of the Bahia seed for every 1000 square ft. of new lawn. It's important to cover the seed 1/4 to 1/2 in. deep by raking it into the ground or applying a topdressing of soil. Gardeners can also establish an instant Bahia lawn with sod. Piece the sod together over damp soil. Cut sections of sod to fill in the smaller areas. Keep seeded and sodded areas moist and apply a complete fertilizer 3 to 4 weeks after growth begins.

ADVICE FOR CARE

Help the turf grow a deep root system by watering only when the blades start to wilt in patches. When the leaves begin to curl, irrigate with 1/2 to 3/4 in. of water. Where adequate water is not available the Bahia turns brown but revives when seasonal rains return. Most Bahia lawns are placed on a lean diet. Gardeners are encouraged to provide a feeding of 16-4-8 or similar fertilizer in March and September. Where additional growth is needed a nitrogen feeding or two may be applied during the summer and early fall months. Most Bahia lawns also benefit from an added iron feeding during early spring growth to prevent yellowing. From April through September Bahia makes rapid growth and sprouts seed heads, making frequent mowing a necessity. Mow at least once a week to 3 to 4 in. high in order to maintain an attractive appearance.

ADDITIONAL INFORMATION

One major pest, the mole cricket, has to be controlled in the Bahia lawn. In recent years several biological controls have been released that help reduce the pest, but most lawns and commercial turf are still affected. Good homeowner control can be obtained through baits applied during the summer season. Due to an open growth habit, weeds may invade the turf. Try cultural controls where needed to encourage dense growth, or apply a herbicide available from garden centers. Few diseases cause major damage to Bahia lawns.

ADDITIONAL SPECIES, CULTIVARS, OR VARIETIES

A few additional varieties have been cultivated in Florida. Common Bahiagrass is available but seldom used due to a very open growth habit and light green color. The similar Paraguay Bahiagrass is available but not popular due to its poor cold tolerance and disease susceptibility.

ADVICE FOR REGIONAL CARE

Care of Bahiagrass is similar throughout Florida. More fertilizer may be needed in the Southern regions than in Northern and Central Florida. Also, areas with a pH above 7 may have to apply more minor nutrients to keep a good green color.

Bermudagrass

Cynodon species

Height: mow to 2 in.
Zones: 8, 9, 10, 11
Light Requirement:

Florida's most impressive lawns are grown from Bermudagrass. These are usually hybrids of the two species *Cynodon dactylon* and *Cynodon transvaalensis*. Gardeners like the fine texture and dense growth this grass offers, which creates a green carpet of durable turf popular on golf courses and athletic fields. Bermudagrass is also selected for its salt and drought tolerance. One traditionally seeded type is marketed as common Bermuda. It has an open growth habit and coarse texture and is used mostly along the roadside. Improved seeded varieties of medium texture and dense growth, including Cheyenne, Sahara, Sundevil, and Jackpot, find use in athletic fields, lawns, and parks. Some varieties are only reproduced vegetatively as sprigs, sod, or plugs. Popular types include FloraTeX, Tifgreen, Tifway, and Tifway II, which have good density, a fine texture, and tolerance to varying cultural conditions.

WHEN TO PLANT

Start the Bermudagrass lawn whenever seeds or vegetative portions can make good growth. This is usually during the warmer months of April through September.

WHERE TO PLANT

Gardeners can plant a Bermuda lawn under most Florida soil conditions. It's advisable to adjust the acidity to around pH 6.5, but the grass tolerates pH extremes if supplied with trace elements in the fertilizer. Nematodes are also a problem, so test the soil and avoid infested areas. Bermudagrass must be planted in full-sun locations. Even in light shade it thins and quickly declines.

HOW TO PLANT

Areas for planting should be cleared of weeds and tilled before establishing the Bermuda lawn. Seeded varieties are usually planted at the rate of 1 to 2 lb. of hulled seed spread over every 1000 sq. ft. of soil and worked in lightly. Improved hybrids maintained vegeta-

tively are started as sprigs, plugs, or sod. Sprigs are small portions
of grass that are spread over the planting site at the rate of 5 to 10
bushels for every 1000 sq. ft. They are then rolled or cut into the soil
to grow. Plugs are set in the ground with a 12- to 24-inch spacing.
Most fill in the lawn within 6 to 9 months. Sod is abutted together to
form instant turf. Keep all planted areas moist and provide a first
feeding in 3 to 4 weeks.

ADVICE FOR CARE

Bermuda is a high-maintenance lawn. Most care programs include
complete applications of a 16-4-8 fertilizer or similar product around
March, May, and September. In addition, gardeners who want to
keep the vigorous green look supply the lawn with nitrogen feedings at least every other month during summer and fall. The grass
also needs frequent watering to remain green and vigorous. Let the
leaf blades start to wilt in small areas of the lawn, then apply up to
1 in. of water. To get the finest looking turf, mow frequently. Lawns
receiving minimal to moderate care should be cut 1 to 1 1/2 in. The
best-looking lawns are cut with a reel mower.

ADDITIONAL INFORMATION

Gardeners should check their lawns weekly for pest problems.
Insects that may affect the lawn include sod webworms and mole
crickets. Some diseases to look for include dollar spot, brown patch,
and leaf spots. These can all be controlled with pesticides or by
adjusting the cultural program. An established Bermuda lawn is
resistant to weeds but occasionally a herbicide treatment may also
be needed. The worst pests are nematodes, for which there is no
chemical treatment. But a good cultural program can help reduce
them. Due to the enhanced care program, most Bermuda lawns
develop a thatch layer just above the soil surface that impedes water
movement and harbors pests. The organic layer has to be periodically removed with a vertical mower.

ADDITIONAL SPECIES, CULTIVARS, OR VARIETIES

Plant breeders continue to produce new varieties. Most are developed for golf courses and athletic fields, but may find use in home
lawns. Some additional types planted in Florida include Guyman,
Midway, Quickstand, Tifdwarf, and Tiflawn.

ADVICE FOR REGIONAL CARE

Bermudagrass turns brown with the first frosts and freezes of winter
in the colder regions of Florida. Recovery is rapid when the weather
turns warm. Give the turf normal care to regain the green growth.

415

Centipedegrass

Eremochloa ophiuroides

Height: mow to 2 to 3 in.
Zones: 8, 9, 10
Light Requirement:

Most gardeners familiar with centipedegrass refer to it as the poor man's turf. What they are describing is the grass's ability to grow in infertile soils with minimal feedings. Centipede looks like a miniature St. Augustine with relatively narrow leaf blades forming in clusters along green runners. Gardeners like the turf's good green color, ability to grow in light shade, and good drought tolerance. With the right care it can be quite vigorous, filling in bare spots and knitting a dense lawn in a few months.

WHEN TO PLANT

Centipedegrass can be established from seed, plugs, or sod. It makes the best growth when planted during the warmer months of March through early September. Planting seed too late in the season may produce grass that is susceptible to cold. Also, centipede can be burned back by frost and freezes, making it unattractive. Growers are reluctant to market the turf until it regreens.

WHERE TO PLANT

Gardeners in North Florida grow the best-looking centipedegrass, and with few pest problems. It grows throughout the state, but nematodes and ground pearls affect lawns in the warmer sandy soils. Highly organic to sandy soils are suitable for centipede culture, but have them checked for nematodes before planting. The grass does prefer a slightly acid soil, so adjust the pH to around 6.0 if needed. When the pH cannot be altered, supply the growing grass with minor nutrients to prevent deficiencies. Centipede grows best in full sun but can tolerate light shade. Keep the turf away from the north side of buildings, and don't let it grow too near the trunks of trees.

HOW TO PLANT

Gardeners can save money by sowing centipede grass seeds. In Florida the seed is sold as a mixture of red- and yellow-stemmed varieties. Prepare a seedbed and then sow the seed at the rate of $1/4$ lb. for each 1000 sq. ft. of lawn. The cost of starting the lawn can also be reduced by using plugs. Set the plugs about a foot apart in a weed-free site. For an instant lawn use centipede sod. Fit the rectangular pieces together tightly and cut sections to fill the small spots. Keep seed and newly plugged or sodded areas moist to encourage growth. A feeding at half the recommended rate can be applied 4 to 6 weeks after good growth begins.

ADVICE FOR CARE

Put the centipede lawn on a lean diet. Many gardeners fertilize only once, in March. Where more growth is desired, or to maintain better color, a feeding may also be applied during fall. Let the grass tell you when to water. Centipede has some drought tolerance, but if shallow-rooted may need frequent waterings. When spots start to wilt, it is time to water the entire lawn. Gardeners like the close cut that centipede lawns allow. Keep the blade sharp and mow at about 2 in. tall.

ADDITIONAL INFORMATION

Ground pearls and nematodes keep centipedegrass from flourishing in the warmer areas of Florida and some sandy soils. Both attack the root system of the turf and there appears to be no good control. Gardeners in Central and South Florida who are thinking of growing centipede should at least have a nematode test to help make the planting decision.

ADDITIONAL SPECIES, CULTIVARS, OR VARIETIES

Some varieties of centipede with improved cold tolerance that might be selected for North Florida are Oklawn and Centennial. Most centipede marketed as seed, plugs, or sod is a generic mixture of red- and yellow-stemmed types.

ADVICE FOR REGIONAL CARE

Turf growing in Central and South Florida may develop yellowing during the warmer months due to a high soil pH. Periodic iron applications may be used to regreen the turf. Residents of North Florida may also use the iron treatment instead of applying a nitrogen fertilizer to keep a greener lawn. Centipede lawns may turn brown in colder regions of the state due to frosts and freezes. Give the turf normal care and spring growth should quickly cover the damaged blades.

417

St. Augustinegrass

Stenotaphrum secundatum

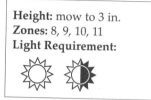

Height: mow to 3 in.
Zones: 8, 9, 10, 11
Light Requirement:

St. Augustinegrass is probably the best all-around turf Florida has to offer. Gardeners like the blue-green color and vigor of most varieties. The leaf blades are a little coarser than many northern turfs, but it has good shade tolerance and pest resistance. Almost every Florida gardener has heard of Bitter Blue St. Augustine, which according to plant lore was found in a South Florida pasture. It has set the standard of good St. Augustines having a dark green color, good cold resistance, and tolerance for light shade. A variety suitable for sunny locations is Floratam, which has notable vigor, good color, and added pest tolerance. Semi-dwarf St. Augustines Delmar and Seville have been the newest selections offering finer leaf blades, a closer mowing height, and good tolerance to shade.

WHEN TO PLANT

St. Augustine can be used to start a new lawn or fill in the bare spots at any time of the year. Perhaps the best time to plant is during the fall and spring months. The grass seems to flourish during the warmish days when supplied with water and fertilizer. Summer is the second-best season, but sometimes the grass seems stressed by the heat and humidity, which can affect good growth.

WHERE TO PLANT

Get the best growth by planting St. Augustine in sunny locations. Away from trees and buildings is the only place to plant varieties Floratam and Floralawn. Other selections, including Bitter Blue, Delmar, Palmetto, and Seville, have more shade tolerance and can survive in up to 25 percent filtered sun.

HOW TO PLANT

Removing the weedy growths and loosening the soil is always the best preparation for the planting site. Some gardeners have succeeded by just killing off the old vegetation and then inserting plugs or strips of sod, but the St. Augustine seems to knit together a tight lawn faster with bare soil and no other competition. St. Augustine plugs can be set 12 to 18 in. apart. The closer the spacing is, the quicker the runners grow together. Many gardeners add a little slow-release fertilizer to each hole before inserting plugs, but it does not appear to be necessary. Lawns established from plugs form a dense turf in 1 to 2 growing seasons. The secret to establishing a lawn from sod is laying the new turf on damp soil and abutting the pieces closely together. Use a serrated knife or hatchet to cut sections of sod to fill in the smaller areas. Keep all plantings moist and give the turf its first feeding in 3 to 4 weeks.

ADDITIONAL INFORMATION

St. Augustine must have irrigation during the drier weather. Let the turf tell you when to water. A lawn with a deep root system can often go a week or more without extra water. At each watering provide 1/2 to 3/4 in. of irrigation. Lawns can be placed on a lean diet and still remain green and healthy. St. Augustine lawns need a complete fertilizer application once in spring and once in fall. If during summer the turf becomes a little yellow, apply an iron application to renew the green. St. Augustine lawns do have a few pest problems. Gardeners should check for chinch bug and caterpillars during the warmer months. Also look for brown patch, a disease that appears during the fall and spring seasons. Nematodes may also affect the root system. Healthy, properly maintained turf is resistant to pests, but chemical treatments may also be needed.

ADDITIONAL SPECIES, CULTIVARS, OR VARIETIES

Perhaps the oldest variety is common, or Roselawn, St. Augustine, which is usually rated inferior to newer selections. A few varieties to consider are Raleigh, which has excellent cold tolerance; Floratine, a named selection of Bitter Blue; and FX-10, introduced for superior drought tolerance. Floralawn, similar to Floratam, is also available and the newest selection Palmetto appears to have good vigor and shade tolerance.

ADVICE FOR REGIONAL CARE

St. Augustine lawns are given similar care throughout most of Florida. Only in the southern portions of the state might an additional feeding or two be desirable.

419

Zoysiagrass

Zoysia species

Height: mow to 1 to 2 in.
Zones: 8, 9, 10, 11
Light Requirement:

Gardeners can ask for no finer lawn than zoysiagrass. It grows a bright-green carpet that, once established, can beat out weeds and withstand wear. It's also drought tolerant, cold hardy, and resistant to high salt levels. A number of zoysia selections are available for planting. The most popular include Meyer (also marketed as Z-52), Amazoy, Emerald, and Cashmere. All are available as sod or plugs to start the new lawn. They offer a medium- to fine-textured turf with good green color.

WHEN TO PLANT

Zoysia can be planted year-round as sod or plugs. Since cold makes the grass often turn brown during the winter months, most is marketed as green sod or plugs during the spring and summer seasons.

WHERE TO PLANT

Sunny sites are the best locations for zoysiagrass, but the grass can tolerate light shade. It grows in sands, clays, and organic soils. Zoysia does tolerate alkaline soils, so there is no need to be too concerned about pH levels a little above 7.

HOW TO PLANT

Sodding produces the instant zoysia lawn that's best able to compete with weeds growing from seeds. Make sure the turf pieces abut each other. Cut sections with a serrated knife or hatchet to fill in the small spaces. Plugging is an economical way of starting a new zoysia lawn. The small squares of turf are set 6 in. apart and grow together in about a year. One type, *Zoysia japonica*, is available for planting by seed. A seedbed should be established and the zoysia seed lightly mixed with the soil and kept moist. Since this is a coarser and lighter-green turf, it is less likely to be selected by homeowners for planting unless the convenience of seeding is more important.

ADVICE FOR CARE

Gardeners who want the best performance from their zoysia should provide several complete feedings per year. Usually a 16-4-8 fertilizer or similar product is applied to the turf once during spring and once during fall. Nitrogen applications are also made about every other month, usually in April, June, August, and November. Zoysia is a very drought-tolerant turf, but during dry weather a lawn without adequate water does turn brown. For the best-looking lawn use the leaf blades as an indication of when to water. Apply about $1/2$ to $3/4$ in. of water at each irrigation. Although zoysia makes slower growth, a well-cared-for lawn needs weekly mowings during the warmer months. Use a reel mower for the best cut.

ADDITIONAL INFORMATION

While zoysia is a great-looking grass, it does have a few problems. Billbugs can cause the turf to decline in patches by feeding on roots and blades, in which case a chemical control is needed. Nematodes are also a major problem and probably the most limiting factor to good zoysia growth in Florida. These microscopic roundworms feed on the roots, causing the turf to lose vigor and decline. Since no home chemical control exists, check the soil for nematodes that might damage the turf before planting. Pick up test kits from your local Extension Service office to have the test made at the University of Florida. Zoysia is susceptible to many turf diseases, but they are not a major problem in properly managed lawns. Where needed, chemical controls are available for the common diseases. After years of growth, zoysia develops an organic layer just above the soil line know as thatch. This restricts water movement, harbors insects, and detracts from the appearance of the turf. Gardeners can mechanically remove the thatch as needed.

ADDITIONAL SPECIES, CULTIVARS, OR VARIETIES

Several additional varieties of zoysia grass may be marketed in Florida for home lawns. Variety Belaire is a selection of *Zoysia japonica*. It has good cold tolerance and green color, but is coarser and more open than the more common Meyer variety. Another selection is El Toro, which appears to grow more quickly and has some improved disease resistance.

ADVICE FOR REGIONAL CARE

Zoysia grows throughout Florida but is sure to turn brown in the northern sections of the state.

CHAPTER FOURTEEN

Vines

*M*Y, MY, HOW THEY GET AROUND, THESE VINES. Shameless climbers, stealthy twiners, exuberant clingers, superlative sprawlers, midnight ramblers . . . cling to me like a vine, we say, and mean every word at the time.

The vining lifestyle must be the envy of the plant world. After all, everyone else stays put. Only the vines scramble hither and yon, scampering up trees and across fences, under guard rails and around poles. Look at kudzu. Look at morning glories. Look at passion vines. But look fast, or you'll miss them going by. Yes, we exaggerate—but only slightly.

In the war of vines, one wonders who might win, kudzu or wood rose? Rosary pea or poison ivy? Air potato or Virginia creeper? Coral vine or flame vine?

Vines are opportunists, seizing the moment, racing for the light. There is one in South Florida called cow itch vine because it can irritate even cattle. There is pull-and-haul-back, so named for its recurved thorns that won't let you move forward once it has you in its grip.

Then there is the parasitic dodder or love vine. It not only twines; it filches, too, stealing carbohydrates from its victims. Pothos, when it escapes (perhaps its revenge for imprisonment), runs up trees and does a quick change into the so-called hunter's robe, a vine with such big leaves that they are used as protection in rain.

The subtext of vine lore is that vines are poised to take over the world if presented with the possibility. And that was certainly the

Chapter Fourteen

case with some hammocks after Hurricane Andrew blew away the canopies. The vines, poised to strike, did. It took years of hot, sweaty (not to mention costly) work to clear them away.

You will have to exercise some control over the vines you introduce into your garden. Periodically take the machete to some of them.

On the other hand, there are spectacular spring effects to be had by running a bougainvillea or flame vine up a tree. Just make sure you want it there before you give it its head. Be especially careful with vining jasmines. They quickly become pests. The passion flower vine and the nasturtium bahuinia (*Bauhinia galpinii*) may also fling themselves about with abandon. Lightly prune vines periodically throughout the growing season, and cut them back hard after flowering or in early spring before they shoot out. Most vines like enriched soil and regular irrigation to keep going as they do. Fertilize once or twice a year, in spring and fall. Keep the root zones mulched to reduce weeds and keep soils evenly moist.

Passion vine is susceptible to nematodes; keep it well fertilized and mulched, growing vigorously, to prevent damage. Like other pests and diseases, nematodes are more apt to attack a weakened root system than a strong one.

The ability to camouflage may be a vine's most useful characteristic. The creeping ficus (*Ficus pumila*) is stellar in this respect. If given enough water and periodic fertilizer, it can hide a concrete block wall in just one or two seasons. Place it at the base of the wall in an enriched planting hole, keep it well irrigated, and watch it go.

Vines have many possibilities. Grow philodendrons on a tree or stump, coral vine or flame vine on a lamppost, or stephanotis on porch lattice . . . your garden will benefit from their unique qualities.

Bougainvillea

Bougainvillea spp.

Height: 6 to 20 ft.
Zones: 9 through 11
Light Requirement:

A woody flowering perennial with grass-green leaves, thorns, and tiny flowers surrounded by spectacularly colored bracts, bougainvilleas may be Brazil's most successful export. They grow in every tropical and sub-tropical climate and dazzle wherever they are. These vines are as skilled as cats in lounging and luxuriating in puddles of sunlight. They can claw their way over any fence or trellis, up any tree or palm. Named for a French admiral of the 18th Century—Louis Antoine de Bougainville, the first Frenchman to cross the Pacific—bougies emblemize South America just as well as they emblemize California, Hawaii, or Florida. They can also make you say "ouch!" when working with them because their thorns, unlike those of cats, are not retractable, and they are always sharp. Recent hybridization efforts in Thailand and India are creating an array of good characteristics that will reduce some of the ouch: woody canes that are semithornless (thorns disappear as the plant ages), bigger bracts, more cultivars with variegated leaves, and more "dwarf" types that can be contained in pots, baskets, or a rea-sonably small plot of ground. Pruning won't be quite the blood sport it used to be. The shimmering and stunning color is in the papery bracts that surround small white flowers. The flowers occur in groups of 3, and are pollinated in their native habitats by hummingbirds, who are able to hover well away from any thorns. Semithornless—often called "thornless" in garden centers—varieties don't grow and climb as read-ily as thorny types. This makes them good container plants for patios or balconies.

WHEN TO PLANT
Plant bougainvillea in the warm season.

WHERE TO PLANT
Plant in a site where the entire plant, including much of the root zone, can get sun and heat. The plant is not fussy about soil, but it will not flower well if it receives too much regular irrigation from an automatic sprinkler system.

424

How to Plant

Dig a planting hole just as deep as the container and a little wider.
Gently remove the pot from the plant, being careful of thorns, and
position it in the hole. The trellis should be in place behind it.
Water in when backfilling. Water regularly, keeping soil moist,
but not wet, to get the plant established. Mulch lightly with wood
chips or gravel.

Advice for Care

Bougies love sun and heat; they require a steady diet of fertilizer to
put on a show. A balanced fertilizer in the summer growing season
is best, followed by a bloom-booster type of fertilizer in the fall.
Bougies do not thrive on benign neglect—they like to be watered,
and then to dry out before being watered again. Flowers develop on
new growth, so in September you can prune back and shape the
summer's growth. Then fertilize with a 4-6-8 or another low-nitrogen fertilizer for flower production.

Additional Information

Bougainvilleas will wilt when too dry. They are tolerant of cold, but
they will drop leaves if chilled. If frozen, they will come back from
the ground. They are fed upon by tiny green caterpillars, the larvae
of small moths. Both the moth and the caterpillar are nocturnal. Use
Dipel, or wait for the cycle to run its course. The plants may be defo-
liated, but they put out new leaves. Long arching stems are weak
and break easily in wind unless supported.

Additional Species, Cultivars, or Varieties

There are a great number of cultivars these days, but just 3 basic
species: *Bougainvillea glabra*, which is a compact grower and flowers
throughout much of the year; *B. peruviana*, which flowers in the dry
season; and *B. spectabilis*, which flowers after a dry spell. The purple-flowering *B. spectabilis* is more cold tolerant than the others.
Miniaturized bougainvilleas have been developed in Thailand.
Florida bonsai enthusiasts often turn out glorious dwarfed subjects
that are quite breathtaking.

Advice for Regional Care

In more temperate areas, select a cultivar of *B. spectabilis*. Bougainvillea is readily grown in large terra-cotta pots, which won't keep
the roots too wet.

Calico Flower

Aristolochia elegans

Length: shoots to 6 to 10 ft. long
Zones: 10 and 11
Light Requirement:

The calico flower is a perennial vining plant with heart-shaped leaves and odd-looking rubbery flowers that are shaped like curved ear trumpets. It is small (about 3 in. across), and non-smelly in comparison to the pelican flower, *Aristolochia grandiflora*, which can reach 12 in. in length. You can grow calico flower on a trellis in full sun, and watch the caterpillars eat the leaves right in front of you. That's okay, the vine is a fast grower. My aristolochia has never flowered. It grows rampantly, and I have cut it back to the base on occasion. But I have not bothered to prop it up on so much as a fence post since it helped itself to the front porch wrought iron. When the caterpillars of certain butterflies such as pipevine and gold rim swallowtails feed on *Aristolochia* vines, they absorb a toxin and in turn become toxic or at least bitter tasting to birds that would eat them. Another common name for several species is snakeroot, the roots having been used for snakebite by indigenous peoples. One use of calico flower in India is to induce abortion. And while pipevine leaves probably won't relieve you of the sniffles, the alkaloids that are found in this and other tropical plants now are receiving more investigation as the source of valuable medicines. The screening of plants for useful properties is a result of work by ethnobotanists—scientists who study how indigenous people use plants in their everyday lives.

WHEN TO PLANT
Plant any time during the warm growing months—March to November.

WHERE TO PLANT
Plant in partial shade, with a support such as a trellis.

426

How to Plant

Enrich the planting soil with peat or compost. Plant vine at base of support, keeping the root zone watered daily until the vine becomes established. Leaves wilt when the plant gets too dry, and some shade at midday is best.

Advice for Care

Use a slow-release fertilizer to keep nutrients available to the plant. Give it a bloom-booster at the beginning of summer, as flowers occur in summer and fall. Water regularly.

Additional Information

Alkaloid-rich aristolochia vines will attract butterflies to your garden.

Additional Species, Cultivars, or Varieties

In Belize, *Aristolochia trilobata*, a relative of the calico flower, is used as a medicine by local shamans for flu, colds, fevers, parasites, and other ailments. Its botanical name *Aristolochia* comes from the Greek *aristos*, for "best" and *lochia*, meaning "childbirth." The flower's curvature suggests a human fetus before birth. An old common name is birthwort.

Advice for Regional Care

Use as an annual in more temperate areas.

Carolina Yellow Jasmine

Gelsemium sempervirens

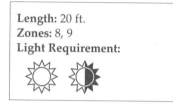

Length: 20 ft.
Zones: 8, 9
Light Requirement:

One of the first native flowers to brighten the new year landscape is the Carolina yellow jasmine. It offers a big splash of bright yellow blossoms which open sometime in early February, certainly before winter is over in most locations. And you don't have to worry about a winter freeze damaging the flowers, as this plant is totally hardy. Set the jasmine to work hiding a fence or covering a wall where you need a few weeks of color or just some great greenery. The leaves are bright green, lancelike in shape, and about 3 in. long. The shoots can grow to more than 20 ft. in length, but this is not a vine that normally gets way out of control. The Carolina yellow jasmine makes a good space divider or view barrier when set on a trellis or other type of support. The plant has also been used as a groundcover to quickly fill in the barren spots in landscapes. *Note: all portions of the plant are poisonous if eaten.*

WHEN TO PLANT

Carolina yellow jasmine is usually an easy plant to find at garden centers. It can be added to the garden throughout most of the year. Perhaps the best planting time is during the cooler winter months when the plants can establish a good root system before spring growth.

WHERE TO PLANT

Carolina yellow jasmine vines need a trellis, fence, or similar support for good growth. It's recommended that all vines be kept off trees to prevent damage to the trunks and to keep from encouraging pests that feed on the limbs and foliage. The Carolina yellow jasmine should be planted in a full-sun or lightly shaded location. Even in the shady spots, it will send its shoots out towards the available sun.

How to Plant

The Carolina yellow jasmine grows well in sandy Florida soils. Best growth is obtained when the soil is enriched before planting. Add peat moss or compost and manure to the planting site and till it in several inches deep. Dig a planting hole that's several times wider but not deeper than the rootball. Set the Carolina yellow jasmine in the ground at the same depth it was growing in the container. Fill in around the rootball with soil and add water to ensure good soil-to-root contact. Create a berm around the outer edge of the rootball to hold water and add a 2- to 3-in. layer of mulch.

Advice for Care

Carolina yellow jasmine vines should be watered daily for the first few weeks after planting; gradually taper off to watering as needed. The jasmine vines are drought tolerant and need watering only during periods of drought—but for best growth, weekly watering is recommended. Give the plantings a first feeding 4 to 6 weeks after transplanting, applying a light scattering of a 6-6-6 or similar fertilizer under the spread of the vine. Repeat feedings for established vines during March, May, and September.

Additional Information

Gardeners should expect Carolina yellow jasmine vines to make lots of growth, and adequate room should be provided at the planting site. The plants cannot climb a wall unless some type of support is provided. When the plants fill the trellis and begin to grow out of bounds, pruning may be needed. Every few years the vine should be given an early spring pruning after flowering to renew growth before new spring shoots sprout. No major pests affect the vines.

Additional Species, Cultivars, or Varieties

Some selections of the Carolina yellow jasmine have been made for a deep yellow bloom or unique flowering habit. One, the Pride of Augusta, opens clusters of fully double blossoms.

Advice for Regional Care

The Carolina yellow jasmine is best suited to the colder portions of the state. Plant in Northern and Central Florida landscapes.

429

Confederate Jasmine

Trachelospermum jasminoides

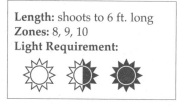

Length: shoots to 6 ft. long
Zones: 8, 9, 10
Light Requirement:

When springtime finally arrives one plant can be counted on for attractive snow white flowers plus a great fragrance—it's the Confederate jasmine. This vine is very versatile, growing at most light levels and finding use as a groundcover or wall hanging. The plant needs just a little support for a dense view barrier or attractive vertical accent. It's an ideal wall covering for gardeners with just a little space. Once the blooms begin you can count on over a month long display. Then the plant provides some great greenery from the masses of shiny oval leaves. When trained to trellis the Confederate jasmine is kept at about 12 to 15 ft., but the vining shoots are capable of growing 30 to 40 ft. long. Better give this vine a good fence or side of a building to climb. Some gardeners also use the Confederate jasmine in planters and allow the vines to hang down from balconies or the railings along porches.

WHEN TO PLANT

Vines can be added to the garden throughout most of the year. The Confederate jasmine is easy to find at local garden centers and is often available trained to a small trellis. Perhaps the best planting time is during the cooler winter months when they can establish a good root system just before spring growth and flowering begins.

WHERE TO PLANT

Unless you are using it as a groundcover, the Confederate jasmine needs a trellis, fence, or similar support for good growth. It's recommended that all vines be kept off trees to prevent damage to the trunks and to keep from encouraging pests that feed on the limbs and foliage. The Confederate jasmine can be planted in full-sun to shady locations.

HOW TO PLANT

The Confederate jasmine grows well in Florida's sandy soils, but it needs less care when given an enriched soil. Most gardeners like to add peat moss or compost and manure to the planting site and till it in several inches deep. Dig a planting hole that's several times wider but not deeper than the rootball. Set the Confederate jasmine in the ground at the same depth it was growing in the container. Fill in around the rootball with soil and add water to ensure good soil-to-root contact. Create a berm around the outer edge of the rootball to hold water and add a 2- to 3-in. layer of mulch. Vines used as a groundcover are planted in a similar manner and given a spacing of 3 to 4 ft.

ADVICE FOR CARE

Confederate jasmine vines should be watered daily for the first few weeks after planting. Gradually taper off to watering on an "as needed" schedule. Confederate jasmine vines are drought tolerant and only need watering during periods of drought—but for best growth, weekly watering is recommended. Give the plantings a first feeding 4 to 6 weeks after transplanting, applying a light scattering of a 6-6-6 or similar fertilizer under the spread of the vine. Repeat single feedings for established vines during March, May, and September.

ADDITIONAL INFORMATION

Gardeners should expect Confederate jasmine vines to make lots of growth, and adequate room should be provided at the planting site. When the plant fills the trellis and begins to grow out of bounds, pruning may be needed. To renew growth, every few years the vine should be given a spring pruning after flowering. Scale insects are a common leaf and stem problem and may need a control. Gardeners can apply an oil-containing insecticide or another University of Florida recommended pesticide, following label instructions.

ADDITIONAL SPECIES, CULTIVARS, OR VARIETIES

Several selections of the Confederate jasmine have been made for their interesting leaf features. Variegatum has green-and-cream-colored foliage and makes a good accent for a garden wall. Gardeners can use a related species, the Asiatic jasmine, *Trachelospermum asiaticum*, for a reliable groundcover.

ADVICE FOR REGIONAL CARE

The Confederate jasmine grows well throughout all but the most southern portions of Florida. It's seldom affected by cold.

Coral Honeysuckle

Lonicera sempervirens

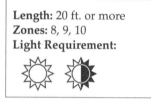

Length: 20 ft. or more
Zones: 8, 9, 10
Light Requirement:

Add a Florida native to a fence, masonry wall, or side of a building to enjoy a spring-through-summer display of reddish orange and yellow blossoms. The coral honeysuckle leads off with a massive flush of flowers during March and April that gradually tapers to sporadic blooms by fall. If you want to attract hummingbirds, this flower will do it. And when its blossoms fade, they are followed by shiny red berries that are a wildlife favorite. The vines are full of foliage that's bright green on top and blue-green on the bottom. It's a rapid vining plant that fills a trellis with shoots that can grow 20 ft. or more in length. Use the coral honeysuckle where you need some reliable color for the warmer months. It serves as a good space divider and view barrier, usually keeping its foliage near the ground.

WHEN TO PLANT

Vines can be added to the garden throughout most of the year. A garden center often offers the coral honeysuckle trained to a small trellis. Perhaps the best planting time is during the cooler winter months when the plant can become established by making good root growth before opening spring blooms.

WHERE TO PLANT

Coral honeysuckle vines need a trellis, fence, or similar support for good growth. It's recommended that all vines be kept off trees to prevent damage to the trunks and to keep from encouraging pests that feed on the limbs and foliage. The coral honeysuckle should be planted in a full-sun or lightly shaded location. In the shadier sites, flowering is greatly reduced.

HOW TO PLANT

The coral honeysuckle tolerates sands, but for the best growth, provide an enriched soil. Add peat moss or compost and manure to the planting site and till it in several inches deep. Dig a planting hole that's several times wider but not deeper than the rootball. Set the coral honeysuckle in the ground at the same depth it was growing in the container. Fill in around the rootball with soil, and add water to ensure good soil-to-root contact. Create a berm around the outer edge of the rootball to hold water, and add a 2- to 3-in. layer of mulch.

Advice for Care
Coral honeysuckle vines should be watered daily for the first few weeks after planting. Gradually taper the watering off to an "as needed" schedule. Coral honeysuckle vines are drought tolerant and need watering only during periods of drought—but when growth is desired, weekly watering is recommended. Give the plantings a first feeding 4 to 6 weeks after transplanting, applying a light scattering of a 6-6-6 or similar fertilizer under the spread of the vine. Repeat single feedings for established vines during March, May, and August.

Additional Information
Gardeners should expect coral honeysuckle vines to make lots of growth, and adequate room should be provided at the planting site. When the plant fills the trellis and begins to grow out of bounds, pruning may be needed. The vine should be given a renewal pruning every 3 or 4 years to ensure good coverage on the trellis. This pruning is usually performed after the major bloom in late spring. Coral honeysuckle plants usually remain pest-free.

Additional Species, Cultivars, or Varieties
Several selections of the coral honeysuckle have been made for the landscape, including varieties Sulphurea and John Clayton with yellow flowers; Magnifica with intense red blooms; and Alabama Crimson with improved color. Most Florida gardeners can also grow the Japanese honeysuckle, *Lonicera japonica*, on a fence or trellis. It's not as vigorous in most areas as it is in Northern states. The white-and-yellow flowers are produced during the summer season.

Advice for Regional Care
Honeysuckles grow best in the Northern and Central portions of Florida. They lack vigor if they don't experience some chilling winter weather.

Coral Vine

Antigonon leptopus

Length: shoots to 8 to 40 ft. long
Zones: 9, 10, 11
Light Requirement:

Not everyone feels the same way about the coral vine. Some say it grows too much like a weed, climbing up trees and sprouting where it is not needed. Others feel it's one of the most attractive wall and fence coverings a gardener can grow. Most gardeners do agree you can expect vigorous growth on poor soils and enjoy some great displays of pretty pink flowers. For its persistence alone you might give the coral vine a try on a barren fence or against a blank wall. In a matter of weeks after the weather warms it will be in bloom, producing strings of dainty blossoms. The foliage is quite attractive, offering bright-green heart-shaped leaves from spring through fall in most Florida locations. In warmer areas of the state, the plant remains evergreen for the winter. But where frost or freezing weather is common in winter, it dies back to the ground for the colder months.

WHEN TO PLANT

The coral vine can be added to the garden throughout most of the year, but it's a little hard to find. A few garden centers carry it, but you may have to start your own from seeds or cuttings supplied by a friend. The best planting time is probably during late winter or early spring so the plants can establish good root systems as new growth begins.

WHERE TO PLANT

Coral vine needs a trellis, fence, or similar support for good growth. It's recommended that all vines be kept off trees to prevent damage to the trunks and to keep from encouraging pests that feed on the limbs and foliage. The coral vine should be planted in a full-sun location.

HOW TO PLANT

Coral vines don't mind our sandy soils, but they appear to make the best growth in an enriched soil. Add peat moss or compost and

434

manure to the planting site, and till it in several inches deep. Dig a planting hole that's several times wider but not deeper than the rootball. Set the coral vine in the ground at the same depth it was growing in the container. Fill in around the rootball with soil, and add water to ensure good soil-to-root contact. Create a berm around the outer edge of the rootball to hold water, and add a 2- to 3-in. layer of mulch.

ADVICE FOR CARE
Coral vines should be watered daily for the first few weeks after planting. Gradually taper the watering off to an "as needed" schedule. Coral vines are drought tolerant and need watering only during excessive dry periods—but for best growth, especially when the vines are filling the trellis, weekly watering is recommended. Give the plantings a first feeding 4 to 6 weeks after transplanting, applying a light scattering of a 6-6-6 or similar fertilizer under the spread of the vine. Repeat single feedings for established vines during March, May, and August.

ADDITIONAL INFORMATION
Gardeners should expect coral vines to make lots of growth, and adequate room should be provided at the planting site. When a plant fills the trellis and begins to grow out of bounds, pruning may be needed. In most locations, the vines decline for the winter and can be cut back to the ground before spring growth begins. In warmer locations, a spring renewal pruning is also recommended. Caterpillars are common leaf feeders on the coral vine and may need a control. Gardeners can spray with the Bacillus thuringiensis caterpillar control or another University of Florida recommended pesticide, following label instructions.

ADDITIONAL SPECIES, CULTIVARS, OR VARIETIES
If you want a different look to your coral vine plantings, choose the white-blossomed variety Album for the warmer months.

ADVICE FOR REGIONAL CARE
In regions where frost and freezing weather affect the vines, this is a three-season wall covering. Prune out the cold-damaged portions and new growth will form from the tubers in spring.

Flame Vine

Pyrostegia venusta

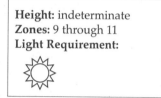

Height: indeterminate
Zones: 9 through 11
Light Requirement:

Flame vine is a South American perennial with late-winter flowers that are a searing bright orange color. What could make a wooden telephone pole look good? What creeps along the top of fences and burns with brightness? Flame vine. Pyro means "flame," stegia, "roof." The current species name, venusta, means "charming." The old name was ignea and means "fiery." The plant seems to appear out of nowhere when it flowers, as if by spontaneous combustion. But like an old flame, it quickly burns itself out. The floral conflagration lasts for a few weeks in late winter, usually February—then it's gone.

WHEN TO PLANT

Plant any time during the growing season—March to October.

WHERE TO PLANT

Plant on a fence or trellis in full sun.

HOW TO PLANT

Plant in enriched soil to keep it vigorous. At one time, when wooden telephone poles were common, the vine would grow up the poles and magically light up in flower—and it is highly probable that no one had bothered to enrich that soil! To enrich, add peat moss, compost, or aged manure to your planting soil and work in well.

ADVICE FOR CARE

Fertilize once a year in the spring; further fertilization is not necessary. Many years ago in an older Miami neighborhood the late Freida Bachmann, a nursery woman who was famous for her water lilies, grew an incredible flame vine in her melaleuca trees. Her secret was to fertilize it every 3 or 4 weeks. People would drive from miles around to stop and admire it.

436

ADDITIONAL INFORMATION

Cut the vine back hard after it flowers.

ADDITIONAL SPECIES, CULTIVARS, OR VARIETIES

The family is Bignoniaceae, which contains an assortment of plants
that have showy flowers: tabebuia, cape honeysuckle, pandora vine,
and trumpet vine.

ADVICE FOR REGIONAL CARE

Flame vine is fairly cold tolerant. Even if it freezes, it will grow
back rapidly.

Jade Vine

Stronglyodon macrobotrys

Length: indeterminate, to length suitable to space
Zones: 10B and 11
Light Requirement:

Jade vine is a woody climbing plant that produces long chains of velvet-textured blue-green flowers. So beautiful are these aquamarine claws that tear at the heart; so memorable is the color that is otherwise found only in shallow tropical seas or on the backs of the rarest birds. Its flower clusters form in the late winter, and are shown most effectively when the mother vine dangles them to eye level from a pergola or trellis high above. Petals develop first in the shape of a rabbit's foot. Then they curl like unsheathed upside-down cat claws, as the standard, or uppermost, petal lifts to reveal sepals and a recurved keel (fused petals around the stamen and stigmas). These long racemes or chains of flowers can grow to 3 ft. and hold about 100 flowers in one of nature's most exotic displays. The jade vine is from the island of Luzon in the Philippines, where it grows in ravines and climbs on ropy stalks to reach sunlight. Its roots, therefore, are accustomed to being shaded. It is possible that the vine is pollinated by birds. A cutting brought to Miami from Jamaica was started and shared among gardeners who dabble in tropical items, so that the jade vine no longer is held captive in the conservatory at Fairchild Tropical Garden. It graces arbors and clings to the trees of several outdoor gardens, and nicely survived a hurricane in 1992. Some have found the vine to be a temperamental grower; others who have a flair for growing it say this is not so.

WHEN TO PLANT
Plant as soon after purchasing as possible, says David Bar-Zvi, Fairchild Tropical Garden horticulturist and author of *Tropical Gardening*. The plant doesn't hold still for long in a container.

WHERE TO PLANT
Plant jade vine at the base of a support, where it can begin climbing as soon as it "learns to crawl."

438

How to Plant

Enrich the soil with potting soil, peat moss, compost, or well-aged manure. The soil must drain well. Carefully ease the plant from its container, position in the planting hole, and water in backfill. Keep the root zone moist while the plant is growing vigorously. Mulch around the roots, keeping mulch away from the vine itself.

Advice for Care

Keep the roots well irrigated. Also, keep the root zone mulched to retain moisture. Apply a slow-release fertilizer, such as that formulated for palms which contains extra magnesium and micro-nutrients, 3 times a year. In late winter, a 4-6-8 or low-nitrogen fertilizer will help flower development. Pinch off stray sprouts. This is a big vine, and one owner we know confesses to "hacking" at it instead of pruning.

Additional Information

Jade vine cuttings have been sold at Fairchild Tropical Garden in recent years. They are not available in most nurseries.

Additional Species, Cultivars, or Varieties

A similar vine is the New Guinea creeper, which also is a legume, or a member of the pea family. This one has scarlet flowers of intense beauty. It can be grown in Hawaii.

Pandorea

Pandorea jasminoides

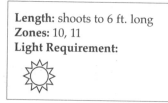

Length: shoots to 6 ft. long
Zones: 10, 11
Light Requirement:

If you need a good disguise for a fence, the pandorea vine (also called bower vine) is ideal. It rambles along, adjusting to the height of the fence and filling in with delicate pinnate leaves. As a bonus, gardeners get some great flowers during the spring and summer months. They are borne in clusters, and each white-and-pinkish blossom is trumpet-shaped. Pandorea can be trained to hide a wall or scramble up a trellis. It forms an impermeable space divider and excellent view barrier. And you won't need many plants to fill in the area—they can be set 6 to 8 ft. apart to grow together by the end of a growing season. This plant's dense growth makes it a good home for birds that fly in and out of the landscape.

WHEN TO PLANT

Vines can be added to the garden throughout most of the year. Pandorea vines are available from garden centers, usually in gallon or larger containers, ready for planting and training. Perhaps the best planting time is during the cooler winter months when they can establish a good root system before spring growth.

WHERE TO PLANT

Pandorea vines need a trellis, fence, or similar support for good growth. It's recommended that all vines be kept off trees to prevent damage to the trunks and to keep from encouraging pests that feed on the limbs and foliage. The pandorea vines should be planted in a full-sun location.

HOW TO PLANT

The pandorea vine tolerates sandy soils but grows best in an enriched planting site. Add peat moss or compost and manure to the planting site, and till it in several inches deep. Dig a planting hole that's several times wider but not deeper than the rootball. Set the pandorea vine in the ground at the same depth it was growing in the container. Fill in around the rootball with soil, and add water to ensure good soil-to-root contact. Create a berm around the outer edge of the rootball to hold water, and add a 2- to 3-in. layer of mulch.

ADVICE FOR CARE

Pandorea vines should be watered daily for the first few weeks after planting. Gradually taper the watering off to an "as needed" schedule. Pandorea vines are drought tolerant and need watering only during periods of drought—but when growth is desired, weekly watering is recommended. Give the plantings a first feeding 4 to 6 weeks after transplanting, applying a light scattering of a 6-6-6 or similar fertilizer under the spread of the vine. Repeat single feedings for established vines during March, May, and August.

ADDITIONAL INFORMATION

Gardeners should expect pandorea vines to make lots of growth in both height and width, and adequate room should be provided at the planting site. When the plant fills the trellis and begins to grow out of bounds, pruning may be needed. After years of growth, the planting may need renewal pruning. This is usually performed during late winter before spring growth begins. Pest problems are few, and the plant usually does not need a spray program.

ADDITIONAL SPECIES, CULTIVARS, OR VARIETIES

A few selections of the pandorea vine have been made for the home landscape. Gardeners can plant the cultivar Alba, with white blossoms, and the cultivar Rosea, with pinkish blooms.

ADVICE FOR REGIONAL CARE

Pandorea is a cold-sensitive vine that is best grown in lower Central and South Florida. Freezing weather will cause major damage to the vines, and affected portions should be removed before spring growth begins. Keep a good mulch layer at the base of the plants to protect the basal buds during the winter months.

Passion Vine

Passiflora spp.

Length: indeterminate, to length you prefer—cut back when it exceeds its space
Zones: 9 through 11, depending on species
Light Requirement:

The passion flower is marvelously complex. With as many as 10 sepals and petals, and a corona fringed with exotic filaments, the sexual parts are elaborately displayed. Some of the filaments are short and straight, some crimped, some two-toned, some miniature. The flowers are variously tiny to several inches across in colors from pink to red, blue or purple, white, and greenish yellow. All the reds are perfumed, and carpenter bees and bumblebees are crazy in love with them. Florida's julia, zebra longwing, and Gulf fritillary butterflies use them as larval host plants, laying eggs on the leaves which hatch into caterpillars with voracious appetites. These plants make perfectly splendid, if rambunctious, garden specimens because they flower freely in the summer and attract loads of butterflies. Some produce delicious fruit. The native Florida *Passiflora* is a tiny thing, with perhaps the least impressive flowers—as small as 1/4 in. to 1 in., and greenish yellow. This is *P. suberosa*, commonly called the corky-stemmed passion flower. Its leaves come in differing shapes, a quality thought by some vine-watchers to be a technique for eluding butterflies and their hungry offspring. An edible cultivar that was developed in South Florida by Robert Barnum at Possum Trot Nursery is *Passiflora edulis* 'Possum Purple'. The sweet purple-fruiting passion vines are ordinarily subject to nematode damage and fungus in South Florida, but this one grows well. Try it to get flowers, butterflies, and fruit for passion fruit milkshakes. (*P. edulis* is the most widely grown commercial species. It is self-pollinating, but it can be hand-pollinated for better fruit set. Yellow passion fruit, which grow better in Florida, are bee pollinated. You will need 2 types for cross-pollination. The fruits are tart.)

WHEN TO PLANT
Plant in the spring.

WHERE TO PLANT

Plant in full sun, against a support such as a fence or trellis, but away from trees—unless you're prepared to find the vine looking down at you one morning.

HOW TO PLANT

Plant in fast-draining soil. Potting soil or organic amendments may be added to a planting area. Keep the roots well irrigated until the vine is growing vigorously. Mulching around the root zone will benefit the young plant.

ADVICE FOR CARE

Passion vines are quick growers. Use a balanced fertilizer, or slow-release 14-14-14, or palm fertilizer with slow-release nitrogen and slow-release potassium plus micronutrients. Too much nitrogen may result in foliage production only. The vines can grow in slightly alkaline soil, but they will become chlorotic in very alkaline soils. If chlorosis occurs, use a foliar spray of micronutrients with a spreader sticker or 2 teaspoons of liquid detergent per gallon of water. If well fertilized and watered, passion vines should outperform any damage that could occur from nematodes. When neglected, the roots can be damaged by nematodes.

ADDITIONAL INFORMATION

A wonderful second edition of *Passion Flowers* by John Vanderplank (MIT Press) was published in 1996. For fans of this vine, this book a must. Vanderplank says that flower buds are initiated when the shoot is pendant, or drooping down. He advises training the vine but allowing the tip to hang over.

ADDITIONAL SPECIES, CULTIVARS, OR VARIETIES

In addition to 'Possum Purple', there are red hybrids available from the Rare Fruit Council. *P. coccinea* is the red species; *P. alatocerulea* is the common blue passion flower that seems to perform well in South Florida. The corky-stemmed passion flower, *P. suberosa*, can be found at native plant sales.

ADVICE FOR REGIONAL CARE

The blue passion flower is more cold tolerant than the red or purple.

Philodendron

Philodendron spp.

Length: to top of tree, and then down again—cut back when you want to contain
Zones: 10B and 11
Light Requirement:

A herbaceous climbing plant that has leaves that are usually heart- or arrow-shaped, philodendron is often lobed or undulating. If you see vines creeping, sprawling, looping, cling- ing, hanging, connecting, lassoing, lurching, dangling—that means you are in only one place: a tropical rain forest, where the canopy is alive with them. The vine lifestyle allows these plants to reach the light, that precious and life-giving commodity which so rarely reaches the tropical forest floor. Some plants have adapted to the low light—about 1 percent of the light at the top of the canopy strikes the forest floor. These are the plants we have rounded up and called houseplants. Some simply outgrow the others, such as the trees that can grow to 200 ft. Some live only in treetops—the air plants that have adapted to life in the most sweltering part of the torrid zone. Still others, including many vines, have 2 kinds of leaves: a juvenile leaf that is small and flattened against a tree trunk, and a mature and much larger leaf that harvests the sun with fierce gluttony. (One vine, the *Monstera deliciosa*, has a juvenile form that is sold as an entirely different plant from its mature form.) Among the most beauti- ful of the vining plants are the philodendrons. They may or may not . have juvenile forms, but they all have a way of transforming tree trunks—and hence gardens—into places reminiscent of a rain forest. They are not fussy; they are self-reliant and even sometimes too suc- cessful and can—like pothos—shade out entire blocks of trees with their piggish appetites for sun and water. So select carefully, and you will soon have a little rain forest of your own.

WHEN TO PLANT
Plant in the warm season—from April to October.

WHERE TO PLANT
The best places to start philodendron are at the base of trees, totems, or even fences.

H<small>OW TO</small> P<small>LANT</small>

If not starting a cutting by burying the severed end in mulch, you may be planting a containerized plant. In this case, you can mix peat moss and pine bark in a planting hole, slip off the container, and place the rootball in the planting medium. Cover and mulch. Water daily until the vine begins to produce new leaves and roots.

A<small>DVICE FOR</small> C<small>ARE</small>

Use an organic fertilizer such as a well-aged manure or a palm fertilizer around the rooted end. Palm fertilizer has slow-release nitrogen and slow-release potassium blended with low amounts of phosphorus and micronutrients. An alternative is a biweekly spray of 20-20-20 during the growing season.

A<small>DDITIONAL</small> I<small>NFORMATION</small>

Philodendrons are in the Araceae family. They are commonly called aroids. Aroids grow one leaf from the base of the proceeding leaf, writes *Aroids* author Deni Brown. Philodendrons make up a large portion of the family, and can be found from Mexico through Central and South America.

A<small>DDITIONAL</small> S<small>PECIES</small>, C<small>ULTIVARS</small>, <small>OR</small> V<small>ARIETIES</small>

Amy Donovan, aroid grower and editor of "Aroideana," the journal of the International Aroid Society, lists the following as vining philodendrons commonly found in nurseries: *Philodendron* 'Black Cardinal', *P.* 'Emerald Duke,' and *P.* 'Red Emerald'. The following plants can be found in specialty nurseries, at local plant sales, or at sales by the Aroid Society: *P. squamiferum,* which has hairy petioles; *P. melanochrysum,* once called *andraenum,* a velvet-textured, oblong heart-shaped leaf with white midvein; *P.* 'Florida' with variegated leaves; *P. davidsonii,* a long, leathery, triangular leaf with light midvein, native to Costa Rica; *P. ilsemanii,* another variegated form with ovate leaves; *P.* 'Santa Leopoldina' with very narrow, arrow-shaped leaves, quite long; *P. imbe,* which has one form with reddish leaves and petioles; *P. domesticum,* similar to imbe; *P. verrucosum* x *melanochrysum,* with a velvet texture and silver veins; and *P. grazielae,* with thick, heart-shaped leaves that are cupped.

A<small>DVICE FOR</small> R<small>EGIONAL</small> C<small>ARE</small>

Some species that are quite cold tolerant include *P. selloum,* a common philo with large, lobed leaves; *P. hastatum,* with arrow-shaped leaves; *P. pinnatifidum,* with wide leaves and a matte finish; and *P. bipinnatifidum.*

445

Queen's Wreath

Petrea volubilis

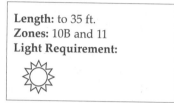

Length: to 35 ft.
Zones: 10B and 11
Light Requirement:

One reason to spend early spring in South Florida is to see the flowering of the queen's wreath. Its blue-purple clusters of flowers are reminiscent of wisteria. The darker violet petals fall after a few days, leaving the lighter blue sepals for several more weeks of color. This twining climber can grow in filtered shade, on rock walls, and over chain link fences. It is a lovely vine to train up the wrought iron at the front porch or across a long trellis of its very own where it can flood the space with flowers. With age, the vine develops a trunk that is quite thick. Twining vines will circle whatever support they are climbing, growing in a direction that has been genetically encoded, rather like being either right- or left-handed.

WHEN TO PLANT

Plant queen's wreath in fall for flowers the following spring, or at the start of the rainy season to provide a long growing period until the next flowering season.

WHERE TO PLANT

This kind of vine can slink around a wooden arbor or even wires, but not up the sides of walls as do clinging vines like *Ficus pumila*, the creeping fig.

HOW TO PLANT

Dig a hole slightly larger than the rootball and add peat moss, compost, or well-aged manure. Slide the rootball out of the container, making sure the top of it is at the same level in the ground as it was in the container when placing it in the planting hole. Water in the backfill, and mulch to keep soil moisture and temperature well modulated.

ADVICE FOR CARE

Fertilize 3 times a year, in spring, summer, and fall. Water 2 or 3 times a week in summer, twice a week in winter. The queen's wreath is a vigorous vine which can be cut back hard after it has flowered.

ADDITIONAL INFORMATION

Leaves have a texture like sandpaper.

ADDITIONAL SPECIES, CULTIVARS, OR VARIETIES

There is a white-flowered variety, *P. albiflora*.

ADVICE FOR REGIONAL CARE

A tender plant that will be hurt by cold, this vine needs a protected sunny spot in Central Florida. It is not a plant for North Florida.

VINES

Trumpet Creeper

Campsis radicans

Length: 30-plus ft.
Zones: 8, 9
Light Requirement:

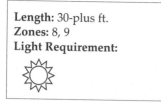

The flowers are big, orange, and beautiful—it's no wonder the hummingbirds like them, and you will, too. Just plant the trumpet creeper in an area where it has some room to climb and you're in for a summer of great color. The blossoms are borne in clusters, each about 4 to 5 in. long and trumpet-shaped, as the name suggests. Plant the trumpet creeper to hide a wall or fill a trellis. Since it gets to be quite tall, each vining stem growing to 30 or more ft. in length, it can be planted at the end of a long vista and easily seen. Use the plant as an accent near the patio, at an entrance, or trained to a support along the walkway. It's one of our native plants that adapts to moist growing conditions.

WHEN TO PLANT

Vines can be added to the garden throughout most of the year. The trumpet creeper is often available from garden centers and mail-order companies. Perhaps the best planting time is during the cooler winter months when it can establish a good root system before spring growth.

WHERE TO PLANT

The trumpet creeper needs a trellis, fence, or similar support for good growth. The stems have clinging roots that help the vining portions climb walls and other smooth surfaces. It's recommended that all vines be kept off trees to prevent damage to the trunks and to keep from encouraging pests that feed on the limbs and foliage. The trumpet creeper should be planted in a full-sun location.

HOW TO PLANT

The trumpet creeper can grow in most Florida sites, but it makes the best growth in an enriched soil. Add peat moss or compost and manure to the planting site and till it in several inches deep. Dig a planting hole that's several times wider but not deeper than the rootball. Set the trumpet creeper vine in the ground at the same depth it was growing in the container. Fill in around the rootball with soil, and add water to ensure good soil-to-root contact. Create a berm around the outer edge of the rootball to hold water, and add a 2- to 3-in. layer of mulch.

ADVICE FOR CARE

Trumpet creeper vines should be watered daily for the first few weeks after planting. Gradually taper the watering off to an "as needed" schedule. Trumpet creeper vines are quite drought tolerant and only need watering during periods of drought. When additional growth is needed during the drier times of the year, give the plantings a weekly watering. Give the plantings a first feeding 4 to 6 weeks after transplanting, applying a light scattering of a 6-6-6 or similar fertilizer under the spread of the vine. Repeat feedings for established vines are normally not needed—the vines appear to take needed nutrients for growth from decomposing mulches and feedings given nearby turf and shrubs.

ADDITIONAL INFORMATION

Gardeners should expect the trumpet creeper vines to make lots of growth, and adequate room should be provided at the planting site. When the plant fills the trellis and begins to grow out of bounds, pruning may be needed. The vines are seldom given additional pruning. No major pests appear to affect the plantings.

ADDITIONAL SPECIES, CULTIVARS, OR VARIETIES

A few selections of improved flower color have been made for planting. These selections include the cultivar Flava with yellow flowers and a hybrid Crimson Trumpet with good reddish blossoms. North Florida residents might also plant the Chinese trumpet creeper, *Campsis grandiflora*, which has open-faced orange flowers.

ADVICE FOR REGIONAL CARE

The trumpet creeper grows best in Northern and Central Florida where the vines receive some winter cold. The plants are deciduous and lose their leaves for the winter.

Wisteria

Wisteria sinensis

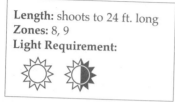

Length: shoots to 24 ft. long
Zones: 8, 9
Light Requirement:

What is the one vine most gardeners would like to grow? It's probably the wisteria. Unfortunately, it is restricted to the cooler portions of the state, but lucky gardeners in these areas can enjoy a spring display of exquisite purplish blossoms. The flowers open in long hanging clusters just before the foliage so the color is especially easy to see. Flower clusters of some vines are fragrant. Plantings need room to grow, and too much trimming just delays flowering. This is a vine many gardeners like to train to an arbor, but it also looks at home on a trellis near a wall or building. Perhaps the best place to use a wisteria is where you can sit and study the growth habit and enjoy the blossoms. Add a planting off the patio or along the walkway near a bench. After flowering, the vines quickly fill with large pinnate leaves that add extra enjoyment during the summer and fall months. Even during the winter months when the vines are bare, the twisting limbs add interest to the landscape.

WHEN TO PLANT

Vines can be added to the garden throughout most of the year. Wisterias are available from garden centers and mail-order companies. Perhaps the best planting time is during the cooler winter months when they can establish a good root system before spring growth.

WHERE TO PLANT

Wisteria vines need a trellis, fence, or similar support for good growth. It's recommended that all vines be kept off trees to prevent damage to the trunks and to keep from encouraging pests that feed on the limbs and foliage. The wisteria vines should be planted in a full-sun or lightly shaded location.

HOW TO PLANT

Wisteria vines are tolerant of sandy sites but make the best growth in an enriched soil. Add peat moss or compost and manure to the planting site, and till it in several inches deep. Dig a planting hole that's several times wider but not deeper than the rootball. Set the wisteria in the ground at the same depth it was growing in the container. Fill in around the rootball with soil, and add water to ensure good soil-to-root contact. Create a berm around the outer edge of the rootball to hold water, and add a 2- to 3-in. layer of mulch.

ADVICE FOR CARE

Wisteria vines should be watered daily for the first few weeks after planting. Gradually taper the watering off to an "as needed" schedule. Wisteria vines are drought tolerant and need watering only during periods of drought—but when extra growth is desired, a weekly watering is recommended. Give the plantings a first feeding 4 to 6 weeks after transplanting, applying a light scattering of a 6-6-6 or similar fertilizer under the spread of the vine. Repeat feedings for established vines during March, May, and September for the first year or two, then taper the feedings off to once or twice a year.

ADDITIONAL INFORMATION

Gardeners should expect wisteria vines to make lots of growth, and adequate room should be provided at the planting site. When the plant fills the trellis and begins to grow out of bounds, pruning may be needed. Most pruning is performed during late summer before the vines set buds for spring flowering. Some pruning can also be performed immediately after flowering. Supplying too much care may result in reluctant bloomers. Where this occurs, reduce the watering and feedings to minimal levels. Several years may pass before the first blooms are obtained. Wisteria plants may have mite or thrip pests. Where needed, apply a soap, oil, or another University of Florida recommended pesticide, following label instructions.

ADDITIONAL SPECIES, CULTIVARS, OR VARIETIES

Several selections of the wisteria have been made for home planting. Gardeners may wish to try Alba, with its white blossoms.

ADVICE FOR REGIONAL CARE

Wisteria grows best in Northern and Central Florida where the vines receive some cold. It's hardy in these areas and needs no special care.

- **African rubber vine** (*Cryptostegia madagascarensis*) is a vine for shade that produces purple bell-shaped flowers. It has compound leaves and will grow as a free-standing plant that reaches 6 or 7 ft. and then lets its branches tumble toward the ground. Don't allow it to grow near your pool or septic tank because the roots are aggressive. Sun. Zones 10B and 11.

- **Bleeding heart** (*Clerodendron thomsoniae*) is a twiner, yet it stays in confined areas. This makes it good for doorways, but unsuited for fences because it doesn't spread. The white and deep-rose flowers hang from the vine like teardrops throughout the summer months. Bleeding heart can be pruned into a shrub. Partial shade. Zones 10 and 11.

- **Bower vine** (*Pandorea jasminoides*) is good for use on trellises, arbors, or fences. It has small, glossy green leaves and whitish-pink tubular flowers. The flowers are held on panicles, which are produced in the spring. Sun. Zones 10B and 11.

- **Cape honeysuckle** (*Tecomaria capensis*) has brilliant orange-red flowers in terminal clusters that appear from October through June, making winter brighter. The compound leaves are delicate, with prominent veins and serrated edges. Sun. Zones 10B and 11.

- **Climbing fig** (*Ficus pumila*) is a wall cover that grows over stucco like English ivy. The leaves range from 1 to 4 in. (they're usually quite small when growing against a wall, larger if on stems sticking out into the air); they are dark-green above, lighter below. This plant doesn't have the aggressive roots of other figs. It is tolerant of various soil conditions, but requires lots of water to get started. It will do best in an enriched planting hole. After it is well established, trim it once or twice a year. Sun, partial shade. Zones 10 and 11.

- **Garlic vine** (*Cydista acquinoctialis*) has clusters of lavender or pink flowers in fall, winter, and spring. The name comes from the distinct garlicky odor emitted if leaves are crushed. Sun, partial shade. Zones 10B and 11.

• **Mexican flame vine** (*Senecio confusus*) has toothed leaves and daisy flowers that start out light orange and turn deep red with age. It's a good butterfly plant, but it can be aggressive. It will bloom off and on during the warm season—March through October. Sun. Zones 10 and 11.

• **Nasturtium bauhinia** (*Bauhinia galpinii*) is a vining cousin of the orchid tree. It has small lobed leaves and salmon-colored flowers during the summer. It becomes chlorotic without regular fertilizer and foliar micronutrient sprays. Cut back after flowering, or it will take off with excessive growth. Leaves turn brown with cold. Sun. Zones 10B and 11.

• **Parrot's beak** (*Gmelina philippensis*), from the Philippines, has bright-yellow flowers throughout much of the warm season. The flowers emerge from brownish red bracts. This plant can also can make a shrub. Sun. Zones 9 and 10.

• **Pink mandevilla** (*Mandevilla splendens*) has lovely pink trumpet-shaped flowers during the warm months—from April to October. It responds well to high-phosphorus fertilizer, which causes it to produce more blooms. Pink mandevilla is drought resistant, and therefore easily killed by standing water. Plant in well-drained soil. Sun. Zones 10B and 11.

• **Rangoon creeper** (*Quisqualis indica*) is a showy vine with pink flowers that turn to red (or white flowers that turn to pink) in terminal clusters. The flowers have exceedingly long floral tubes and appear in the warm months as the vine sprawls across a fence or support. Sun, partial shade. Zones 10B and 11.

• **Stephanotis** (*Stephanotis floribunda*) produces the wonderfully fragrant waxy white flowers that are used in bridal bouquets. It likes acid soil; enrich the planting hole with peat moss, manure, or compost, and mulch around the base of the vine. This vine does well on a galvanized chain link fence. It's a slow grower, adding about 3 ft. a year. Flowers appear in March. Sun. Zones 10B and 11.

SOURCES

Bibliography

Bar-Zvi, David, Chief Horticulturist, and Elvin McDonald, series editor. *Tropical Gardening*. New York: Pantheon Books, Knopf Publishing Group, 1996.

Batchelor, Stephen R. *Your First Orchid*. West Palm Beach: American Orchid Society, 1996.

Bechtel, Helmut, Phillip Cribb, and Edmund Launert. *The Manual of Cultivated Orchid Species*, Third Edition. Cambridge, MA: The MIT Press, 1992.

Bell, C. Ritchie and Byron J. Taylor. *Florida Wild Flowers and Roadside Plants*. Chapel Hill, NC: Laurel Hill Press, 1982.

Berry, Fred and W. John Kress. *Heliconia, An Identification Guide*. Washington and London: Smithsonian Institution Press, 1991.

Black, Robert J. and Kathleen C. Ruppert. *Your Florida Landscape, A Complete Guide to Planting & Maintenance*. Gainesville, FL: Cooperative Extension Service, Institute of Food and Agricultural Sciences, University of Florida, 1995.

Blackmore, Stephen and Elizabeth Tootill, eds. *The Penguin Dictionary of Botany*. Middlesex, England: Penguin Books, Ltd., 1984.

Blombery, Alec and Tony Todd. *Palms*. London, Sydney, Melbourne: Angus & Robertson, 1982.

Bond, Rick and editorial staff of Ortho Books. *All About Growing Orchids*. San Ramon, CA: The Solaris Group, 1988.

Brookes, John. *The Book of Garden Design*. New York: Macmillan Publishing Co. and London: Dorling Kindersley Ltd., 1991.

Broschat, Timothy K. and Alan W. Meerow. *Betrock's Reference Guide to Florida Landscape Plants*. Cooper City, FL: Betrock Information Systems, Inc., 1991.

Brown, Deni. *Aroids, Plants of the Arum Family*. Portland, OR: Timber Press, 1988.

Bush, Charles S. and Julia F. Morton. *Native Trees and Plants for Florida Landscaping*. Gainesville, FL: Florida Department of Agriculture and Consumer Services.

Sources

Calkins, Carroll C., ed. *Reader's Digest Illustrated Guide to Gardening*. Pleasantville, NY and Montreal: The Reader's Digest Association, Inc., 1978.

Campbell, Richard J., ed. *Mangos: A Guide to Mangos in Florida*. Miami: Fairchild Tropical Garden, 1992.

Courtright, Gordon. *Tropicals*. Portland, OR: Timber Press, 1988.

Dade County Department of Planning, Development and Regulation. *The Landscape Manual*. 1996.

Editors of Sunset Books and Sunset Magazine. *Sunset National Garden Book*. Menlo Park, CA: Sunset Books Inc., 1997.

Gerberg, Eugene J. and Ross H. Arnett, Jr. *Florida Butterflies*. Baltimore: Natural Science Publication, Inc., 1989.

Gilman, Edward F. *Betrock's Florida Plant Guide*. Hollywood, FL: Betrock Information Systems, 1996.

Graf, Alfred Byrd. *Tropica*. East Rutherford, NJ: Roehrs Co., 1978.

Hillier, Malcolm. *Malcolm Hillier's Color Garden*. London, New York, Stuttgart, Moscow: Dorling Kindersley, 1995.

Holttum, R.E. and Ivan Enock. *Gardening in the Tropics*. Singapore: Times Editions, 1991.

Hoshizaki, Barbara Joe. *Fern Growers Manual*. New York: Alfred A. Knopf, 1979.

Kilmer, Anne. *Gardening for Butterflies and Children in South Florida*. West Palm Beach, *The Palm Beach Post*, 1992.

Kramer, Jack. *300 Extraordinary Plants for Home and Garden*. New York, London, Paris: Abbeville Press, 1994.

Lessard, W.O. *The Complete Book of Bananas*. Miami, 1992.

MacCubbin, Tom. *Florida Home Grown: Landscaping*. Sentinel Communications, Orlando, Florida, 1989.

Mathias, Mildred E., ed. *Flowering Plants in the Landscape*. Berkeley, Los Angeles, London: University of California Press, 1982.

Meerow, Alan W. *Betrock's Guide to Landscape Palms*. Cooper City, FL: Betrock Information Systems, Inc., 1992.

Morton, Julia F. *500 Plants of South Florida*. Miami: E.A. Seemann Publishing, Inc., 1974.

Sources

Myers, Ronald L. and John J. Ewel, eds. *Ecosystems of Florida*. Orlando: University of Central Florida Press, 1991.

The National Gardening Association. *Dictionary of Horticulture*. New York: Penguin Books, 1994.

Neal, Marie. *In Gardens of Hawaii*. Honolulu: Bishop Museum Press, 1965.

Nelson, Gil. *The Trees of Florida, A Reference and Field Guide*. Sarasota: Pineapple Press, Inc., 1994.

Perry, Frances. *Flowers of the World*. London, New York, Sydney, Toronto: The Hamlyn Publishing Group, Ltd., 1972.

Rawlings, Marjorie Kinnan. *Cross Creek*. St. Simons Island, GA: Mockingbird Books, 1942. Seventh Printing, 1983.

Reinikka, Merle A. *A History of the Orchid*. Portland, OR: Timber Press, 1995.

Rittershausen, Wilma and Gill and David Oakey. *Growing & Displaying Orchids, A Step-by-Step Guide*. New York: Smithmark Publishers, Inc., 1993.

Scurlock, J. Paul. *Native Trees and Shrubs of the Florida Keys*. Pittsburgh: Laurel Press, 1987.

Stearn, William T. *Stearn's Dictionary of Plant Names for Gardeners*. New York: Sterling Publishing Co., Inc. 1996.

Stevenson, George B. *Palms of South Florida*. Miami: Fairchild Tropical Garden, 1974.

Tasker, Georgia. *Enchanted Ground, Gardening With Nature in the Subtropics*. Kansas City, Andrews and McMeel, 1994.

Tasker, Georgia. *Wild Things, The Return of Native Plants*. Winter Park, FL: The Florida Native Plant Society, 1984.

Tomlinson, P.B. *The Biology of Trees Native to Tropical Florida*. Allston, MA: Harvard University, 1980.

Vanderplank, John. *Passion Flowers*, Second Edition. Cambridge, MA: The MIT Press, 1996.

Sources

Walker, Jacqueline. *The Subtropical Garden*. Portland, OR: Timber Press, 1992.

Warren, William. *The Tropical Garden*. London: Thames and Hudson, Ltd., 1991.

Watkins, John V. and Thomas J. Sheehan. *Florida Landscape Plants, Native and Exotic*, Revised Edition. Gainesville, FL: The University Presses of Florida, 1975.

Workman, Richard W. *Growing Native*. Sanibel, FL: The Sanibel-Captive Conservation Foundation, Inc., 1980.

INDEX

Index

Index

Index

Index